# Henry Hobson Richardson and the Small Public Library in America

Kenneth A. Breisch

# Henry Hobson Richardson and the Small Public Library in America

## *A Study in Typology*

The MIT Press
Cambridge, Massachusetts London, England

This book was set in Garamond 3 by Graphic Composition, Inc., and was printed and bound in the United States of America.

Library of Congress Cataloging-in-Publication Data

Breisch, Kenneth A.

Henry Hobson Richardson and the small public library in America : a study in typology / Kenneth A. Breisch.

p. cm.

Includes bibliographical references (p. ) and index.

ISBN 0-262-02416-0 (hc : alk. paper)

1. Library architecture—United States—History—19th century. 2. Richardson, H. H. (Henry Hobson), 1838–1886. 3. Public libraries—United States—History—19th century. 4. Small libraries—United States—History—19th century. I. Title.

Z679.2.U IN PROCESS

727′.82473—dc20 96-43752

CIP

For Judy Keller and in memory of David C. Huntington

# CONTENTS

* *
*


*Preface* .... viii

Introduction .... 2

*one* Strongholds of Noble Political and Civil Life .... 18

*two* Handsome Bindings and Vistas of Shelves: American Library Design to 1875 .... 54

*three* Woburn: "A Model Village Library" .... 104

*four* The Epitome of Design: Libraries in North Easton and Quincy .... 150

*five* Et in Arcadia Ego .... 192

*six* Competition in East Saginaw .... 218

*seven* Epilogue .... 254

*Notes* .... 270

*Bibliography* .... 314

*Index* .... 336

# PREFACE

* *
*

The American public library is essentially an invention of the latter half of the nineteenth century, and the arrangement of the structures that evolved to house it underwent its most significant course of development during this same period. By the end of the century, more than 450 purpose-built public library buildings had been raised in the United States, more than half of them in New England. Like that of the railway station or the department store, the story of their evolution represents a study in the invention and development of a new and essentially modern building type. While it is the larger American library buildings, such as McKim, Mead and White's grand palace in Boston (1887–1898; fig. 7.8), that have attracted the most significant scholarly attention to date, these more prominent monuments were far outnumbered during the nineteenth century by their smaller, typically suburban cousins. As a consequence, it was in the libraries of "the second class" that architects discovered a unique opportunity to experiment with issues of program, planning, and iconography specifically geared to the needs of this institution.

This study focuses on five designs for public library buildings produced by Henry Hobson Richardson (1838–1886) in the decade between 1876 and 1886. The four of these that were actually constructed are all located within the intellectual and economic orbit of Boston, at

North Easton (1877–1879), Woburn (1876–1879), Quincy (1880–1882), and Malden (1883–1885), Massachusetts; the latter three are all within ten miles of the State House and Athenaeum on Beacon Hill. The fifth design was entered into a competition held early in 1886 in East Saginaw (now part of Saginaw), Michigan. While rejected by the board of trustees, plans for this edifice appear to have been reused after Richardson's death for the Howard Public Library in New Orleans (1887–1889), the city of his birth. An examination of Richardson's contribution to the form, as well as the political and cultural context in which this form was molded, provides an exceptional opportunity to study the early development of the small public library in the United States in general and its buildings in particular.

As Richardson's first biographer, Mariana Griswold Van Rensselaer, observed in 1888, Richardson's library buildings also "afford an excellent chance to trace the development of his talent," a gift for design and invention that was widely acclaimed by both his colleagues and the American public at the time of his death at the age of 47 in 1886. Because the iconographic and programmatic requirements that shaped the configuration and meaning of Richardson's small public libraries represent a discrete problem with its own set of factors, I have chosen to study them as a group, ignoring, for the most part, the architect's proposal for the much larger and more complex Young Men's Association Library in Buffalo, New York (1884; never built), and, to a lesser degree, the Billings Memorial Library, erected at the University of Vermont between 1883 and 1886.

Although he is widely recognized as one of the most significant figures in the history of American architecture, Henry Hobson Richardson's life and work have proven difficult to interpret. In sharp contrast to Louis Sullivan or Frank Lloyd Wright, Richardson wrote almost nothing about his buildings. Scholars attempting to decode their meaning have thus been forced to rely, as James F. O'Gorman has noted, on the "testimony of his contemporaries" and the "witness of [his] mature works." While the principal testimony remains Van Rensselaer's rich biography, additional information on the architect's career—the full scope of which I have not attempted to recapitulate in this monograph—can be found in Henry-Russell Hitchcock's *The Architecture of Henry Hobson Richardson and His Times* (New York, 1936), Jeffrey Karl Ochsner's *catalogue raisonné* of the architect's buildings, *H. H. Richardson: Complete Architectural Works* (Cambridge, 1982), and more recently in O'Gorman's *H. H. Richardson: Architectural Forms for an American Society* (Chicago, 1987) and *Three American Architects: Richardson, Sullivan, and Wright, 1865–1915* (Chicago, 1991). In his masterful examination of the drawings that emanated from Richardson's office and are now housed in the Houghton Library at Harvard, *Henry*

*Hobson Richardson and His Office: Selected Drawings* (Cambridge, 1982), O'Gorman also took the first close look at several of this architect's public libraries as a building type. The Houghton drawings, some 150 of which pertain to Richardson's five small libraries, necessarily form a third significant source of information on this architect's working method. I would like to thank the staff of this institution for the access they have given me to these documents, and for their willingness to schedule their cleaning so that new and clearer reproductions of them might appear in this book.

Much of the background for this study derives from material found in my doctoral dissertation, "Small Public Libraries in America 1850–1890: The Invention and Evolution of a Building Type" (The University of Michigan, 1982). Statistics on library construction that appear in the introduction and chapter 2 of the present study have been based on my own survey of American public library buildings, which has been ongoing since 1978. In addition to correspondence with individual institutions, I have visited more than 250 of these buildings. I have also consulted state library commission and United States government reports, especially those published in Connecticut (1895), Massachusetts (1899), and New Hampshire (1906), and by the United States Bureau of Education in its exhaustive *Statistics of Public, Society and School Libraries* (1900). These publications were cross-referenced with notices on library activities that appeared in publications such as the *Library Journal*, the *American Architect and Building News*, or the *Inland Architect and Building News* to create a database on more than 450 public library buildings erected in this country and Canada between c. 1850 and 1900. The history of library architecture to 1875 that appears in chapter 2 is based on this work.

If there is an element of nostalgia in this study, it is driven in part by the precarious situation in which so many public libraries currently find themselves. Budgets are being cut by small-minded and short-sighted politicians and bureaucrats, and—in the popular imagination—electronic media have begun to replace our long-standing reliance on the book as a source of essential information and entertainment. As Neil Harris has observed: "The image of the eternal stacks ebbs, replaced by intercommunicating data banks, whose network maintenance now dominates professional planning."[1]

A more personal nostalgia derives from my own fascination with books, which began as a child in the public library in Des Plaines, Illinois, when for the first time I was confronted with what to a child seemed an unending wall of these fascinating objects. That moment of discovery, as it has for so many individuals fortunate enough to experience a public library, transformed my life and ultimately led me here, to an exploration of these buildings and of the intentions of the people who founded and designed them. To the individuals who had the foresight to establish that institution and to the anonymous librarians there, and in so many of the libraries I have had the pleasure of visiting and working in during the last twenty years or so, I owe many of the seeds of inspiration for this book.

To "build a library" is both to accumulate a significant collection of books and to erect an edifice in which to house them. In the former sense, at least, I feel that I have discovered a kindred spirit in Henry Hobson Richardson, who was himself a bibliophile of no small stature. This fact surely underlies his approach to the design of library buildings. Much recent literature has argued that during the nineteenth century women as well as men became ever more dependent on reading—and writing—to define their place in society. As Victor Hugo suggests in his novel *Notre-Dame de Paris* (1831), the ever-increasing availability of books due to the invention of the printing press greatly increased their significance as cultural artifacts. By the middle of the nineteenth century, books and libraries had been imbued with central roles in American cultural and political life. As Henry Ward Beecher makes more than clear in a novel like *Norwood; or, Village Life in New England* (1868), not only did the size of one's library signal one's economic and intellectual status, but its very form reflected the fundamental moral character of its owner.[2]

Necessarily, any project of this kind is indebted to a long list of individuals who have given generously of their time and insight. To them I largely owe the small successes of this book, while I must reserve for myself the blame for its shortcomings. It was Nathan Whitman who, many years ago, first suggested that I look more closely at the Hackley Public Library in Muskegon, Michigan, a building that became the topic of my master's thesis in the Department of Art History at the University of Michigan, where he reigned with terror over his infamous seminars in the history of architecture. He, along with Leonard K. Eaton, David C. Huntington, William A. Coles, and Frederick Wagman, later served as members of my dissertation committee. Leonard Eaton, Mark Mumford, Judy Keller, and Kevin McMahon all graciously consented to read portions of this manuscript in its early stages of development.

I would like to acknowledge Michael Rotundi and Margaret Crawford, who arranged for a sabbatical from my teaching at the Southern California Institute of Architecture that made possible the final work on this book, and Robert Mangurian and John Buchanan, who helped to facilitate production of the manuscript and illustrations. Other financial support has come from the Rockefeller Foundation; The University of Michigan, Horace H. Rackham School of Graduate Studies; and the National Endowment for the Humanities, Travel to Collections Program.

Special thanks go to Anne Anninger, Philip Hofer Curator of Printing and Graphic Arts at the Houghton Library, Harvard, as well as to Julie Mellby and to Ardys Kozbial and Greg Kehm, who have been patiently overseeing the cleaning of Richardson's drawings at that institution, and who granted me permission to reproduce them. I would also like to thank Kathy O'Dougherty, Tom Smith, and Sylvia Pope at the Woburn Public Library, Mary Clark at the Thomas Crane Public Library, Joel Thiele at the Malden Public Library, Anna Mae Maday at the Hoyt Public Library, and Dorothy Berry with the Easton Historical Society, as well as John Doherty, Janice H. Chadbourne, Katherine Dibble, John Dorsey, Aaron Schmidt, and Sinclair Hitchings at the Boston Public Library, and Lorna Condon and Ann Clifford at the Society for the Preservation of New England Antiquities, as well as the library staff at the Getty Research Institute for the History of Art and the Humanities in Santa Monica.

Thanks are also due to my editor at the MIT Press, Matthew Abbate, as well as Daniele Levine and, for his patience, Roger Conover, and to the anonymous readers of this manuscript who approved of it and also offered numerous insightful criticisms and unselfish suggestions.

Others have contributed to this project in a myriad of ways too varied to catalogue; these include, but are not limited to, John Hoops, Carol Keller, Ann Gilkerson, Kelvin Jones, Leland Roth, Mary Daniels, Marcia E. Moss, Dale Pretzer, Robert Roche, Nancy R. Horlacher, Ruth T. Degenhardt, Joyce Connolly, Hollie B. McHenry, John Ferguson, Paul Larson, Richard Longstreth, Patricia Leighton, Jacqueline Baas, Richard Candee, Linda Hart, and Barbara and Gordon Petersen.

For permitting me to quote from the diary of his great-grandfather, George M. Champney, I would like to thank Edwin A. Champney, and also the Massachusetts Historical Commission for permission to quote from the Albert Crane Correspondence. Glenn Waguespack ably produced or redrew a number of plans that appear in this book.

To my parents Walter and LaVerne Breisch, whose support and confidence over the years allowed me to return to school and pursue my interests, and to Rush Clinger and Judy Keller, what can I say? Thank you as well. I could not have done this without you. To Judy, in particular, my friend, supporter, and companion for more than twenty years, and to David C. Huntington, a scholar, humanitarian, and fine entertainer, a man deeply missed but not forgotten by anyone who had the privilege to know and learn from him, I dedicate this book.

# Henry Hobson Richardson and the Small Public Library in America

# INTRODUCTION

* *
*

The ambition of the old Babel builders was well directed for this world: there are but two strong conquerors of the forgetfulness of men, Poetry and Architecture; and the latter in some sort includes the former, and is mightier in its reality; it is well to have, not only what men have thought and felt, but what their hands have handled, and their strength wrought, and their eyes beheld, all the days of their life. The age of Homer is surrounded with darkness, his very personality with doubt. Not so that of Pericles: and the day is coming when we shall confess that we have learned more of Greece out of the crumbling fragments of her sculpture than even from her sweet singers or soldier historians.

John Ruskin, "The Lamp of Memory," 1849

I.1
Henry Hobson Richardson. Courtesy of the Society for the Preservation of New England Antiquities.

When Henry Hobson Richardson (fig. I.1) was notified in January 1877 that the firm of Gambrill and Richardson had won the competition for the Public Library in Woburn, Massachusetts, his career stood at a critical juncture. Having enjoyed a relatively successful practice since his return from the Ecole des Beaux-Arts in Paris in 1866, by the end of 1876 Richardson appears to have been faced with relatively little work. Major construction on his most important commission, Trinity Church, Boston (fig. I.2), was all but complete (it was consecrated on 9 February 1877), and with the exception of his ongoing association with the New York State Capitol in Albany, a project he was undertaking in collaboration with Leopold Eidlitz and his good friend and colleague Frederick Law Olmsted (1822–1903), Richardson's other projects had also recently drawn to a close. The William Watts Sherman House in Newport, Rhode Island, the Hayden Building in Boston, and the R. and F. Cheney Building in Hartford were all finished in 1876. Following a move to Brookline in the spring of 1874—in part to be nearer his Trinity Church work—Richardson had also become progressively more independent of his New York partner, Charles Gambrill (1834–1880), ultimately severing all professional ties with him in October 1878: hence, the anxiety over the outcome of the Woburn competition that he reveals in letters he addressed to Olmsted in late November and again in December of 1876.[1]

Although not as significant as the Trinity Church competition that Richardson had carried in 1872, the Woburn contest was nonetheless notable. In addition to Gambrill and Richardson, four other architectural partnerships, representing an impressive selection of Boston's most successful firms—Snell and Gregerson, Peabody and Stearns, Ware and Van Brunt, and Cummings and Sears—had been invited by the executors of the will of Charles Bowers Winn to submit designs for the building. Winn had died in December 1875, leaving $140,000 to the town of Woburn for the construction of a public library to commemorate his father. Richardson's victory not only brought much-needed work into the office (the firm's commission would ultimately total almost $5,000), but helped consolidate his reputation at a point when his own personal interpretation of the Romanesque style was just beginning to mature. With his triumph at Trinity Church all but behind him, the architect must have been anxious to move on to other signal projects.[2]

While not as widely admired as this ecclesiastical monument (indeed, all of his major biographers have criticized the library's overly picturesque grouping of parts), Richardson's Woburn Public Library was almost immediately published in *American Architect and Building News,* appearing in the 3 March 1877 edition (fig. 3.1).[3] Later that same year he received a

I.2
H. H. Richardson, Trinity Church, Boston, 1872–1877. Van Rensselaer, *Henry Hobson Richardson and His Works*, 1888.

second library commission from the heirs of Oliver Ames II for a memorial edifice in North Easton, Massachusetts, where, according to these same critics, he was able to rectify many of the shortcomings inherent in his first foray into library design. This form would be further refined at Quincy, Massachusetts, where he erected a third public library building for the wife and sons of Thomas Crane, and subsequently in the Converse Memorial Building in Malden, Massachusetts. Like the previous three structures, this last was also intended as a memorial, in this case to commemorate the son of Elisha and Mary Converse, who had been murdered twenty years earlier in a bank robbery. Of the Crane Library, in particular, observed *Harper's Weekly* in 1883: "It is the third Village library that Mr. RICHARDSON has designed in Massachusetts, and, upon the whole, the most successful; and saying that is pretty safely saying that it is architecturally the best Village library in the United States" (fig. I.3).[4] While some 450 public library buildings were to be erected in this country during the last half of the nineteenth century (about 75 of these before 1883), Richardson's achievement in Quincy alone would rank him as perhaps the most important and influential library designer of the era.

* * *

By 1876, the year in which Richardson had begun work on his preliminary drawings for the Woburn Public Library, the public library movement in the United States was just over twenty-five years old. As Jesse Shera, Sidney Ditzion, and others have pointed out, this movement drew its nourishment from a myriad of public and private sources.[5] Earlier, more informal parish and town libraries, literary societies, Athenaeums, social and circulating libraries, mechanics' and mercantile institutes, public school, university, and college libraries all contributed to the form of this new American institution as it evolved between 1850 and 1900. These antecedents, however, ranging back to the eighteenth century, had generally been social or proprietary libraries, restricted, for the most part, to paying members and privileged scholars.

If there was one thing that most Americans seemed able to agree upon during the nineteenth century—as George Ticknor and Edward Everett affirmed in the 1852 *Report of the Trustees of the Public Library of the City of Boston*—it was their implicit faith in the ability of the book to "affect life and raise personal character and condition."[6] The American public library represented an almost inevitable expansion of this ideal, one that found a progenitor in the educational reform movement that had coalesced around men such as Horace Mann (1796–1859) during the 1840s. As a direct reaction to the disintegration of traditional values brought on by large-scale industrialization, urbanization, and immigration, Mann and others had urged that public schools be employed in the battle to maintain the status quo. "As population increases, and especially as artificial wants multiply," he argued, "the temptations increase, and the guards and securities must increase also, or society will deteriorate."[7] According to Michael Katz, the goal of a reformed educational system became the "reformation of society through the formation of personality," one that believed implicitly in the reality of unfettered economic opportunity but also in the virtues of punctuality, hard work, and the respect for private property.[8]

George Ticknor (1791–1871), an outstanding man of letters and a well-entrenched member of Boston's aristocracy, and his colleague and the first president of the Boston Public Library, Edward Everett (1794–1865), applied a similar logic to the public library they were urging the city of Boston to found in 1852. Hailing it as "the crowning glory of our public schools," this institution, averred Everett, was "absolutely needed to make our admirable system of Public Education complete; and to continue in some degree through life that happy equality of

I.3
H. H. Richardson, Crane Memorial Library, Quincy, Massachusetts, 1879–1881. Photograph by Thomson and Thomson, courtesy of the Society for the Preservation of New England Antiquities.

intellectual privileges, which now exists in our Schools, but terminates with them."[9] In order to achieve this goal, these men envisioned the establishment of an innovative institution that would be composed of two independent book collections, one for serious scholarly research and the other catering to more general tastes. Following the example of the Astor Library in New York, which had been founded as a public but noncirculating research library in 1849, as well as European libraries in Paris, Munich, and London, Everett in particular, argued that the Boston Public Library should maintain a first-class reference collection. At the same time he became convinced by Ticknor that this institution should also house a smaller circulating or lending library, composed of current and more popular literature. According to Ticknor, this lending department (the first of its kind to be seriously considered in any major American or European city) would allow for "the freest circulation of the books that is consistent with their safety. . . . Thus, by following the popular taste,—unless it should ask for something unhealthy,—we may hope to create a real desire for general reading" among "the greatest possible number of persons in the city."[10]

While echoing the idealism of Jefferson, Ticknor's proposal also reflected his own anxiety over what he and his fellow Brahmins viewed as an alarming acceptance of Jacksonian notions of democracy among the city's poor and immigrant populations. These people, observed the Boston library's Joint Standing Committee in 1852, "for the most part are devoted to the laborious occupations of life; and, if it be true that they know nothing of the enervating influence of luxurious habits, it is also true that they think little of moral and intellectual culture."[11] Thus the establishment of a circulating library in Boston was of "paramount importance" for the maintenance of order: "As a matter of public policy and duty, on the same principle that we furnish free education . . . general information should be so diffused that the largest possible number of persons should be induced to read and understand questions of social order, which are constantly presenting themselves, and which we, as a people, are constantly required to decide, and do decide, either ignorantly or wisely." In order to achieve this goal it was crucial that "as many [books] as possible" find their way "into the home of the young; into poor families; into cheap boarding houses; in short, wherever they will be most likely to affect life and raise personal character and condition."[12] Initially controversial, Ticknor's proposal was destined to serve as a model for nearly every public library founded in this country.

While the debate concerning the creation of a great public library in the City of Boston extended back to the 1830s, the first legislative steps toward the realization of this goal began with the submission in 1848 of a petition requesting the Massachusetts state assembly to grant the municipality the right to establish and maintain such an institution with public moneys. An act empowering the city to do so was signed into law in March of that year, though Boston took no further substantive action for another four years. All the same, observes Jesse Shera in his landmark study *Foundations of the Public Library,* this legislation represented "the first official recognition by a state governing body of the principle of municipal library support."[13] In the year following the enactment of the Boston Public Library Act, the New Hampshire legislature approved a similar law, which was (unlike the Massachusetts legislation) not exclusive, allowing "that any town in this State, at any legal meeting notified and holden for the purpose, and the city council of any city in this State, may raise and appropriate money to procure books, maps, charts, periodicals, and other publications, for the establishment and perpetual maintenance within the limits of such town or city of a public library." Communities were also empowered by this law to raise or appropriate, through taxation, money "for the purchase of land and the erection of such buildings as may be necessary for the suitable accommodation" of a library, and additionally they were allowed to accept "gifts, devices, bequests and legacies" that might be made for such purposes.[14]

Following the example of New Hampshire and an attempt by the village of Wayland, Massachusetts, to establish its own free library in that state, the Massachusetts legislature in 1851 voted to expand the Boston Public Library Act to include all of its cities and towns. By 1876, similar authority had been extended by state legislation to all of the municipalities of New England, Ohio, Wisconsin, Iowa, Indiana, Illinois, and Texas. The result of these laws, as was their intention, was the rapid establishment of an ever-increasing number of public libraries all across the country, but especially in the northeastern states. In Massachusetts alone, more than 30 free public libraries were created within a decade of the passage of its 1851 act. By 1876, some 457 such institutions had been founded in the country as a whole, though few were housed in buildings of their own. More than half of these institutions were located in New England, many—like those for which Richardson designed buildings—in the immediate vicinity of Boston.[15]

Like the Athenaeums and social libraries that had preceded them, the overwhelming majority of these early institutions were relatively small in size, consisting, at most, of a few thousand books (heavily prescriptive and religious in nature), housed unceremoniously in a back room, basement, or upper story of the town hall or post office, or some out-of-the-way corner of a local drug store or other emporium. Because the requirements of American book collections before midcentury were comparatively uncomplicated, little attention was directed toward their shelving arrangements and planning; in fact, the first published discussion of library design did not appear in the United States until 1853.[16] The Woburn Public Library, for example, was housed in a small room in the town hall from 1856—the year in which the library was founded—until its transfer to the new Richardson building in May 1879. In 1874, the year in which the town library committee began to seriously recognize a need for expanded quarters, the collection numbered just 2,684 volumes.[17] The Quincy Public Library, which was formed in 1871 by a vote of the town meeting, opened that same year with 4,607 books in a borrowed room in the Adams Academy. This structure had been erected by the Adams family, and designed by the Boston firm of Ware and Van Brunt in 1869, to house a private, classical school that had been established several decades earlier through a bequest of President John Adams. In 1874, because the Academy was in need of more classroom space, the library was relocated to a vacant church at the corner of Hancock and Canal streets, where it resided until moving into the Crane Memorial building in 1882.[18] In Malden, the public library opened in a small room in the city hall on 14 February 1879 with 3,643 books, a number that had grown to 5,513 by the end of the year. With an annual circulation of 51,000 volumes, noted the trustees in their report for 1881, demand had already far exceeded their limited space.[19] The following year, they noted that "the room occupied by the alcove" was "becoming somewhat straitened," and "hope[d] that, should a remodeling of the City Hall be decided upon by the City Council, such changes will be made as give the Library the room now occupied by the Overseers of the Poor."[20]

As in Malden, and as so often happened elsewhere during the nineteenth century, the trustees in both Woburn and Quincy actively advertised their need for more and better library space. When Jonathan Winn, who had himself initiated the founding of the public library in Woburn with a donation $300 for the purchase of books in 1854, died in 1873, he bequeathed an additional $2,500 to the library, with his brother Timothy—who died the same year—adding another $3,000.[21] While gratefully accepted by the town library committee, these gifts, which were likewise to be used for the purchase of books, only exacerbated the cramped conditions within which the library had operated for nearly two decades. "The need of additional accommodation for the Library is pressing itself with greater force every year upon the attention of the Committee," noted its members in their 1874 Report; "it seems impossible to continue to occupy the present rooms beyond the year now before us, without doing violence to every rule of comfort, taste and propriety." While recognizing the inability or indisposition of the town to furnish the library with a new building, they noted that "there [was] reason to believe that if a Committee is appointed to take the matter into consideration, several of our public spirited citizens would be ready to combine liberal gifts with an appropriation by the town" for this purpose.[22] Although a building committee was chosen at the annual town meeting that year, little progress appears to have been made toward this goal until January 1875, when Jonathan Winn's son, Charles, committed himself to this task by establishing a library bequest in his will, which was signed and witnessed that month.[23]

The board of the Quincy library, led by Charles Francis Adams, Jr. (1835–1915), likewise remarked in their annual report of 1878 on the necessity of finding "a commodious and better adapted library room in a more central part of town,—that should be nearer the station, the post office, the banks and the business center, where it can be most conveniently reached by the greatest number of persons."[24] Echoing the Woburn Library Committee—and a reality faced by most small village libraries at the time—the Quincy trustees went on to acknowledge the town's financial inability to undertake such an endeavor, while at the same time noting that in a surprising number of neighboring communities, such as Hingham, Braintree, Randolph, and North Easton, "the needs of the public libraries in this respect have been met by the gifts or bequests of wealthy inhabitants desiring to do something to evince their interest in their native places." Thus, they were "not without hope that the great want of a suitable and commodious building [would] ultimately be met in Quincy as it has been met elsewhere. Private munificence may supply a public need. Certainly no better field for its exercise could be desired."[25]

As the number of new public library buildings in the vicinity of Quincy alone indicates, "private munificence" had, in fact, played a major role in the shaping of the early public library movement in America. It was, for example, an offer of $50,000 for the purchase of books, made by the London financier and Boston expatriate Joshua Bates (1788–1864) in 1852, that ultimately acted as the primary stimulus for the founding and construction of the Boston Public Library. The "only condition" that he asked was "that the building shall be such as to be an ornament to the City, that there be shall be room for one hundred to one hundred and fifty persons to sit at reading-tables,—that it shall be perfectly free to all, with no other restrictions than may be necessary for the preservation of the books."[26] Bates noted in a subsequent letter to his friend and business colleague Thomas Ward Wren that his proposal had been prompted by a chance discovery of the 1852 *Report of the Trustees,* but stimulated by his own memories of his experience as a "poor boy" in Boston attempting to get ahead without "the great advantage of such a Library." Had such an institution then existed, Bates averred, "I am confident that had there been good, warm, and well-lighted rooms to which we could have resorted with proper books, nearly all the youth of my acquaintance would have spent their evenings there to the improvement of their minds and their morals." Bates's offer proved to be decisive, as Walter Muir Whitehill observed: "Before his intervention there were words, after it there was a library."[27]

At the time of his initial overture to the City of Boston, Bates was, no doubt, aware that in June 1852, just four months earlier, his friend George Peabody (1795–1869), a fellow American financier and expatriate living in London, had offered to give $20,000 to his native village of South Danvers (renamed Peabody in 1868), Massachusetts, for the establishment of a lyceum, which would include both an auditorium for public lectures and a free public library. When opened in 1854—also no doubt under the influence of Ticknor and Everett's 1852 *Report*—the Peabody library was set up as a circulating collection, from which any citizen of Danvers over the age of fifteen, with a suitable recommendation from its Board of Reference, had the "free right to take books . . . , so long as they compl[ied] strictly with its regulations."[28]

Widely publicized, as were the numerous other benefactions that ultimately came to bear his name, the Peabody Institute eventually received more than $200,000 from its patron. His other gifts and bequests included the erection of small library buildings in Post Mills, Vermont (1867), and Danvers (1868–1869) and Georgetown (1866–1869), Massachusetts, all places with which Peabody had had personal contact during his youth. He also distributed several million dollars to found institutions and museums in Baltimore and Salem and at Harvard and Yale, and he made generous donations to numerous other British and American charities, colleges, and museums.[29] Although based on an old Anglo-American tradition of public philanthropy, which had endowed similar if typically private institutions such as the Radcliffe Camera in Oxford, the Redwood Library in Newport, Rhode Island, and the Lawrence Institute in Cambridge, Massachusetts, both the Peabody and the Bates gifts were widely touted by library advocates and emulated by philanthropists all across the country.

In 1853, for example, exactly one year and a day after Peabody's offer to Danvers was made public, the radical abolitionist Gerritt Smith notified residents of Oswego, New York, that he intended to make available $25,000 for the establishment of a similar institution in that community.[30] And although the economic crash of 1857—the year in which Oswego City Library was dedicated—and the onset of the Civil War brought at least a temporary halt to this initial spate of library building, these events did not entirely discourage those interested in the promotion of libraries. Before the end of the war, in fact, plans for five new public library buildings had been initiated in small American towns and villages: in Bernardston (1862–1863), Sudbury (1862–1863), and Stockbridge (1864), Massachusetts, Richmond (1863–1864), Indiana, and Ithaca (1863–1866), New York. All five of these buildings were built with private funds, the Sudbury building through the bequest of John Goodnow, a wealthy Boston merchant, and the others through gifts made by local entrepreneurs and industrialists. Only Boston and New Bedford (1856–1857), Massachusetts, were able to raise public library buildings using municipal funds before 1865.[31]

Fed by the enormous profits accumulated by northern industrialists during and after the Civil War, private philanthropy subsequently fueled an even more dramatic increase in the building of public libraries. It was, in fact, through the type of beneficence envisioned in the New Hampshire Public Library Act of 1849 that the majority of purpose-built public libraries came into existence in American during the later half of the nineteenth century. Of 34 new public library buildings opened in the United States between 1865 and 1875, for example, some 23 were endowed entirely with private funds, totaling more than $600,000. During the same decade, the median price of these structures more than doubled, from $15,000 for buildings erected before 1865 to over $32,000 for those between 1871 and 1875. The cost and size of the largest of these town libraries, in communities like Brookline (1866–1869), Concord (1872–1873), Northampton (1872–1874), Braintree (1873–1874), or Pittsfield (1874–1875), Massachusetts, ranged from $40,000 to $70,000, with projected capacities of 30,000 to 65,000 volumes.[32]

Still, in the United States as a whole, fewer than 10 percent of all public, municipal libraries in 1875 were housed in specially designed structures.[33] As will be discussed in chapter 2, these varied widely in style, size, and arrangement. Following Peabody's example, a number of institutions, such as those in Oswego, Ithaca, or Bernardston, included auditoriums in their program. Other institutions, such as the Northampton and Pittsfield libraries, housed art galleries and natural history collections, as would Richardson's building in Woburn. Erected at a cost of over $95,000, with shelf space for some 100,000 volumes, the latter edifice was by far the largest and most expensive of these new village libraries to date. Its conception in many ways marked a pivotal moment in the evolution of the American public library movement.

The year it was designed, 1876, witnessed not only the publication of the landmark government report *Public Libraries in the United States of America: Their History, Condition, and Management,* but the founding of the American Library Association at the Philadelphia Exposition, and the appearance of the *Library Journal,* the official mouthpiece of this new professional organization. This same year marked the birth of *American Architect and Building News,* a professional periodical that would eventually publish and celebrate all of Richardson's built library designs. During the following decades an increasing volume of technical literature on library design appeared in both publications. By 1886, the year of Richardson's death, librarians in this country had authored more than 15 important essays on the planning and arrangement of public library buildings, many of which appeared in the *Library Journal.*[34]

During this same period some 60 new buildings would open their doors to the public, with structures like the Converse Memorial Building, which was dedicated in 1885, now costing as much as $125,000. Between 1885 and 1895 this number jumped to 225, with 32 library buildings opened in 1894 alone. Of the slightly more than 450 purpose-built structures that marked the American countryside by the end of the century, more than 80 percent had been endowed by local philanthropists, a trend that was only eclipsed after 1900 by the remarkable success of Andrew Carnegie's nationwide benefactions.[35] Boston remained at the center of this movement throughout the second half of the nineteenth century, especially during the period in which Richardson was designing his libraries in its suburbs. In 1875, for example, more than one-third of all of the public library buildings standing in this country (some 16 new structures) were located within 25 miles of the city. By the end of the century, nearly 200 of these structures had been raised in Massachusetts alone.

* * *

In spite of his early prominence, Richardson's contribution to this movement was mixed. Predictably, his widely acclaimed library in Quincy found numerous imitators, at least on the surface. His other libraries and many of his planning strategies did not meet with the same degree of success. The alcove and gallery shelving system that he preferred, and the general lack of good natural light that too often characterized his libraries, were widely criticized by American librarians—and even some architects—during the latter half of the 1880s. As James F. O'Gorman observed in his seminal discussion of Richardson's library drawings, "the type of Richardson building universally admired by twentieth-century architectural critics was condemned by the people who had to use it."[36] That contradiction is of central interest to this study.

Chapters 1 and 2 describe the cultural and architectural context in which Richardson's designs evolved. The first of these explores the ambiguous and complex role of the public lending library in nineteenth-century New England society. As library historian Dee Garrison has pointed out, public libraries became a "rich focus for expressive meaning in Victorian America," one that is in many ways evident in the structures Richardson designed to house them. "The belief that America was a radical democratic experiment in government; the sense of urban crisis and chaos; the fear of immigrant intruders; the emphasis upon the family as guarantor of tradition; the discontent of women and labor; the hope that education would right the wrongs of poverty and crime; the hunger for education among the poor; the ambiguous paternalistic and humanitarian motives of reformers—all were as important to the content of library ritual as the need for a contented, disciplined, and busy wage force."[37]

Because all of Richardson's library commissions resulted from private benefactions, an understanding of the intentions of his patrons and their representatives is also essential. Part of the genius of these family monuments is that they were able to fulfill at once so many of the cultural and political aspirations of these conservative New England men and women. Born to privilege and educated at Harvard, Richardson moved in the same circles as those who solicited library designs from him. He was thus especially well suited to grasp their fears and desires. In addition to the material form of the structures themselves, my interpretation has had to rely heavily on the official accounts of the era, a testimony that prejudices the story of these buildings in favor of the class that commissioned them. Conspicuously absent from the contemporary record are the voices of the institutions' intended audience, the middle- and working-class residents of the communities in which the edifices were erected. Similarly ignored at the time was the role played by the bereaved widows and mothers of the families who built these memorial libraries. Unless new evidence is subsequently uncovered, we can only assume (and I will try to touch upon this at the end of the first chapter) that these women and the otherwise silent majorities of these towns made equally significant contributions to this history. As one scholar has noted, just because "women did not often sit on the boards of trustees of cultural institutions, . . . we can hardly conclude . . . that they had no influence. Involvement in culture must ultimately be seen as a family matter."[38]

By 1876, when Richardson created his first designs for a library building at Woburn, some 40 public library buildings already existed in the United States, along with two dozen academic and private library structures. While prominent European precedents, such as the Bibliothèque Ste.-Geneviève in Paris or the Munich Staatsbibliothek, had a direct impact on the form of larger American public libraries, like the Astor Library in New York or the two Boston Public Library buildings, these monuments were to prove inadequate as paradigms for the new programmatic requirements of smaller American lending libraries, as well as for the iconographic aspirations of their founders and builders. Just the same, they did serve as powerful symbols of the continuity of Western culture, a validation that extended back through the earlier monastic and university libraries of the Middle Ages to the legendary institutions of classical antiquity. While invoking this much-venerated tradition, planners during the later nineteenth century assumed that the "modern" library would incorporate the latest innovations in lighting, heating, and the efficient and secure storage and retrieval of books. As chapter 2 will set out, a fundamental conflict consequently arose in the design and construction of public libraries of this era between an obsession with efficiency and utility and a nostalgic, at times reactionary yearning for the sentimental reassurance of the past. This duality of intention is, of course, characteristic of the era, one that witnessed bewildering, at times dehumanizing industrialization and institutional growth.

Chapter 3 focuses on the Woburn library and the competition out of which its design emerged. The program for this building necessarily confronted its architect with new and complex problems related to its multiple functions as library, art gallery, and museum, as well as its public and commemorative iconography. Because it was intended to house a circulating collection, this edifice had to accommodate borrowers as well as readers. Given its relatively modest size, memorial intention, and expanded pedagogical program, few precedents existed for its form. Richardson would turn to his earlier experience in Europe for inspiration—most particularly to Henri Labrouste's two Paris libraries—transforming these archetypes to meet new demands of program, meaning, and place.

In chapter 4, I will analyze Richardson's designs for the libraries in North Easton and Quincy in light of his training at the Ecole des Beaux-Arts in Paris. As one of the first Americans to be educated at this school, which by midcentury stressed typology as a foundation for its method, Richardson found himself in a unique position to contribute to the quest for a vocabulary and arrangement appropriate to the American public lending library. Among the architect's many and varied achievements, one of the most singular was his invention and refinement of a legible form in which to house this institution. It seems clear that Richardson had imbibed deeply of what David Van Zanten has termed Henri Labrouste's "ideal" of "transparency": that is, "the situation where the whole work of architecture—its structure, its function, its philosophical nature—might be grasped by a glance at its exterior, as if one were conceptually seeing right through its walls."[39]

At the same time, like no other contemporary American institution, Richardson's public libraries also picturesquely reflect the qualities of their place in the natural world. In this respect one must turn to the architect's reading of the seminal English critic John Ruskin, as well as the American transcendentalist ideals of his friend and colleague Frederick Law Olmsted. It is O'Gorman's thesis that Olmsted's vision ultimately shaped Richardson's broader architectural program as well, "to create evolved architectural forms which by association would express the pluralistic American society of the post-Civil War years."[40]

While Richardson's libraries articulate the specific character of their use and place, I will argue that they likewise express the individual character and aspirations of their patrons. All four of his built libraries were erected to commemorate deceased family members. Subsequently, these institutions—though still intended to perform as town libraries, with all of their own public, cultural, and political ramifications—established a new iconography explicitly associated with their commemorative function. Chapter 5 examines the new meanings that this new role brought to bear on the library, and the broader context in which these meanings developed. Nowhere was the paradoxical symbiosis of capitalist display and feminine sentimentality, democratic institution and Christian memorial to the entrepreneurial spirit, carried out more completely than in the last of these edifices at Malden.

Finally, chapter 6 will return to the role played by the library profession in the development of a modern theory of library planning during this period. This will be examined within the context of the competition that Richardson entered early in 1886 (just months before his death) for the Hoyt Public Library in East Saginaw, Michigan. Here, the presence of a strongly opinionated and vocal librarian, William Frederick Poole, acting as planning consultant to a building committee composed of local lawyers and businessmen, greatly altered the dynamics of the design process. Recently discovered correspondence in Saginaw provides new insight into both the mechanics of the architectural competition and the circumstances leading to the board's rejection of Richardson's proposal in favor of one submitted by the firm of Van Brunt and Howe. As I have noted elsewhere, and will revisit at the end of this volume, the subsequent resurrection of Richardson's Hoyt scheme by Shepley, Rutan and Coolidge in New Orleans brought a growing rift between librarians and architects to a head.[41] Perhaps because of their unique point of view and because they, like the architects at this time, were also struggling to establish themselves as a recognized profession, librarians seem rarely to have been pleased with the environments that architects designed for them—and in particular, it would appear, those created by Richardson.

What they failed to recognize was that, had Richardson catered entirely to their demands and not to the desires of his monied patrons, the institution itself would have attained far less public recognition and hence the ultimate stature it did in the cultural life of small towns all across the nation.

*one*

# Strongholds of Noble Political and Civil Life

Now, if culture, which simply means trying to perfect oneself, and one's mind as part of oneself, brings us light, and if light shows us that there is nothing so very blessed in merely doing as one likes, that the worship of the mere freedom to do as one likes is worship of machinery, that the really blessed thing is to like what right reason ordains, and to follow her authority, then we have got a practical benefit out of culture. We have got a much wanted principle, a principle of authority, to counteract the tendency to anarchy which seems to be threatening us.

MATTHEW ARNOLD, *Culture and Anarchy,* 1869

The rapid expansion of industrial capitalism during the latter half of the nineteenth century irrevocably altered the political and social landscape of New England, transforming scores of small agrarian villages into centers of large-scale manufacturing. While excess wealth produced by this new economic order provided the means to erect and fund public libraries, the buildings themselves embody something of the ambivalence with which their patrons and the people who surrounded them viewed this new world. In the second volume of *Three Episodes of Massachusetts History* (1892), Charles Francis Adams, Jr.'s, epic chronicle of Quincy, for example, the author bitterly recounts the circumstances he believed had led to the decline of his hometown. Here Adams describes how the opening of granite quarries and the growth of the local shoe manufacturing industry during the first half of the nineteenth century had attracted "a new race" of laborers "of different blood and religion" to a previously homogeneous "community made up of those who tilled the soil, and those who supplied the tillers' wants."[1] By 1885 "thirty-seven inhabitants only reported themselves as farmers and one hundred and twenty-four as farm laborers, while the stone-workers and quarry-men were fourteen hundred in number. The agriculturist had practically disappeared." During this same period the town's population expanded dramatically, from 2,000 residents in 1830 to more than 12,000 in 1885. The "large infusions of alien material which from time to time had taken place in the Quincy constituency," observed Adams, had produced a population in which a "clear majority of the whole were either of foreign birth or the children of immigrants." Even of those born in this country, one out of three was not originally from Quincy.[2]

The expansion of Quincy's population and industry brought with it the destruction of much of the town's historic fabric. Older homes and trees were removed to make way for widened roads and workers' tenements, and much of the surrounding countryside was being destroyed by suburban development and expanding granite quarries. "The creaking of the derrick, the blows of the sledge, and the click of the hammer [were] everywhere heard from the week-day morning to its night."[3] Already by the mid-1870s, the quiet, rural community that Adams and his siblings visited in their childhood—the small village in which Thomas Crane (1803–1875) was also raised—had all but vanished.

For Adams the most discouraging sign of change was the decision of many towns during this period—including Quincy in 1889—to charter themselves as municipalities, abandoning a town meeting form of government that had guided them for over two and a half centuries. As he observed in his own community, the inevitable expansion of the public school system and increased demand on roads, water systems, police and fire services that accompanied the town's growth had combined to overwhelm this venerable New England decision-making body. A member of one of Quincy's oldest and most distinguished families, Adams, who amassed his own fortune in railroad and mining investments in the West, viewed this change of governmental form as marking the final dissolution of an agrarian society whose traditional bonds and hierarchies had previously maintained a clearer sense order: "The time had been when almost every man in those town-meetings knew by face and name and reputation every other man in them, while the bulk of those who attended were tillers of the soil." By the last quarter of the nineteenth century, "in the place of the eighteenth century freeholders,—colonial yeomanry,—there now assembled a great mass of men who, engaged in multifarious occupations, not only neither knew of, nor cared for, the ancient ways and old-time traditions, but many of whom regarded those traditions and ways with an impatience and contempt they were under no pains to conceal as part of the rubbish of the antiquated past." "It is almost needless to say," lamented this consummate patrician, "that in the presence of such elements as these the downfall of the local gentry influence was a mere question of time."[4] In 1907, more than a decade after he himself had fled the town for a new country residence in Lincoln, Massachusetts, Adams would confide to Thomas Crane's son, Albert, that "the gradual transformation of Quincy into a thoroughly suburban city of the fourth class has been extremely painful to me. It has lost all its individuality, and almost every trace of that which was agreeably associated with my younger life. The Thomas Crane Memorial Hall, and the grounds you have gradually acquired in its vicinity, constitute the single distinct betterment the place has undergone."[5]

The unprecedented development and radical demographic shifts charted by Adams in his history of Quincy were common in communities surrounding Boston. Both Woburn and Malden, for example, experienced similar growth during these same years. An 1883 bird's-eye view of the former reveals a sprawling community of some 12,000 residents, up from 8,560 in 1870 (fig. 1.1).[6] Throughout the town, tall smokestacks of more than a dozen tanneries spew forth the acrid residue of their manufacturing processes. Employing some 1,500 workmen, this was the same industry that had served as the source of the Winn family fortune. By way of contrast, the slender steeples of fewer than half as many churches mark the historic center of the community, which stands just east of the new library building.[7]

The traumas attendant upon industrial growth lamented by Adams appear to have been greeted with an equal measure of anxiety and nostalgia by Woburn's gentry. In August 1876, for example, the Converse homestead, one of the oldest residences in Woburn, was torn down

NEW BOSTON
SALEM
BROAD ST
MAIN ST
MAIN
PARK
MONTVALE
WALNUT
AUBURN
WARREN
STURGIS
WARREN
LAWRENCE
JONES
STURGIS ST
CANAL

1.1
Bird's-eye view of Woburn, Massachusetts. Detail of map by L. R. Burleigh, 1883. Geography and Map Division, Library of Congress.

1.2
Family reunion at the Converse homestead, Woburn, 1876. Courtesy of the Society for the Preservation of New England Antiquities.

after a reunion of the family had been arranged so they might visit the ancient "relic" one last time and have themselves photographed with it (fig. 1.2). Whether the distantly related Elisha and Mary Converse traveled from nearby Malden to attend this event cannot be ascertained, but it did receive considerable coverage in the local press. Woburn's future librarian, George M. Champney (d. 1881), apparently purchased a photograph of this gathering for the Woburn library, an institution he felt to be the appropriate repository for such records of the town's early history.[8]

Between 1853, when Elisha Slade Converse (1820–1904) and Mary Diana Converse (1825–1903) first settled there, and 1885, the year in which the Converse Memorial Building was dedicated, Malden likewise mushroomed from just 3,500 inhabitants to well over 16,000, during the last five years alone gaining 4,390 new residents. Among its major industries was the Boston Rubber Shoe Company, which had been organized in 1853, with Elisha as its treasurer and general manager. Within three decades this corporation was transformed under his leadership into one of the largest of its kind in the world, with factories in Malden and neighboring Melrose employing between 2,000 and 2,500 workers capable of producing some 30,000 shoes and boots a day.[9]

In response to its own growth, Malden had likewise been incorporated as an independent municipality seven years before Quincy in 1881, and Woburn followed suit in 1888. In contrast to the more aristocratic reaction of Adams, however, Elisha Converse was instrumental in securing Malden's municipal charter from the state legislature and served as its first mayor.[10] John Cummings (1812–1898), himself a leather manufacturer as well as uncle of Charles Bowers Winn (1838–1875) and president of the library's board of trustees from 1886 until 1898, appears to have played a parallel role in Woburn, presenting the petition for incorporation to that town's selectmen in January 1883. According to D. Hamilton Hurd's history of the area, this event had been anticipated for more than a decade by the town's business community.[11]

While the village of North Easton remained relatively small, with a population of just under 4,000 in 1875, the Ames shovel works, as can be seen in an 1881 bird's-eye view (fig. 1.3), dominated the core of the town. By 1860 these factories, then being managed by the future founder of the Ames Public Library, Oliver Ames II (1807–1877), and his brother Oakes (1804–1873), likewise represented the largest manufactory of its type in the country, turning out nearly a million and a half shovels a year. Demand for these products only increased with the outbreak of war with the South and the continuing expansion of the American railroad system. With the growth of the Ames' fortune an almost feudal relationship developed between the family and the village, as in Quincy replacing earlier less formal bonds with a new hierarchy based upon personal wealth. In North Easton, the heavily Irish workforce that manned the Ames factories lived in Ames houses and tenements, shopped at Ames stores, attended schools built for them by the Ames family, and kept their savings in the Ames-owned bank. Vast Ames estates and sumptuous mansions ringed the industrial core of the village, near where, on a slight prominence, the Ames library and Ames Memorial Hall overlook the town.[12]

As is most evident in North Easton and Malden, modern manufacturing, marketing, and investment led to ever greater disparities in wealth, creating class divisions heretofore unknown

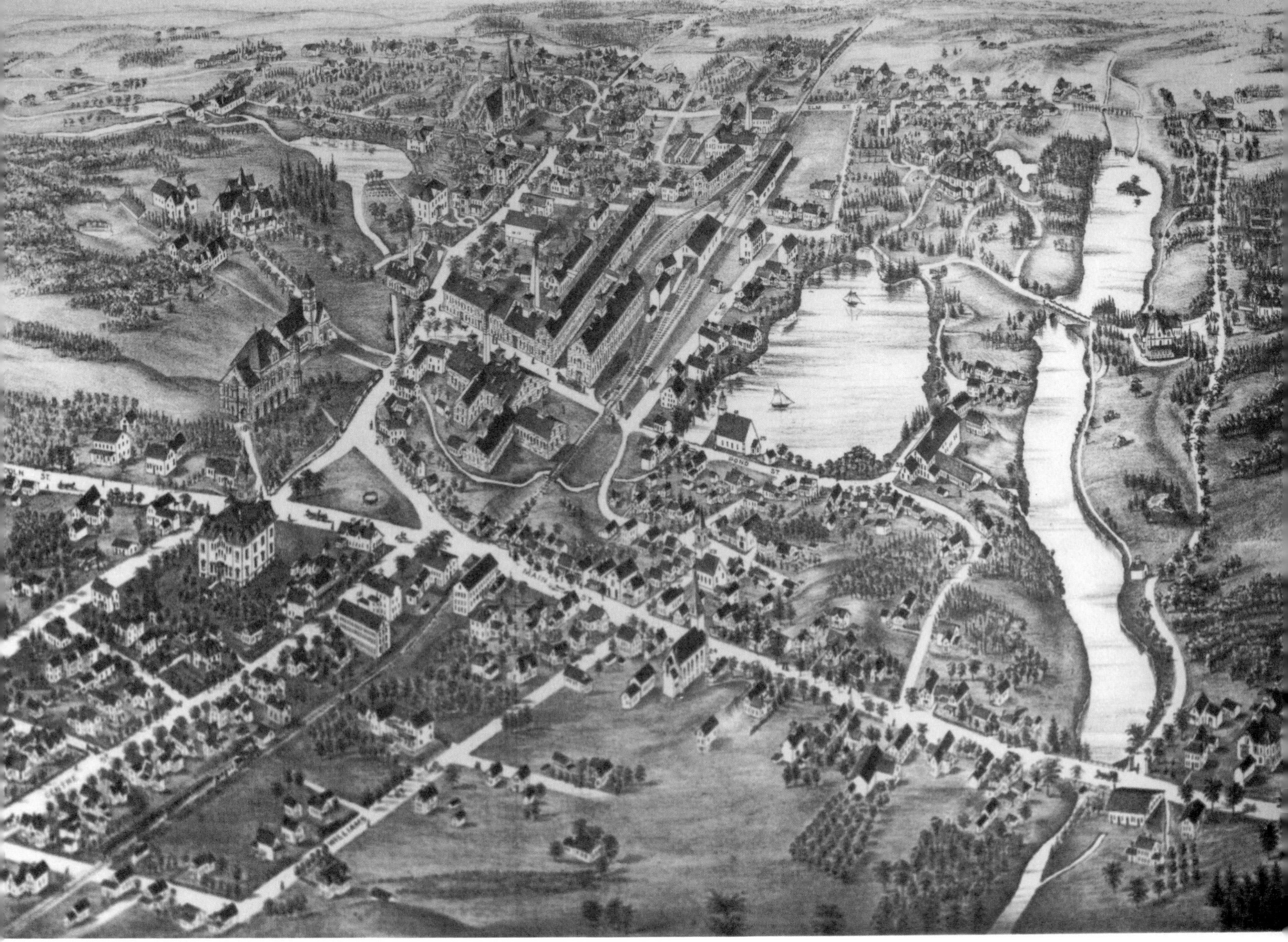


1.3

Bird's-eye view of North Easton, Massachusetts. Detail of map by O. H. Bailey and Co., 1881, courtesy of the Easton Historical Society.

in New England. As Ronald Story has noted: "In Boston, if not elsewhere, the emergence of modern culture and philanthropic institutions was inextricable from the emergence of a modern upper class; the emergence of institutions and class, inextricable from the larger patterns of urbanization and growth."[13] And the enormous sums of money accumulated by the Ames and Converses, as well as the Winns and Cranes, and expended by them on these new philanthropic institutions, must have been all but incomprehensible to the people who were actually expected to patronize them. In 1875, for example, Charles Bowers Winn left behind an estate whose total worth was in excess of $400,000 (more than $225,000 of which would eventually be directed to the Woburn library), while the personal wealth of Clarissa L. Crane, (1837–1895), widow of Thomas Crane, was nearly $410,000 when she passed away twenty years later. At his death in 1904, Elisha Slade Converse's estate was valued at between seven and eight million dollars.[14] Even these fortunes paled beside the profits the Ames family accumulated in their North Easton factories and from investments in enterprises such as the Union Pacific Railroad. During this same period, the median income of a skilled shoemaker who labored 60 hours a week in Woburn's or Quincy's shoe and leather industries, or the factories of Elisha Converse in Malden, amounted to just over $420 a year.[15] In 1880, the year in which the Cranes made their initial offer of $20,000 to erect a memorial to Thomas Crane in Quincy, the two librarians at the public library—both women—were making annual salaries of $450 and $480. At North Easton the first librarian, Charles R. Ballard, on the other hand, was offered $900: still a paltry sum compared to the more than $80,000 the Ames family expended on the library itself.[16]

This widening gap between rich and poor contributed, among other things, to increased labor unrest and a rise in violent crime all across the country, a fact that only served to exacerbate the anxiety of the newly wealthy manufacturing class and the older Brahmins alike. By 1870 between one-third and one-half of all the men engaged in American shoe manufacturing had joined the Knights of St. Crispin, a militant trade union, which continued to be active into the mid-1870s, leading major strikes in Lynn, Massachusetts, for example, in 1872 and 1878. During the following decade this union was replaced by other labor organizations, such as the Lasters' Protective Union or the Knights of Labor. The threat of anarchy in events such as these, and especially in the violent national railroad strikes and riots of 1877, must have been much on the minds of all of Richardson's patrons, many of whom had extensive interests in the railroad industry.[17] Charles Winn's uncle, John Cummings, for example, was a director of the Boston and Albany Railroad from 1876 until his death in 1898. In 1889, he was joined on this board by Edward D. Hayden (1833–1908), the first president of the Woburn Public Library board of trustees and former brother-in-law of Winn.[18] Both the Ames family and Charles Francis Adams, Jr., likewise maintained intimate and lucrative ties to the Union Pacific and many other railroads.[19]

Fear of class warfare led Civil War veterans and businessmen to form the National Guard Association in 1876 to lobby Congress to pass a new Militia Act. In the industrialized New England states, in particular, the continuing threat of domestic insurrection led to the creation of dozens of National Guard units and the erection of municipal armories all across the region—with budgets and building programs often supplemented by the local business community. The correspondence between this new American institution—and building type—and the public library did not pass unnoticed. At the dedication of the Scoville Institute in Oak Park, Illinois, in 1888, for example, its founder James Scoville maintained that the public library itself acted as "an armory in which you will store weapons for defense, more powerful than dynamite in the preservation of the liberties of a free people."[20] And in John Hay's novel *The Bread-Winners: A Social Study* (1883), the chairman of the public library board and well-to-do property owner Captain Arthur Farnham organizes, arms, leads, and pays out of his own pocket a private militia composed of fellow Civil War veterans to maintain order during a general strike. He is later robbed and left for dead in his own home by a disgruntled striker whom he had earlier arrested.[21]

In Malden, the fear of violence must have appeared even more immediate following the murder in 1863 of the eldest son of Elisha and Mary Converse, the child to whom they would dedicate the Converse Memorial Building in 1885 (on the thirty-ninth anniversary of his birthday). Frank Converse, who was only 17 at the time, had been shot in the head during a robbery while working as a cashier in his father's bank. The notoriety of this crime was compounded by the fact that the perpetrator appears to have been Edward W. Green, himself a well-known resident of Malden. Following his apprehension by a local "vigilance committee," Green—subsequent to a series of appeals—was hung for his action, one that became the subject of numerous sensationalized accounts, which also accused him of womanizing, embezzlement, and of being a "secretly drinking man."[22] To this day, in fact, the events surrounding the robbery, trial, and Green's execution—all of which was practically unprecedented at this date—are recalled in Malden with a clear sense of dismay. The Malden Bank robbery, suggested former Massachusetts Governor John D. Long (1838–1915) at the dedication of the new library, stands out as "one of those monstrosities of human aberration which now and then shock the moral sentiment of a community as an earthquake would shock a New England landscape."[23]

* * *

In line with Edward Everett and George Ticknor, all of Richardson's clients appear to have viewed the library as a staunch ally of the public school system in their battle to counter this perceived collapse of moral and social order; or, as Everett's nephew Charles Francis Adams, Jr., viewed the library in Quincy, it was "the natural compliment of the first,—the People's College."[24] Before he left Quincy in 1893, Adams, who himself served as the chairman of both the Quincy school committee and public library board of trustees during the 1870s and 1880s, worked to reform town government, as well as the public educational and library systems, in an attempt to reduce the growing influence of the immigrant and working classes and reinstate the traditional leadership of the local aristocracy. He summarized many of his efforts in a pamphlet which he had printed at his own expense in 1879 entitled *The Public Library and the Common Schools: Three Papers on Educational Reform.*[25] Echoing the founders of the Boston Public Library, Adams identified these institutions as a means of "prepar[ing] children in the community for the far greater work of educating themselves," in particular those "born and bred in the habitations of labor,—those offspring of the dollar and the dollar and a half a day people whom we especially wish to reach."[26]

In North Easton, the Ames family had long maintained an interest in public education. Oliver Ames II, whose 1875 bequest would establish the Ames library, had begun to play an active role on various local school committees as early as the 1840s. In 1869 Oliver Ames and Sons at their own expense erected a new three-story school building, which can be seen to the left of the library and memorial hall in the 1881 bird's-eye view of the town (fig. 1.3). The construction of this edifice had been supervised by Oliver's nephew and namesake, Oliver Ames III (1831–1895). Upon their deaths in 1873 and 1877, moreover, Oliver Ames II and his brother, Oakes, each bequeathed $50,000 to the public schools of North Easton. Oliver's decision to will an additional $50,000 for a public library can be viewed as a natural extension of his earlier philanthropic and civic endeavors, a gesture that did not pass unnoticed by the local School Committee, which recognized the library as "an important auxiliary in the education of our children" and called the attention of its teachers to the usefulness of the collection for its students.[27]

When lobbying for a new library space for their institution in 1874 (more than a year before the Winn bequest), the Woburn trustees likewise reasoned that "if it is considered what an important part a library plays among our modern educational institutions, it seems highly proper that it should receive due attention with regard to its attractions, its comforts, its proper equipment, as well as opportunity for its increase and enlargement. It cannot be doubted that a good Library bears a close and influential relation to the education of the community."[28] Seven years later the trustees of the Malden Public Library noted that "the library is sustained as a public educator, with functions like those of our public schools. It is to improve and elevate tastes, capacities, and moral and mental qualities, and to minister innocent delight to weary toilers."[29] Under their guidance "time w[ould] bring a closer union between school and library." Great as were the "material" trusts of this board, maintained its president, Deloraine P. Corey (1836–1910) at the Converse Memorial's dedication, "I hold them as a feather's weight against their moral and aesthetic power. They stand apart as a great conservative and educational force, throwing out its gathered energies and influences into every part of the community. . . . I know that the influence of the public library will ever be on the side of private virtue and public honor, and where it exists, a living active force, ignorance and crime will be held as reproached things."[30]

Employing culture to conserve order was clearly a prominent goal of all of these libraries, and the men who controlled them, no doubt, agreed with Matthew Arnold that at least one "practical benefit" of culture was "to counteract the tendency to anarchy which seems to be threatening us." As an antidote to the rampant materialism of the age, culture was characterized by Arnold as "a pursuit of our total perfection by means of getting to know, on all the matters which most concern us the best which has been thought and said in the world."[31] In America, this tenet had been embraced by Charles Eliot Norton (1827–1908), who was also an early and ardent admirer of John Ruskin. From his pulpit at Harvard, where he was appointed Professor of Fine Arts in 1874, Norton was in a particularly significant position to spread his own brand of conservative aesthetic idealism to many of the men who would be involved with Richardson's libraries.[32] It was in line with the assertions of both Arnold and Norton that Adams would argue (though he did not entirely prevail) that it was the duty of the trustees and the librarian at Quincy to purge the library of "trashy and sensational novels," and to direct readers to the "standard works" of literature and nonfiction, which would have the greatest positive impact on them. Likewise, noted the Malden trustees in 1881, "there is a considerable class of books, which, though they may not be positively impure and corrupt in their tone and contents, are so utterly worthless, and so lacking in any good quality and influence for heart, mind, or character, that the committee would advise their exclusion from circulation and from the shelves." While there might be room for a limited number of "amusing or pleasing" books, even these should be employed so as to "lead the way to something a little higher and better."[33]

With art galleries at both Woburn and Malden, these beliefs were extended into the realm of the fine arts as well, although neither collection could be said to achieve the level of quality anticipated by Arnold, or even Norton. Woburn's gallery, for example, was initially filled with some fifty paintings from the estate of Charles Bowers Winn; primarily landscape and genre scenes by minor nineteenth-century European painters (fig. 3.17). After examining these for the first time in 1876, George M. Champney, the chairman of the library committee and future librarian, rather ambiguously pronounced it "a good average collection—in fact much superior to what are found in the parlors of the wealthy as a general thing."[34] After the paintings were put on display three years later, a critic writing for the *Woburn Advertiser* hedged even further. "In concluding this article," this critic wrote, "we cannot refrain from referring people to their own judgment in considering these paintings. All artists cannot be masters, and all masterpieces cannot be understood by all people. Thus the work of mediocrity in art has a wide range, for from the most ordinary paintings something can be learned."[35]

Fortunately, at Malden the collection fared somewhat better, although it began with only a small number of paintings by mostly local artists, including copies of Gilbert Stuart portraits of Washington, Jefferson, and Madison, as well as a large canvas depicting "Lincoln at Gettysburg," by Albion Harris Bicknell (1837–1915), who also contributed portraits of the donors and their son, Frank Converse. While more explicitly patriotic in their intent, the Malden trustees still appear to have considered the presence of these political icons secondary to the mission of the library. The gallery was to act as a "companion" to the books, they noted in one report, and through its influence, "visitors, who might otherwise never come to a Library, are gradually brought within its influence."[36] Upon her death in 1903, Mary Converse bequeathed the institution $15,000, the income from which was to be used specifically to purchase art, and this fund was supplemented the following year with $50,000 from the bequest of her husband Elisha. With this money, the Malden Public Library was able over the years to increase the quality of its collection with paintings such as Jean-François Millet's *Woman Churning Butter.*[37]

* * *

While they were incorporated as public institutions, the collections in all of these buildings—the books as well as paintings and sculpture—clearly reflected the social and cultural norms of their founders and the men chosen by them to serve as their trustees. It was these individuals—overwhelmingly Anglo-Saxon and male, conservative and Republican—who defined what was meant by "standard" works of literature or a "better class of books."[38] These men might all be characterized, as Geoffrey Blodgett has described Charles Francis Adams, Jr., as advocates of conservative social activism; that is, they "shared a profoundly conservative concept of reform. The core of the concept was a stubborn faith in political and social democracy—provided that democracy remained responsive to the cues of trained and cultivated leadership."[39] This power to set standards provided a means of maintaining cultural hegemony over the working classes, an affirmation of the privilege attendant upon the accumulation of wealth and status that set these men apart.[40] During the early years of all of these public libraries, these positions were maintained with tenacity. The presence of a prominent patron only served to increase the power of the boards, and this expanded their control over, and distance from, those beneath them, the classes who actually frequented the libraries. With his own Harvard background and close friendship with these men, it could be assumed that Richardson shared these same values.

As a condition of the gift of a new building to Malden, for example, Elisha Converse required that the public library—in spite of its status as a municipal institution—be independently incorporated through an act of the state legislature that he himself had drafted. This law specified that the trustees, who up until then had been chosen by vote of the city council, would subsequently consist of nine members, self-elected by the corporation (Elisha S. Converse among them), with the mayor, president of the common council, and chairman of the board of aldermen (all of whom had previously been voting members of the board) serving only in an *ex officio* capacity. While Converse argued that this would place the library above the vagaries of city politics, not everyone in the community appears to have agreed. One letter to the *Malden Mirror,* for example, characterized the Converse proposal with unabashed redundancy as "the attempt of a half dozen old family politicians to perpetuate themselves by this means of perpetuity." In particular, this correspondent objected to the "power" of this "clique," which had also "made the offices and filled them with their appointees in Malden for so many past years," to select the library's books. "The people may be ignorant, poor, vulgar, and no better than they ought to be," maintained the writer, "but they can discount the literary critics of the trustees of the public library, by a large majority, every day of the week."[41] After considerable public debate, Converse's proposal was none the less accepted by the city, and he himself continued to serve on the public library board until his death in 1904, only to be replaced by his son, Harry E. Converse. During this entire time as well, William F. Merrill, who had been the chief clerk in Elisha Converse's bank when his son was murdered, acted as secretary, and Converse's close friend Deloraine P. Corey served as president.[42]

This interest on the part of patrons and their representatives in maintaining control over their institutions is equally evident elsewhere. In Quincy, Charles Francis Adams, Jr., in spite of the fact that members of this body were chosen by a vote of the town meeting, was able to serve as chairman of the library board from 1875 until 1894. His biographer, Edward Chase Kirkland, has observed that when Adams used the phrase "library trustees," as he had in reference to the Quincy school committee—of which he was also an active member—it was "a modest euphemism, probably, for the pronoun 'I.'"[43] Adams, in fact, continued, through his close association with the Crane family, to exert an inordinate influence over the institution well into the first decade of the twentieth century, even after moving his residence to Lincoln in 1893.[44]

Likewise, in Woburn, the uncle of Charles Bowers Winn, John Cummings, and Winn's ex-brother-in-law, Edward D. Hayden, seem to have remained very much in control of the library from the time it was incorporated in 1885 until their respective deaths in 1898 and 1908. Hayden, in fact, served as the library's first president until 1886, when he was replaced by Cummings. He then acted as vice-president until Cummings's death, when Hayden resumed the responsibility of the presidency of the board, maintaining it until 1908.[45] "The Woburn Public Library was his pride," noted the author of his obituary in the *Boston Evening Transcript.* "Within its walls he spent many hours, and its interests were closely watched by him."[46]

As might be expected, the exercise of philanthropic and cultural paternalism was most conspicuous in the company town of North Easton, where the Ames Free Library was incorporated as a private institution totally independent of the town government; its charter specifying that its five trustees be chosen by the Unitarian Society, a congregation in which the Ames family were active members and to which they had been major contributors for decades. In 1875 the library's founder, Oliver Ames II, had donated nearly $100,000 to this church for the erection of a new sanctuary, which was designed by his nephew John Ames Mitchell. Beginning with his son, Frederick Lothrop Ames (1835–1893), a member of the family served as president of the library board continuously from the institution's establishment in 1883 until its charter was changed in 1977. Ames family members also dominate the list of other library directors chosen over the years by the church.[47]

While a disgruntled citizen might occasionally object, a seemingly endless stream of local histories, vanity compendiums of the lives of famous and successful men, and family genealogies continually reaffirmed the positions of authority these men held. All of the families for whom Richardson designed libraries, for example, like Thomas Crane, whose lineage Charles Frances Adams, Jr., painstakingly delineated in his address at the dedication of the Quincy library, prided themselves on being descended from "pure, old New England stock."[48] This "ancestor worship," what E. Digby Baltzell has labeled "the social defense of caste," was reiterated time and again in pamphlets such as *Henry Crane of Milton, Mass., 1654, and Some of His Descendants* (1893), and *The Starkeys of New England and Allied Families* (1910), which were commissioned by Thomas's son, Albert, to trace both his father's and his mother's Anglo-Saxon heritage; or in the *Family Records of Deacons James W. Converse and Elisha S. Converse,* which Elisha had privately printed and bound with an account of the dedication of the Converse Memorial Building in 1887.[49] Having been descended from a long line of Braintree and Quincy residents, observed one biographer, "Thomas Crane concentrates all these sterling New England ancestors, all of them sprung from sturdy English stock and from stalwart men who came to create homes founded on strong religious faith, and rigid adherence to codes of honor, integrity and probity. Grave Puritans they, who in their toil and concern to establish strongholds of noble political and civil life could not unbend to light enjoyments, but wrought at their self appointed, God-given tasks with knit brows, and close set lips, weighted with sense of personal responsibility and dignified by their labor."[50]

According to its founders and supporters, this same Anglo-Saxon birthright could be claimed by the public library itself. While the Malden library might be "unique in its purposes," as the audience was instructed by ex-Governor John D. Long at its dedication, "it is yet—to the honor of our American civilization be it said—only in the line and easy evolution of our New England system. It is as much a flower of the Pilgrim and the Puritan seed, as much a part of the providential scheme of the Mayflower and John Winthrop's landing, . . . as is Harvard College, or our common school system, or as if every stone under its roof, every book on its shelves, every picture upon its walls, had been in the minds eye of the founders of Massachusetts."[51]

In addition to certifying the cultural, class, and racial pedigree of the institution and its founders, these kinds of pronouncements reflect the growing interest in the nation's history associated with the celebration of its centennial in 1876. In addition to the founding of local history and genealogical collections in many of the libraries, this antiquarianism would soon blossom in architecture and design into the American colonial revival. It was in this spirit that George M. Champney, Woburn's future librarian, upon reading of the imminent destruction of the Converse homestead in 1876, noted in his diary that the library should act as a repository for records and photographs of the town's early history (fig. 1.2).[52] Less than two years after its opening, moreover, the trustees assembled a "colonial kitchen," similar to the widely publicized New England kitchen that had been exhibited at the Philadelphia Exposition of 1876, in the basement of their building, directly below the main reading room. This "old time kitchen," remnants of which can still be observed in what is now the children's room, was fitted up with diamond-paned windows, a timbered ceiling, and a massive, open hearth, equipped with pothooks and trammel, a Dutch oven, and heavy cast-iron cooking pots. A collection of antiques—a corner cupboard, chairs and table, a loom, and spinning wheels—completed this pageant of feminine and domestic virtue. All of this was intended to "carry . . . us back to the good old times of honest industry, home comfort, and thrift."[53] By the end of the century, America's colonial heritage would be perceived by reformers as a particularly potent weapon in the struggle to naturalize the thousands of immigrants who were still landing on this nation's shores.[54]

At Quincy, the trustees voted just one week before the Crane Memorial's dedication, in May 1882, to reserve four upper alcoves on the northeast side of the building for the library of John Adams, which had previously been stored in the Adams Academy in Quincy, and in 1886 Charles Francis Adams, Jr., "following the original intentions" of the Crane family, presented a portrait of his grandfather John Quincy Adams to the library. Seven years later they agreed that the alcove over the building's entryway should be assigned to the Quincy Historical Society.[55] In 1909, the Woburn trustees, likewise, agreed to reserve the front room on the second floor of their library for a genealogy collection, a function it still performs, and at Malden the local historical collection has long been stored in a basement room that opens off the children's room.[56]

* * *

In an age of laissez-faire capitalism and a naive belief in the Darwinian virtue of a free market system, of course, the intended influence of these memorial libraries extended far beyond the moral suasion of their books and lessons in American history to include the example of the lives of the founders themselves. These men were constantly being held up, not only as paragons of strict New England virtue but also as models of capitalist success. As Charles Francis Adams, Jr., reminded his audience at the dedication of the Quincy library, Thomas Crane "was merely a self-educated, self-made son of New England, well-intentioned and clear-headed, who a youth, went out from home into the great world and there amassed a fortune." Having begun his career as a lowly stone cutter in Quincy's granite quarries, he had journeyed to New York City in 1829, where he and several colleagues opened a stone yard. Through his own perseverance and integrity Crane eventually bought out his partners and subsequently accumulated large holdings in New York real estate; always "preserving, amid all temptations, his New

England birthright traits of simplicity, thrift, straight-forward honesty and deep religious feeling."[57]

In like manner, residents in Woburn and Malden were regularly prompted to recall the modest economic—if not familial—roots of Jonathan Bowers Winn and Elisha Slade Converse, or in North Easton, the simple virtue of the founder of the Ames dynasty, Oliver Ames, Sr. (1779–1863), who in his youth had been the village wrestling champion. Jonathan Winn, for example, was characterized as "a country schoolmaster" who "possessed a genius for finance, which he later developed in the prosecution of the leather industry, in which business he made for himself and those connected with him a fortune of considerable magnitude."[58] Or, as Arthur H. Wellman, a member of the board, noted at the presentation of Elisha Converse's bust to the Malden library in 1890, during his youth "poverty was the rule and we need not be surprised to find the young lad, at an age when according to modern customs he should have been busy with his books, working in a factory, thirteen hours a day, for wages of a dollar a week. Thus commenced the life of ceaseless industry we still behold among us. Add to this trait a true courage, plain New England common sense, a kindly regard for the feelings and opinions of others, and an unswerving integrity, and you have the stuff out of which he has builded success."[59]

As a literal embodiment of the Horatio Alger mythology of bootstrap success, these men and the monuments that commemorated their achievements stood as constant reminders of the heights to which the industrious might rise; while the libraries—as unlikely as the prospect might in reality be—were held out as the means by which this ascension could be accomplished. As Andrew Carnegie would further enunciate in his widely read "Gospel of Wealth" (first published in 1889), the amassing of great fortunes like those controlled by the Converse and Ames families carried with it certain innate responsibilities, not the least of which was its proper administration for the benefit of the less fortunate. Carnegie, with the assistance of his faithful lieutenant, James Bertram, set out to raise this art of giving to that of a corporate science, where "the man of wealth" became "the mere trustee and agent for his poorer brethren, bringing to their service his superior wisdom, experience, and ability to administer, doing for them better than they would or could do for themselves." In Carnegie's mind, "the main consideration should be to help those who will help themselves; to provide part of the means by which those who desire to improve may do so."[60]

From the perspective of the manufacturer, of course, a more industrious and better-educated working class also offered the prospect of improved productivity in the workplace. As early as 1856, for example, Rufus Choate argued at a reception held for George Peabody when he visited his new library in Danvers that it could be proven "by precise statistical details, derived from a long course of personal observation, that throughout the whole range of mechanical industry, the well educated operative does more work, does it better, wastes less, uses his allotted portion of the machinery to more advantage and more profit."[61] As was often noted by orators at the time, at least one other major function of the library was to offer an alternative to the saloon and pool hall. In this sense, Sidney Ditzion has noted that free library advocates and temperance workers were often of one mind. In his history of Quincy, for example, Adams railed against the "crying evil" of alcohol among the town's Irish and its granite workers, while Oliver Ames II, founder of the Ames library, had been vice-president of the Massachusetts Total Abstinence Society. In Malden, the local chapter of the Women's Christian Temperance Union was placing "scientific temperance text-books" in the public library within a year of the opening of the new Converse Memorial Building, a gesture that must have pleased the Converses, who were active members of the local Baptist church and whose own son was said to have been murdered by a "secretly drinking man."[62]

Given these multiple missions, men such as Carnegie would come to trust in the public library as one of the most effective conservators of the industrial capitalist order they had at their command. These institutions, Carnegie maintained, acted to "make men not violent revolutionists, but cautious evolutionists; not destroyers, but careful improvers."[63] Acting on beliefs such as these, he went on to endow more than 1,600 library buildings in the United States between 1886 and 1917, and an additional 828 in other parts of the English-speaking world.[64]

Even while public libraries were clearly intended to act as guardians of the status quo, however, Lawrence W. Levine has suggested that it is also "important to recognize the degree of tension" inherent in the decision of the cultural elite to open up these kinds of institutions to working men and women and their children. While this course might contribute to political and social stability, the realm of high culture had traditionally been reserved as an exclusive domain of the patrician classes, distinguishing, for example, proprietors of the Boston Athenaeum—the Ticknors and Everetts, as well as Frederick Lothrop Ames, Charles Francis Adams, Jr., or Edward D. Hayden of Woburn—from the common masses.[65] Even if they were able to sustain some degree of control over them, allowing open access to these new repositories of culture could be interpreted as undermining their authority and status. Indeed, it is important to recognize that the public library—no matter what the intentions of its founders—housed by its very nature "sources of resistance to dominant social modes and values," and that people of every class from Marx to Carnegie have indeed subverted libraries to their own ends.[66] "That an outcast should become a privileged citizen, that a beggar should dwell in a palace," wrote the Jewish immigrant Mary Antin of childhood years spent in the Boston Public Library at the end of the nineteenth century—"this was a romance more thrilling than poet ever sung. Surely I was rocked in an enchanted cradle."[67] Because, or perhaps in spite, of Ticknor's vision, the public library remains one of the last bastions of democratic space in America. In the country's larger cities, in particular, its tables are still shared by the homeless and the immigrant, scholar and schoolchild. The "Trojan horse inside th[is] cultural citadel," suggests Kenneth L. Kusmer, may very well be the librarian. The "culture of professionalism," while itself capable of myriad interpretations, "operated as a check upon the inherent elitism of privately endowed cultural institutions," at the very least by defending the right of all citizens to free and unrestrained access to books. The "goals and motives" of library professionals, observes Neil Harris, have always been "highly mixed, and subservience to political establishment was not the invariable result."[68]

The same, of course, might be said of the motives and goals of the library's founders. As Levine has argued, "culture is too variegated, too complex, too human to be tied to one explanatory device."[69] A number of scholars have suggested, for example, that the gift of the Ames library to the village of North Easton was intended, at least in part, as expiation for the family's association with the infamous Crédit Mobilier scandal during the early 1870s. There was a widespread belief that the Ameses had unfairly profited from investments in the Crédit Mobilier of America, a limited liability company chartered in 1864 to finance the construction of the Union Pacific Railroad. Oliver Ames II had been named president of the line in 1866 and held that office until 1871, when he was forced to step down in response to these charges. His brother Oakes, who as the Congressional representative of the Second District of Massachusetts served as a member of the committees on Manufactures and Pacific Railroads, was likewise accused of a conflict of interest, and of having suborned fellow representatives to invest in this venture at discount rates. In 1873, Oakes was censured by Congress for his activities. Said to have been crushed by the scope of this scandal and the indictment of his colleagues, he died the same year. While Oliver lowered his public profile, he continued to hold fully 10 percent of the Union Pacific stock, an interest that was first managed and then inherited by his son Frederick Lothrop Ames.[70]

While other patrons may have gained their fortunes in somewhat less controversial ways, the fact that Elisha Converse gained much of his early wealth by supplying Union forces with rubber canteens, boots, and wool blankets to fight the bloodiest war in American history may have moved him to think of his gift in similar terms. In New England, in particular, the ever-present Puritan heritage of the region's elite insured that a variety of altruistic motives drove their philanthropic and charitable endeavors and the ultimate consequences of them. As Robert F. Dalzell, Jr., has observed in Boston, "Christianity; the faith in 'higher' values; the conviction that democracy, properly tutored, could be made to work; the belief that wealth was a 'trust' to be administered for the good of society: each of these was taken seriously as a guide to action. They were never just elements of a convenient public posture."[71] The wealthy philanthropist, suggested John D. Long at the dedication of the Converse library building, thus becomes "almost the involuntary servant and expression" of a "general sentiment," which commands that he "appropriates a part of his fortune back to the public use and service."[72]

It was in line with these kinds of sentiments that all of Richardson's patrons also donated to more traditional charities. Along with his bequest to the public library, for example, Charles Bowers Winn divided one-third of the residue of his estate among a variety of social institutions designed to aid the poor. These included the New England Hospital for Women and Children in Roxbury, the Temporary Home for the Destitute in Boston, and a handful of other charitable societies devoted to the care of orphans and the aged.[73] Elisha and Mary Converse likewise "gave generously" to similar foundations, like the Malden City Hospital, the Malden Home for the Aged, and the Consumptives' Home in Roxbury, while Elisha was also a supporter and trustee of Wellesley College.[74] And Clarissa L. Crane, widow of Thomas Crane, bequeathed a portion of her estate to the Women's National Relief Association and the Chapin Home for the Aged and Infirm in New York City, an institution with which she had been actively involved before her death in 1895.[75] She and her husband had been members of the Universalist Church in New York City and close friends and admirers of a number of its more reform-minded ministers, such as Edwin Hubbell Chapin (1814–1880). Thomas Crane was himself a founder of Tufts College and served as a trustee from 1852 until his death in 1875. He was remembered as a close friend of Horace Greeley (1811–1872), and is said to have deeply sympathized with his ideas. Unswerving abolitionists, the Cranes may have shared some of Greeley's more controversial beliefs concerning the defense and help of the working classes.[76] While other library founders during this era may not have held views as extreme as those espoused by Greeley, they do appear to have taken an equally active role in their respective churches.

In North Easton, the Ames family, in addition to a major donation to its building campaign, charged the Unitarian Society with the selection of the Ames Free Library's trustees, and its minister, William L. Chaffin, was a member of its first board. As a surviving drawing from Richardson's office illustrates, Elisha Converse, who served as a deacon of the First Baptist Church in Malden, and his wife Mary initially considered commissioning the same architect to design a new ecclesiastical edifice to serve as a companion to the memorial library (fig. 1.4). In 1891 they donated $30,000 toward the construction of this church, which was finally designed by H. S. McKay.[77]

* * *

During the years following the Civil War, America's liberal Protestant clergy had become more comfortable with the idea of accepting secular institutions like public libraries as new allies in their struggle to maintain the church as a pertinent moral, if not ecclesiastical, force in a society that was becoming increasingly less Protestant. According to T. J. Jackson Lears, in fact, minis-

1.4
H. H. Richardson, Converse Memorial Building and design for a proposed Baptist Church, Malden, Massachusetts, 1883–1885. MAL F1, Department of Printing and Graphic Arts, The Houghton Library, Harvard University.

ters such as Edwin Chapin, or Richardson's close friend and rector of Boston's Trinity Church, the Reverend Phillips Brooks (1835–1893), found themselves much in accord with the objectives of the public library and its founders: "Their self-deceptions and evasions stamped many liberal Protestants as of a piece with ideologues of domesticity, genteel literati, success mythologists, and Spencerian positivists—by denying personal and social conflict, all promoted a vision of progress and harmony that sanctioned status quo social arrangements. Embracing official doctrines for a wide variety of personal reasons, they unwittingly reinforced the cultural dominance of their own class, the educated bourgeoisie."[78]

As has been widely observed, it was often women who formed the closest alliances with this ministry, particularly in the realms of literary pursuits and of the home. Within the context of industrial capitalism in particular, it was women who were viewed—and viewed themselves—as the ordained guardians of the type of family values that ministers and libraries alike were attempting to promote. "In the bourgeois imagination," observes Lears, "the home became an oasis of tenderness and affection in a desert of ruthless competition."[79] In this culture, Ann Douglas has argued, it was the woman who was responsible for the propagation of the sentimental and moral values "which her competitive husband, father, and son had little time to honor or enjoy; she was to provide an antidote and a purpose for their labor."[80]

While it might appear—if one were to rely solely on the official record—to have been the sons of Oliver Ames II and Thomas Crane, or the father of Frank Converse, who took the lead in the conception of the Ames, Crane, and Converse memorials, it is likely that the widows and mother played a significant role as well. Both Sarah Ames and Clarissa Crane, for example, left generous endowments in their own wills for their husbands' memorials, as did Mary Converse for the monument dedicated to the memory of her son in Malden. Clarissa Crane, in particular, was remembered for her strong beliefs in higher education and advocacy of "broader training of women." During her lifetime she was associated with the Sorosis Club in New York City, an organization founded in the 1860s as the first women's group in the United States devoted to self-education in the arts and literature, "a finely equipped training school, wherein . . . women [could] absorb the knowledge which is power."[81] In spite of the public prominence of her husband, Mary Converse, as grieving mother, also no doubt stood conspicuously in the background in Malden. In a portrait of her and her husband that appeared at the time the library was erected, it is Mary who holds the book.[82]

That these women remained publicly dependent on the men—the sons or the husband—was common nineteenth-century convention. In the words of Ann Douglas, the widow during this period "had no communal tasks deemed appropriate to her widowed state; she was obligated to undertake nothing but the heavily self-involved business of mourning."[83] The ritual of mourning, of course, only served to focus the spotlight on the Christian spiritual values that these surviving women were expected to exemplify and to disseminate to their families and society at large. "In a very true sense Mrs. Converse belonged to a wide world beyond the immediate horizon of her home," observed the Reverend Francis H. Rowley, pastor of First Baptist Church in Boston, at her funeral, "but behind this outer world where she was known so well, there was the sweet and sacred home life, where she realized the highest glory of her womanhood as wife and mother." During her lifetime this grieving mother had especially endeared herself to the youth of Malden, notes the sketch that appears in a memorial booklet published after her death: "One whose high and honorable position gives force to his words writes. . . . 'She was the ideal lady of my boyhood, who seemed to live and move in a world so calm and gracious as to be far above all earthly tumult and anxiety. . . . [I] could not imagine her anything other than I always saw,—a serene and beautiful Christian lady.'"[84]

As memorial buildings, all of Richardson's libraries likewise represented a significant, sentimental manifestation of the Victorian cult of mourning. By invoking the powerful image of death, their new commemorative function transformed them into quasi-religious institutions, a concentrated reflection of the sacralization of culture that has been identified as one of the hallmarks of late nineteenth-century American society.[85] The institutional roots of this ritualization of death and commemoration, in fact, extend back to the rural cemetery movement, which was founded in this country in the Boston area with the opening of Mount Auburn Cemetery in 1831. Already, at the dedication of this institution, Joseph Story had argued that the association of nature with art, in the form of monuments and cenotaphs, might "be made subservient to some of the highest purposes of religion and human duty." If "rightly selected and properly arranged," these memorials to the virtuous dead of a previous era could teach lessons in civic and moral responsibility "to which none may refuse to listen, and which all, that live, must hear."[86] Since the church burial ground had traditionally acted as "the country Laborer's only library, and to it was limited his knowledge of history, chronology, and bibliography," John Claudius Loudon likewise would argue a decade later that the rural or garden cemetery, with its tombs, trees, and shrubs, would also serve as "a school for instruction in architecture, sculpture, landscape-gardening," and other related arts.[87]

During the years preceding and following the Civil War, the public park, under the influence of Andrew Jackson Downing (1815–1852), or Richardson's colleague Frederick Law

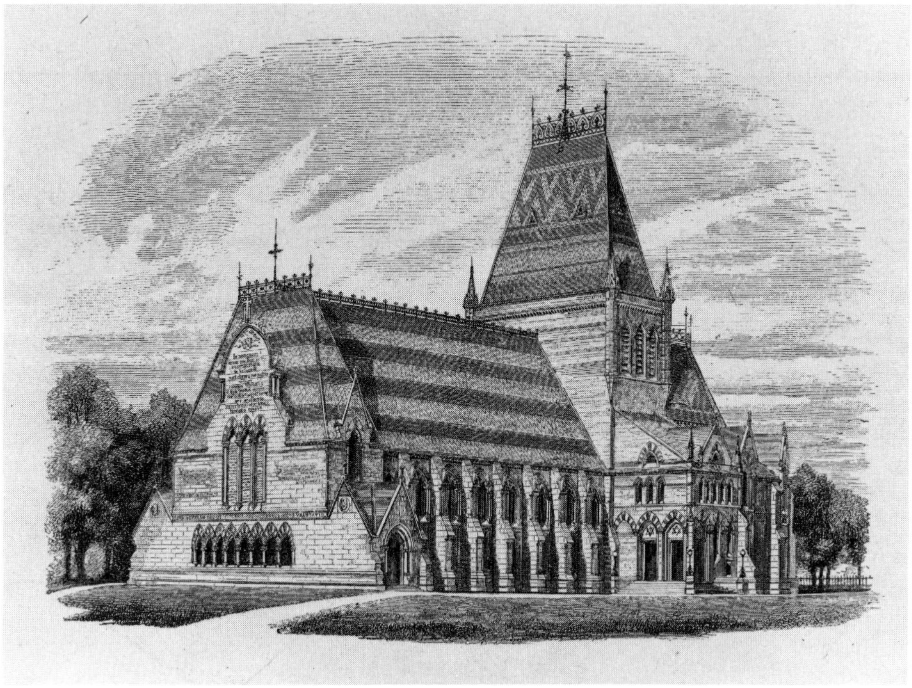

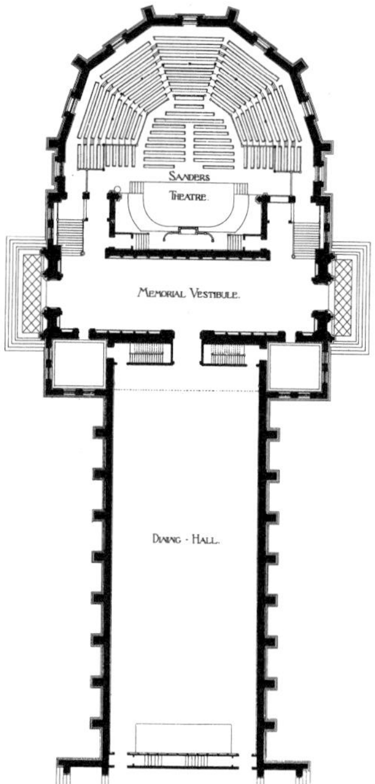
SANDERS
THEATRE
MEMORIAL VESTIBULE
DINING - HALL

Olmsted, and the memorial library inherited something of the conservative mission as well as the Transcendentalist aspirations of the rural cemetery movement. The transitional models for Richardson's memorial libraries can be found in a handful of public libraries dedicated as Civil War memorials in Massachusetts immediately following the cessation of hostilities in 1865. Buildings like Lancaster Memorial Hall and Library (1867–1868), Andover Memorial Hall (1871–1873), or the Northampton Free Public Library (1872–1874) all mixed patriotic and commemorative iconography with library functions.[88] The immediate precedent for these buildings seems to have been Memorial Hall at Harvard, where a room dedicated to the memory of the students and graduates who had fallen in the War of Rebellion was joined with an auditorium and a dining room for the use of alumni (figs. 1.5, 1.6). According to his brother-in-law, it was Charles Eliot Norton who led the fight for the union of these spaces in one edifice, arguing "that the memorial should be one which did not suggest victory or triumph in war, but the sacrifice of life for a cause wholly disconnected from ordinary warfare, and above it, and that the memorial should be avowedly dedicated to the uses of peace and the objects of the university."[89]

An initial appeal for funds for this project, along with a woodcut and description of Ware and Van Brunt's preliminary design for the building, had been mailed in February 1866 to Harvard alumni—among them Frederick Lothrop Ames and Edward D. Hayden (both Harvard '54), Charles Francis Adams, Jr. (Harvard '56), and Henry Hobson Richardson (Harvard '59).[90] This was just one month before the Boston financier Nathaniel Thayer (1808–1883)—a leading railroad investor and associate of both Adams and Ames—first suggested that his hometown of Lancaster combine its own interest in erecting a Civil War memorial with its need for a public library building. Although himself not a graduate of Harvard, Thayer, whose father had matriculated there in 1789, had by this date developed close ties to the institution. In addition to donating $1,200 toward the construction of Memorial Hall itself, in 1864 he

1.5
Ware and Van Brunt, Memorial Hall, Harvard University, 1866–1878. Harvard University Archives.

1.6
Memorial Hall, Harvard, 1866 plan. Harvard University Archives.

1.7
Lancaster Common, Lancaster, Massachusetts, with the Lancaster Meeting House by Charles Bulfinch, 1816, to the left, and Memorial Hall by Ryder and Harris, 1867–1868, in the background. Reproduced courtesy of the Trustees of the Boston Public Library.

had endowed a boarding club and dining room for Harvard students that became known as Thayer Commons, and in 1868 he would be elected a Fellow of the Harvard Corporation, an unusual honor for a nongraduate. The following year Thayer announced his intention to donate $100,000 to the college for a new dormitory dedicated to the memory of his father and brother. Opened in 1870, this building was designed by Edward D. Harris, a junior partner in the Boston firm of Ryder and Harris, the architects of Lancaster Memorial Hall, which was itself dedicated in 1868 (fig. 1.7).[91]

The Reverend George Bartol described this building's elaborate memorial iconography in its dedication booklet, where he noted that the "twofold design" of this edifice as public library and memorial hall "everywhere appear[ed]." It was immediately introduced on the facade by a stone plaque "bearing in bas-relief an urn surrounded by a wreath of oak leaves, draped in mourning," while just inside the entrance a set of engraved tablets lining the vestibule announced that this structure had been "DEDICATED BY THEIR FELLOW-CITIZENS, TO THE SACRED MEMORY OF THOSE MEN OF LANCASTER WHO GAVE THEIR LIVES FOR THE INTEGRITY OF THE REPUBLIC IN THE CIVIL WAR, 1861–1865." The library itself was housed in a two-story octagonal hall set at the far end of this entryway, and even here, behind the delivery desk, a large marble tablet displayed the names of the thirty-nine Lancaster soldiers who had died in the conflict. Above this list of casualties stood a "war window," which pictured in stained glass the Holy Bible and military emblems such as a sword, helmet, shield, victor's wreath, and national flag. These symbols of conflict were counterbalanced by a "peace window," which filled the center of a domed skylight that hovered over the hall and depicted a dove bearing an olive branch, descending through the parting clouds of battle.[92]

Within this memorial edifice, Christopher Thayer reminded his audience at its dedication, the Union dead "for their worthy and glorious deeds, are placed side by side with, and share the immortality of, those who by their writings have been made, so far as on earth they could be, immortal." Were anyone to stand in this edifice and "be tempted to swerve from the strict line of patriotic integrity, to plot against the union and freedom of the Republic, and meditate involving it in anarchy, distraction, and ruin, hardly could we wonder" if the very stones with which this building had been constructed were "to cry out, and that cold marble [of its commemorative tablet] suddenly to glow with fervent heat, and the names written thereon changed to speaking tongues of fire, in rebuke of such disloyalty and treason, such ingratitude and demoralization, not only social and civil, but of soul."[93] The moral authority of this memorial was confirmed further by its placement on Lancaster's village green, next to Charles Bulfinch's stately and austere meeting house (1816).

After carefully situating Andover's new Memorial Hall within an even more mythic geography and history, Richardson's close friend, the Reverend Phillips Brooks, likewise distinguished this public library at its dedication as an institution destined to foster the same character as had expressed itself in the valor of Andover's heroic soldiers. This was a stern quality born of the rocky soil of New England and nourished by its rugged granite outcroppings, its sweeping hills and valleys, and its mighty rivers. It was upon this "solid granitebase [sic] of character" that the village of Andover had itself been founded and subsequently fashioned, "under the hard and healthy ecclesiastical system," which had sprung from "the severe but vigorous theology of the 17th century" into a "true" New England town. It was this same stoic landscape that had prepared Andover's citizens for the epic War of Independence and the prolonged struggle against slavery that had culminated in civil war.[94] It was this hard and rocky soil that, likewise, had given birth to the public library.

Upon this institution, prayed the Reverend Brooks,

> let the morning sun strike with its call to duty, and the evening gather with its benediction of repose. Let its shelves be filled with the noblest and purest literature, that shall speak the same infinite lessons that the tablets utter from its walls. Let the thoughtful and eager young men and women of many generations come to its quiet rooms for refreshment and instruction, and drink deep of its influence and go out stronger for the good work of life. Let the men of business, of the shop and the farm pass under its shadow and feel that there is something better in this world than success. Let the little children play about its steps and tell each other wondering stories about brave men who died long ago, and for whom this building, now grown gray with age, was built in those long gone years that seem to the child like an eternity. We dedicate it to Truth, to Loyalty, to Conscience, to Courage, and to Culture.[95]

While the citizens of Northampton (fig. 1.8) and Andover set aside separate rooms as memorial halls in the front block and on the second story of their buildings, the intimate association of these public libraries with the names of those who had sacrificed their lives that the country might remain intact still served to strengthen the libraries' role as arbiter of traditional cultural, social, and moral values. As their founders would with much of the literature that was to fill their shelves and the free dissemination of this literature to the public, they were transforming these libraries into new and powerful "American" institutions. By baptizing it with the blood of martyrs to the Union cause, Americans were imbuing the public library with a quasi-ecclesiastical aura. These new associations intimately tied the public library to the American landscape and a historical continuum that many believed manifested the nation's destiny.

1.8
James H. McLaughlin, Northampton Free Public Library, Northampton, Massachusetts, 1872–1874. Forbes Library, Northampton.

By the late 1870s, it appears to have been relatively easy for liberal Protestant ministers like Brooks, as well as men such as Charles Francis Adams, Jr., in Quincy or John D. Long in Malden, to associate parallel ethical and moral traits with America's entrepreneurial elite. While the idea of dedicating a public library as a private memorial was at first approached with some reticence, by the 1880s it became increasingly common to consecrate these edifices to the memory of the families who built them.[96] While not nearly as overt as Lancaster's commemoration of its Civil War martyrs, Richardson's Woburn Public Library was among the first to prominently incorporate within its architectural fabric an iconography that explicitly memorialized its benefactor. In conformance with the express wishes of Charles Bowers Winn, this building was never named for the family, but its memorial porch and a large dedicatory plaque designed by the architect clearly announce its commemorative function to visitors (fig. 1.9). Several years earlier, the library's board had determined to erect this building on the site of the Jonathan Bowers Winn house, a location that Champney characterized as "fitting as a sentimental and a memorial place." The history of this property, which traced its ownership back to the founding of the town, was recorded by John Johnson, a member of the building committee, in the library's *Bulletin of Accessions* in 1884.[97] Richardson's other public library buildings were all named for the families that raised them and became much more overt shrines to these clans.

At North Easton, for example, a bas-relief of Oliver Ames II, originally executed in stone by Augustus Saint-Gaudens (1848–1907; fig. 1.10), was set into the overmantel of the hearth in the reading room. This sculpture was replaced in 1890 with a bronze portrait by the same artist (fig. 4.9).[98] In June 1881, Richardson apparently asked Saint-Gaudens to produce a similar bas-relief of Thomas Crane for the fireplace at Quincy, but this was never executed. An earlier description of the building, on the other hand, suggests that a large stained-glass window dedicated to Crane's memory was to have been placed directly opposite the building's entryway and an oil portrait of the patriarch hung over the fireplace.[99] Following the death of Thomas and Clarissa Crane's second son, Benjamin F. Crane (1842–1889), a memorial window commemorating him, by John LaFarge, was installed to the left of this hearth, and a bronze plaque commemorating Clarissa was placed in the same room after she passed away in 1895. In early photographs of the building, a portrait of Thomas Crane can be seen on an easel near the entryway to the building (fig. 4.16).

In addition to the memorial plaque that marks its porch, a sketch for the hearth at Malden, now in the Houghton collection at Harvard, indicates that the architect once contemplated placing a relief of Frank Converse in the overmantel of the reading room fireplace there. In

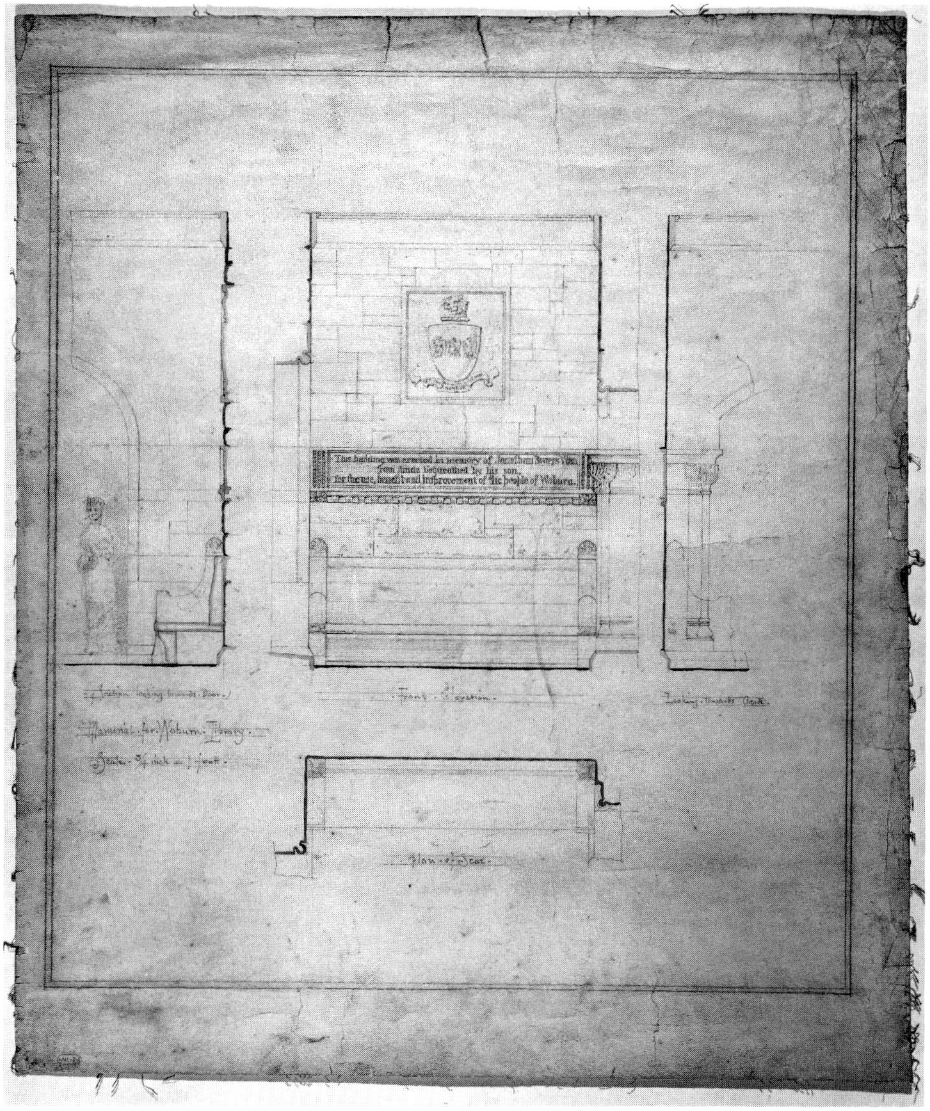

1.9

Woburn Public Library, design for porch bench and memorial plaque, c. 1880. WML D6, Department of Printing and Graphic Arts, The Houghton Library, Harvard University.

1.10
Ames Memorial Library, North Easton, reading room hearth with stone bas-relief of Oliver Ames II by Augustus Saint-Gaudens. *Monographs of American Architecture,* 1886, courtesy of the Society for the Preservation of New England Antiquities.

place of a relief, a painting of Frank Converse by Albion Harris Bicknell was hung in the art gallery on axis with the book wing, flanked by portraits of Elisha and Mary Converse by the same artist (fig. 5.1). These were donated to the library by citizens of the town, and bronze and marble busts of the couple were later given to the institution by members of the community as well.[100] These buildings helped to set a precedent for hundreds of similar memorial institutions that would be erected on American soil in subsequent decades, a custom that would culminate, and in many ways end, with the Carnegie library benefactions of the early twentieth century.[101]

So common did the dedication of public libraries to America's wealthy philanthropists become that by 1891 Henry Stedman Nourse, newly appointed chairman of the Free Public Library Commission of Massachusetts, could observe:

> The number of buildings which have been erected as memorials of individual families clearly points to the fact that the "free initiative," even in New England, is not always the intelligent vote of a town-meeting accepting the financial burden for the public good. Quite as often it is the generous impulse of some individual, one resolved to justify to the world his possession of super-abundant wealth, or who seeks to secure for himself or those dear to him grateful and imperishable remembrance. Endowments and bequests have not been more numerous than might have been anticipated, and they might be expected to increase as wealth and taste and general culture increases; for it would be difficult to imagine a cenotaph more permanently conspicuous, and yet popularly useful, than that assured by the gift of a memorial structure, consecrated in the donor's name to the gathering and garnering of deathless relics of genius, which generation after generation will make the goal and resting place of their daily walks. The name Munroe will not soon fade from the people's memory in Concord, nor that of Winn be forgotten in Woburn. The Ames family will long have honor in Easton, the Nevins in Methuen. Converse will ever be a household word in Malden.[102]

It is not entirely coincidental that many of the men who ultimately led the movement to appropriate history and consolidate moral authority through the public library were the same individuals who spearheaded the relentless and brutal expansion of the Union into the West. It was to commemorate a key triumph in this conquest of a new territory, and their role in it, that Richardson was commissioned by the Union Pacific Railroad's stockholders in 1879 to design a memorial to Oakes and Oliver Ames II, in the form of a sixty-foot-high granite monument raised on a hilltop in Wyoming, which was completed in 1882 (fig. 1.11).[103] Given the symbiotic relationship that Edward Said has identified between expanded territorial control, stability and prosperity at home, and a Eurocentric sociocultural vision, the Ames Monument in Wyoming and its contemporaneous public library and memorial hall in North Easton, like Richardson's other libraries in Woburn, Quincy, and Malden, ultimately must be viewed as potent testimonials to the extended cultural, economic, and political aspirations of a newly arrived imperial power.[104]

1.11
H. H. Richardson, Ames Monument, Sherman (Buford), Wyoming, 1879–1882. Wyoming Division of Cultural Resources.

*two*

# Handsome Bindings and Vistas of Shelves

*American Library Design to 1875*

We have already alluded to some of the perplexing questions connected with libraries, but there is none demanding for its solution so thorough a knowledge of the wants of libraries, combined with good taste and common sense, as drawing plans for a library. It is for this reason that most libraries are either pleasing to the eye and unsuited to the purpose for which they were erected, or conveniently planned and contrary to the rules of good taste.

S. G. W. Benjamin, "Libraries," 1864

While no public libraries in the United States had the need, or wherewithal, to erect purpose-built structures before the middle of the nineteenth century, some two dozen private and academic libraries did raise their own buildings. The earliest of these, such as the tiny edifice that James Logan built in Philadelphia in 1745 to house a personal library of some 3,000 volumes, or the Walterboro, South Carolina, Society Library (c. 1820), tended to be extremely modest in form.[1] Of somewhat more pretension were monuments such as the Redwood Library in Newport, Rhode Island (1748–1750), or William Strickland's Providence Athenaeum (1836–1839). The interior spaces of even these two buildings, however, were still relatively unsophisticated with respect to planning. Although 19 feet in height, the reading room of the Redwood Library, for example, measured just 37 by 25 feet. Its original specifications called for "a sort of Partition erected about ten feet high, with openings over against each window, on both sides of which must be placed Shelves for Books" These were to be constructed "about four feet from the Walls of the Sides of this Great Room." An attached memorandum that altered this plan, however, simply stipulated that "Shelves for the Books be placed against the Walls of the Building." The two flanking wings, each only 12 feet square, housed a meeting room and additional reading space. As completed, the reading room of the Providence Athenaeum was only a single story in height and measured 34 by 44 feet.[2]

In this respect, William Thornton's otherwise unremarkable design of 1790 for the Library Company of Philadelphia was somewhat more significant in that its reading room, which was a full two stories in height, was encircled from floor to ceiling with bookcases and a light iron gallery that provided convenient access to its uppermost reaches.[3] This type of hall library, or *Saalbibliothek*—apparently the first of its kind in the United States—reflected on a small scale a European tradition that stretched back to the latter part of the sixteenth and early seventeenth centuries. Credited to the Spanish architect Juan de Herrera, the prototype for these monumental library spaces seems to have appeared at the Escorial in the 1560s, where low bookcases lined the long walls of a 213-foot, barrel-vaulted hallway.[4] Extended vertically into two stories with a narrow gallery, the book hall of the Ambrosian Library in Milan (1603–1609) expanded the concept further. Widely admired for its open plan, impressive size, and unified design, the general form of this space was to have a far-reaching impact on library design. This room, enthused one contemporary observer, "is not blocked with desks to which the books are tied with iron chains after the fashion of the libraries which are common in monasteries, but is surrounded with lofty shelves."[5] Subsequent variations on the form ranged from the Arts End of the Bodleian Library at Oxford (1610 and 1613) to Hermann Korb's magnificent oval book hall at Wolfenbüttel (1706–1710), a room that prefigures by a century and a half the central plan of the British Museum Reading Room in London (1854–1856).[6] While it was conceptually impressive, only a handful of early, private American library collections, such as those housed in the New York Society Library's first Nassau Street building (c. 1795), or the Portsmouth, New Hampshire, Athenaeum (remodeled in 1817), warranted the creation of such a monumental space.

The first American academic building to be designed specifically as a library was Thomas Jefferson's Rotunda at the University of Virginia in Charlottesville, which was completed in 1826 at an estimated cost of $55,000. As is well known, the final plan for this campus placed the library in a brick and wood rotunda modeled on the Pantheon in Rome. Positioned symbolically as the physical and philosophical focus of the university, this building, in particular, symbolized Jefferson's faith in the ability of public education to guide the new republic he had helped to foster. The basement and ground floors of this structure were occupied by lecture and meeting rooms, while books were shelved on the second story in two tiers of shallow alcoves that radiated inward from the exterior walls of the building.[7] While Jefferson's disposition seems to echo the form of James Gibbs's Radcliffe Camera at Oxford (1737–1749), which was itself surrounded by eight radial alcoves arranged in two stories beneath a monumental dome, its panoptic form may also reflect a series of neoclassical *partis* for centralized libraries, museums, and prisons that were popular in France during the late eighteenth and early nineteenth centuries.[8]

While it was widely admired, the immediate influence of Jefferson's rotunda on library design appears to have been limited. Of more consequence during the early nineteenth century were the libraries at Yale and Harvard, schools that possessed two of the largest book collections in the United States. The Harvard College library, which in 1825 numbered some 25,000 volumes, was housed from 1766 until 1820 in a 30-by-45-foot room located over the chapel in the "new" Harvard Hall. In the late medieval and early Renaissance tradition, its books were shelved in 11-foot-high, two-sided cases arranged in ten alcoves, five to either side of a 13-foot-wide central corridor. While somewhat smaller in size, the Yale College library appears to have been similarly shelved in a room over its campus chapel from 1763 to 1804 and again from 1825 until 1843.[9]

Although the alcove system that these colleges employed derived most directly from British academic libraries at Cambridge and Oxford, its origins can be traced to the lecterns and chained books of medieval European monasteries. As collections expanded during the later Middle Ages and early Renaissance, the capacity of these reading stands was enlarged by adding shelves, first above and then below the lecterns. When double-faced shelving finally appeared in conjunction with tall, paired reading desks, a series of alcove-like stalls was created, each of which now required its own window for adequate light. Two early examples of stall libraries, dating from 1517 and c. 1625, can still be found at Corpus Christi and Merton colleges in Oxford.[10] A further refinement of the stall system was introduced by Sir Christopher Wren at Trinity College Library in Cambridge in 1675. Here, the architect raised the windows over his book cabinets, which allowed him to continue the shelving around all three sides of each "stall." He also moved the lateral shelving further apart and replaced the traditional lecterns with reading tables placed in what could now be considered full-fledged alcoves, thereby inventing the system of shelving commonly employed in many larger European libraries during the eigh-

2.1
Horace Jones, Guildhall Library, London, 1870–1872. Guildhall Library, Corporation of London.

2.2
Guildhall Library, book hall. Guildhall Library, Corporation of London.

teenth and nineteenth centuries. As was done at Trinity College, Dublin, in the early eighteenth century, or as late as 1870–1872 at Guildhall Library in London, Wren's alcove system could also be extended upward with the addition of a gallery (figs. 2.1, 2.2).[11] A similar strategy would be introduced into the United States during the 1830s at Gore Hall, Harvard (1837–1841), an edifice that Henry Hobson Richardson must have come to know well during his years as a student between 1856 and 1859 (fig. 2.3).

Designed by the Boston architect Richard Bond (1798–1861), Gore Hall was described by the college's president, Josiah Quincy, as "a very pure specimen of the Gothic style of the fourteenth century in its form and proportions."[12] Resembling a medieval basilica, the library was planned in the form of an elongated cross, with a 140-foot nave bisected with somewhat shorter transepts (figs. 2.4, 2.5). Shelving was arranged in two-story alcoves that opened off either side of the 35-foot-high nave. Each of these alcoves was formed by brick partitions that, according to Quincy, ran "from the columns [of the nave] to the walls of the building, somewhat in the form of the chapels in the aisles of many of the Catholic churches."[13] While this shelving continued into the west transept, the eastern arm of the building served as an entrance hall, reading room, and librarian's office.

The pressing need for more library space felt by institutions such as Harvard was due in no small part to the rapid expansion of their collections brought on by a dramatic and unanticipated increase in the availability of books and magazines during the first half of the nineteenth century. Technological improvements in printing, paper manufacturing, and bookbinding, combined with more efficient methods of marketing and distribution, served to lower the cost and greatly expanded the production of books during this period.[14] By the 1840s, the size of American book collections began to necessitate the erection of a number of new buildings specifically dedicated to the housing and reading of books, buildings whose programs prefigure the later requirements of American public libraries. Gore Hall, for example, an edifice designed to shelve 100,000 volumes, opened with a collection already numbering some 41,000, then the largest in this country. Structures with comparable capacities were raised soon after at Yale (1842–1846) and by the members of the Boston Athenaeum (1847–1859).

2.3
Richard Bond, Gore Hall book room, Harvard University, 1837–1841. Harvard University Archives.

2.4
Gore Hall. Harvard University Archives.

2.5
Gore Hall, plan. Drawing by Glenn Waguespack after a plan in the Harvard University Archives.

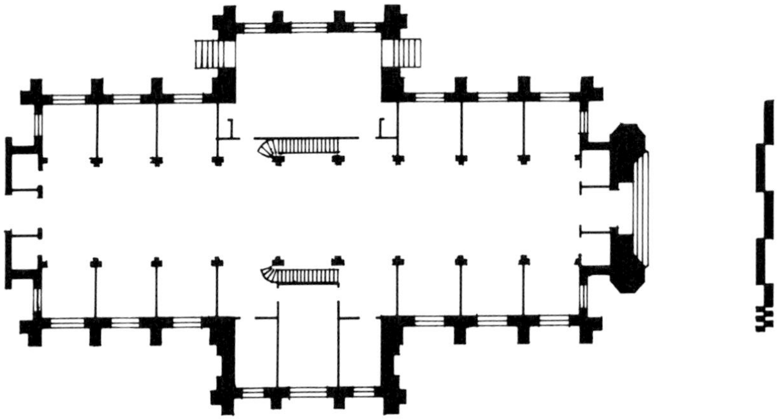

The plan for Yale College Library, which was devised by Henry Austin, called for a series of five parallel rooms, with a central hall exhibiting two-story alcoves that echoed the scheme of Bond's Harvard library. This type of arrangement, albeit in neoclassical guise, had been employed as well for the University of South Carolina Library in 1840, and the following year for the remodeled library hall at Brown University.[15] The program for the Boston Athenaeum, the most lavish proprietary library erected in the United States up to this date, called for a series of independent spaces for book storage and reading arranged in a three-story building. The requirements for this structure also called for galleries in which to display the Athenaeum's collections of painting and sculpture, as was common practice among institutions of this sort at the time. The principal library rooms, which were located on the second floor, consisted of a spacious hall that extended 114 feet along the rear of the building and two smaller rooms in front. One half of the large hall, which was bisected by a central diaphragm arch, displayed books and periodicals in glass wall cases, while the other, in emulation of the Harvard library across the Charles, was arranged in a series of wide alcoves set to either side of a central aisle (fig. 2.6). With an estimated capacity of 50,000 books, this space was surrounded by an iron gallery, which could be reached by any of five spiral iron staircases. "For convenience and beauty," noted *Norton's Literary Gazette and Publishers' Circular* in 1852, "this Library-Room is probably unequaled by any in the country."[16] The two front rooms likewise were furnished with iron galleries and staircases, and together expanded the overall capacity of the Athenaeum to 80,000 volumes.

In addition to the ever-increasing size of collections, the initial proliferation of multistory alcove libraries in the United States may have been stimulated by two influential manuals on library management, both of which advocated this system of book storage: Leopold August Constantin Hesse's *Bibliothéconomie* (1839), and J. A. F. Schmidt's *Handbuch der Bibliothekwissenschaft, der Literatur- und Bücherkunde* (1840).[17] In his booklet, which was published under the pseudonym L. A. Constantin, Hesse described a scheme for the administration and arrangement of a library of 25,000 to 35,000 volumes. This institution, he suggested, ought to be divided into at least three separate departments: a public reading room, offices for staff and administrators, and a book storage area. Although Hesse gives little indication of what the relationship between public, storage, and work space should be, it was especially important, he argued, that public access be limited to the reading room, where patrons could be easily supervised by the staff. He also illustrated two small plans for the book room, in which "the most convenient form" would be "that of a long and generous gallery, lit either from above or from

8A-8C
EUROPE.
RUSSIA.
SCANDINAVIA.
8D
8E
8F
HISTORY
VERMONT

both sides," with shelving attached to the walls and running down the center of the room, or divided into alcoves (fig. 2.7). If more than a single story in height, he noted, this room could be encircled with a balcony, so that the maximum height of the bookcases would be no more than eight or nine feet on any level. "This gallery could even serve as an adornment in a very large hall."[18] While J. A. F. Schmidt basically echoed Hesse's recommendations, he suggested placing tables for the use of the public in the center of the book room, and shelving the books in either one- or two-story alcoves.

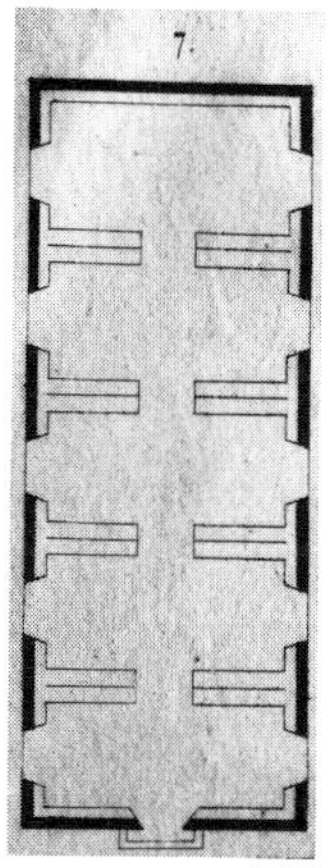


Whether or not these two volumes immediately influenced the form of American libraries, it is known that they soon became familiar to American librarians and accessible to Boston's intellectual elite. In March 1846, for example, Charles Coffin Jewett, who as librarian at Brown had overseen the introduction of alcoves into the library there, met with Charles Folsom, who was soon to become the librarian of the Boston Athenaeum, to look over designs for the latter's new building. Jewett not only critiqued these plans but supplied his colleague with an extensive list of European books on library administration. In June 1846, Folsom sent to Paris for 21 of these library manuals, and by September of this same year was able to acknowledge the receipt of 17 of these volumes. These included, among others, books by Hesse, Schmidt, and Leopoldo della Santa, as well as Martin Schrettinger's works on the administration and arrangement of the new Staatsbibliothek in Munich (1832–1840) and Benjamin Delessert's suggestions for the enlargement of the Bibliothèque Royale in Paris.[19] Not surprisingly, as worked out by Folsom, the building committee, and the architects, Edward C. Cabot and George M. Dexter, the final arrangement of the Boston Athenaeum library rooms incorporated ideas found in the work of these authors.[20] Because of its wealth and prestige, this institution came to epitomize high culture and taste in the United States during the nineteenth century; thus its rooms were to have a great impact on subsequent library design in the country. At the same time, a number of its members, including Edward Everett, George Ticknor, Edward D. Hayden, Charles Francis Adams, Jr., Nathaniel Thayer, and Frederick Lothrop Ames, were destined to play crucial roles in the ideological, political, and physical development of the American

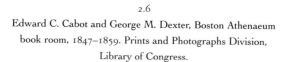

2.6
Edward C. Cabot and George M. Dexter, Boston Athenaeum book room, 1847–1859. Prints and Photographs Division, Library of Congress.

2.7
L. A. Constantin, plan for an alcove book room. *Bibliothéconomie,* Paris, 1841.

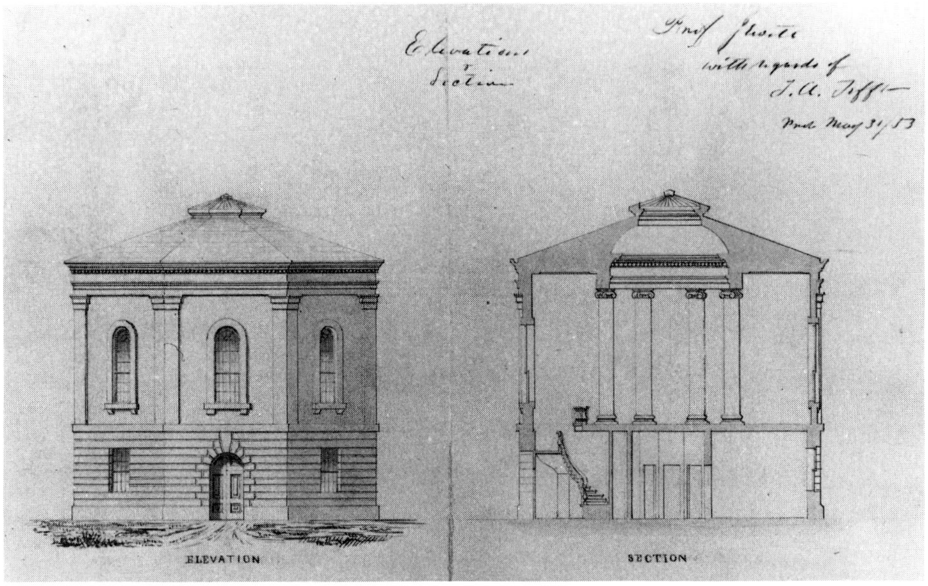


2.8
Thomas Tefft, Lawrence Hall, Williams College, elevation and section, 1846. Brown University Archives.

2.9
Lawrence Hall, first- and second-floor plans. Brown University Archives.

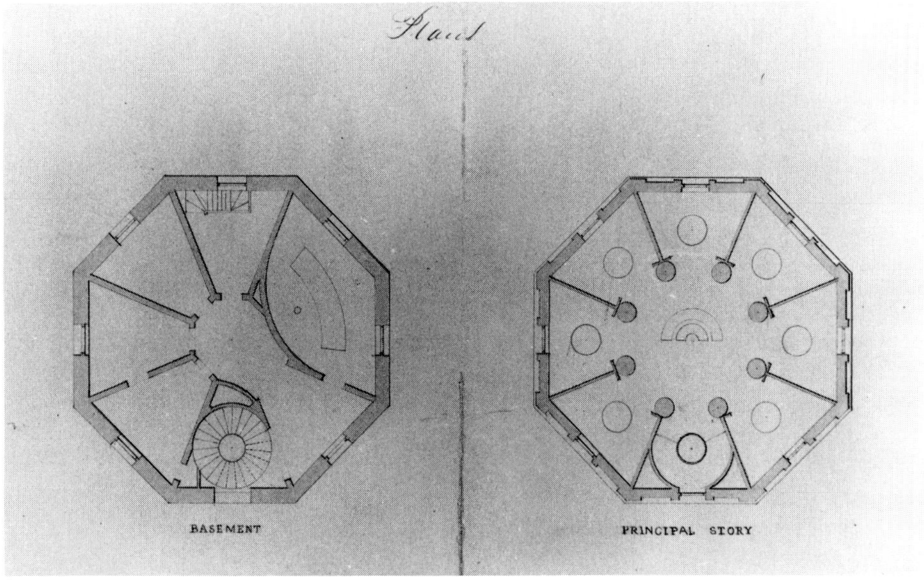

public library movement. Still others, like Amos Lawrence, were to contribute to the development of library architecture in different, if sometimes indirect, ways.

In January of 1846, for example, two months before Folsom and Jewett's meeting in Boston to review the proposed plans for the Athenaeum, Lawrence offered $5,000 to Williams College for a new library building. This structure, which was to be named Lawrence Hall in honor of its donor, was erected between the spring of 1846 and August of the following year, and was designed, according to an article that appeared in *Norton's Literary Gazette and Publishers' Circular* in 1853, "under the direction of Prof. C. C. Jewett, by Mr. T. A. Tefft of Providence." When completed in 1847, this building represented the first comprehensive attempt to incorporate modern library planning theory into the arrangement of an American library building. According to Jewett, it was "one of the few" libraries "in the planning of which the *internal conveniences* have been primarily consulted."[21]

As devised by these two men, Lawrence Hall (1846–1847) took the form of a two-story octagon, somewhat reminiscent in its interior disposition of both Jefferson's Rotunda for the University of Virginia and the Radcliffe Camera at Oxford (figs. 2.8, 2.9). The basement level was divided into half a dozen wedge-shaped spaces, which housed a meeting room for the trustees of the college, a periodical reading room, the librarian's office, and packing and storage spaces; the principal story, which occupied the upper two-thirds of the building, was given over to the library itself. Reached by a spiral iron staircase that ascended from the vestibule, this space was lighted from the side and through a central lantern that surmounted a dome supported on eight Ionic columns. Books were shelved in wooden bookcases that radiated outward from these columns and ran along the exterior walls, forming eight triangular alcoves that opened off the central floor area. "The shelves as first built" were "only seven feet high," noted Jewett, "and will contain say 10,000 volumes. When more shelves are required, a light iron gallery is to be laid upon the top of the case, and another set of shelves, also seven feet in height, is to be placed upon the first." This internally expandable system would ultimately reach a height of three tiers with two galleries, capable of holding some 30,000 volumes, "all of which may be reached without the use of movable ladders." With the librarian's desk in the center of this space, observed the Providence librarian, "he can see, by turning round, every person and every book in the room."[22]

According to Edward Everett Hale, who several years later collaborated with Tefft on a design for a new building for the American Antiquarian Society (1852–1853) in Worcester, Massachusetts, the "general idea" for the configuration of this hall, with "alcoves radiating from

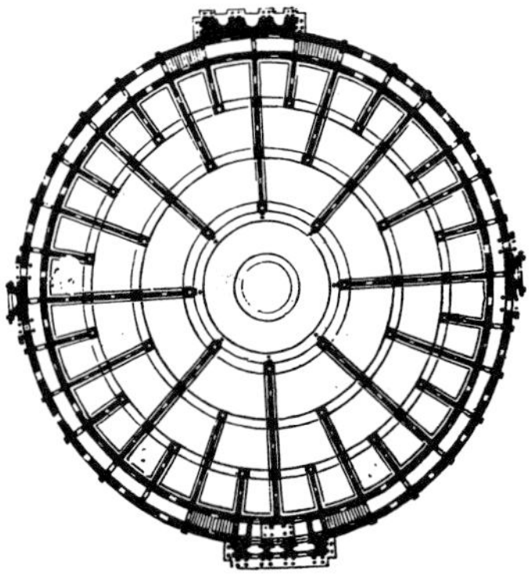

the centre, all equidistant from it," had been derived from Benjamin Delessert's *Mémoire sur la Bibliothèque Royale,* in which he had proposed a centralized book room as a means of enlarging the Royal Library (now the Bibliothèque Nationale) in Paris.[23] Inspired in part by Jeremy Bentham's Panopticon, as well as a variety of earlier neoclassical schemes, Delessert's library was to have been circular in configuration, with four-story bookcases of alternating lengths radiating inward from its exterior walls to form alcoves (fig. 2.10).[24] This arrangement, he argued, not only represented the most efficient form of book storage, but—as the term *panopticon* suggests—also allowed for the supervision of both readers and books from a single, raised observation desk located in the center of the library. As at Williams College, light iron galleries and staircases would provide access to the upper shelves. "So far as we are aware," noted Hale in 1853, "the Library building of Williams College, was the first Library Hall ever erected on the suggestion of M. Delessert. . . . The collection however, being only 6,000 volumes, is too small to test the principle."[25]

* * *

Less than a year after Lawrence Hall was completed, in March 1848, John Jacob Astor died, leaving $400,000 for the foundation and support of a free reference library in New York City, of which $75,000 was to be set aside for the construction of a library building.[26] Early the following year Joseph Green Cogswell, the library's first director, was authorized by the institution's new board to advertise for designs for this edifice, and on 30 March 1849 an announcement appeared in the *Evening Post* offering premiums of $300 and $200 for the two best plans submitted before 1 May of that year. The winning scheme by Alexander Saeltzer was in the "Byzantine" style, and, as Montgomery Schuyler was to note some four decades later, was substantially indebted to Friederich von Gärtner's *Rundbogenstil* ("round-arched style") designs for the new Staatsbibliothek in Munich, which had opened in 1842.[27] In addition to its proto–Romanesque revival style, as at Munich a long flight of stairs transported the visitor from the entry foyer to the center of a second-floor reading room, which was designed to accommodate about 100,000 volumes (fig. 2.11).

This hall, which was lit by a broad skylight and windows in the front and rear of the building, rose to a height of 50 feet, with multiple alcoves encircling a 100-by-60-foot room. Each alcove was divided into two primary stories, with light iron galleries further subdividing the library into four 11-foot tiers, with corridors along the walls through which "communication {was} established between the different parts of the library." As was common practice throughout the nineteenth century, access to the shelves was restricted by a fence that encom-

2.10
*Opposite:* Benjamin Delessert, plan for a panoptic library, 1835. *Revue générale de l'architecture,* 1850.

2.11
Alexander Saeltzer, Astor Library book room, New York, 1849–1854. Prints and Photographs Division, Library of Congress.

passed the main floor of the hall. "It would have crazed me," wrote Cogswell to George Ticknor in 1854, "to have seen a crowd ranging lawlessly among the books and throwing everything into confusion."[28] Combining an alcove system with the height and breadth of a hall library, the Astor reading room formed one of the most impressive spaces in New York City when it opened on 9 January 1854. This expansiveness was made possible by an extensive and innovative use of iron in the galleries and roof structure of the building, which, following an admonition common among library theorists at the time, was also intended to render the structure fireproof.[29]

Because this institution served only as a reference library and not a lending library and had other restrictions such as short and inconvenient hours, it drew criticism during its early years, and its reputation grew increasingly conservative and elitist as the century progressed. John Jacob Astor's own personality and business practices only added to this negative image. In 1850, for example, Horace Mann singled out Astor in a lecture he delivered before the Boston Mercantile Society "as the most notorious, the most wealthy and considering his vast means, the most miserly of his class, in the country. Nothing but absolute insanity can be pleaded in palliation of the conduct of a man who was worth nearly or quite twenty millions of dollars, but gave only some half million of it for any public object."[30]

Despite mixed reviews, the Astor Library's size and presence in New York City served to mark it as one of several critical catalysts in the burgeoning of the American public library movement. Not only were the first serious discussions concerning the founding of the Boston Public Library begun during the same years that this edifice was rising, but the first American articles on library design began to appear in a New York book journal, *Norton's Literary Gazette and Publishers' Circular.* In January 1853, for example, this publication printed a synopsis of the architectural section of Leopold Constantin Hesse's *Bibliothéconomie.* This appeared as an unsigned article, entitled "Hints upon Library Buildings," and was introduced as having been "prepared for another purpose by an intelligent German gentleman, who has paid much attention to the subject of Libraries." Like Hesse, but with an interesting early reference to John Ruskin, the author of the *Gazette* article began by reminding readers—many of whom would have been librarians—that architects were more likely to be concerned to give the exterior of their building "a splendid appearance, than to combine convenience and comfort in the interior." While the librarian, on the other hand, "knows generally very little about regular architectural beauty, even though he may pride himself upon the diligent study of Ruskin's eminent works, . . . he ought to understand well how to make the best use of room, and must be thoroughly acquainted with the most convenient arrangements for his books."[31]

Such an institution, continued the author, should be fireproof and located away from "noisy and dangerous neighborhood[s], . . . theaters, factories, &c., but, notwithstanding, conveniently situated for the visitors of the library," and should be so sited as to allow for "the possibility of an enlargement, if it should be necessary." In addition to a book room "destined for the library itself," this structure should house a separate reading room, so that "the readers will not be interrupted constantly by the noise of comers and goers," and "some other smaller apartments." The "most suitable form" for the book room, notes this author—and as two of the three plans that accompany this essay illustrate (fig. 2.12)—"seems to be a long and wide saloon, well lighted from above or both sides." In contrast to Hesse's book room, the entryway in these plans has been set in one of the long walls and the shelving arranged on all four sides of the hall; affixed to the walls in one plan and arranged in alcoves and wall shelving in the other. In either case, notes the author, "the apartments should be either only so high that the top of the shelves are easily accessible by a light and transportable ladder, or be crowned with galleries, on which cases for books may be placed." If patrons were allowed to enter the book room to borrow books, he warns, "it is essentially necessary that the books and the officers employed should be separated from the visitors by a rail." This "might be the continuation of a desk in the form of a semi-circle."[32]

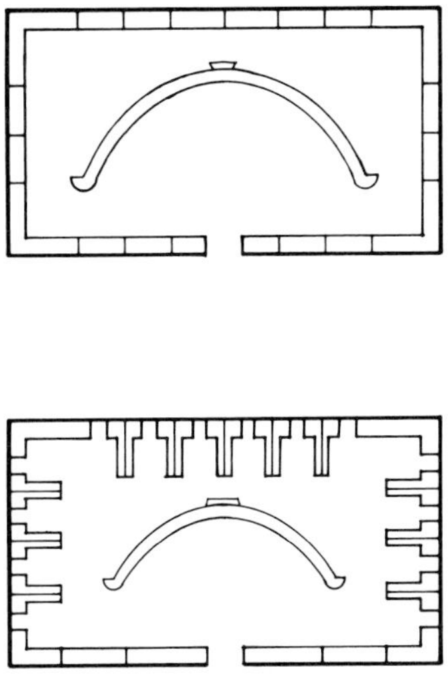

The third plan that accompanied this article was very loosely based on the arrangement of the reading room of the Bibliothèque Ste.-Geneviève in Paris, a library that had been opened to the public in February 1851 (fig. 2.33). This building, notes the American, is "perhaps the most conveniently arranged and latest built library on the Continent of Europe."[33] Nine months later, in October 1853, the same journal ran a longer article on this library alone, which was accompanied by an impressive illustration of its reading room.[34] In addition, during 1852 and 1853 *Norton's Literary Gazette* also featured a series of short pieces on the Redwood Library in Newport and the Philadelphia Society Library, as well as such important "modern" structures as the "Royal Library" at Munich (the Staatsbibliothek), the college libraries at Harvard, Yale, and Williams, the Boston Athenaeum, and the Astor Library in New York. In 1853, a review of John and Wyatt Papworth's *Museums, Libraries and Picture Galleries* also appeared in the publication. This book, which had been published the same year in London, described the Papworths' design for a large, panoptic library loosely based on Benjamin Delessert's scheme for the Bibliothèque Royale in Paris, as well as the proposed plan for the British Museum reading room in London.

It was in the midst of this growing American interest in library design that George Ticknor and Edward Everett began to formulate their vision for a public library in the City of Boston. In January 1855, following Joshua Bates's offer of $50,000 for the purchase of books, an invitation was issued by the city for architects to submit designs for a new building. This

2.12

Two plans for a public library. Drawing by Glenn Waguespack after plans in *Norton's Literary Gazette,* 15 January 1853.

2.13
Charles Kirk Kirby, the first Boston Public Library building on Boylston Street, 1855–1859. Photograph c. 1860s, courtesy of the Print Department, Boston Public Library.

called for "a simple but substantial structure, ample in its dimensions, just in its proportions, absolutely fireproof, and depending for its effect rather upon its adaptation to the use for which it was designed, than upon any ornamental architecture or costly materials."[35] Of the 24 proposals submitted to the building commission in response to this document, that of Charles Kirk Kirby of Boston was chosen. His structure was designed to hold an unprecedented 240,000 books; it was dedicated on 1 January 1858, though not opened until one year later (fig. 2.13).[36] In 1856, while this edifice was still under construction, Dr. Nathaniel B. Shurtleff, a trustee and member of the building commission, published *A Decimal System for the Arrangement and Administration of Libraries,* the first library science manual to be published in the United States. As its title indicates, this book addressed not just issues of physical planning but all aspects of public library management and organization. While Shurtleff admitted at the outset of this work that his ideas were intended "only to be descriptive of a system which the writer has introduced into the Public Library of the City of Boston," it is clear that he expected his scheme to stand as a model for other public libraries as well.[37]

Like most European authors before him, Shurtleff begins by reminding his readers that a library building should be freestanding and should not include other, unrelated functions within its shell. It should "be entirely fire proof, not only as regards danger from without, but also from any cause that may exist within, and should be so constructed that the destruction of one part by fire shall not cause the ruin of the remainder." To this end, heating equipment should be isolated from the rest of the building in a vaulted cellar and materials such as stone, brick, and iron employed in construction. This basement might also house maintenance and packing rooms, as well as "water closets, and the usual conveniences." Following the program laid out by Ticknor and Everett in the 1852 *Report of the Trustees of the Public Library of the City of Boston,* Shurtleff also suggests that a large public library should include both a research collection and a lending department for the circulation of more popular books.

As was done in Boston (fig. 2.14), he recommends that the first floor of such a library building be devoted to the latter function, with "a room for the delivery of books, which will answer the purpose of a conversation room, and connected with it a room for containing duplicates and the volumes which may be most frequently needed for current circulation; a general reading room, with tables and stands for periodicals; a smaller reading room which may be used exclusively by females; and a small room for the librarian and managers of the library." Ideally, the reading rooms on this floor should be entered through the delivery room, "so that no person can pass in or out without the knowledge of one of the employees of the library."[38]

2.14

Boston Public Library, first building, plan of the first-floor lending department. *Proceedings at the Dedication of the Building for the Public Library of the City of Boston, January 1, 1858.*

2.15

Boston Public Library, plan for Bates Hall. *Proceedings at the Dedication of the Building for the Public Library of the City of Boston, January 1, 1858.*

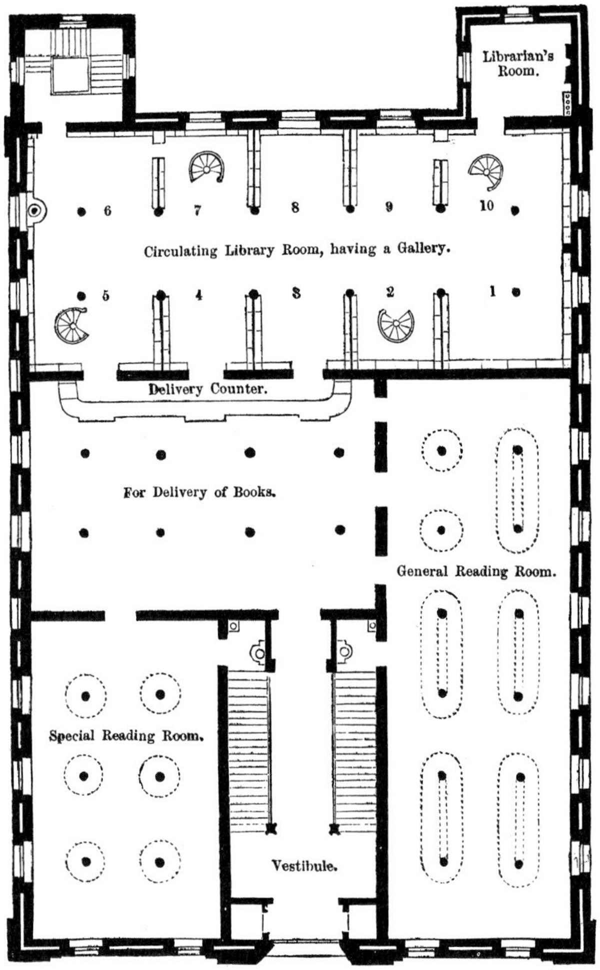


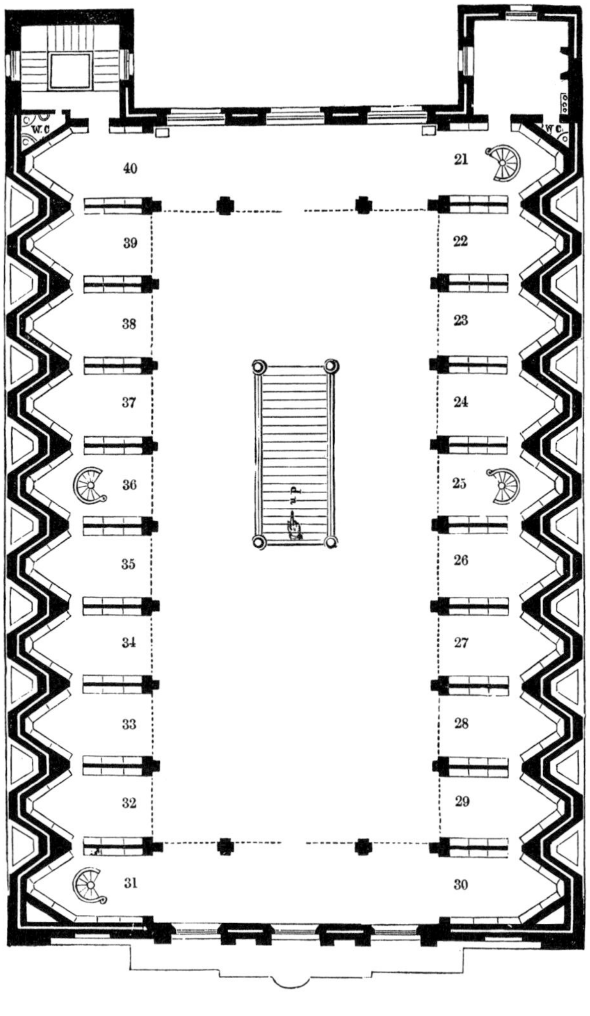




**

2.16
Boston Public Library, Bates Hall. Photograph c. 1895, courtesy of the Print Department, Boston Public Library.

In the actual Boston building the "room for conversation and the delivery of books" was located directly behind the entryway, where a grand staircase led up to the main book room housing the research collection. A general reading room, capable of accommodating some 200 readers, was situated to the right of this delivery area, which also opened into a smaller ladies' or "special" reading room. Extending across the back of the building was a long book hall for a circulating library of approximately 40,000 volumes. This space, which measured 78 feet in length and 21 in height, was flanked on two sides with alcoves and encircled by an iron gallery, which divided it into two stories. It was connected to the delivery room by a broad counter that prevented the public from entering this storage space.

As in New York and also at the Boston Public Library, the second floor of Shurtleff's ideal library was to be the "*principal story.*" Housing the research collection, it would "consist of a spacious hall . . . , so constructed as to allow of expedition in the administration of the library, and every thing about or in connection with it should be perfectly centralized." It "should be well lighted at the ends by capacious windows, and also from the roof above, and from such small windows on the sides as shall not interfere in the arrangement of the books." These were to be shelved in alcoves opening off the sides of the hall, with "one or more galleries, accessible at convenient places by means of suitable stairs." The alcoves themselves were to be "connected with each other by open doors [so] as to give the assistants of the librarian free scope throughout the whole range of the hall."[39] In the actual building this room, named in honor of Joshua Bates, occupied the entire second story of the building and was designed to accommodate some 200,000 volumes in 20 alcoves, ten on each side of the hall. These alcoves were divided by galleries into three tiers, which could be accessed via circular iron staircases (figs. 2.15, 2.16). Engaged Corinthian columns supported a coved lantern of iron and copper that hovered 52 feet above the main floor. "In an extensive library hall" such as this, "where every alcove will show its shelves," observed Shurtleff, "great architectural beauty and symmetry" could be attained: as Bates had envisioned in 1852 when he offered $50,000 to the City of Boston for the purchase of books, "the student on entering will be impressed and elevated, and feel a pride that such a place is free to him."[40] As at the Astor Library, however, readers were still to be restricted to tables on the main floor and separated from the collection with "suitable fences."[41]

While largely forgotten today, the clear differentiation of functions exhibited in the disposition of this first Boston Public Library building placed it firmly in the vanguard of modern library design. Not only were specific areas set aside for book storage, administration, and reading, but an entire floor was devoted to Ticknor's radical experiment in free distribution. In this respect it was the first major urban institution of its kind freely and with a minimum of restriction to make books available to the general public for home use. Still, the dichotomy between the first and second floors of the building is significant. In the lower realm, middle- and working-class patrons were entirely segregated from the circulating collection, which was housed in an enclosed storage area at the back of the building, while the more privileged readers in the research collection were allowed to sit among the books in the manner of a private gentleman's library or Athenaeum. Not only was access to this upper room nominally restricted by social code, but access to books below was more clearly and symbolically mediated through the librarian, who acted as arbiter for the trustees and donor.

Although the notion of lending books to the public would eventually have the most wide-ranging influence on the American public library and its arrangement, it was the impressive form of Bates Hall that was to have the most immediate impact on library design. During the decade following the end of the Civil War, for example, public libraries in Springfield, Massachusetts (1866–1871; fig. 2.17), Cincinnati (1868–1874; fig. 6.1), Detroit (1874–1877), and Baltimore (1875–1878) all constructed impressive book rooms similar in scale and configuration to that erected in Boston and described by Shurtleff.[42]

This further acceptance of the book hall in the United States was reinforced by the literature on library design available in this country during the period. In 1859, for example, William Rhees authored the *Manual of Public Libraries, Institutions, and Societies in the United States and British Provinces of North America,* the second American text to appear on library management. While his book was largely devoted to administrative and cataloguing matters, Rhees did include a short chapter on "The Construction and Furnishing of Library Buildings," which also advocated the hall library form. This section of the book, as Rhees acknowledged, had been borrowed directly from Edward Edwards's landmark publication, *Memoirs of Libraries,* which was printed in London the same year.[43] In addition to promoting lofty book rooms with iron galleries, Edwards also recommended separate reading rooms, work spaces, and offices for the librarians and their staff. More importantly, this massive two-volume work contained an illustrated history of library architecture from the Middle Ages to the middle of the nineteenth century. This was the first survey of its type to appear in English and certainly the most widely read in Britain and America before the 1890s. It included descriptions, plans, and views of the Bibliothèque Ste.-Geneviève in Paris, the Munich Staatsbibliothek, and the recently completed reading room of the British Museum library in London, as well as the Bodleian Library and Radcliffe Camera at Oxford and the eighteenth-century *Saalbibliothek* at Wolfenbüttel in Ger-

2.17
George Hathorne, Springfield Public Library, Springfield, Massachusetts, book room, 1866–1871. Prints and Photographs Division, Library of Congress.

many. Edwards also presented detailed descriptions of the new American library buildings in New York and Boston, while an additional chapter surveyed the extant European literature on library design and management. This included synopses of the work of Leopold Hesse, Léon de Laborde, Leopoldo della Santa, Benjamin Delessert, Edmund von Zoller, and John and Wyatt Papworth.[44]

Five years after the appearance of Edwards's work, Samuel G. W. Benjamin published an article entitled "Libraries" in *Harper's New Monthly Magazine* in which he briefly discussed the history and design of many of the same institutions described by his English colleague. Sounding a call that would reverberate throughout the remainder of the century, Benjamin urged librarians to take an active role in the design process. Among all of "the perplexing questions connected with libraries," he wrote,

> there is none demanding for its solution so thorough a knowledge of the wants of libraries, combined with good taste and common sense, as drawing plans. . . . It is for this reason that most libraries are either pleasing to the eye and unsuited to the purpose for which they were erected, or conveniently planned and contrary to the rules of good taste; the former is, however, the most usual error, at least in Europe, where there are many really beautiful library buildings designed by architects of the first order, but at a great waste of space and convenience. There is only one way entirely to obviate the difficulty: the architect should be at once librarian and architect—that is, a librarian by profession, but at the same time conversant with architecture, sufficiently so at least to consult with and direct some architect sensible enough to heed the suggestions of one who knows thoroughly what is required.

While Benjamin's recommendations concerning library design are relatively sketchy, he did argue that for the "main portion of a library," the "form of a rotunda," similar to the recently completed reading room of the British Museum in London, was most appropriate: "Thus from a central point can the librarian best oversee the visitors and readers, who should always be under his eye, and the books, on this plan, can be most accessible to the assistants."[45]

Although no librarian appears to have been directly involved in its planning, the octagonal book room for the Memorial Hall erected by Nathaniel Thayer in Lancaster and dedicated in 1868 closely follows Benjamin's recommendations (fig. 1.7). While patrons were allowed to enter the book room to borrow books, a separate reading room was placed on the second story in front of this rotunda, with a librarian's office and vault for town records flanking the vestibule below.[46] A similar disposition was employed at the Free Public Library of Concord (1872–1873), where books were stored in a three-story, alcoved rotunda with an elongated octagonal

2.18
Snell and Gregerson, Free Public Library of Concord, Concord, Massachusetts, book room, 1872–1873. Reproduced courtesy of the Trustees of the Boston Public Library.

2.19
Free Public Library of Concord, plan: *A*, book room; *B*, reference area; *C*, delivery area; *D*, reading room. Drawing by Glenn Waguespack after a plan in *Dedication of the New Building for the Free Public Library of Concord, Massachusetts. . . . October 1, 1873.*

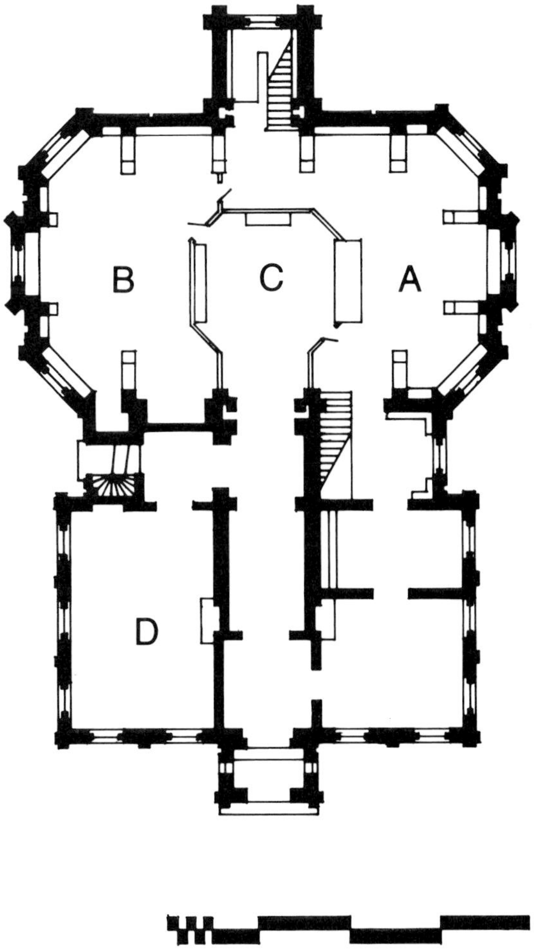


footprint (figs. 2.18, 2.19).[47] This hall was divided into a reference and a lending library and had a projected capacity of 35,000 volumes (by 1890 discovered to be nearer to 20,000), all of which, according to its architects, Snell and Gregerson of Boston, could be "seen at a glance." While patrons were allowed access to this book hall as well, a railing and delivery desk, reminiscent of the plans published in 1853 in *Norton's Literary Gazette* (fig. 2.12), segregated them from the collection. A separate reading room, librarian's office, and additional work space for the library staff were arrayed along a central hallway that led to the rotunda. The reading room, noted the architects on their plan, was oriented so that its users would be "in view of the

2.20
Free Public Library of Concord. Courtesy of the Society for the Preservation of New England Antiquities.

librarian's desk in the main Book Room," a proposition that appears from this plan to be marginal at best.

Combining a multistory book hall with an independent reading room, Snell and Gregerson's scheme and Ryder and Harris's at Lancaster both reflect characteristics of the upper and lower floors of Boston's Boylston Street building. A gift to his native town from William Munroe, the Concord library was erected for about $70,000. Surviving letters make it clear that Munroe himself was involved in its planning, having begun discussions with Ebenezer Rockwood Hoar concerning its layout as early as 1869. Munroe was a resident of Boston at the time, with an office at 100 Boylston Street very near the Public Library, so it is no surprise that this building might have figured heavily in his thinking.[48]

Given its location, the psychological and symbolic impact of Concord's vertically oriented hall of books, in particular, was not lost on its audience. "To be born in Concord," observed

Harriet Mulford Lothrop in 1893, "presupposes a love of books, and the first inhalations of the air, it is said, introduce a yearning for the infinite." In this book room, among busts of Emerson, Hawthorne, Plato, Louis Agassiz, and Horace Mann, "the very children know there is a presence other than the silent books, the voiceless statues, and the subtle influence of the place, to help them upward; a wise, kindly presence that shall enter into the needs of each, and intuitively supply them." Assisting them in their lofty quest was an 85-foot-high medieval stair tower, with which the architects culminated the stepped-back massing of the exterior (fig. 2.20): a tall Gothic spire that stood, as an unidentified companion of Ms. Lothrop observed in her book, "like a beacon on some slender promontory."[49]

With round and segmentally arched windows, corbeled arcades, Gothic trefoils over the entryway, and steeply pitched gables breaking through French mansard eaves, the Free Public Library of Concord was particularly eclectic in spirit. As a Miss H. R. Hudson characterized it in *Harper's New Monthly Magazine* in 1875: "The building is remarkable for its originality of design and elaboration of detail; it is, indeed, so odd that at first it did not receive much favor. It has often—perhaps on account of its many angles and colors—been profanely likened to a German toy; and Mrs. Moulton, in a letter to the *Tribune,* observes that 'the literature of Concord is, no doubt, its religion; therefore, very appropriately, the library is built like a church.' "[50]

While not based on a centralized plan, and perhaps not quite as impressive as Concord's book room, hall libraries also appeared in other small towns near Boston during the early years of the library movement. Both the Brookline (1866–1869) and Braintree (1871–1874) public libraries, for example, stored their books in variations on the type of longitudinal, alcove system advocated by L. A. Constantin Hesse.[51] The disposition of the Braintree building (fig. 2.21), which was designed by Hammatt Billings (1818–1875) and constructed at a cost of $32,500, echoed the first floor plan of the Boston Public Library. The book hall, which seems to have consisted of a single row of two-story alcoves attached to the rear wall, was oriented along the back of the structure, behind a central vestibule flanked by trustees' and reading rooms. It had an estimated capacity of 20,000 books. At Brookline, on the other hand, five two-story alcoves were set to either side of a single large hall that appears to have occupied the bulk of the edifice (figs. 2.22, 2.23). Constructed at a cost of $45,000 by Boston architect Louis Weissbein, this library was expected to hold 44,000 volumes, with "arrangements possible" for 20,000 to 25,000 more if additional shelving was added. It opened just five years before Henry Hobson Richardson moved his home and office to this town.

* * *

2.21

Hammatt Billings, Braintree Public Library, Braintree, Massachusetts, 1871–1874. Braintree Historical Society.

2.22

Louis Weissbein, Brookline Public Library, Brookline, Massachusetts, 1866–1869. Photograph by E. R. Hills, c. 1873, courtesy of the Society for the Preservation of New England Antiquities.

2.23

Brookline Public Library book room. Prints and Photographs Division, Library of Congress.

In spite of its early popularity and often impressive demeanor, the book hall system of shelving was not without its critics. One of the first and sharpest of these was Justin Winsor, who, as a trustee in 1867 and then as Boston Public Library superintendent from 1868 until 1877, had ample opportunity to discover firsthand the faults of this institution's arrangement. In his annual report to the trustees in 1872, for example, Winsor complained that Bates Hall seemed to be "planned to produce the largest instead of the smallest average distance of books from the point of delivery." This defect, he observed, had resulted from "the inability of architects and building committees to recognize the paramount demands of administrative uses over the meretricious attractions of vistas of books and displayed alcoves," an all-too-common oversight that, in Winsor's opinion, had also "disfigured some of the more important and recently erected library buildings in this State and at the West."[52] "The first principle of architecture," argued this librarian, should consist of "the primary adaptation of the building to its uses."[53] This meant that in a library, book storage should be as compact and utilitarian as practicable, placing a maximum number of volumes within the closest possible proximity to the delivery desk so that they would be conveniently and rapidly accessible to the library staff who delivered them to the public; or as Winsor put it in 1876: "compact storage to save space, and short distances to save time."[54]

In designing a library, he wrote, the "plan of administration should be decided upon, and in accordance with that its book rooms, public waiting rooms, official and service quarters should be planned to fall into the most convenient relations one to the other. Describe this to the architect, and ask him if he can build his edifice around these quarters without disturbing size or relative position. If he complains that the public apartments do not give sight of the books, and that he must fail of half his effects if he cannot have handsome bindings and vistas of shelving, tell him to fail; that the public wants books to read, not to look at."[55]

Winsor found his first opportunity to demonstrate these principles in 1872, when he collaborated with the Boston architects Bradlee and Winslow to develop a plan for the Roxbury Branch of the Boston Public Library, a building intended to function primarily as a lending library (fig. 2.24). Despite his ongoing criticism of Boston's main building, the librarian seems to have derived the general idea for this branch library from the disposition of the circulation department of this earlier structure (fig. 2.14). The first floor at Roxbury, in fact, was given over almost entirely to the lending of books, while the upper story was relegated to reading. As in the main library, a separate book storage room was isolated from the public along the back of the branch building, with a long delivery counter acting, in the librarian's words, as

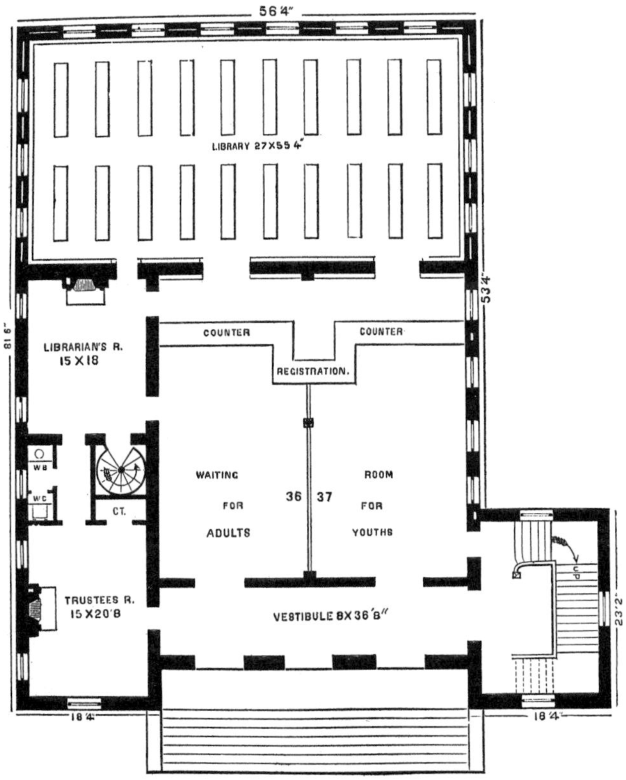


2.24
Bradlee and Winslow, Roxbury Branch of the Boston Public Library, first-floor plan, 1872. *Dedication Services of the Fellowes Athenaeum and the Roxbury Branch of the Boston Public Library, July 9, 1873.*

the "one point of contact between the readers and officials."[56] Touted by Winsor "as a model of convenient arrangement . . . well worth the examination of persons interested in town libraries," the plan and elevation of the Roxbury building were published in the *Annual Report of the Trustees* in 1873.[57] "This is a much better plan for town libraries where the public is not admitted to the shelves than is the plan involving a large central hall with alcoves," observed the *Nation* in a review of this structure that appeared the previous year. "Architects like the vista down the hall, but no library committee should listen to them. If a hall is desired, do not have alcoves; parallel stacks will store more books," but these should never be so tall as to make it "necessary to climb to reach a book."[58]

In addition to its publication in the widely distributed report of the Boston Public Library, Winsor described the Roxbury plan at length in 1876 in his article "Library Buildings," which appeared in the landmark government publication *Public Libraries in the United States of America: Their History, Condition and Management.* Of particular significance to the librarian was the building's book storage system, which he presented as a model for future library design. Measuring just 27 by 55 feet, with a height of only 24 feet, its total capacity was projected to be 100,000 volumes. This could be achieved, in a manner reminiscent of the expandable system at Williams College (fig. 2.8), by stacking three stories of freestanding, double-faced wooden shelves in the center of the book room—each eight-foot story separated by a glass floor. Although constructed of wood, this independently supported stack clearly foreshadows the much more widely acclaimed iron stack, which Winsor, in collaboration with William Robert Ware (1832–1915) and Henry Van Brunt (1832–1903), erected as an addition to Gore Hall at Harvard between 1875 and 1877 (fig. 2.25). Both of these arrangements appear likewise to have been inspired by the work of Henri Labrouste in Paris, who employed a single level of 12-foot-high, double-faced wooden bookcases in the first-floor book room of his Bibliothèque Ste.-Geneviève in the 1840s, and then, between 1860 and 1867, erected a freestanding, iron stack at the Bibliothèque Nationale, which would serve as the model for Harvard's Gore Hall.[59]

The stack system at Harvard also formed a freestanding, independent structure, set within a masonry shell composed of brick piers divided by wide expanses of glass. Consisting of six tiers of alternating metal book shelves hung from "iron skeleton uprights" that extended the full height of the building, the Harvard stack also supported an iron and terra-cotta roof and skylight. At the third annual conference of the American Library Association in 1879, Van Brunt proudly announced "that in this structure no sacrifice of convenience or economy has been made for the sake of any architectural pretense. The external aspects of the building are a legitimate growth from necessity, and have been adjusted so as to secure a proper and decent harmony of proportions and just significance of detail, no more, and no less." It thus represented "the greatest degree of economy as regards space, material, and cost yet attained in the fireproof and damp-proof stacking of books for the uses of a public library." While it might be difficult to educe universal principles of library design from this single example—"for this part of the problem . . . must be governed by local conditions, by the amount of money available, by the character and shape of the ground to be occupied, and by various other circumstances"—the Harvard system, Van Brunt suggested, could serve "as a convenient point of departure for further development" of a new utilitarian approach to planning.[60]

2.25
*Opposite:* Ware and Van Brunt, book stack addition to Gore Hall, Harvard, 1875–1877. Under demolition in 1913. Harvard University Archives.

2.26
John Ames Mitchell, Turner Free Library, Randolph, Massachusetts, 1873–1875. *The Architectural Sketch Book,* November 1873, Fine Arts Department, Boston Public Library; reproduced courtesy of the Trustees of the Boston Public Library.

While it would be another decade before metal stack shelving was to become common in American public libraries, by the mid-1870s the ever-expanding nature of these institutions was already forcing them to adopt a wide variety of arrangements for book storage—even among institutions of intermediary size.[61] John Ames Mitchell's scheme for the Turner Free Library in Randolph, Massachusetts (1873–1875), for example, shelved the collection in free-standing, double-sided bookcases arrayed about a central delivery area (fig. 2.26). Reproduced in *The Architectural Sketch Book* in 1873, this scheme is similar in configuration to the alcove plan published twenty years earlier in *Norton's Literary Gazette and Publishers' Circular* (fig. 2.12),

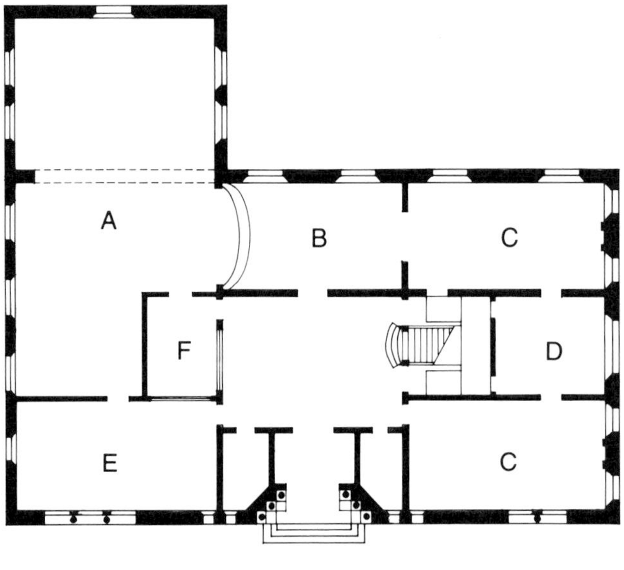
A
B
C
F
D
E
C

2.27

William A. Potter, Berkshire Athenaeum, Pittsfield, Massachusetts, 1874–1876. Photograph illustrating overcrowding in the book room, c. 1900. Courtesy of the Berkshire Athenaeum.

2.28

Berkshire Athenaeum, first-floor plan: *A,* book room; *B,* delivery area; *C,* reading rooms; *D,* trustees' room; *E,* reference room; *F,* librarian's office. Drawing by Glenn Waguespack after a plan in the Berkshire Athenaeum.

2.29

Berkshire Athenaeum. Courtesy of the Berkshire Athenaeum.

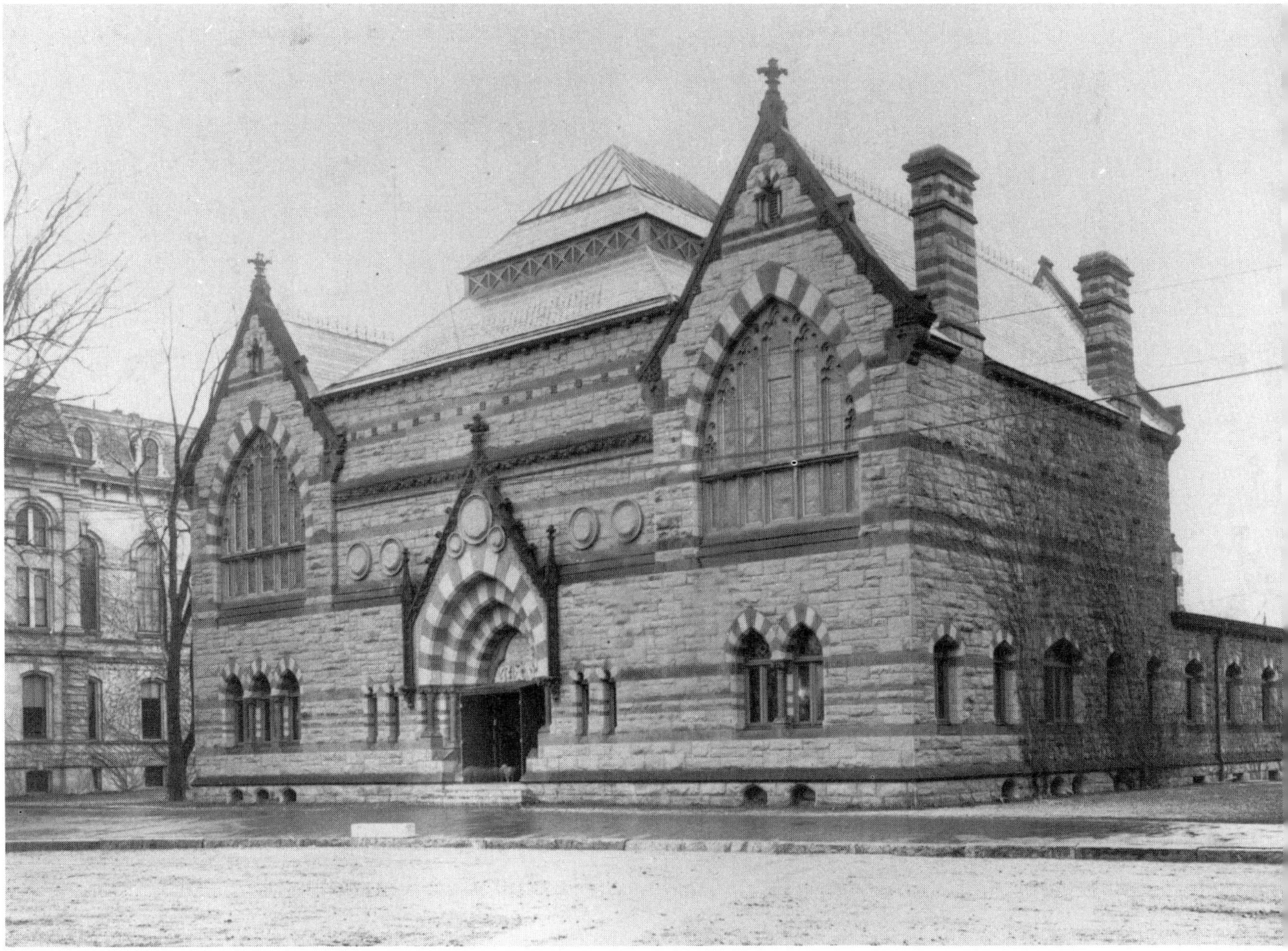

but now with a reading room, librarian's office, and work space appended to it. Located on the second story of a commercial block above a bank and store, this building was erected as a memorial to Colonel Royal Turner by his heirs, at a cost of some $40,000.

Shelving similar to that employed by Mitchell in Randolph can be seen in a turn-of-the-century photograph of the book room at the Berkshire Athenaeum in Pittsfield, Massachusetts (1874–1876; fig. 2.27). With an estimated capacity of 30,000 volumes, these shelves were arranged in a relatively low room that extended from a rear corner of the main two-story block of the library (fig. 2.28).[62] As in Boston (on the lower level) or at Roxbury, the book room at Pittsfield was isolated from a delivery area and "conversation" room by a prominent delivery desk. Along with these spaces, a small consulting and reference library, reading room, librarian's office, and trustees' room were arrayed about a central atrium and staircase, which led up to a picture gallery and natural history cabinet on the second floor. Erected at a cost of $50,000, with funds from the bequest of Phineas Allen of Pittsfield, this edifice was designed by William A. Potter of New York. Completed in August 1876, just four months before the deadline for the Woburn Public Library competition, it was designed in the Gothic style, with vibrantly polychromed, quarry-faced masonry inspired by John Ruskin and the English Gothic revival (fig. 2.29).

In the nearby Northampton, Massachusetts, Public Library (1871–1874), on the other hand, the collection was shelved in seven-foot-high, double-faced bookcases placed in parallel rows in the center, or "nave," of the book room. This was arranged, as in Justin Winsor's Roxbury library or at Williams College (fig. 2.8), so that a second tier of shelving could be built on top of the first when the initially projected capacity of 32,200 volumes was exceeded. Unlike the arrangement of the Boston branch library, however, patrons were allowed to enter this storage area, though they were confined to the outer aisles of the room by a "neat iron railing" that encircled the central "stack." This room, which no longer survives intact, was located over a reading room in a long, heavily fenestrated library wing that extended from the rear of the Memorial Hall (fig. 1.8). In a manner reminiscent of the Boston Athenaeum, a picture gallery and museum were located on the second floor of the memorial pavilion. This structure, noted the *Northampton Courier,* had "a plain, solid and substantial look suggestive of the purpose for which it is to be used and there is nothing of an ecclesiastical or domestic character about it."[63] It is possible that the arrangement of this library was worked out by its architect, James H. McLaughlin of Cincinnati, in collaboration with William Frederick Poole, who was then director of the Cincinnati Public Library, an institution McLaughlin had also designed. Along with Justin Winsor, Poole would himself become one of the most vocal critics of the hall library during the 1880s—an arrangement that, ironically, had been employed in Cincinnati (fig. 6.1).[64]

* * *

While only sporadically integrated into actual contemporary building practice, and even then with no great artistry, Winsor's principles of library planning began to emerge more clearly in a program for a small public library that was distributed to fourth-year architecture students at the Massachusetts Institute of Technology in January 1875. This program was published, along with portions of six student projects, in *The Architectural Sketch Book* the same year. At this time William Ware, then head of the Department of Architecture at MIT, along with his partner Henry Van Brunt, also began collaborating with Winsor on the design for the new stack wing at Gore Hall.

The program asked the students to combine the functions of a small public library, as at Northampton or Lancaster, with "that of doing honor to the memory of the town's people who fell during the war." In addition to "a library-room, for keeping about twenty thousand books," this structure was to be designed to house "a private room for the librarian, for the transaction of business, and three work-rooms, for the covering or binding of books, for writing, or for private students," a public reading room, and a room reserved for "students and for ladies, . . . wash-rooms, water-closets, and other conveniences." Following closely the precepts of Winsor, the book room was "not to be used by the general public, but by the librarian and his assistants only." It was specifically stipulated, moreover, that this space was "accordingly for use, and not for show; and the books must be arranged in as compact and convenient a manner as possible, so as to be easily got at without unnecessary steps: none to be more than seven feet from the floor, or gallery floor, so that ladders may not be required." In this same room, "or adjacent to it, must be desks and tables, with sufficient floor space, where books may be placed as they are taken out or brought back, and where the records and registers may be kept." Arrangements for the delivery of books from this area could be located "in the reading-room and writing-room, in the vestibule, or both, or in a separate room, as may be judged most convenient." And finally, it had to be "well lighted, as indeed, must be all of the rooms in the building."[65]

Two of the six student designs reproduced in the *Architectural Sketch Book*—those of F. W. Stickney and R. S. Atkinson—exhibited a full range of elevations, sections, and plans (figs. 2.30, 2.31). In line with the Beaux-Arts-inspired curriculum that had been introduced by Ware to MIT in 1868, both of these projects reflect contemporary French classical principles of de-

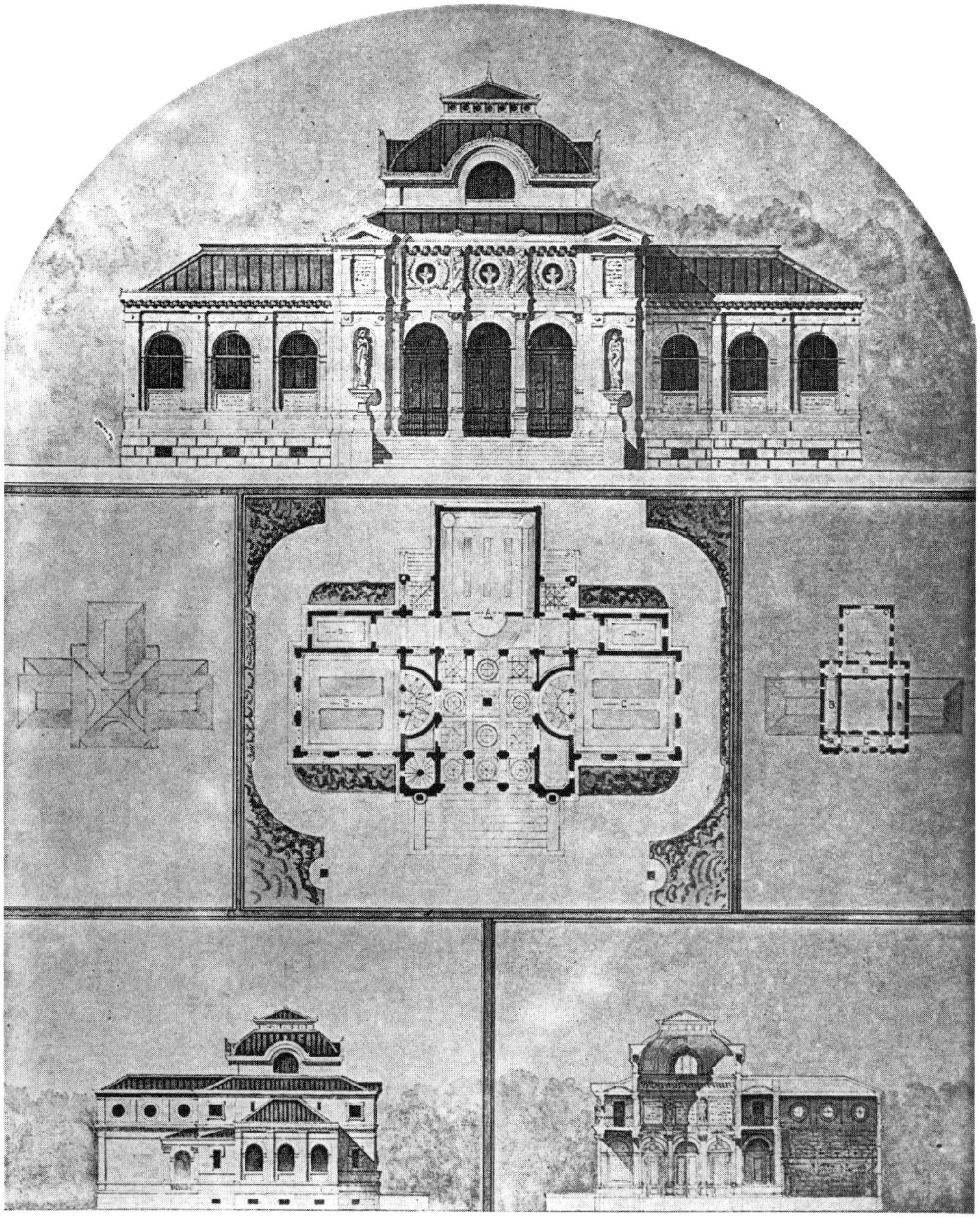

2.30
F. W. Stickney, "Problem XVI.—A Memorial Library." *The Architectural Sketch Book,* May 1875, Fine Arts Department, Boston Public Library; reproduced courtesy of the Trustees of the Boston Public Library.

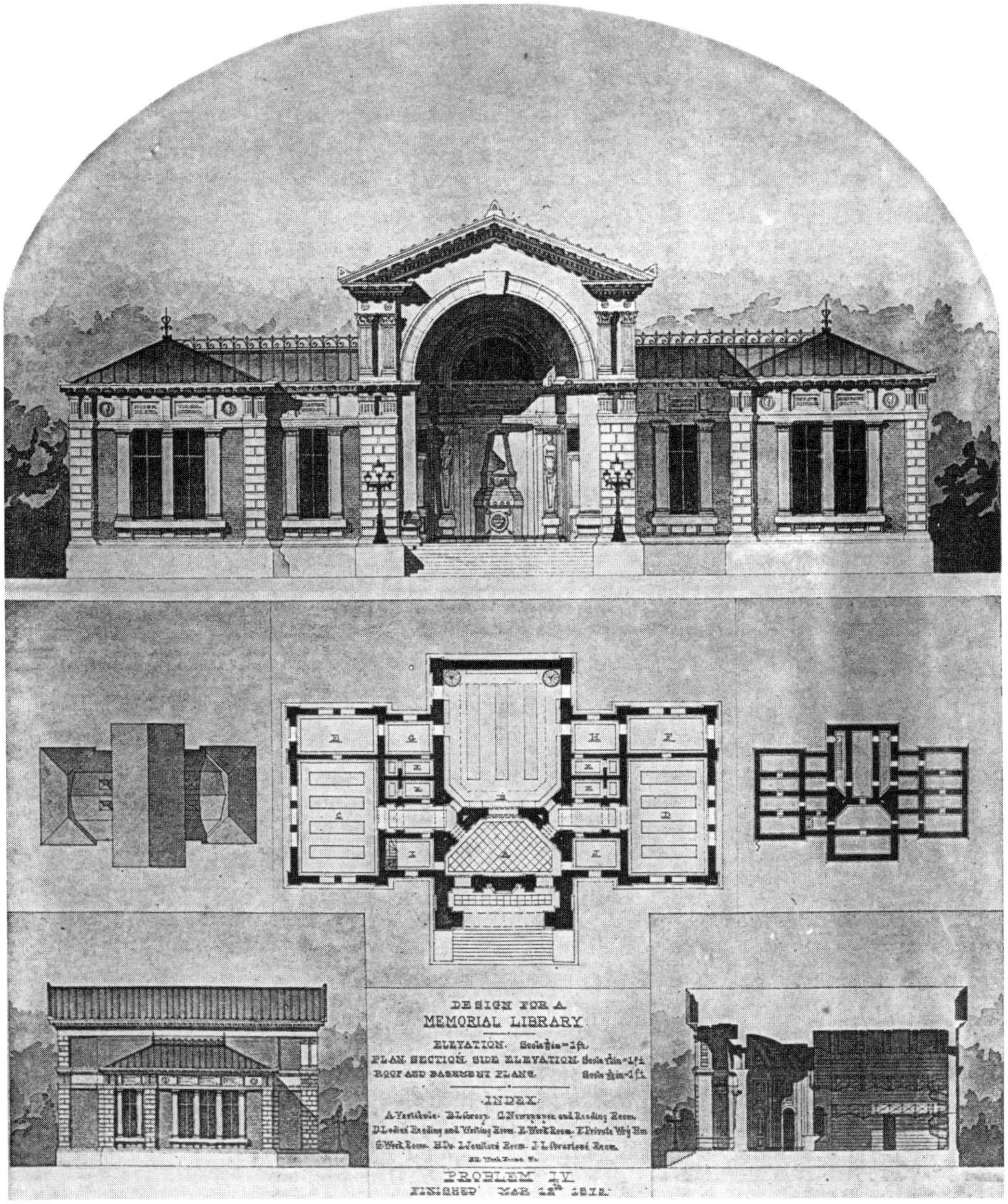


2.31

R. S. Atkinson, "Problem XVI. — A Memorial Library." *The Architectural Sketch Book,* May 1875, Fine Arts Department, Boston Public Library; reproduced courtesy of the Trustees of the Boston Public Library.

sign.[66] In contrast to the plan for Potter's Berkshire Athenaeum, for example, the MIT students have created a rational and orderly relationship of spaces arranged along two intersecting axes. In both of these plans, the book rooms have been extended axially from the rear of the buildings, in a manner reminiscent of the Northampton library, to form one leg of a T. As Winsor's colleague, Charles Ammi Cutter, would characterize this arrangement a few years later, these storage spaces "project longitudinally from the delivery room as a train-house projects from the head-house of a railway station."[67] As specified in the program, the books in both of these designs were to be stored in double-faced bookcases and wall shelving similar in configuration to, but smaller in scale than, the Roxbury book room. Located directly in front of these storage spaces are vestibules and delivery rooms, which have been symmetrically ordered along a central axis, flanked by work and administration areas and the reading and writing rooms.

Stickney's scheme, in particular, with its focus on a large central delivery area that opens directly into the book room, reveals a clear comprehension of both the problem at hand and Beaux-Arts method. This is especially evident in the manner in which he uses his circulation system to articulate the underlying geometric armature of his overall arrangement, as well as in the logical relationship he establishes, based on an implied hierarchy of his spaces, in the development of his plan, section, and elevations. His facade, while composed of a pastiche of common Beaux-Arts elements arrayed in a none-too-original pyramidal massing, reflects an unambiguous expression of the building's primary functions (storage, circulation, and reading). As in the only other published plan, that by Atkinson, Stickney's reading and writing rooms are ensconced in two symmetrically disposed wings that flank the dominant central pavilion, which itself marks the entryway, delivery area, and elevated upper story of the book room.

Stickney's tripartite, Palladian disposition was common for smaller buildings at the Ecole des Beaux-Arts in Paris as well. A group of similarly scaled student designs for a small tribunal, which appeared in the *Croquis d'architecture* in June 1866, all exhibit prominent, centrally disposed and gabled pavilions, flanked with lower wings (fig. 2.32). The planning strategy displayed in these projects likewise parallels closely that of the American students, with the courtroom replacing the central delivery area as the focal point of the composition. Where the Paris proposals, in line with the seriousness of their function as halls of justice, all employ the Doric order as their central element, the MIT facades reflect a variety of ornate decorative forms more appropriate to the character of a cultural institution.[68] Stickney, for example, along with several other of the MIT students, articulated his facade with sculptural ornament, and inscribed it with literary quotations and the names of prominent Western authors. The authors' names, in particular, following a tradition initiated by Henri Labrouste at the Bibliothèque Ste.-Geneviève, serve to mark these buildings as institutions dedicated to the literary arts (fig. 2.33). As Labrouste explained in 1852, "in the part of the upper story corresponding to the interior shelves containing the books," he had inscribed "the names of the principal authors and writers whose works are preserved in the library. This monumental catalogue," he noted, formed "the principal ornament of the facade, just as the books themselves are the most beautiful ornament of the interior."[69]

In his important article "Greek Lines," which had appeared in the *Atlantic Monthly* in 1861, Ware's partner, Henry Van Brunt, had singled out the Bibliothèque Ste.-Geneviève as one of the "most important" and "serious of modern buildings" constructed in France during the nineteenth century. Its intention, he maintained, was "at once patent to the most casual observer, and the story of its destination told with the eloquence of a poetical and monumental language. . . . The lore of the classics and the knowledge of the natural world, idealized and harmonized by affectionate study," declared Van Brunt, "are built up in its walls, and internally and externally, it is a work of the highest Art."[70]

In addition to the Bibliothèque Ste.-Geneviève, additional motifs in the MIT student designs can be traced to plates in the *Croquis d'architecture* or the *Revue générale de l'architecture et des travaux publics,* as well as to other French libraries such C. A. Questal's Musée-Bibliothèque in Grenoble. An extensive description of the latter building, which was begun in the early 1860s, was published in the *Encyclopédie d'architecture* in 1874.[71] The low, winged profiles of all the MIT designs likewise recall those of the recently completed public libraries in the Boston suburbs of Brookline and Braintree (figs. 2.21, 2.22). With the exception, perhaps, of Richard Morris Hunt's much larger Lenox Library in New York (1869–1876), these two buildings—the Brookline library, with its mansarded, Second Empire silhouette, and the Thayer in Braintree in an extremely severe French, "neo-grec" style—both reveal more Gallic influence than almost any other contemporary American building of the sort. Successful or not, the students at MIT were striving to employ all of these precedents to create an American public library whose multiple functions and meaning would be clearly legible in its architectural forms. This intention included the lucid expression of the building's secondary mission as a Civil War memorial.

Following the precedent of Lancaster Memorial Hall, for example, this function was made immediately evident in the entryways of Atkinson's scheme and in a third published facade by W. C. Richardson (figs. 2.31, 2.34). Here, centrally positioned obelisks recall a neoclassical form that had been commonly employed to commemorate American heroes throughout the

*Echelle de 0m005 p. M.*

Projet de M[r] Bisset.

RÉCOMPENSES.

1[ères] Mentions

| | |
|---|---|
| *Leflon* *élèves de MM.* | Ginain |
| *Paygné* | André |
| *Dutert* | Ginain |
| *Paumier* | Louvet |
| *Boudoy* | Garnier |
| *Moreau* | André |

2[èmes] Mentions

| | |
|---|---|
| *Laynaud* *élèves de MM.* | Ginain. |
| *Vimann* | Ginain. |
| *Broustet* | Questel |
| *Wallon* | Questel |

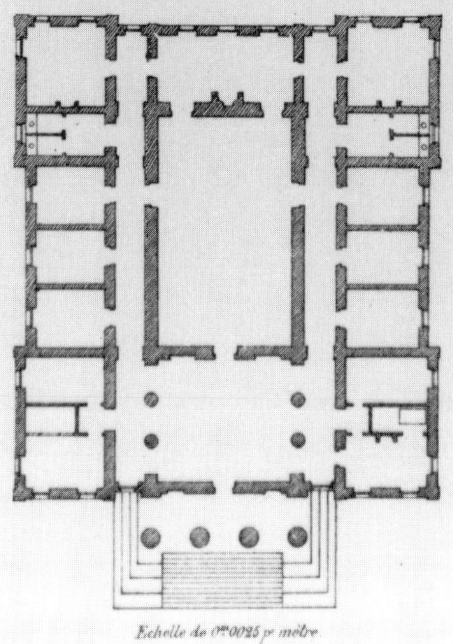

*Echelle de 0m0025 pr mètre*

2.32
*Opposite:* M. Bisset, "Tribunal de 1$^{ère}$ instance." *Croquis d'architecture,* June 1866.

2.33
Henri Labrouste, Bibliothèque Ste.-Geneviève, Paris, 1844–1850. MFA Collection, Fine Arts Department, Boston Public Library; reproduced courtesy of the Trustees of the Boston Public Library.

nineteenth century (as at Mt. Auburn Cemetery in Cambridge, for example), and had also recently appeared in numerous designs for a series of tombs and memorials that had been published in both the *Croquis d'architecture* and the *Revue générale de l'architecture.* In 1874, for example, the latter publication reproduced an illustration of an obelisk designed by André Bellemain to commemorate the French soldiers and national guardsmen who had died defending the town of Nuits during the Franco-Prussian War of 1870. Two years earlier, the *Croquis d'architecture* had devoted its October issue to an Ecole *concours,* or competition, for a memorial to French citizens who had given their lives during the Prussian siege of Paris that same year. Many of these student tributes to French patriotism resemble the inscribed obelisks that mark the entryways to the two American students' designs.[72]

In both the MIT projects, as well, these stone monuments are framed with broad triumphal arches, iconographically derived from a European tradition that extended back through

the Renaissance to the Roman era. With triumphal, commemorative, and funerary associations, this motif had been commonly illustrated in contemporary French journals as an entry portal to cemeteries and in small garden and roadside chapels.[73] Henry Hobson Richardson had himself proposed freestanding arches, appropriated even more directly from Roman precedents, as Civil War memorials in Worcester in 1868 and at Buffalo six years later (fig. 2.35).[74] This motif would reappear in his entryways in North Easton and Quincy. In 1881, Richardson's colleague Frederick Law Olmsted likewise utilized a heavy rustic arch, set in a cairn of rocks, as a Civil War memorial in North Easton (fig. 2.36). This same year, Arthur Rotch, who had been a student at MIT in 1873 and 1874, and his partner, George Tilden, employed a broad, arched entryway as a "Memorial Vestibule" for their public library in Bridgewater, Massachusetts (1881–1882; fig. 2.37). As at Lancaster (fig. 1.7), marble plaques engraved with the names of local Civil War martyrs were attached to the walls of the atrium of the building.[75] Earlier, at Woburn, Richardson had likewise framed the commemorative inscription with a broad segmental arch that formed the entryway to the porch (figs. 1.9, 3.28). Here, above an empty stone bench, was inscribed the dedication of this monument to the father of Charles Bowers Winn, a man whose fortune had made possible its erection.

2.34
*Opposite:* W. C. Richardson, "Problem XVI. — A Memorial Library." *The Architectural Sketch Book,* May 1875, Fine Arts Department, Boston Public Library; reproduced courtesy of the Trustees of the Boston Public Library.

2.35
H. H. Richardson, proposed Civil War Memorial, Buffalo, 1874. ARC F1, Department of Printing and Graphic Arts, The Houghton Library, Harvard University.

2.36

Frederick Law Olmsted, The Rockery, North Easton, 1881. Author.

2.37

Rotch and Tilden, Bridgewater Public Library, Bridgewater, Massachusetts, entryway and Civil War memorial plaque, 1881–1882. Author.

A MEMORIAL
BRIDGEWATER
SUPERINTENDENT
OF SCHOOLS



**
*

*three*

# WOBURN

*"A Model Village Library"*

We are forced, for the sake of accumulating our power and knowledge, to live in cities: but such advantage as we have in association with each other is in great part counterbalanced by our loss of fellowship with Nature. We can not all have our gardens now, nor our pleasant fields to meditate in at eventide. Then the function of our architecture is, as far as may be, to replace these; to tell us about Nature; to possess us with memories of her quietness; to be solemn and full of tenderness, like her, and rich in portraitures of her; full of delicate imagery of the flowers we can no more gather, and of the living creatures now far away from us in their own solitude.

JOHN RUSKIN, *The Stones of Venice,* 1851

When Charles Bowers Winn died in December 1875, the same year in which the MIT student designs for a memorial library had appeared in *The Architectural Sketch Book,* he left a bequest of $140,000 to the town of Woburn, Massachusetts, for the construction of a similar institution. While not intended to commemorate the victims of civil war, the building that he described in his will was still envisioned as a memorial, in this case to his father. Only 37 years of age, unmarried and childless, Winn was the sole surviving heir of Jonathan Bowers Winn, a prominent manufacturer who had amassed a small fortune in the local leather industry. Jonathan Winn had himself initiated the founding of the public library in Woburn with a donation in 1854 of $300 for the purchase of books, and had bequeathed an additional $2,500 to this library when he died in 1873.[1] By this date his son, Charles, appears to have been bedridden with a lingering illness that had forced him to leave Harvard in 1859, during his second year at the school. He had subsequently spent little of his adult life in Woburn. Having first ventured for reasons of health to the Mediterranean, he continued to travel incessantly until the last years of his life. While his death was apparently not unexpected, the size of Winn's gift to the public library appears to have come as something of a surprise.[2]

Indeed, this bequest, which ultimately totaled more than $225,000, ranked among the most liberal donations that had been made to an American public library to date. Only a handful of earlier endowments, such as those of John Jacob Astor and James Lennox in New York, George Peabody to Baltimore, or James Rush for the Ridgeway Branch Library in Philadelphia, had exceeded Winn's.[3] With just 10,000 inhabitants, of course, Woburn was much smaller than any of these cities. More typical for a town of its size—and nearer to home—was William Munroe's gift of a new library building to the town of Concord, which cost in the neighborhood of $70,000, or the $28,000 that John Smith had donated for a library and war memorial building in Andover. Both of these structures had opened with considerable fanfare in 1873. Ralph Waldo Emerson, for example, had delivered the dedication address before a large assembly of visiting dignitaries and citizens in Concord (fig. 2.20), while Richardson's close friend Phillips Brooks had undertaken similar honors in Andover. These gifts and dedication exercises had been reported in the press and could have served as inspiration for Winn's own generosity.[4]

While he did not leave specific instructions in his will as to how his endowment was to be expended, Winn did make a number of suggestions and expressed the wish that "all but a comparatively small proportion of these bequests" be spent for a new building and its contents within a few years of his death; fully expecting, as he says, that the town would be willing to "make provision for the payment of regular annual expenses pertaining to the use of the library by the public, also for new books and necessary repairs." So that the library might be "an architectural ornament to the town," it was Winn's hope "that no expense . . . be spared in the most important of matters, namely the selection of a plan." To this end, he proposed that "several architects of the highest reputation be requested to make drawings so that by comparing one with another a satisfactory result in the matter of a choice of a plan be more likely to be attained." Although this course could "possibly be quite expensive," he argued, "that ought not be an obstacle or objection, for I think the within bequest for the Library and the other purposes in connection therewith will be found to be of a sufficiently liberal amount to allow of having everything of the very best, and consequently of the most expensive order." Winn went on to suggest that the new structure should contain a library room, as well as reading rooms, "which of course it would be of great advantage to add to the other opportunities offered." These included a space "exclusively devoted to the object of having a suitable place for the exhibiting of pictures, and more especially oil paintings," the basis for which was to be Winn's own collection. "Naturally," he added, this would be located on "the upper floor, so as to have the light only from above."[5]

Although it was common practice by this date to designate such an institution for the donor or their family (especially in light of the size of the bequest), Winn specifically stated that "the above named custom would be very much against my wishes and feelings." He preferred that the new building continue to be known as "the Woburn Public Library, or by some name of a similar general nature and having no personal reference."

In consideration however, of the fact that the library building is to be erected entirely from property accumulated by my late honored father, to whom alone therefore the citizens of the town are indebted for the advantages and opportunities resulting from this bequest and (as a memorial to whom this building is by the undersigned intended) I would suggest that should it meet with the approval of those who may have charge of such matters of detail in connection with the building, that an inscription having reference to him only, and containing his name alone, be placed in some portion of the building, (on perhaps a small metallic plate, and in a not over conspicuous position) which shall make known in some words as the following, that the building "was erected for the use and benefit and improvement of the people of Woburn, from funds bequeathed for the purpose from the estate of Hon. Jonathan B. Winn."[6]

Following Winn's directives, the building committee, which consisted of the three executors of his will, his ex-brother-in-law, Edward D. Hayden, John Johnson, and Parker L. Converse, invited five prominent Boston architectural firms to submit designs for a new library building in early to mid-1876. These included Snell and Gregerson, Peabody and Stearns, Ware and Van Brunt, Cummings and Sears, and Gambrill and Richardson. The program for this structure, which was projected to cost about $75,000, apparently included a book room and delivery area, at least two reading rooms, an art gallery, and a natural history museum, which was to house a collection of fossils, minerals, and birds that belonged to Winn's uncle, John Cummings. Nine plans submitted by these five partnerships (two each by Peabody and Stearns and Cummings and Sears and one by each of the other firms) were in the possession of this committee by December of the same year.[7]

While relatively little is known concerning the mechanics of this competition or the building committee's deliberations, some sense of their thinking can be surmised from secondary sources and related circumstances. Of the five competitors, for example, three could claim some degree of expertise in library design. Snell and Gregerson had only three years earlier completed work on the nearby Concord Free Public Library, while Peabody and Stearns had designed a smaller library building for the town of Yarmouth, Massachusetts, in 1872. An elevation and plans for the Turner Library, which had been submitted by this firm to a competition in Randolph, Massachusetts, also had appeared in *The Architectural Sketch Book* in November 1873.[8] In 1875 Ware and Van Brunt, as noted previously, had begun collaborating with Justin Winsor on the design for the innovative, metal stack addition to Gore Hall at Harvard (fig. 2.25).

Four of the five invited firms had close ties to this school, which both Winn and Edward D. Hayden had attended. This association, in fact, may have carried at least as much weight in the building committee's initial selection process as library experience.[9] Although it is uncertain how closely acquainted any of these men may have been with one another, four of the younger architects whose firms were invited to submit proposals had graduated from Harvard during the years that Winn or Hayden were students there. Both Henry Van Brunt and Charles Dexter Gambrill, for example, had been classmates of Hayden, graduating from Harvard in 1854, and Van Brunt's partner, William Robert Ware, had matriculated two years earlier. After having studied together in the New York atelier of Richard Morris Hunt, Ware and Van Brunt established their own practice in Boston in 1863. Two years later they won the important commission for Harvard's Memorial Hall (figs. 1.5, 1.6), a building Hayden certainly would have known and which was still under construction at the time of the Woburn invitation. In 1870, the firm began work on its second Harvard commission, Weld Hall (1870–1871), which was followed in 1875 by its Gore Hall library addition. In 1868, Ware founded the first American school of architecture at MIT, a school for which John Cummings had acted as one of the original incorporators and continued to serve as secretary.[10]

Charles Gambrill, who had also studied with Hunt in New York, had formed his partnership with Henry Hobson Richardson in 1867. While they were still nominally partners in 1876, Richardson had moved his own office to the Boston suburb of Brookline two years earlier so that he might be better situated to supervise the construction of Trinity Church in Boston. He had won the competition for this commission in 1872 while still completing work on another Boston landmark, Brattle Square Church (1869–1873). Given the date of the Woburn project, it can be assumed that their proposal represents Richardson's and not Gambrill's conception. Following this competition, Richardson, among others, would go on to design two important monuments for his alma mater, Sever (1878–1880) and Austin (1881–1884) halls.[11]

The firm of Peabody and Stearns, which was formed in 1870, had received a commission to design Matthews Hall at Harvard (1870–1872) this same year. Robert Swain Peabody (1845–1917), following graduation from the college in 1866, had been one of the first Americans after Richardson to study at the Ecole des Beaux-Arts in Paris. His partner, John Goddard Stearns (1843–1917), received his degree from the Lawrence Scientific School at Harvard College in 1863.[12] Though neither of the partners in the firm of George Snell (1820–1893) and James R. Gregerson (dates unknown) were Harvard men, Snell had designed the University Museum at Harvard in collaboration with Henry Greenough (1807–1883) in 1858. The oldest of the firms invited to participate at Woburn, Snell and Gregerson had been practicing together in Boston since 1860 and had designed numerous houses in the Back Bay area of the city. Charles Amos Cummings (1833–1906) and Willard T. Sears (1837–1920), likewise, had been active in the Boston construction industry since before the Civil War. While neither had attended or worked at Harvard, their firm at the time of the Woburn competition had just completed what is perhaps its best-known building, New Old South Church (1874–1875), which stood opposite Richardson's Trinity Church on Copley Square.[13]

While it is not clear exactly when each of these firms was invited to submit proposals to this competition, George M. Champney, chairman of the Woburn library committee and the future librarian, noted in his diary that by the middle of June 1876, both Cummings and Sears and Ware and Van Brunt were being consulted by the building committee concerning the siting of the new building.[14] In the meantime, Champney (whose library committee had by this date become divorced from the building committee) was, with the hope of being appointed its librarian, taking charge of book purchases for the new institution. He spent time during these middle months of 1876, as well, examining many of the newest buildings in Boston, including Cummings and Sears's New Old South Church and Richardson's Trinity Church. Perhaps not insignificantly, his son, Edwin G. Champney, was assisting John La Farge on the murals he was creating in the interior of the latter monument.[15]

The future librarian also took it upon himself to visit nearby libraries and consult with prominent local librarians concerning the management and arrangement of such institutions. On 20 June, for example, Champney took a train to Haverhill to inspect the new building there and consult with its librarian, Edward Capen, a former assistant of Justin Winsor at the Boston Public Library. The Haverhill Public Library, which appears to have been modeled, at least in part, on Winsor's design for the Roxbury branch library in Boston (fig. 2.24), had opened on 1 January 1876. "The general arrangement of the Library is excellent," noted Champney in his diary: "The Reading and Reference rooms are all that could be desired. The circulating book room is good so far as it goes, but it has no opportunity of extension and is already nearly full. The work rooms and all necessary apartments in the basement are convenient, well lighted and admirably arranged."[16]

Although he was "without any architectural opinions on the subject," and "as to their arrangement [would] want to be guided by the experience of an architect," by early August Champney had begun to form his own "rough idea of what the interior of the [Woburn] building should be," a concept that clearly reflected the notions of Winsor and his colleagues concerning the separation of functions necessary in a modern lending library. In his diary he noted that he "would venture to suggest the following":

An ample vestibule before entering the main building.

A Room in the center for the Circulating department of the Library at least 30 ft. by 60 ft.

A Reception Room 20 by 30.

A general Reading Room 25 ft by 40.

A Reference and Study Room 25 by 50.

A Librarian's Room 12 by 16.

Trustees Room 16 ft. by 20.

An Art Gallery 30 by 50.

A Cabinet Room 20 by 30.

Work Rooms in the basement for Covering books, Cataloguing, etc.

In the same department, Wash rooms, Water Closets, etc.[17]

Also in August, the building committee apparently settled on a site for the new library on Pleasant Street, just west of the downtown, on a lot that had been previously occupied by the Winn homestead. This plot was surveyed the following month and a plat forwarded to the architects.[18] Because the ground slopes downward from the street, a characteristic evident in all of the surviving competition entries, it seems clear that these designs must have been produced after this date.

In further preparation for the competition Champney traveled in October and again in November to Amherst to confer with Melvil Dewey, then librarian at Amherst College and the editor of the *Library Journal,* which had been founded this same year.[19] The second visit was quickly followed by a trip to Boston to meet with Justin Winsor. In sharp contrast to the more genial Dewey, Champney found Winsor a "pleasant" enough man who, nonetheless, meant "business all day long. . . . He is no enthusiast as Mr. Dewey is; he has decided and mature opinions on Library subjects and is free to state them. I was with him an hour: he was opposed to fine buildings for libraries, thinks good accommodations of more importance and books to be of more value than towers and pinnacles; but when he was told that the donor of our funds expected a good building and did not want the money to remain as a permanent investment he of course criticized that part of our plans no further."[20]

During the month of November, Champney was also busy reading the new government report, *Public Libraries in the United States of America: Their History, Condition and Management* (1876).[21] Among other articles on library philosophy and management, this publication presented Winsor's first extensive discussion of library planning, as well as a description of the recently completed Roxbury library.

By late December, when Edward Hayden invited the library committee to his home to examine the plans that had now been submitted for the new Woburn library, Champney himself had developed a clear preference. "All were there but Mr. Pollard," he writes: "The plans were all gone over. None of the Com. had any marked or decided opinions of their own; but after examination and the remarks made upon each, it was quite unanimously *agreed that the Gambrill and Richardson offering* was the *most complete and satisfactory.* I do not believe this result would have been arrived at if the Comm. had looked at the plans individually, for no words of approval were given it when first gone over; but *the leanings of Mr. Hayden and myself gave it character* and it was gradually fallen in with as the best and at last endorsed."[22]

By 16 January 1877, the library building committee, which appears to have been under the firm control of Hayden, officially accepted the designs of Gambrill and Richardson. Although they still may have been in need of "some slight modifications, . . . as a whole" Champney considered them "admirable . . . both in architectural form and interior arrangement."[23] Nine days later the result of this competition was publicly announced, and in May of this same year a contract for $71,625.50 was signed by the Norcross Brothers of Worcester, Massachusetts, a firm that would be employed as the contractor on all three of Richardson's subsequent libraries, as well as many of his other buildings. The final expenditure for the Woburn edifice, inclusive of the architect's fees and furniture, was $95,305.24. Of this amount, the partnership of Gambrill and Richardson was paid a commission of $4,903.29 and Theodore Minot Clark (1845–1909), who worked for the office and supervised the construction of the building for them, received an additional $681.50. Each of the other firms was given $200 as compensation for its participation in the competition. Although the edifice was completed in 1878, the new library quarters were not opened to the public until the first of May 1879.[24]

* * *

3.1
Gambrill and Richardson, design for the Woburn Public Library, 1876. *American Architect and Building News,* 3 March 1877.

3.2
Woburn Public Library, 1876–1879. Photograph, 1891, by Baldwin Coolidge, courtesy of the Society for the Preservation of New England Antiquities.

While the entries of Snell and Gregerson and Ware and Van Brunt have not survived, two entries each by Peabody and Stearns and Cummings and Sears appeared in *American Architect and Building News* in March 1877, along with perspectival renderings of the facade and the reading room and a plan of Gambrill and Richardson's scheme. An additional 39 sheets of sketches, presentation drawings, and working drawings for the latter have been preserved in the Houghton Library at Harvard. With the exception of minor alterations to the fenestration and entryway arch, some subtle shifts in the proportions of the elevation (most notably in the stair tower), and the elimination of a monitor clerestory on the octagonal natural history museum, Richardson's competition renderings differ relatively little from the completed edifice (figs. 3.1, 3.2).[25] As built, it was finished in quarry-faced ashlar masonry with a combination of reddish-brown Longmeadow and cream-colored Ohio sandstone set on a red Westerly granite base. Its rough, polychrome surfaces, monumental massing, round arches, and clustered colonnettes all derived from Richardson's earlier work at Trinity Church in Boston. A description that accompanied the announcement of his selection as architect described "the style of the architecture [as] original, of a composite in nature." Richardson's biographer, Mariana Griswold Van Rensselaer, labeled it "a paraphrase of southern Romanesque."[26] At Trinity Church (fig. I.2) the architect himself had characterized his work as "a free rendering of the French Romanesque, inclining particularly to the school that flourished in the eleventh century in Central France."[27]

Richardson's plan for the Woburn Library is arranged along a central axis that extends from the book room through the delivery area and art gallery into the octagonal pavilion of the natural history museum (figs. 3.3, 3.17). One enters the building through a porch and vestibule, which have been set at a right angle to this spine, and then into the art gallery which was connected with the library areas of the structure. A trustees' room and apartment for a custodian were located on the second story over the delivery and reading rooms. As Champney suggested in his diary, work spaces and lavatories—but also a room reserved for periodicals and maps—were located in the basement.

In respect to organization, in fact, all five of the published designs roughly conform to the program Champney sketched out in August 1876. They also incorporate many of the principles of library design championed by Nathaniel B. Shurtleff and Justin Winsor, and generally reflect the arrangement of the MIT student projects published in *The Architectural Sketch Book* in 1875 (figs. 2.30, 2.31). Although Richardson rotated his *parti* so that its primary axis runs parallel to the facade of the building, all but Cummings and Sears's "alternative design" employ the

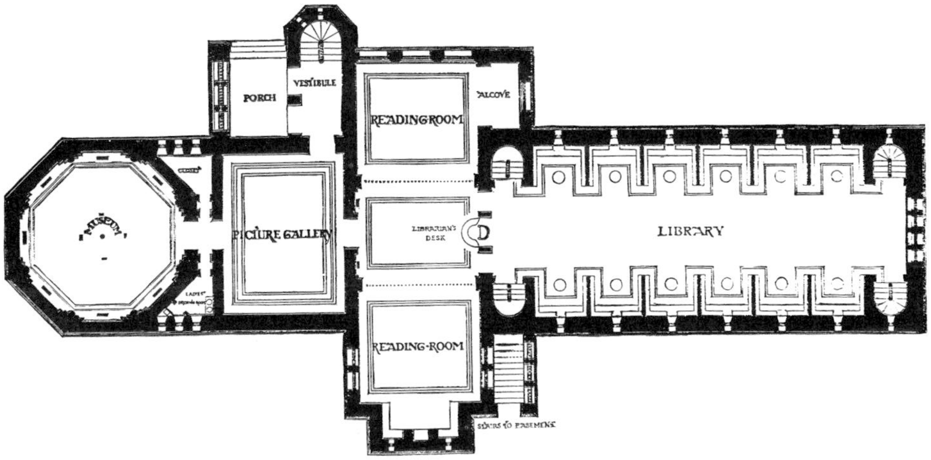


3.3
Woburn Public Library, plan. Van Rensselaer, *Henry Hobson Richardson and His Works*, 1888.

delivery area as the primary focus of an axial plan. In each case this space is flanked on either side with reading rooms and has been located in front of the book room.

In Cummings and Sears's principal submission, the museum rooms, in a manner reminiscent of William A. Potter's massing of the Berkshire Athenaeum, have been sheltered beneath a broad hipped roof on the upper story (figs. 3.4; compare fig. 2.29). Similarities in the first-floor plans of these two buildings, with central foyers flanked by a trustees' room and grand staircase, further suggest that the Boston architects may have been looking at this Pittsfield library, which had been published in A. J. Bicknell's *Wooden and Brick Buildings with Details* in 1875 (figs. 3.5, 2.28).[28] The monumentality and pyramidal form of their proposal may also have been inspired by Richardson's Trinity Church, which stood opposite their own New Old South Church. As one of the earliest examples of Richardson's stylistic influence, this design shares with his work what appears to be quarry- or rock-faced ashlar masonry and a variety of semicircular and segmental arches. The largest of these mark the women's and general reading rooms, which, as at Pittsfield, have been set in pavilions that flank the primary mass of the edifice. Cummings and Sears's design also shares a strong resemblance to William Potter's United States Court House and Post Office in Grand Rapids, Michigan, another early Richardsonian building that was published in *American Architect and Building News* in July 1876, just

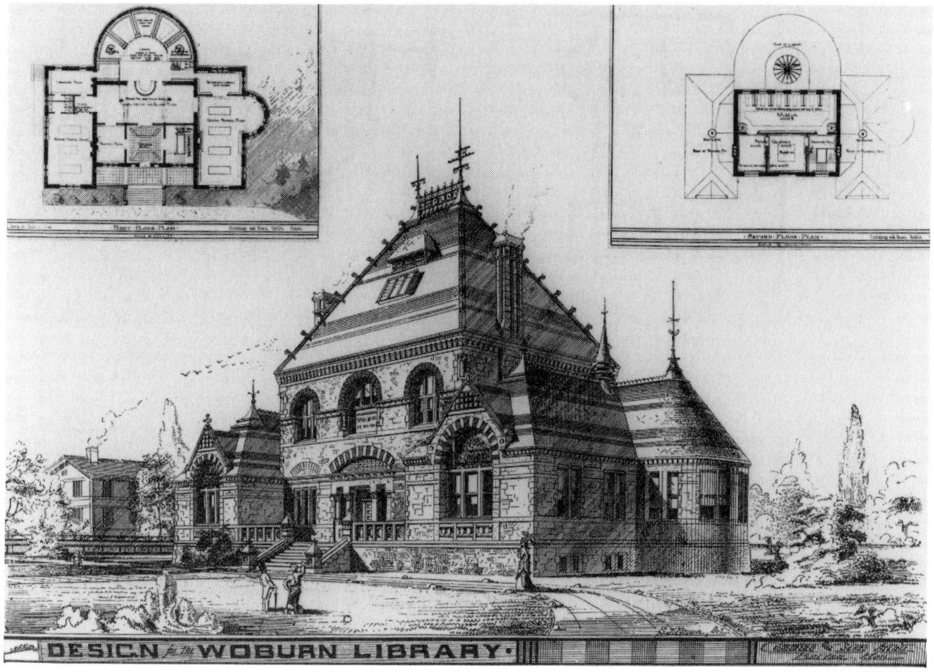
DESIGN for the WOBURN LIBRARY

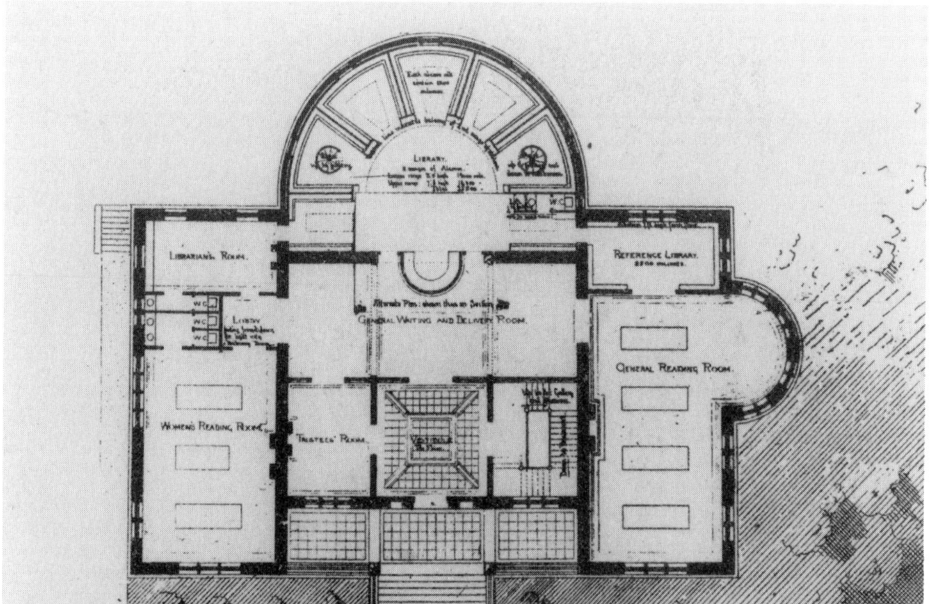
LIBRARY.
LIBRARIAN'S ROOM.
REFERENCE LIBRARY.
GENERAL WAITING AND DELIVERY ROOM.
GENERAL READING ROOM.
WOMEN'S READING ROOM.
TRUSTEES' ROOM.
WC
WC
WC



**
*

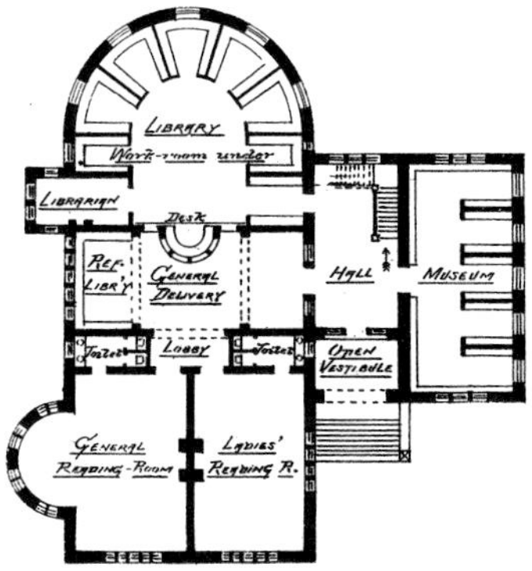


3.4, 3.5
*Opposite:* Cummings and Sears, primary design for the Woburn Public Library, perspective view and first-floor plan, 1876. *American Architect and Building News,* 10 March 1877.

3.6, 3.7
Cummings and Sears, alternative design for the Woburn Public Library, perspective view and first-floor plan, 1876. *American Architect and Building News,* 10 March 1877.



**
*

as Cummings and Sears would have been developing their design for Woburn.[29] In their alternative design, the museum and picture gallery occupy a separate, rectangular block set to the right of a stair tower and entryway (figs. 3.6, 3.7). The function of this pavilion can presumably be distinguished by its clerestory monitor and the inscriptions and bas-reliefs that adorn its otherwise windowless upper shell. In contrast to Richardson's round arches, this proposal was in the pointed style, with two prominent lancet windows lighting the general and ladies' reading rooms.

By comparison to the designs of Richardson or of Cummings and Sears, the two competition entries of Peabody and Stearns appear relatively subdued and insubstantial. Although developed in a Gothic revival mode, they are more strictly symmetrical in plan and massing than any of the other surviving entries—in a number of ways, rather anemic and unimaginative medieval variations on the MIT student designs of 1875. Their principal scheme, like that of Cummings and Sears, is two stories in height, here distinguished by a tall bell tower set over the entrance porch (figs. 3.8, 3.9). Three reading rooms and the trustees' room flank the central vestibule, while the museum and art gallery occupy space in the basement and on the second story. Peabody and Stearns's second proposal is more sprawling, with reading rooms and the art gallery and museum arranged on a single floor. Neither design appears to involve heavy use of polychromy or rusticated masonry (figs. 3.10, 3.11).

While all of these proposals provided for a separation of functions and the segregation of the public from the book room (with a delivery counter acting, in Justin Winsor's words, as the "one point of contact between the readers and officials"), their shelving schemes, in line with contemporary practice, varied widely. Peabody and Stearns, for example, proposed employing two slightly different compact storage systems, with several stories of double-sided,

3.8, 3.9
Peabody and Stearns, primary design for the Woburn Public Library, perspective view and first-floor plan, 1876. *American Architect and Building News,* 31 March 1877.

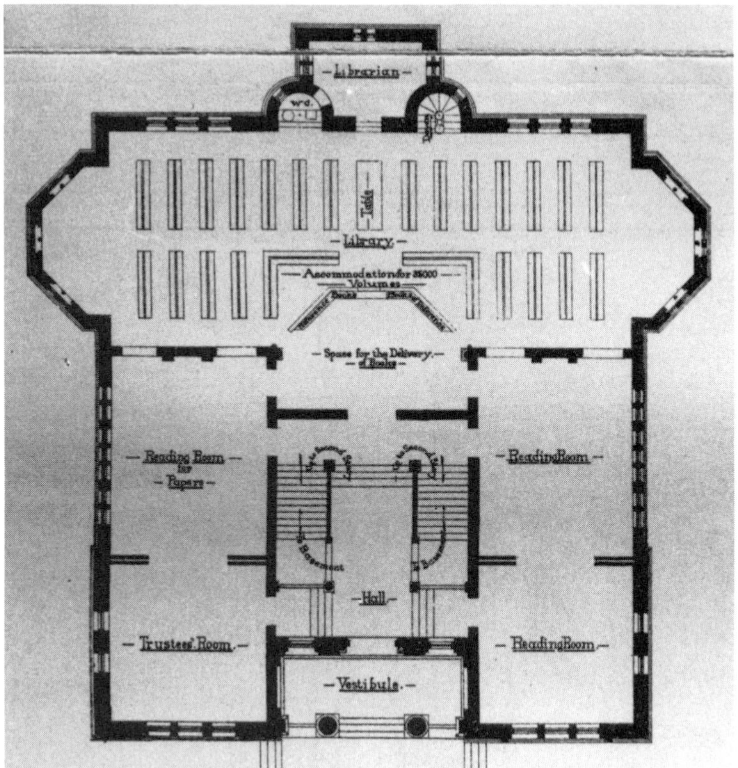


WOBURN: "A MODEL VILLAGE LIBRARY"



**
*

3.10, 3.11

Peabody and Stearns, alternative design for the Woburn Public Library, perspective view and first-floor plan, 1876. *American Architect and Building News*, 31 March 1877.

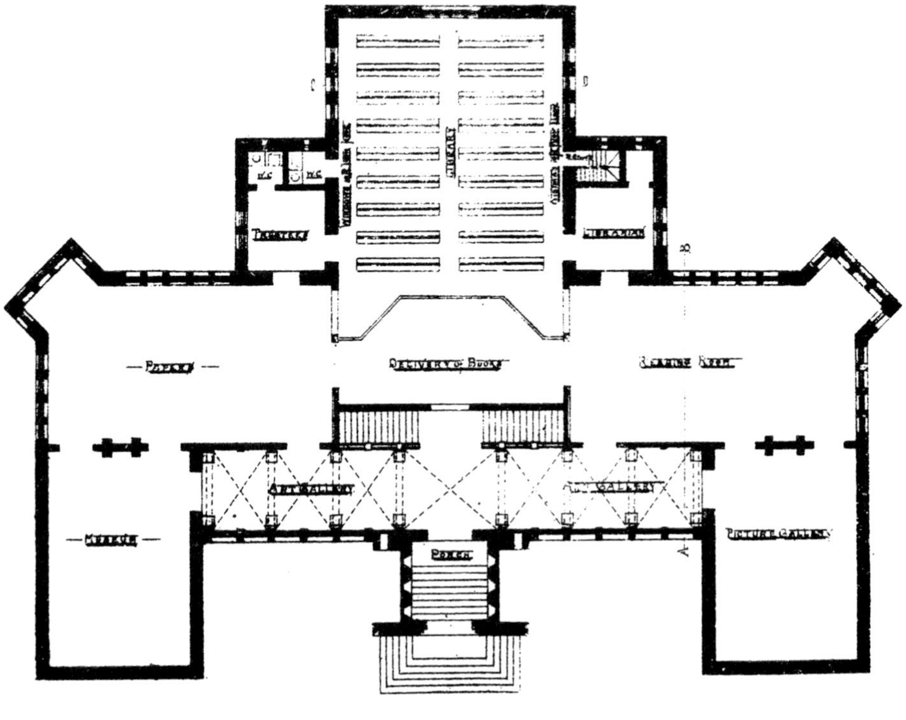




**
*

freestanding shelves oriented both perpendicular to and parallel with the building facade. While the alternate plan recalls the T plan of both the Stickney and Atkinson MIT designs or the configuration of the Northampton Public Library (figs. 2.30, 2.31, 1.8), the book room in the principal design seems more closely related to Justin Winsor's Roxbury book room (fig. 2.24), or to their own earlier scheme for the Turner Library in Randolph, Massachusetts.[30] Cummings and Sears presented a more unusual organization in both of their published plans, with multistory, double-sided shelving radiating from the delivery desk in a semipanoptic form. While derived from Benjamin Delessert's proposal for enlarging the Bibliothèque Royale in Paris or Thomas Tefft's library at Williams College (figs. 2.9, 2.10), the more focused orientation of these rooms also recalls the alcove plan published in *Norton's Literary Gazette* in 1853 (fig. 2.12), or John A. Mitchell's book room scheme for the Turner Free Library (fig. 2.26).

In contrast to these more "modern" solutions, Richardson—as suggested in Leopold Hesse's *Bibliothéconomie* (fig. 2.7)—disposed his books in twelve two-story alcoves, six to either side of a wide central nave (figs. 3.12, 3.13). As at the Boston Public Library (figs. 2.15, 2.16), a single gallery follows the line of the wall to either side of this room, passing through the alcove partitions on the second story and undulating around the edge of each bay. Spiral iron staircases in the corners provide access to this level. Conceptual models for this scheme were, of course, legion. They could be found at Brookline (fig. 2.23), where Richardson had recently relocated his home and office, at the Boston Athenaeum, or at Gore Hall (figs. 2.4, 2.6), a library both Richardson and Edward Hayden would have known from their student years at Harvard. Ironically, by 1876 Gore Hall was being altered through the addition of Ware and Van Brunt's innovative metal stack. Although the latter went on to employ this method of shelving at other public libraries, it is unclear whether they proposed it at Woburn.

In addition to American examples, there were a number of prominent alcove libraries that Richardson may have seen during his student excursion to Britain in 1859 or later while traveling with his friend Henry Adams. These included the Guildhall Library in London (1870–1872; fig. 2.2), as well as Trinity College Library, Dublin (1858–1861).[31] In 1858 Deane and Woodward had proposed enclosing the book room of the latter with a barrel vault similar in configuration to Richardson's Woburn book room ceiling. Construction on this alteration, however, was not begun until 1860, a year after the American's visit to Dublin, so it is not certain that he would have known it.[32] Henri Labrouste had, of course, employed parallel barrel vaults in his more widely acclaimed reading room at the Bibliothèque Ste.-Geneviève, a work with

3.12
Woburn Public Library, book room. Courtesy of the Society for the Preservation of New England Antiquities.



**
*

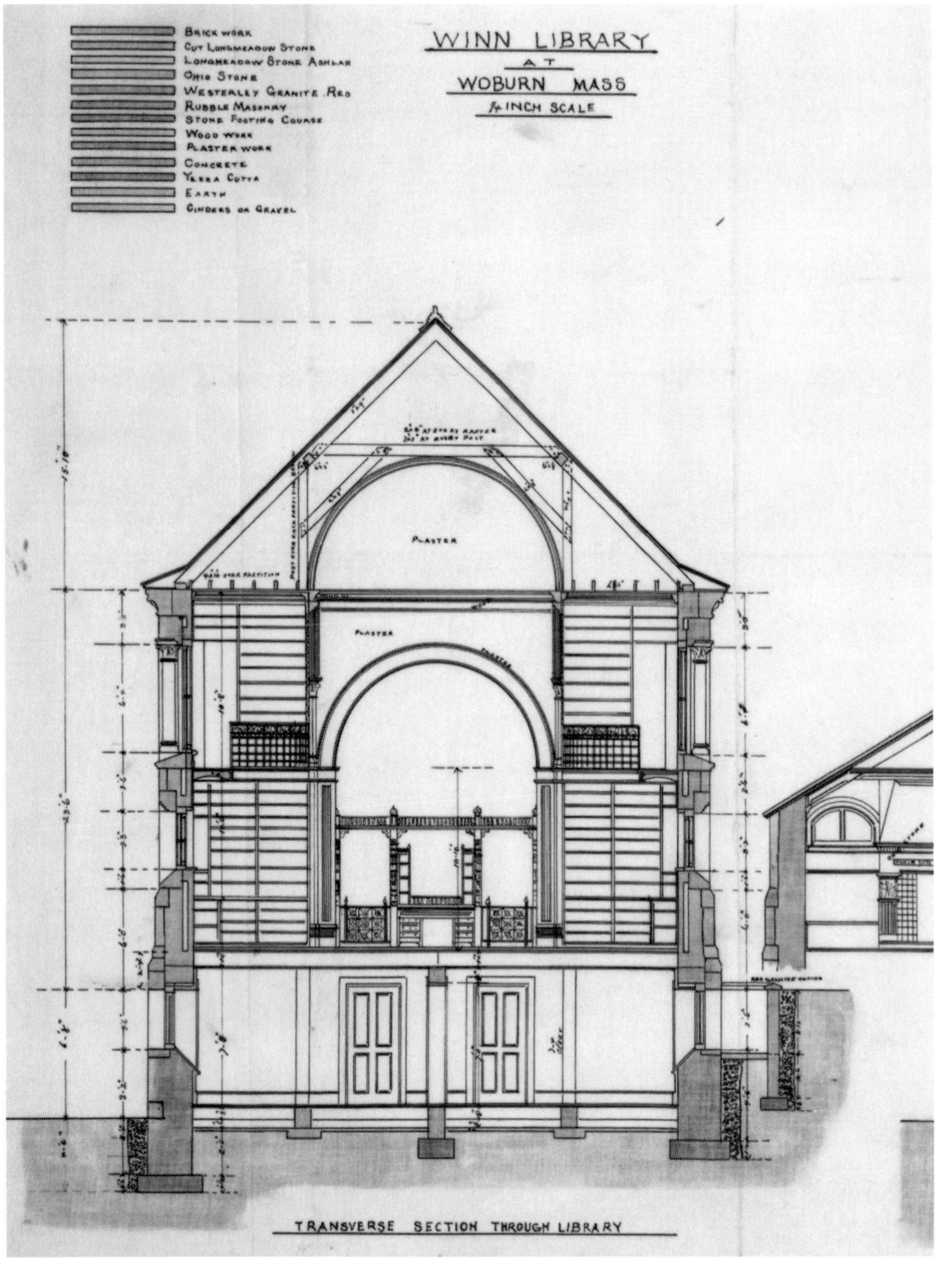


3.13
Woburn Public Library, transverse section through book room, 1877. WML C6, Department of Printing and Graphic Arts, The Houghton Library, Harvard University.

THOMA

**
*

which Richardson would have become well acquainted during his student years in Paris (figs. 3.14, 2.33). By 1859, the year he arrived in that city, the Bibliothèque Ste.-Geneviève had become one of the most highly acclaimed buildings in Europe. The following year, moreover, construction began on Labrouste's reading room (the Salle des Imprimés) at the Bibliothèque Nationale (fig. 3.15), a project that would continue during the years the American was working for Henri's brother, Théodore. Any assessment of Richardson's achievement in Woburn is impossible without considering the impact of these two buildings on his thinking. The proportions of a longitudinal section of Richardson's book room, for example, are almost identical to those of the elevation of the Bibliothèque Ste.-Geneviève, the books at Woburn literally replacing Labrouste's famous inscriptions (figs. 3.16, 3.17). The transverse arches of Richardson's vault spring from thin entablatures, which—in a manner reminiscent of Labrouste's facade, or the early work of Filippo Brunelleschi—rest directly on the crowns of the alcove arcades. While Labrouste's first library in Paris was widely recognized for the exposed, iron structural system of its reading room, Richardson's fabric in Woburn was more traditional. Composed of horizontal butternut slats laid over beaded transverse arches of the same material, his vault was hung from the wooden trusses of the roof above (fig. 3.12).

At the same time, the articulation of Richardson's alcove arcades also owes a debt to European Romanesque basilicas of the twelfth century. The fluted pilasters (engaged to piers on the ground floor, shortened and clustered with thin flanking colonnettes above), for instance, seem to be loosely modeled on Burgundian precedents, such as the nave elevation of the cathedral church at Autun in France (c. 1120–1130). This building was prominently illustrated in Eugène-Emmanuel Viollet-le-Duc's *Dictionnaire raisonné de l'architecture française du XIe au XVIe siècle* (1854–1868), a work that Richardson himself owned (fig. 3.18).[33] Viewed from the delivery room, as in Etienne-Louis Boullée's 1784 proposal for the expansion of the reading room of the Bibliothèque du Roi (a predecessor to both Delessert's panoptic library and Labrouste's Salle des Imprimés), the axial disposition of Richardson's book room displays a dramatic enfilade of

3.14
Henri Labrouste, Bibliothèque Ste.-Geneviève, reading room, 1844–1850. Edward Edwards, *Memoirs of Libraries,* 1859.

3.15
Henri Labrouste, Bibliothèque Nationale, reading room, 1860–1867. *Revue générale de l'architecture,* 1878.



**
*

3.16

Bibliothèque Ste.-Geneviève, elevation. *Revue générale de l'architecture,* 1852.

3.17

Woburn Public Library, longitudinal section, 1876. WML C1, Department of Printing and Graphic Arts, The Houghton Library, Harvard University.

3.18

*Opposite:* Autun cathedral, nave elevation, c. 1120–1130. Viollet-le-Duc, *Dictionnaire raisonné,* 1868.

books (fig. 3.19).[34] Each alcove is partially visible behind the thin wooden diaphragm of the arcade and its supporting pilasters, and obliquely illuminated by the large double windows of the second-story galleries. In a manner reminiscent of Labrouste's reading room in the Bibliothèque Nationale, or the sanctuary of an early Christian basilica, this vista has been framed with a broad arch, which in Paris was filled with glass (fig. 3.15). At Woburn it was articulated with an ornate delivery desk screen, which was both flanked and crowned by carved flaming torches, emblematic, perhaps, of the light of knowledge which this institution represented. Henri Labrouste had employed a similar motif to mark the entryway of the Bibliothèque Ste.-Geneviève (fig. 3.20), one that was intended to commemorate the introduction of gas to light the building at night, while Greek caryatids guard access to the book room at the Bibliothèque Nationale.[35]

In contrast to the more utilitarian metal stack that Labrouste employed in the latter institution, the perspectival vista of Richardson's book room is marked by the regular meter of the transverse arches of the vault and intersecting counterplay of curves created by the arcades and undulating gallery balustrades. This results in a space that is both scenographic and yet rational. It brings to mind the early Renaissance basilicas of Brunelleschi—particularly Santo Spirito in Florence (begun c. 1435)—as well as the great Baroque *Saalbibliotheken* of J. B. Fischer von Erlach. The undulation of the galleries might likewise be compared with the curving oriels of Richard Norman Shaw's New Zealand Chambers in London (1871–1873), a building that contributed greatly to the revival of the Queen Anne style in Britain.[36] Although Richardson would continue to employ variations on this paradigm, with and without barrel vaults, in all of his libraries, none of the later book rooms works quite so well as this space at Woburn. With the screen of the circulation desk separating the public from the library's ecclesiastical display of books, the magnificent organization of space at Woburn transformed the act of borrowing a book into a transcendent public ritual. By creating a distinctly hierarchical—almost ministerial—relationship between borrower and staff, it ordained the librarian as steward of the moral and ethical values its patrons believed to be embodied in this new American institution.[37]

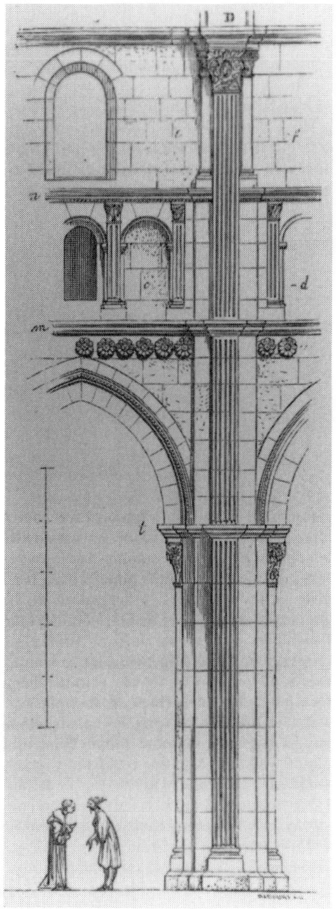

* * *

Allusions to these values were further reinforced by many of the furnishings and decorative motifs in the library (fig. 3.21). In parallel with Shaw's Queen Anne motifs in England, for example, much of this could be interpreted as either medieval or American colonial in inspiration. The mortise and tenon construction and turned spindles of the reading room chairs, as well as the turned and spiral legs and framing of the reading tables, in particular, reflect late

3.19
Woburn Public Library, view of delivery desk and book room.
Photograph, 1891, by Baldwin Coolidge, courtesy of the Society
for the Preservation of New England Antiquities.

3.20
Bibliothèque Ste.-Geneviève, entryway. *Revue générale de l'architecture,* 1852.

3.21
Woburn Public Library reading room. Photograph, 1891, by Baldwin Coolidge, courtesy of the Society for the Preservation of New England Antiquities.

seventeenth- and early eighteenth-century English and American furniture designs, as well as the "medieval principles" recommended by Charles Eastlake in his book *Hints on Household Taste* (1868). There is a strong similarity, in fact, between the furnishings at Woburn and the reading room tables and chairs employed by Horace Jones only a few years earlier at the Guildhall Library in London (fig. 2.2). Even more "medieval" are the curving frames and cantilevered arms of another group of chairs that appear in early photographs of the Woburn book room and later in the reading room at North Easton (figs. 3.12, 4.9).[38] Their broad proportions, beveled corners, and simple, chip-carved decoration recalls the straightforward and sturdy form of early American vernacular furnishings as well as the contemporary work of William Morris, while the spindled chairs seem to represent variations on Morris's revival of the Sussex chair, or related Winsor-inspired designs found in Bruce Talbert's *Gothic Forms Applied to Furniture, Metalwork and Decoration for Domestic Purposes* (1876), a book that Richardson owned. While it is not clear what hand Richardson himself had in the design of these furnishings, it is evident that all of these accouterments were carefully orchestrated to maintain a unified sense of design.[39]

The emphasis on simplicity and unity of design, structural integrity, and honest use of materials derives, as well, from John Ruskin's "Lamp of Truth." Like the products of the British aesthetic movement, Woburn's furnishings prefigure the emergence of the arts and crafts movement later in the century. Following this English lead, Richardson's adaptation of American colonial examples of late medieval and early Renaissance craftsmanship represents an attempt on his part to rediscover a parallel language of design in this country's own vernacular forms. "With our Centennial year," asked Robert Swain Peabody (of Peabody and Stearns) in 1877, "have we not discovered that we too have a past worthy of study?—a study, too, which we can subsequently explain and defend by all the ingenious Queen Anne arguments, strengthened by the fact that our Colonial work is our only native source of antiquarian study and inspiration."[40]

Jeffrey Karl Ochsner and Thomas Hubka have observed that Richardson and his chief assistant at the time, Stanford White, had begun to experiment with early American motifs several years earlier at the William Watts Sherman House in Newport, Rhode Island (1874–1876).[41] In addition to beamed ceilings and paneled wainscoting, they also had introduced a great, pyramidally hooded medieval fireplace of the type that reappears in the reading room at Woburn (fig. 3.21). With its flanking windows and benches, the fireplace inglenook is a motif that had appeared often in the domestic work of men whom Richardson closely admired, like William Morris, Richard Norman Shaw, and William Burgess. At the library, this hearth is set beneath an immense segmental arch that echoes the form of the building's entry porch (fig. 3.28), while the arcade above seems to have been derived from the facade of a twelfth-century

3.22

Twelfth-century Romanesque townhouse, Cluny. Viollet-le-Duc, *Dictionnaire raisonné,* 1868.

3.23

Woburn Public Library, natural history museum. Courtesy of the Woburn Public Library.

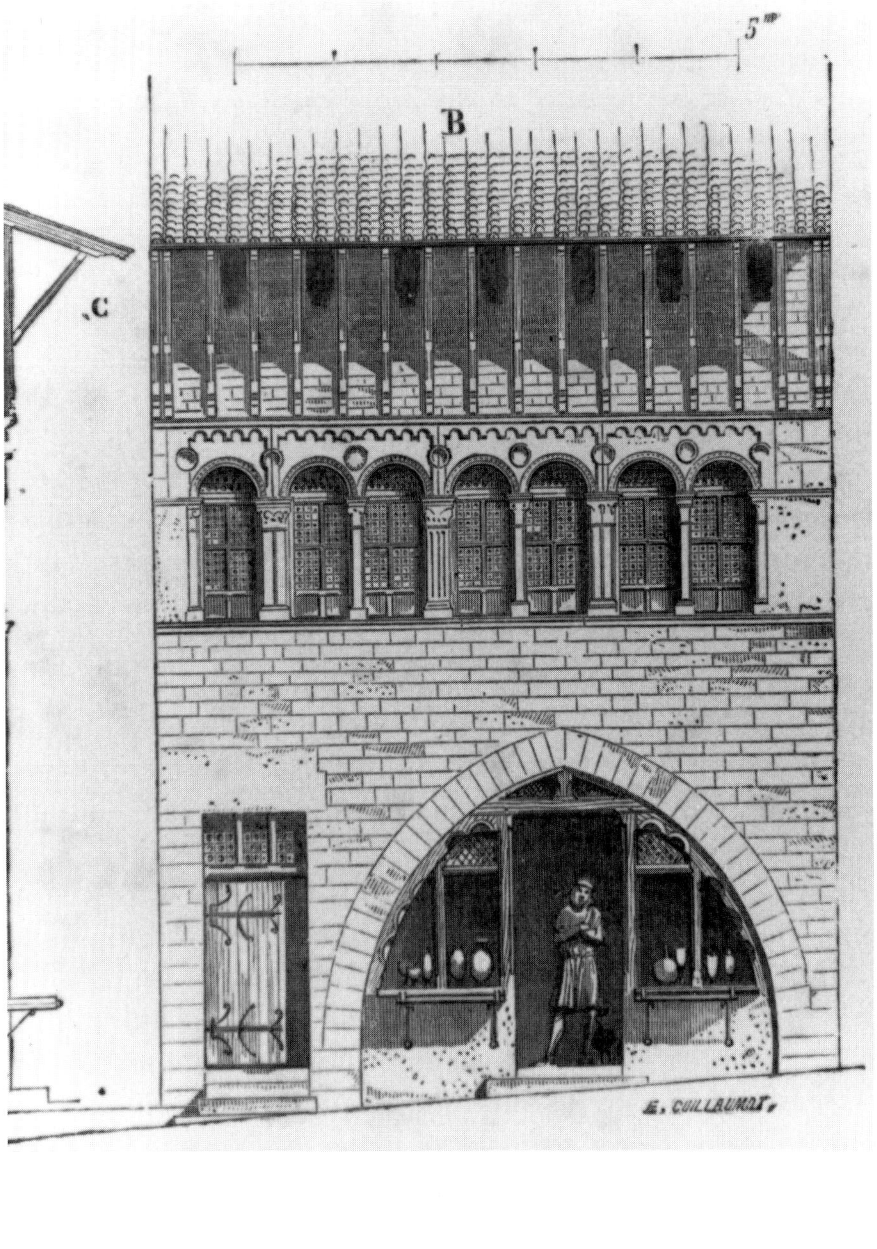




**
*

Romanesque townhouse illustrated in Viollet-le-Duc's *Dictionnaire raisonné* (fig. 3.22).[42] In an early rendering of this room that appeared in *American Architect and Building News,* the second-story arcade rests on an asymmetrical arrangement of fluted pilasters and colonnettes that have been clearly copied from the Frenchman's plates. In the completed building, however, Richardson doubled the piers to either side of the clock and balanced them with paired colonnettes. Whether or not the domestic origins of this elevation were consciously symbolic of the function of the reading room is not clear. More significantly, perhaps, Richardson repeated the distinctive alternating pier and colonnette motif in the window band of his book wing, and continued to experiment with variations on it in all of his subsequent library designs.[43]

In Richardson's as well as Labrouste's libraries, the iconography of history was further consecrated by nature. At the Bibliothèque Ste.-Geneviève, the French architect had transformed his vestibule into a painted garden, with trees set over niches in which were placed busts of French intellectuals. He had similarly enclosed two sides of the Salle des Imprimés at the Bibli-

othèque Nationale (fig. 3.15) with lunettes filled with vistas of treetops and blue sky. David Van Zanten has suggested that these murals combined with the effect of the white porcelain vaults to produce the illusion of a "garden tent," recalling, for him and others, Arcadian associations ranging from the Garden of Academe to Pliny the Younger's description of his villa at Laurentium. These illusions created a quiet, parklike refuge in which readers could study without the distraction of a more overtly symbolic iconography.[44] At Woburn, Richardson's "sacred grove" took the form of a kind of botanical garden, where a diverse local flora has been carved into the capitals and cornices of the delivery and book rooms and wreathes the art gallery and natural history museum (figs. 3.12, 3.23). In the book room, in particular, realistically portrayed specimens of horse chestnut, oak, butternut, and elm leaves, as well as a variety of fruits and flowers, have replaced the more abstract and figural capitals of the Romanesque basilica. This ornament combines with a profusion of rich oak finishes found throughout the building to create a warmth and intimacy—as well as a unity of design—that belies the monumentality of the spaces. "Among the many lessons which we might learn from Nature's mute teachings," noted Charles Eastlake in his *Hints on Household Taste,* "there is one which bears especially upon the decoration and furnishing of our dwellings, namely this, that unity is perfectly compatible with the utmost variety."[45]

Precedent for Richardson's lavish display of foliate forms likewise can be found in the work of John Ruskin, who throughout his oeuvre celebrates a delight in the botanical world. His principle of naturalism, for example, prescribes "the love of natural objects for their own sake, and the effort to represent them frankly, unconstrained by artistical laws."[46] In the United States, this tenet had mixed freely and easily with Andrew Jackson Downing's and Frederick Law Olmsted's naturalization of English picturesque theory, and the American transcendentalists' call for a new art freed from the bonds of European history and tradition. James F. O'Gorman contends that Olmsted was most responsible for introducing Richardson to both Ruskin and the transcendentalist tradition, leading him to a deeper appreciation of the significance of place but also spurring his quest to invent a new architectural language, which might be indebted, in part, to the European past but was adapted to the contemporary conditions of American society.[47] In addition to Olmsted—if, indeed, he had any hand in the conception of the Woburn building—it seems not unlikely that Richardson may have turned to his neighbor and friend, Charles Sprague Sargent (1841–1927), for advice concerning the appearance and perhaps even the arrangement of his ornamental program. Sargent was himself a prominent horticulturist who had worked under Asa Gray at Harvard during the early 1870s, and after

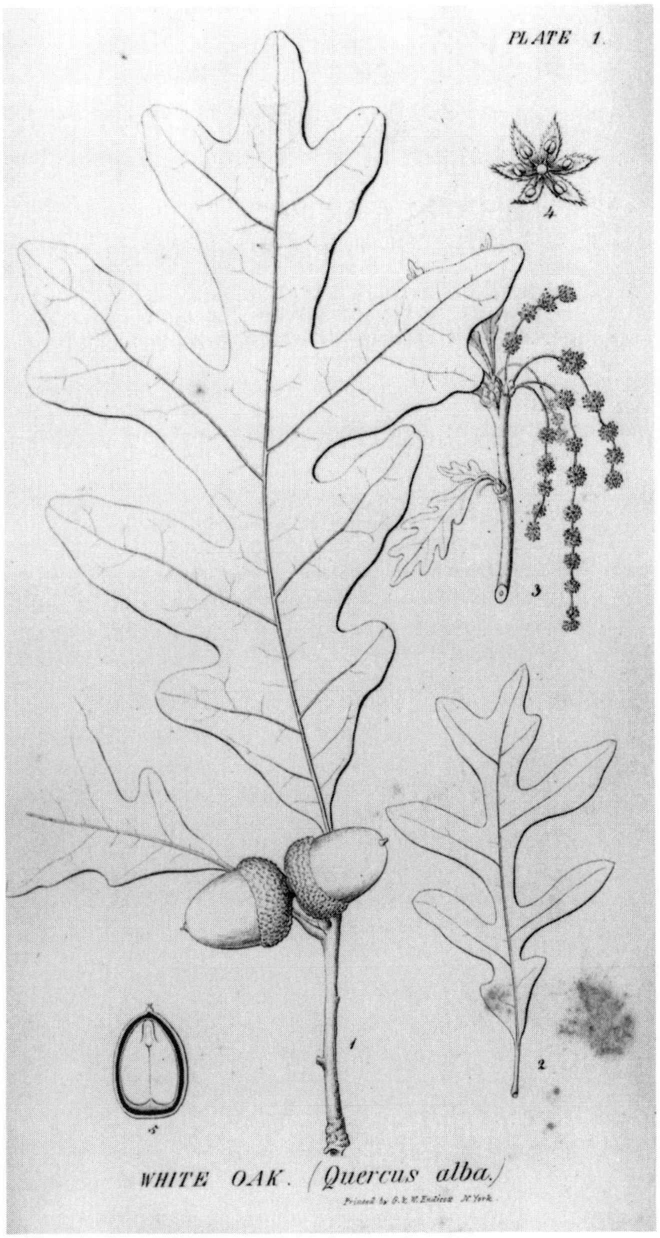


3.24
George B. Emerson, white oak. *Report on the Trees and Shrubs Growing Naturally in the Forests of Massachusetts,* 1850.



**
*

1873 had served as director of the Harvard Botanic Garden. This same year he was appointed as the first director of the newly established Arnold Arboretum, an institution that Harvard wanted to develop with moneys bequeathed to it by James Arnold, on land it had been given in Jamaica Plain. In addition to reclassifying and organizing specimens in the Botanic Garden, Sargent spent a great deal of time after 1873 inventorying existing native trees and plants at the arboretum site. By 1877, moreover, he was working with Olmsted on a landscape program for this property, a plan Sargent had suggested should be integrated into a larger scheme that the landscape architect was then developing for the Boston Park System. As this evolved, Sargent proposed lining the main road—like the aisle of the book room at Woburn—with

3.25
Deane and Woodward, Museum of Natural History, Oxford, 1851–1859. Charles Eastlake, *A History of the Gothic Revival,* 1872.

3.26
Museum of Natural History, Oxford, foliate capital. Charles Eastlake, *A History of the Gothic Revival,* 1872.

specimens of trees grouped according to family and genus, so that "a visitor driving through the Arboretum will be able to obtain a general idea of the arborescent vegetation of the north temperate zone without even leaving his carriage."[48]

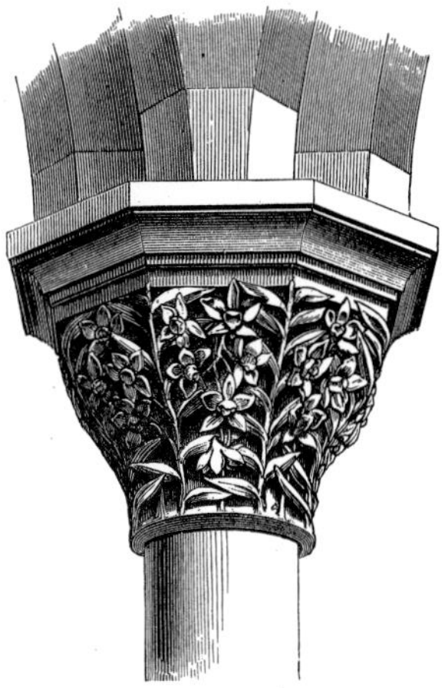

Not only were the botanical specimens with which Richardson decorated his library the same as those being discovered and planted by Sargent in Jamaica Plain, but the specificity of presentation and encyclopedic cast of its decorative scope closely recalls the mission of the Arboretum as both a scientific and picturesque institution, as well as the horticultural illustrations found in books upon which Sargent and Olmsted relied for their own work. One might compare Woburn's ornament, for example, to plates in George B. Emerson's seminal publication, *Report on the Trees and Shrubs Growing Naturally in the Forests of Massachusetts* (1850; fig. 3.24).[49]

The most salient built model for Woburn's botanical verisimilitude is Deane and Woodward's Oxford Museum of the Physical Sciences, which had been completed in 1859, two years before Richardson himself had visited Oxford in the company of Henry Adams. Using specimens from the school's own plant collections as prototypes for the decorative program, this widely touted edifice was specifically intended to demonstrate Ruskin's principles, as well as act as a physical demonstration of the collections ensconced within its walls (figs. 3.25, 3.26).[50] A parallel aesthetic philosophy had first been applied to architecture in this country by Peter B. Wight at the National Academy of Design (1861–1865), which was opened in New York City just as Richardson returned from his studies in Paris. At Harvard, Ware and Van Brunt, likewise, had intended Memorial Hall as an American exemplar of the theories of Ruskin, while a similar foliate decoration had been employed on a somewhat more limited scale by other American architects, such as Cummings and Sears at New Old South Church in Boston.

The rich vegetative ornament that Richardson presents at Woburn, however, was also likely to have been intended to reflect the institution's lofty purpose—as at the Oxford museum or the Bibliothèque Ste.-Geneviève, to prepare its visitors for the contemplation of its collections, which included specimens of art and natural history as well as literature. Within an American transcendentalist context, this veritable catalogue of arboreal species also took on an overt religiosity. Like an open book of nature, it stood as a revelation of God's own creation, a promise of spiritual renewal and immortality. "The affectionate observation of the grace and outward character of vegetation is the sure sign of a more tranquil and gentle existence, sustained by the gifts, and gladdened by the splendour, of the earth," observed Ruskin in "The Nature of Gothic." "In that careful distinction of species, and richness of delicate and undis-

3.27
Woburn Public Library, front elevation, 1877. WML B8, Department of Printing and Graphic Arts, The Houghton Library, Harvard University.

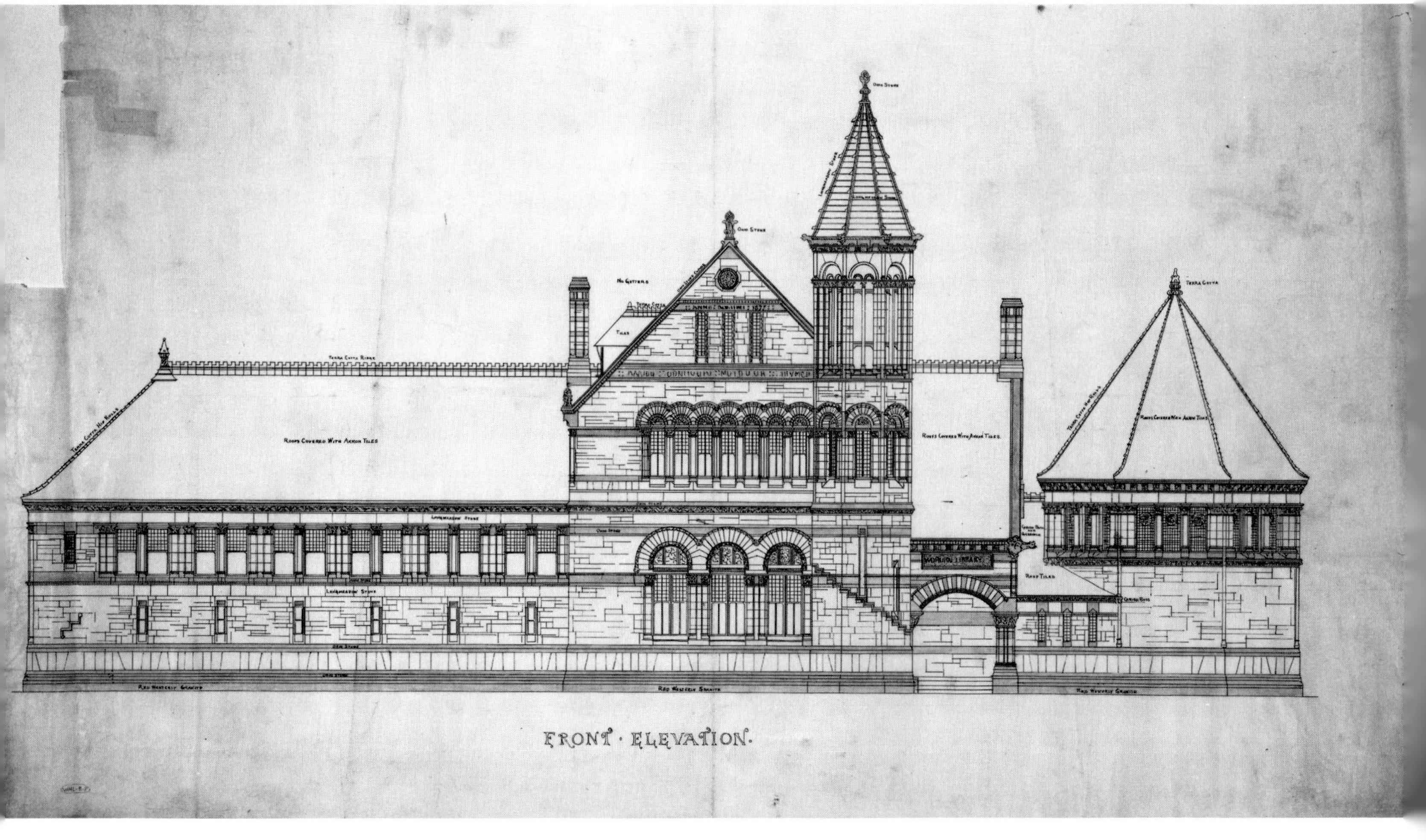




**
*

turbed organization, which characterizes the Gothic design, there is the history of rural and thoughtful life, influenced by habitual tenderness, and devoted to subtle inquiry; and every discriminating and delicate touch of the chisel, as it rounds the petal or guides the branch, is prophecy of the development of the entire body of the natural sciences, beginning with that of medicine, of the recovery of literature, and the establishment of the most necessary principles of domestic wisdom and national peace."[51]

* * *

In line with the ideas of Ruskin, but also his own Beaux-Arts training, the exterior elevations of Richardson's library at Woburn exhibit an equally beguiling palimpsest of associations. Like the complex rhythms that enliven the interior of his book hall, or those that march across the facade of Labrouste's Bibliothèque Ste.-Geneviève, the surfaces of Woburn's walls form an elegant fugue of repetitions and variations on themes composed of windows, colonnettes, foliate bands, and blocks of stone (figs. 3.27, 3.2). Where Labrouste scored his facade in the cold and precise vocabulary of French romantic classicism, Richardson's is rich and voluptuous. The elevations of both buildings, just the same, are curiously mannered.

As within, a lush variety of carefully articulated foliate forms cling to the building's primary structural elements, stringcourses, and cornices. Elsewhere, like the inhabitants of a nineteenth-century garden of earthly delights, playful foxes peek out from behind graceful fern fronds and biomorphic faces form whimsical medieval corbels. In the second story of Richardson's book wing, individual shafts of cream-colored Ohio sandstone, each engaged to a recessed pier, alternate with thin rusticated pilasters flanked by colonnettes to create an A-B-A rhythm. This plays off against the B-A-A-B of the heavy, brownstone lintels, which the vertical elements support. A thin cleft, with rolled moldings and splayed sills, opens in the quarry-faced ashlar base directly beneath each lone column of this window band, while the cadence of the building's fenestration is echoed and counteraccented in the foliated cornice with escutcheons flanked by dragons and, in the middle bay alone, by two owls.

The meticulous attention to detail exhibited by the natural ornament extends to the arrangement of the main blocks of the masonry, where Richardson's building superintendent, Theodore Minot Clark, obviously worked closely with the Norcross Brothers' masons to achieve the effect he wanted. Stone structures, in particular, noted Clark in his popular textbook *Building Superintendence,* "require a minuteness of attention, and a precision and accuracy of workmanship, superior to that which is generally bestowed upon buildings of any other material."[52] "The work of the mason," noted Mrs. Van Rensselaer, "was as important in Richardson's eyes as the work of the sculptor; and many a piece of plain wall was pulled down" under his "orders and rebuilt because the desired effect had in some particular been missed. The result justified and more than justified his care, though perhaps few observers pause to appreciate how much it contributes to the general result which they admire."[53] A single detail, such as the careful building up, or triangulation, of the ashlar blocks around each of the basement windows of the book wing facade, if compared to the same area on the rear of the building, more than elucidates the significance of this art. As Ruskin suggests in his "Lamp of Power," the masonry at Woburn "accommodates itself, naturally and frankly, to the conditions and structure of its work," imparting through the careful shaping and placement of the roughly hewn stones a true sense of the monumental.[54] For memorial buildings, in particular, averred Ruskin's leading American disciple, Charles Eliot Norton, in 1867, it was essential that "every stone . . . should bear evidence of its purpose of honor, every stone should be the object of solicitous care, and should receive every desirable adornment. There should be no expense spared either in material or in the use made of the material so far as ends of art may be served. Every feature of the building should show that patient, inventive, and imaginative thought had been bestowed upon it, and that all the labor needed for its beauty or strength had been given it."[55]

The authority of Richardson's masonry was greatly enhanced, of course, by his love of bold quarry-faced surfaces and massive ashlar blocks, a propensity that betrays—again in the words of the British critic—a "sympathy . . . with the vast controlling powers of Nature herself."[56] Although he would contradict himself elsewhere, rustication formed one of the primary elements of Ruskin's "Lamp of Power." In leaving stones "as they came from the quarry," he declared, there should be revealed "a certain respect for material. . . . If we build in granite or lava, it is a folly, in most cases, to cast away the labour necessary to smooth it; it is wise to make the design granitic itself, and to leave the blocks rudely squared. . . . There is also a magnificence in the natural cleavage of the stone to which the art must indeed be great that pretends to be equivalent; and a stern expression of brotherhood with the mountain heart from which it has been rent, ill-exchanged for a glistering obedience to the rule and measure of man. His eye must be delicate indeed, who would desire to see the Pitti Palace polished."[57]

Along the "harsh seaboard of New England," in particular, argued the American John Bascom in 1877, "the sober gray of solid granite" was particularly well fitted, especially when its "coarse stones, made to face the storms," have been "left to advantage in their fresh native cleavage, the chiseled edge alone marking the attention and care of the workman. There are a certain boldness and rapidity of workmanship in these rough Titan blocks, a distinguishing between what is necessary and what may be dispensed with that often render the effect most pleasing."[58]

At Woburn, the powerful wall of the library, likewise, rests atop a massive, battered-granite foundation similar to the type advocated and illustrated by Ruskin in his *Stones of Venice,* and the corner of the book wing is further anchored with massive piers whose angles have been inscribed with tall, thin colonnettes like those that appear in the *Entretiens sur l'architecture* (1863–1872) of Viollet-le-Duc or Henry Antoine Révoil's *Architecture romane du Midi de la France* (1867–1873), both works that could be found in the architect's library.[59] A curious, stepped and raised pictograph identifies the location of a book room staircase beneath this pile of masonry, as does a second chevron that clings to the central stair tower. Directly atop the stepped foundation, a file of rectilinear brownstone blocks marches around the structure in regular cadence, and above this horizontal bands of Ohio sandstone wrap around the building in a strained attempt to bind together its disparate masses.

According to Ruskin, it was "perfectly natural that the different kinds of stone used in [the] successive courses" of a wall "should be of different colours," for there are "many associations and analogies which metaphysically justify the introduction of horizontal bands of color, or of light and shade. They are, in the first place, a kind of expression of the growth or age of the wall, like the rings in the wood of a tree." They also expressed the "enclosing power of the wall itself" and were "valuable in their suggestion of the natural courses of rocks, and beds of the earth itself. And to all these powerful imaginative reasons we have to add the merely ocular charm of interlineal opposition of color."[60] In his description of the Alps in chapter 5 of *The Stones of Venice,* Ruskin likewise compared the polychrome striations in a masonry wall to the veins of quartz that run through the "mass of loose and slaty shale" of Mont Cervin, knitting "the strength of the mighty mountain like iron bands."[61] Richardson, of course, was not alone in heeding the aphorisms of this popular English critic. Ruskin's work had earlier made a dramatic impression on American landscape painters, and in architecture one has only to look to a building such as William Potter's Berkshire Athenaeum (fig. 2.29) to find a parallel lithic and visual fascination with the polychromed and quarry-faced "wall veil" of Ruskin.[62] Barbara Novak has argued that in the sense in which it represented an account of creation itself, geology in this country embodied the "Great Myth" of the nineteenth century. "It offered Americans a past at once more recent and more remote: the wilderness, ever new in its virginity, also stretched back into primordial time. The past was crucial in establishing an American sense of identity."[63] In Richardson's work, of course, this "geological myth"—the sense of "primordial time"—reveals itself most directly in his fascination with the lithic quality of stone, as well as in his quest for monumental geomorphic form. At Woburn, as Henry Van Brunt declared of the Bibliothèque Ste.-Geneviève in 1861, it is as if "the lore of the classics and the knowledge of the natural world, idealized and harmonized by affectionate study are built up in its walls, and internally and externally, it is a work of the highest Art."[64]

* * *

Significantly, Richardson's decision to rotate his otherwise symmetrical *parti,* so that the book room was shifted from the back of the edifice—as in the MIT designs, for example—to the facade, transformed what had previously been an obscure and utilitarian space into a resonant and picturesque symbol of the library itself. Like the facade of Labrouste's Bibliothèque Ste.-Geneviève (fig. 3.14), the wall at Woburn can be read as a metaphor for the building's functions. In the elevation of the book wing, in particular, a broad band of windows admits light for reading, while below, a thick, battered wall of brownstone wraps itself protectively around the library's contents. Only Snell and Gregerson's elevation at Concord can be seen as anything like an American parallel to this gesture (fig. 2.20). Even here, however, in spite of its brooding presence, the book room was still set at the back of the building.

Whether or not Richardson achieved a comparable success in the development of his overall massing at Woburn, this book wing alone represents one of the most successful and evocative inventions of his entire career. As Henri Labrouste described his design for the Bibliothèque Ste.-Geneviève, "the forms given to each part of the superstructure . . . express forcibly the *nature of the service* for which it was intended."[65] David Van Zanten has identified this notion as the ideal of "transparency": that is, "the situation where the whole work of architecture—its structure, its function, its philosophical nature—might be grasped by a glance at its exterior, as if one were conceptually seeing right through its walls."[66]

At Woburn the low horizontal mass of the book storage area—in contrast to the symmetrical presence of the Bibliothèque Ste.-Geneviève, and symbolic perhaps of the differing relationship of the public to its collections—is played off against the vertical mass of the library's delivery and reading rooms. To the far right, in a manner evocative of the relationship of the chemistry laboratories to the main block of the Oxford Museum (fig. 3.25), the octagonal pavilion of the natural history museum balances this composition. Like the book wing, the natural history collections have been illuminated from above with clerestory windows. Where the Oxford laboratories had been modeled on monastic kitchens, however, Richardson's museum appears to have been inspired by an English Gothic chapter house. In contrast to this museum or the book wing, the reading room spaces in the central block have been illuminated with a broad arcade of windows set at the ground level, while a smaller arcade on the second story provides light to the trustees' room, behind which were located apartments for the library's custodian. Anchoring this central mass, and signaling the public nature of the edifice, is a tall, almost Gothic stair tower, flanked by the low segmental arch of the entry porch (fig. 3.28). The threshold of this porch has been vibrantly articulated with polychromed voussoirs, and bordered on one side with heavy columns and arches whose forms recall the arcades of a Romanesque cloister, a motif that may have been intended to remind visitors of the historical role played by the Christian monastery in the preservation of Western literary traditions. In his *Dictionnaire,* Viollet-le-Duc notes that the cloister was always located "in the vicinity of the library, the infirmary and the cemetery."[67]

The porch also played a commemorative role at Woburn, and a tablet inscribed with words similar to those suggested by Charles Bowers Winn in his will has been placed above a stone settee at the back of this space (fig. 1.9).[68] The broad, segmental arch that frames this inscription recalls a parallel arrangement in the foyer of the Bibliothèque Ste.-Geneviève, where this building's dedication plaque has been similarly framed by a segmental arch leading to the reading room. Behind the entry porch at Woburn, and entered via a circuitous route through a vestibule that opens off of it, is the painting gallery. The end gable of this room has been enriched with polychrome, checkerboard bands, and stone marquetry borrowed from the Romanesque churches of the Auvergne region of southern France.

Of all the surviving competition entries for the Woburn library, only those of Cummings and Sears exhibit a parallel interest in legibility. Their prominent reading room windows, and—in their alternative submission (fig. 3.6)—the independent museum and gallery block, for example, help to identify individual elements of their program. They still fall far short, however, of Richardson's much more explicit didacticism, a method that, ironically perhaps, when coupled with the complexity of the program at Woburn, led to an unsettling collision of forms that in one manner or another has managed to annoy nearly all of his critics. This "florid picturesqueness," what even the architect himself referred to as representative of his "pyrotechnique stage," had "made this building very popular with uncritical observers," claimed Van Rensselaer; but while "the first impression the building produces is very powerful, and delightful," a simpler scheme would have been more appropriate. "The octagon, though thoroughly pleasing in itself, does not group well with the gable, and is so separated from the library proper that the effect is of two buildings in contact rather than of one building of two

3.28
Woburn Public Library, entry porch. Author.

parts. In the main portion the grouping lacks simplicity and breadth; there is no dominant centre of interest, and the relationship between feature and feature seems fortuitous, not inevitable. The portal is not satisfactory and is hardly important enough to suit the character of the building, while the tower is too important and is not felicitous on plan."[69]

Precedents for this type of assemblage, as Henry-Russell Hitchcock observed, abound in contemporary Victorian work.[70] The curious resemblance of Richardson's library to Deane and Woodward's Oxford Museum has already been mentioned (fig. 3.25), while in the United States, the Concord Public Library, Berkshire Athenaeum, and Ware and Van Brunt's Memorial Hall at Harvard all exhibited a similar polychromed masonry, steeply pitched gables, and a profusion of ornament (figs. 2.20, 2.29, 1.5, 1.6). Memorial Hall, in particular, is entered through the transepts and its more picturesque elevation had been turned lengthwise to the street, as was the facade of the Guildhall Library in London (fig. 2.1).[71] Richardson himself had spent just short of a decade exploring the Anglo-American tradition out of which these conventions had arisen. His earliest work, for example, had been heavily indebted to the English Gothic revival. At Trinity Church and then at Woburn, however, he had abandoned the Gothic for the Romanesque, "a system of architecture" that he characterized as "differing from the classical manner in that, while it studied elegance, it was constructional, and from the succeeding Gothic, in that, although constructional, it could sacrifice something of mechanical dexterity for the sake of grandeur and repose."[72]

Many authors have noted precedents for this architect's adaptation of round arches and rusticated stonework in the Boston area, France, and elsewhere. O'Gorman, for instance, has pointed out that buildings such as Paul Schulze's Boylston Hall at Harvard (1857–1858), with its massive granite walls and semicircular windows derived from the German *Rundbogenstil,* must surely have attracted Richardson's eye as a young Harvard undergraduate, as might the monumental warehouse and commercial structures of Boston's "granite school."[73] In Paris the Romanesque revival churches of Victor Baltard or J.-A. Vaudremer likewise may have inspired him, as might Léon Vaudoyer's cathedral at Marseilles (1856–1893), a monument that also displayed a vivid polychrome stonework and embodied complex allusions to both Romanesque and Byzantine motifs. In 1864, Richardson's fellow student and friend Julien Guadet had won the coveted Prix de Rome with a Romanesque design for a hospital in the Alps, a project (autographed photographs of which Richardson brought back to the United States in 1865) that must have played a decisive role in the development of his own architectural vision.[74]

According to O'Gorman, however, Richardson's evolution toward more monumental form had been given added impetus by the popular discovery of America's dramatic western mountain ranges during the post–Civil War era. While the architect himself appears never to have traveled beyond St. Louis, he would have been aware of these geological wonders from the myriad photographs, paintings, and book illustrations that flooded the country at the time, as well as "through the circle of New England intellectuals who were his mentors, clients, and friends," men such as Frederick Law Olmsted, Frederick Lothrop Ames, or Charles Francis Adams, Jr., who knew these natural monuments at first hand.[75] As the Alps, a range Ruskin referred to as the "pillars of the earth," represented a constructional metaphor for the English critic, so the Rockies became a model for architecture in this country. Ultimately, contended Andrew Jackson Downing, "it was our own soil" that formed "the right platform upon which a genuine national architecture must grow, though," he added, "it will be aided in its growth by all foreign thoughts that mingle harmoniously with its simple and free spirit."[76] While Richardson himself exhibited little overt interest in theory, there is ample evidence that he spent much of his career striving to invent just such a style of architecture, and the fruits of this "great Americo-Romanesque experiment" were almost immediately recognized by his contemporaries as a "characteristic expression of American civilization."[77] As Van Rensselaer noted in her biography, "Richardson's choice of language was by no means fortuitous or without deep and interesting significance."[78]

* * *

In France, moreover, a theoretical framework for the development of a modern French regional style, parallel to that for which Richardson seems to have been striving in this country, had begun to emerge during the 1820s and 1830s in a circle of young French "Romantic" architects who had gathered around Henri Labrouste, first in Rome and then in Paris. Neil Levine and David Van Zanten have shown that the principles upon which this theory was based had begun to form in a series of *envois* that Labrouste produced in Rome during the late 1820s, especially in his reconstruction of the Greek temples at Paestum in southern Italy.[79] Here the young student had hypothesized that the classicism which the first Greek colonists had carried with them from their homeland had, in the face of local south Italian building conditions and customs, decayed into a kind of provincial vernacular. This theory was suggested to Labrouste by the "degeneration" of proportions and shift in functions of the Greek temple that he observed in his reversal of the traditional chronology of Paestum's buildings. The overriding dilemma posed by this perceived "devolution" of form has been aptly characterized by Van Zanten: "If Greek colonists at the apogee of Attic art could not meaningfully reproduce the Doric temple form once removed to a foreign place, how could a Frenchman in the nineteenth century hope to do so in Paris?"[80] Labrouste's stripped-down classicism and simplification of arcuated masses at the Bibliothèque Ste.-Geneviève were in many ways intended as an answer to this question (fig. 2.33).

By the time of Richardson's own arrival in Paris, variations on the determinist and positivist theories espoused by Labrouste and his generation, as well as by Viollet-le-Duc and Hippolyte Taine, had entered the mainstream of French architectural theory.[81] Labrouste had himself opened a teaching atelier in Paris in 1830, and although he gave this up in 1856, many of his students subsequently joined the studio of Louis-Jules André. While somewhat more conservative than Labrouste, André passed on much of the substance of his predecessor's historical determinism, as well as his own interpretation of nineteenth-century French romantic classicism, to his own pupils, including Julien Guadet and—after 1859—Henry Hobson Richardson. In respect to his training at the Ecole, noted the architect's former assistant, Theodore Minot Clark, in 1888,

> it seems to be taken for granted by everyone who has written about him that, after the first year or two in this country, he abandoned entirely what he had been taught, except, of course, the mental discipline that he had gained, and turned to a new style of design, which he had to evolve mainly out of his inner consciousness. There is a good deal of truth in this view, but it appears to me to be not entirely correct, and to do injustice to the influence of his patron, André, whose peculiarities of style, and even pet *motifs,* are frequently suggested in Richardson's work of all periods, although the rendering is very different from that which André would have employed, and the part which his old master had in his inspiration was probably unsuspected by Richardson himself. In fact, André's ideas were so congenial to Richardson's tastes that hardly any one else in Paris could have done so much to favor him. If there was any other man suited to be his teacher, it would have been Henri Labrouste, whose simplicity and originality were as dear to Richardson as the "bigness," the "stuff," the broad contrasts of light and shadow, and the largeness of detail which André impresses on all his best pupils. The cavernous triple portals, the all-embracing arches, the deep and richly decorated voussoirs, in everything, except the details, are André's as well as Richardson's, and belonged to certain Romanesque architects six or seven hundred years before their two modern disciples took pleasure in them.[82]

Significantly, by the late 1850s many of the French romantic concepts that inspired these buildings had been independently transported across the Atlantic by other Americans such as Richard Morris Hunt, who himself had studied at the Ecole between 1846 and 1854, or the Danish emigrant architect Detlef Lienau, who had worked in Paris with Henri Labrouste during the years the Bibliothèque Ste.-Geneviève was being erected.[83] This was a decade before Richardson's own return from Europe, but at a time when Frederick Law Olmsted was at work in New York City on his early designs for Central Park. Here, French ideas began to merge with native American determinist theories espoused by the transcendentalists and the precepts of John Ruskin, all of which would later reinforce and alter the lessons absorbed by Richardson in Paris. In 1858, for example, just one year after Olmsted and Vaux's proposal for the park was accepted, Lienau published a lecture, which he had delivered in the same city, in *The Crayon* entitled "On Romantic and Classic Architecture." The ideas expressed here are notable as a kind of summa of French romantic determinist theory; they also reveal a close affinity with themes that were to mature in the work of both Olmsted and Richardson.

"Romantic" architecture, argued Lienau in this paper, "creates new structures, entirely adapted to the purposes for which they were intended, adapted to the climate of the country in which they were erected, and out of the materials supplied by the locality; it gives to the materials the forms most expressive of the degree of perfection of *taste* and mechanical skill of the time; in short, structures reflecting like a mirror the people, the country, the climate, and the wants of the times for which they were erected." In line with Labrouste's reconstruction of the temples at Paestum, Lienau likewise viewed the architecture of the Greeks as the archetypal model for these new "Romantic" forms. Their temples, he noted, "grew naturally out of the soil on which they stood, making, through their broad base, a solid body with the rock, on which and out of which they were built." These monuments were "so fully in harmony with the formations of the locality," he concluded, "that it may be said that they complete its landscape."[84] Three years later, in 1861, Hunt's student Henry Van Brunt attempted to construct a parallel argument in his essay "Greek Lines," which was published in the *Atlantic Monthly.* Here, Van Brunt not only recounts the scandal that Labrouste's *envois* of Paestum created when they were first viewed in Paris, but he calls for a return to the same "Greek" principles that Labrouste as a student had "discovered" in southern Italy and demonstrated at the Bibliothèque Ste.-Geneviève: a building Van Brunt praises as "the most important" building yet erected by the French romantic school.[85]

Given his own training in Paris and subsequent collaborations with Olmsted, Richardson's "naturalization" of the Romanesque idiom through his exploitation of local materials, native ornament, and American vernacular forms can be seen as a parallel attempt to create an American romantic style, adapted geologically and botanically to a new land and reflective of both historical and modern American conditions. The architect's adaptation of a picturesque mode of expression, moreover, allowed him to further intensify the typological character of his buildings, emphasizing not only the genius of place but of program. Like Lienau's—and Labrouste's—vision of the Greek temple, Richardson's libraries appear "so fully in harmony with the formations of the locality" that they, too, can be said to "complete its landscape."[86] Because they look as if they have always been where they now stand, these monuments recall a past more ancient than that of any mere historical allusion.

* * *

While Richardson's decision to arrange his edifice at Woburn along a single spine set parallel to the street clearly announced his own admiration for Labrouste's great French library (fig. 2.33), he also apparently argued that this disposition offered superior illumination in his interior spaces, an advantage that seems to have appealed to the Woburn building committee. Their only surviving comment on the competition, a short notice that appeared in the press announcing the acceptance of the Gambrill and Richardson design, stated that "one prime object in view in having a building so long was to obtain as much sunshine as possible for the better preservation of the books and objects of art the building will probably contain."[87] This opinion was echoed in the *Library Journal,* which in February 1877 noted that the building would "extend 165 feet on Pleasant street with a depth of 75 feet in its widest part; the effect of which, though perhaps making it appear ill-proportioned, will be to furnish an abundance of light—a consideration of more than ordinary weight where not only a library, but reading room, art gallery, and museum must be provided for."[88]

Because of its larger windows, the Woburn building does appear to have better natural light in its book room and alcoves than any of Richardson's later libraries. This consideration, along with the power and legibility of its forms, may indeed have led to Richardson's ultimate triumph in 1877. For all of its flaws, this edifice continues to serve its community well. While its public library functions eventually spilled over into the art gallery and natural history museum and finally into the basement work rooms, the building's ample and impressive interior has allowed it to remain, to date, the only one of Richardson's libraries to have escaped major additions and alterations. In 1890 its second librarian, William R. Cutter, pronounced it a "model village library; . . . one of the most exquisitely designed and harmoniously arranged buildings" that "modern architecture" had produced.[89]



**
*

*four*

# The Epitome of Design

*Libraries in North Easton and Quincy*

The art of characterizing, that is to say, of rendering sensible, by means of material forms, the intellectual qualities and moral ideas that can be expressed in buildings; the art of making understood, by means of the accord and suitability of all the constituent parts of a building, its nature, its propriety, its use, and its purpose; this art, I say, is perhaps, of all the secrets of architecture, the finest and most difficult both to develop and to comprehend.

A. C. Quatremère de Quincy, "Caractère," 1788

While the Woburn library, as the American architectural critic Montgomery Schuyler observed in 1891, may have been "the first of Mr. Richardson's secular works to arrest the attention and secure the admiration of his profession," it was, he went on to note, rapidly "improved upon in a series of charming works for the same purpose and of the same character at North Easton, Quincy and Malden." In his opinion, and that of many others who were to follow, "the essence of Richardson's power of design" lay in his "power of simplification," and this sequence of buildings in particular "shows a progressive simplification which has its climax in the building at Quincy, where the simplicity would be baldness but for the great art of the adjustment of the three features of the front, the reading-room, the book-room and the entrance." These libraries, continued Schuyler, clearly illustrated "the wisdom of employing again and refining upon the motive already employed, rather than of abandoning it because at some points it fails to satisfy the designer, in favor of a radically different motive to be in turn worked out crudely and in turn abandoned."[1]

* * *

The commission for the second building in this series, the Ames Free Library of Easton, in North Easton, Massachusetts, appears to have arrived in Richardson's office sometime before September 1877, less than seven months after the publication of the Woburn Public Library in *American Architect and Building News.* The establishment of this institution followed the death on 9 March of that year of Oliver Ames II, who left a bequest of $50,000 "for the construction of a library building and the support of a library for the benefit of the inhabitants of the town of Easton." Of this sum he specified that not more than $25,000 was to be "expended on the purchase of land and the erecting of the library building," with $10,000 for the acquisition of books. "The remaining fifteen thousand dollars shall constitute a permanent fund to be invested in stock of the Old Colony Railroad Company, the income of which shall be devoted to increasing the library and keeping the building and its appurtenances and contents in repair."[2]

In addition to a long-standing interest in public education, as exemplified by his continued participation in local school committees, the decision by Ames to bequeath money for a public library building in his hometown may have been influenced by the erection of similar structures in Braintree and Randolph, Massachusetts, in 1874 and 1876 (figs. 2.21, 2.26). Both of these communities were located near North Easton on the Boston line of the Old Colony Railroad, which was itself owned by the Ames family. As noted in chapter 2, the Turner Free Library in Randolph had been designed by Oliver Ames's nephew, John Ames Mitchell, whose proposal had been chosen over those of Peabody and Stearns and Samuel F. Thayer, as well, perhaps, as others. Although Mitchell had also been employed by his uncle in 1875 to design the Unitarian Church in North Easton, by 1876 he had returned to Paris—where earlier he had trained in architecture at the Ecole des Beaux-Arts—to study painting. He therefore appears not to have been available to design the North Easton library.[3] In any case, by September 1877 Richardson was awarded this commission by Ames's son, Frederick Lothrop Ames, and his daughter, Helen Angier Ames (1836–1882). Although completed sometime in 1879 at a cost of $34,535, it did not open until 10 March 1883, in order that all of its books could be catalogued before this event. The difference between the initial bequest of Oliver Ames II and the final cost was made up by the two children and his widow, Sarah, who died just a few months after her husband.[4]

As may have been the case in Woburn and was elsewhere in his career, a number of authors have speculated that Richardson owed this North Easton commission to his Harvard connections.[5] Frederick Lothrop Ames, the person who appears to have been most responsible for his selection, had, like Edward D. Hayden of Woburn, graduated from Harvard in 1854, the same year as Richardson's partner, Charles Dexter Gambrill. It is likely that Ames knew both of these men and may even have consulted with Hayden concerning his choice. The architect may also have been recommended to Ames by either Frederick Law Olmsted or his Brookline neighbor, Charles Sprague Sargent. Ames, an avid amateur horticulturist, may have been in contact with either or both of these men by this date concerning his own interest in orchids, especially it would seem with Sargent, who was director of the Botanic Gardens at Harvard.[6] In 1881, the Ames family hired Olmsted to landscape the grounds of Ames Memorial Hall (1879–1881), a second Richardson-designed building commissioned in February 1879 by the children of Oakes Ames (the brother of Oliver Ames II) as a memorial to their father.[7] Frederick Lothrop Ames was also a close friend and business associate of Charles Francis Adams, Jr. Since their years together in college, Richardson had been a frequent companion of Charles's younger brother Henry (Harvard '58).[8] As noted in chapter 1, the elder Adams had himself been a member of the board of trustees of the Quincy Public Library since its founding in 1871, and would serve as its chairman from 1875 until 1894. In the process of carrying out the provisions of his father's will, it seems more than likely that Ames discussed the organization of this new institution with Adams.

In his capacity as chairman of the board of the Quincy library, Adams appears to have played an equally significant role in the choice of Richardson as architect for that building.

Raised by the widow and two surviving sons of Thomas Crane, himself a former resident of Quincy who had died in New York City in 1875, the Quincy library was also intended as a family memorial. On 19 February 1880, Albert (1842–1918), the eldest of the Crane sons, wrote a letter to the Quincy board of selectmen informing them that he, his brother, and mother were "desirous of erecting some memorial" to his father. Although Thomas had long been resident in New York, continued the son, he had "always retained a strong feeling for the town of Quincy, where his family originated and had resided for over a century, and where he himself passed the earlier portion of his life. After much deliberation, therefore, his family thought that a memorial erected to him in Quincy would be both more appropriate than elsewhere, and most in consonance with the tender feelings and cordial interest he always manifested therefor in his lifetime, and which he constantly expressed to us."[9]

Consequently the family offered to expend "no less than" $20,000 to "erect an edifice to his memory," on the condition that "the town, on its part, be willing to dedicate a site therefor, satisfactory to us in some convenient and central locality." This building, "to be known as the Crane Memorial Hall or Library," was "to be held in trust forever by the town, or by some corporation authorized by it, for the free use of the town as a Public Library building."[10]

Although the Quincy library board later averred that it had "no reason to suppose" the Crane family had been aware of the pressing need for a new building which they had broadcast in their 1878 report, or that their plea for a private benefactor to fill this need had "in any way influenced their action," Thomas Crane's heirs—even though they resided in New York and Connecticut—could very well have been aware of the town's dilemma through other sources. Albert Crane observed in 1880, for example, that while his father had not known Adams personally he had "for many years" made annual visits to Quincy, and had also continued to subscribe to the *Quincy Patriot Ledger.*[11] Clearly the family might have known, too, of the recently completed library buildings in neighboring Braintree, Thomas Crane's ancestral home, or in other nearby towns, such as Randolph or North Easton. In Stamford, Connecticut, where the Cranes kept a substantial country residence, moreover, John Day Ferguson had bequeathed $10,000 for a public library in 1877 on the condition that an additional $25,000 be raised by subscription before 15 February 1880, just four days before Albert Crane's letter reached the Quincy board. Although the family did not contribute to the Stamford fund, it seems likely that they would have been aware of the flurry of activity surrounding it, and the ultimate success of the fund drive.[12]

While the Cranes reserved the right "to select the architect (who shall be one of standing and ability), the architectural design and the details of material and construction," for their new building in Quincy, the influence of Charles Francis Adams, Jr., in this process should not be underestimated. A member of Quincy's most prominent family and descendant of two presidents, Adams was accustomed to taking charge. He had been the indisputable architect of the library's earlier organization and philosophical mission, which conformed closely to the innovative program engineered for the Boston Public Library by his uncle, Edward Everett, in

4.1
H. H. Richardson, plans for public libraries: *A,* Woburn Public Library, 1876–1879; *B,* Ames Memorial Library, North Easton, 1877–1883; *C,* Crane Memorial Library, Quincy, 1879–1881; *D,* Converse Memorial Building, Malden, 1883–1885. Drawing by Glenn Waguespack.

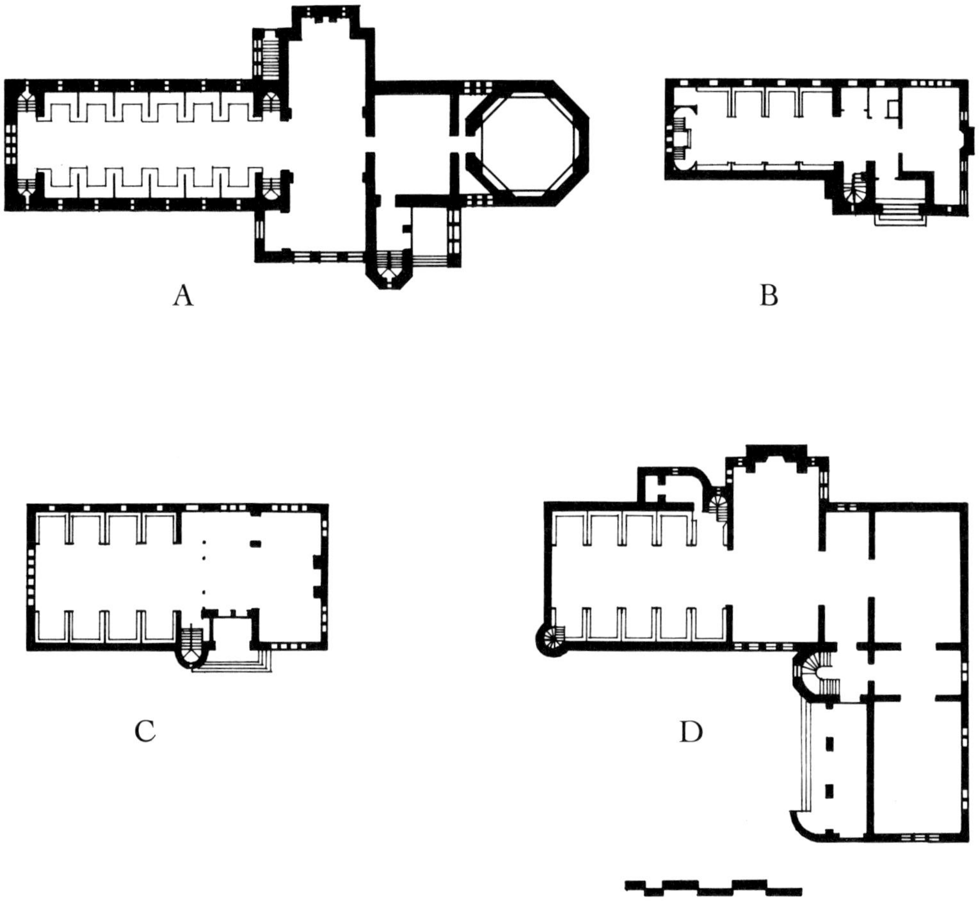



**
*

collaboration with George Ticknor during the 1850s. And, as he himself would note late in life, his role in the establishment and nourishing of the Quincy library was one of his most treasured achievements. Acknowledging his continuous involvement in the affairs of the library, upon his resignation as chairman in 1894 Adams's fellow trustees observed: "Whatever is best in the creation and fruition of the library belongs to him. He has been its master builder."[13] From his ongoing correspondence with the Crane family, moreover, we know that Adams continued to keep a close watch on the library from his new home in Lincoln even after this date.[14]

With the exception of a meeting between Albert Crane, the town's selectmen, library trustees, and the architect in April of 1880, the Crane family appears to have remained in New York and Connecticut during both the design and construction phases of the Quincy building. Details of the project, for which ground was broken in September 1880, would appear to have been left to a subcommittee appointed "to confer with Mr. Albert Crane and the architect of the proposed building, in relation to details of construction in regard to which they may wish to consult." This group included Adams and two other members of the library's board of trustees.[15] The survival of at least five different schemes for the building among the drawings in the Houghton Library at Harvard suggests, in fact, that the building's program was in a considerable state of flux for some time during its early development, a process with which Adams must have been closely associated. According to the *Quincy Patriot,* as the Cranes "became interested in their scheme, it naturally developed on their hands, and they found themselves unwilling to either reduce the size, or impair the architectural effect of the designs submitted to them; so that, when everything which they were willing to curtail had been curtailed, the contract as finally executed exceeds by considerably more than half the amount originally proposed, and which the family had caused the town to understand they were willing to expend."[16]

* * *

When the Quincy building was finally dedicated on 30 May 1882, it was both more costly than the family's original conception (the structure alone cost more than $50,000) and yet less elaborate than Richardson's initial proposals. As at North Easton, the final building was considerably smaller and less complex than the program at Woburn (fig. 4.1). Where the Woburn building had been designed to hold 100,000 volumes, for example, the Quincy book room was projected to accommodate 40,000, and North Easton's just 25,000. Neither of the latter two buildings made provision for an art gallery or museum collections, and their public

4.2
H. H. Richardson, Ames Memorial Library, North Easton, 1877–1883. Department of Printing and Graphic Arts, The Houghton Library, Harvard University.


**
*

4.3
Ames Memorial Library, entry arch. Van Rensselaer, *Henry Hobson Richardson and His Works,* 1888.

4.4
Belfry at Morienval. Viollet-le-Duc, *Dictionnaire raisonné,* 1868.

reading areas were reduced in size. In spite of these differences, however, it is clear—as Montgomery Schuyler recognized—that Richardson considered all three of these structures to be of the same generic type (figs. 4.2, 4.11). There are, in fact, a variety of features they share in common. All of these libraries have their primary functions arrayed along a central axis that runs parallel to the main facade of the building, although in the later structures the reading rooms have been shifted to the right so that one enters through a shallow vestibule directly into the circulation area. Entry to these vestibules is now marked with a simple yet imposing arch (figs. 4.3, 4.14), which replaces Woburn's porch and has been absorbed into a multistory, gabled block; a maneuver that Mrs. Van Rensselaer felt imparted a "due dignity" to the entrances, furnishing the buildings with "a true centre of interest."[17] With no museum or picture gallery to accommodate at North Easton, Richardson shifted the stair tower to the left of, and behind, the gabled block of the building, thereby creating a tenuous balance between his entry pavilion and the book wing—an equilibrium that he better refined at Quincy. The tower at North Easton—now much simplified in form and diminished in scale from that at Woburn—may have been inspired by an illustration of the belfry at Morienval illustrated in Viollet-le-Duc's *Dictionnaire* (fig. 4.4).[18] At Quincy, this element was further reduced and pushed forward along the left edge of the gable, which has itself been moved back into the same plane as the library's book wing.

In North Easton, as at Woburn, the upper stories of the main block of the building originally housed a directors' room (on the second story), with a small librarian's apartment above. While these quarters were eliminated at Quincy, a storage area, which could at some date be converted into a meeting hall, did occupy the attic space under the roof. In all three of these libraries, the book wing has been illuminated with a broad band of fenestration set over a massive, battered masonry base. At North Easton, these windows have been fixed between alternating single and clustered colonnettes (fig. 4.5). While the primary A-B-B-A cadence of these elements is somewhat more complex than those found at Woburn, the overall elevation of the book wing has been greatly simplified. The lower fenestration has been eliminated and, with the exception of the colonnette capitals, Woburn's lush foliate ornament has been stripped away, leaving a more elemental, geomorphic form. "Richness," as Mrs. Van Rensselaer observed, "is not excessive and is artistically concentrated upon a few features supported by dignified and quiet fields of wall." These fields are composed of rusticated Milford granite and reddish-brown Longmeadow sandstone laid under the supervision of the architect and his contractor, O. W. Norcross. By the time he reached North Easton, notes Van Rensselaer, "the somewhat crude and over-bold treatment of wall-surfaces which marked much of Richardson's early work had . . . disappeared. . . . Scale was carefully considered in regulating the average size of the stones, and they were varied among themselves in size and shape with a keen feeling for that degree of difference which should mean animation without restlessness, breadth combined with vitality."[19] This has been accomplished, as Edward R. Ford has pointed out, with great subtlety:

> The North Easton wall begins with two projecting courses of Milford gray granite, dressed on their sloped edges but rough on their thin vertical faces. Atop this is a string course of pink granite, uniform in height but narrow. Above this is an unbroken expanse of wall, slightly battered and composed of gray and pink granite in what looks like, but is not, a random pattern. The larger stones are gray, the smaller ones pink.

The gray stones are flatter than the pink ones and more regular, so that they have less shadow on their faces. Atop this is a string course of Longmeadow sandstone, rough-faced but with a top molding that forms a tiny drip for the windowsill. Projecting drip molds or sills are small if they occur at all in Richardson's work, so as not to detract from the mass.[20]

Because of North Easton's diminished book capacity, Richardson employed full alcoves only along the rear edge of the book room in this building (figs. 4.6, 4.7). In contrast to the front elevation, this back wall has been illuminated with small windows set into the lower story and four dormers that extend above the eave (fig. 4.8). Along the front elevation the alcoves are much shallower, with only wall shelving in the upper tier. The narrow galleries that access this story are connected at the rear of the room with a balcony and reached by way of spiral wooden staircases. As at Woburn, the book room has been enclosed with a wooden barrel vault, now composed of polished butternut slats, the same material employed throughout this space. The detailing here is now more American colonial in spirit than the lush, botanical ornament Richardson had employed earlier. The gallery encircling the book room is supported by austere pilasters with carved rope moldings and simply decorated brackets. Above, a more mannered grouping of turned and inverted colonnettes flank heavy, urn-shaped columns. These vaguely Queen Anne motifs all recall late seventeenth-century New England cabinetwork, magnifying in scale the forms of smaller elements found in this genre of furniture design. Similarly, the curving iron railings of Woburn's galleries have been replaced by a straight wooden balustrade, with turned balusters of eighteenth-century inspiration. Richardson's growing attraction to indigenous American models reflects an increasing interest in this country in its own past, one promoted by the centennial celebration of 1876 and reinforced by important American tastemakers like Clarence Cook, and by contemporary pattern books such as *Early New England Interiors Sketched by Arthur Little* (1877).[21]

4.5
Ames Memorial Library, book wing. Van Rensselaer, *Henry Hobson Richardson and His Works,* 1888.

4.6
Ames Memorial Library, book room. *Monographs of American Architecture,* 1886, courtesy of the Society for the Preservation of New England Antiquities.

**
*

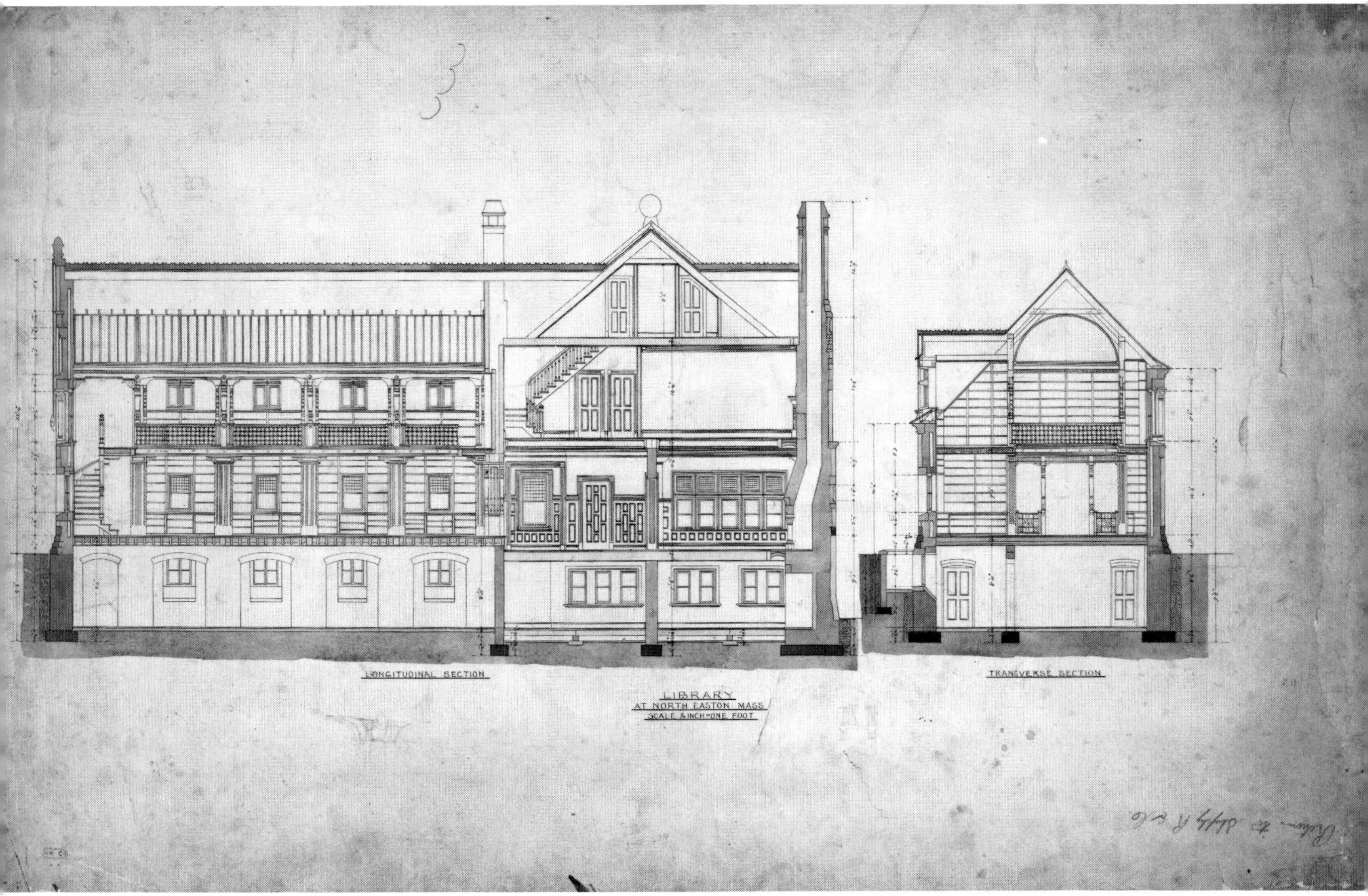


4.7
Ames Memorial Library, transverse and longitudinal sections, 1877. ALNE C1, Department of Printing and Graphic Arts, The Houghton Library, Harvard University.

4.8
Ames Memorial Library, rear elevation, with Ames Memorial Hall in background, 1879–1881. *Monographs of American Architecture,* 1886, courtesy of the Society for the Preservation of New England Antiquities.

4.9
Ames Memorial Library, reading room. Prints and Photographs Division, Library of Congress.



**
*

4.10
Ames Memorial Library, sketch for reading room mantel attributed to Stanford White. ALNE E1, Department of Printing and Graphic Arts, The Houghton Library, Harvard University.

In a similar antiquarian spirit, the small reading room to the right of the entry at North Easton was finished with black walnut paneling and a timbered ceiling (fig. 4.9). This space is dominated by a great hearth, with a bas-relief of the library's patron, Oliver Ames II, executed by the American sculptor Augustus Saint-Gaudens, set into the overmantel (fig. 1.10).[22] The naturalistic foliage of Woburn lingers in the luxurious oak leaves and acorns that surround this icon, or the pomegranate bushes that flank it. This detail has been attributed to the brilliant ornamentalist Stanford White, who was still in the architect's employ at the time. An early sketch for the hearth, which also has been associated with White, depicts a series of quatrefoils in place of the portrait (fig. 4.10). Other furnishings at North Easton appear to have been very similar to those Richardson employed at Woburn. Like them, they reflect his growing interest in combining medieval and early American motifs.

* * *

In his third library at Quincy, Richardson reintroduced the double-loaded alcove system he had utilized in his first library design at Woburn, but had modified at North Easton (figs. 4.11, 4.12). While maintaining the unbroken lower story of the latter's book wing facade, he also returned to the A-B-A rhythm of his original window band scheme on the upper story. A small sketch from the Richardson office, now in the Houghton Library at Harvard, gives some indication of the significance that this form of the window band held for the architect (fig. 4.13). It depicts the relative dimensions and proportions of the fenestration not only at Woburn, North Easton, and Quincy, but at Austin Hall at Harvard (1881–1884) as well. At the same time, at Quincy, the massive corner pier that marks the composition of both of his previous library wings has been greatly reduced in scale. To Henry-Russell Hitchcock, Richardson's band of fenestration now extended in a "curiously modern" way "from turret to corner [leaving] only the thickness of the end wall" to halt the visual repetition of the colonnettes and, apparently, to support the cornice and roof. "Seen in perspective, as it was designed," this motif, to a modernist such as Hitchcock, "represent[ed] a very advanced step away from traditional [masonry] design." For a contemporary critic such as Montgomery Schuyler, who was not as interested in discovering the roots of the modern movement, this motif represented the "chief defect" in an otherwise masterful composition.[23] Both here and at North Easton, Richardson abandoned the vertical roll molding he had employed to accent his corners at Woburn in favor of a sharply defined, geometric edge, which contrasts with the rough facing of the stone walls. This motif not only strengthens the silhouette of the mass but may also reflect the difference in materials: brownstone walls at Woburn, as opposed to the harder, more difficult to work granite of his next two libraries.[24]

4.11
H. H. Richardson, Crane Memorial Library, Quincy, 1879–1881. Courtesy of the Thomas Crane Library.

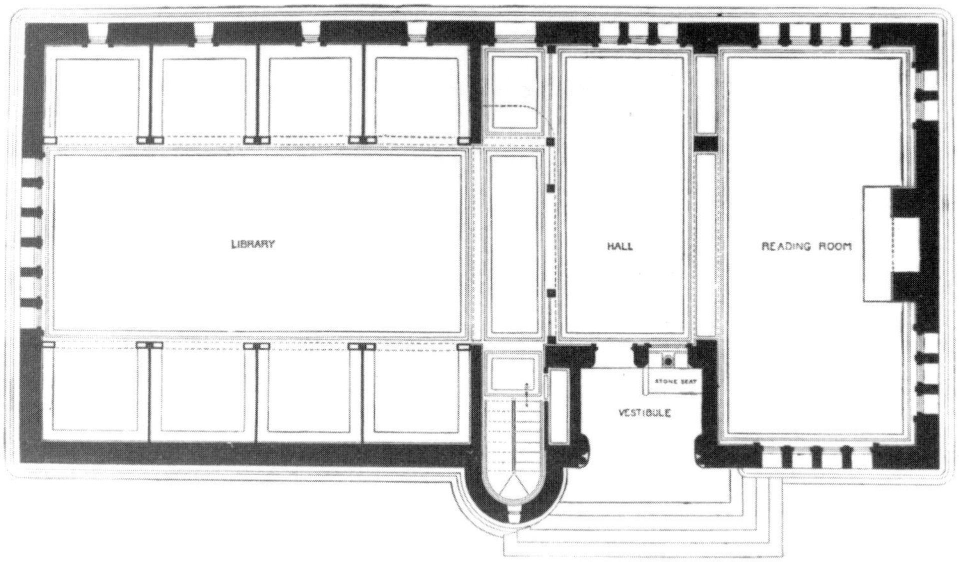


4.12
Crane Memorial Library, first-floor plan. Van Rensselaer, *Henry Hobson Richardson and His Works,* 1888.

4.13
Office of H. H. Richardson, sketch of fenestration at Austin Hall, Harvard (upper left), Quincy (middle left), Woburn (middle right), and North Easton (lower left), n.d. AH D144, Department of Printing and Graphic Arts, The Houghton Library, Harvard University.

Although the foundation of the Crane Library was of Quincy granite, the superstructure of this building was articulated in a manner similar to that of the Ames Library, with rock-faced, North Easton granite blocks and Longmeadow sandstone details and trim. The overall vocabulary also remained essentially the same, although its syntax was greatly refined. Quincy's gabled pavilion and tower, for instance, were further melded into a single, powerful ensemble and now flanked to the right with a large "Tudor" window of the type with which the architect had originally lighted the rear wall of the Ames Library reading room (fig. 4.8). While helping to balance the book wing to the left, this large expanse of fenestration also delineated the function of the area behind it, further distinguishing it from the more protective stone wall of the storage area. The diminished stair turret, itself now pulled into the central block of the build-

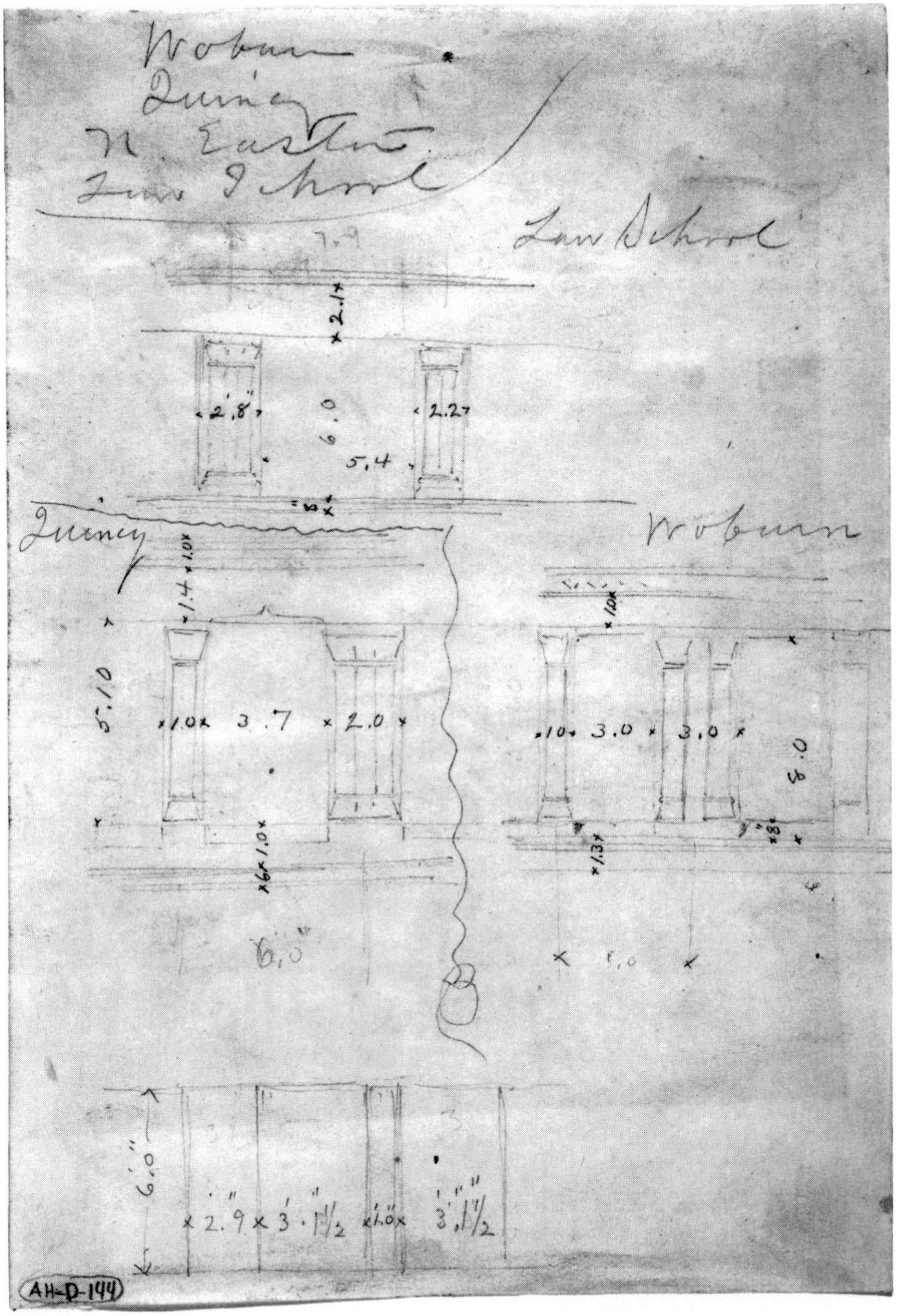
Woburn
Quincy
N. Easton
Law School
Law School
Quincy
Woburn
AH-D-144

4.14
Crane Memorial Library, entry arch. Author.

ing, further strengthens the unity of this composition, its bold, convex and battered mass played off against, and colliding with, the yawning void of the entry arch (fig. 4.14). The oversized voussoirs of the gable arcade reiterate this theme, one that is picked up again in the elegantly understated curve of the eyebrow dormers in the roof.

In 1886, in one of his very rare discussions of his work, Richardson summarized his intent in a very closely related proposal for the Hoyt Library in East Saginaw, Michigan (fig. 6.10). The object of this design, asserted the architect, has been to provide a building the character of which should depend on its outlines, on the massing and accentuation of the main features representing its leading purposes, and on the relation of the openings to the solid parts. The intention has been to produce that sense of solidity requisite in dignified, monumental work, by a perfectly quiet and massive treatment of the wall surfaces. . . .

A FREE treatment of Romanesque has been followed throughout, as a style especially adapted to the requirements of a civic building; for while it maintains great dignity together with a strong sense of solidity, it lends itself at the same time most readily to the requirements of utility, especially in the matter of light. To strengthen this feeling of dignity and to express the civic character of the building, a monumental treatment has been followed throughout.[25]

"All this is so well studied," maintained *Harper's Weekly* of the Quincy building in 1883,

that there is nothing forced, no appearance of 'making architecture,' but the composition seems as simple and spontaneous as if it came so. There is a complete equipoise and balance, with no approach to formal symmetry, in the two wings of the front, which is brought about by skillful arrangement and contrast of the two sets of openings. A striking instance of the length to which variety may be carried in skillful hands without becoming restless is afforded in the courage with which the entrance is placed 'out of centre' in both directions, neither in the centre of the wall which it pierces horizontally, nor in the axis of the central opening of the triple window above it vertically. The impression of rugged strength is everywhere kept by the ample spaces of rocky wall, either in unbroken wall spaces or in powerful wall piers.

While each of Richardson's libraries was "of high architectural interest," the building at Quincy was "the most simplified as well as the most refined in treatment, and gains thereby in singleness and force of expression." Of the three libraries Richardson had built to date, concluded *Harper's,* the Thomas Crane Public Library was, "upon the whole, the most successful; and saying that is pretty safely saying that it is architecturally the best Village library in the United States."[26]

The unification of form evident on the exterior of the Crane Memorial, and its "real successes of detail," as *Harper's* went on to note, were carried over into the interior of this edifice as well (figs. 4.15, 4.16). Here, a late medieval or colonial beamed ceiling of the type that Richardson first introduced into his work at the William Watts Sherman House extends from one end of the building to the other, replacing the barrel vaults he had employed in his earlier book rooms. Although patrons were still separated from the collection by a delivery desk and ornamental screen, Richardson opened up all of his rooms so that the spaces now flowed freely

4.15
Crane Memorial Library, book room. Courtesy of the Thomas Crane Library.

one into another. The woodwork throughout is of southern white pine, with clustered colonnettes in the lower story of the book room, combined with fluted pilasters flanked by thin colonnettes and colonial revival turned-wood balustrades in the upper galleries (fig. 4.17). The capitals of the colonnettes and pilasters have all been articulated with "Byzantinesque decoration, largely based upon suggestions afforded by native plants," but which almost could have been copied from plates in Ruskin's *Seven Lamps of Architecture* or *The Stones of Venice.*[27] At Quincy the galleries run straight across the back, or right side, of the book room, while, as at Woburn, they undulate gracefully around the alcove partitions behind the front facade. The slope of the ceiling over the alcoves has been covered with black leather embossed in gold.

4.16
Crane Memorial Library, view of delivery desk and book room with portrait of Thomas Crane on easel. Courtesy of the Thomas Crane Library.

**
*

4.17
Crane Memorial Library, book room alcoves. Courtesy of the Society for the Preservation of New England Antiquities.

4.18
Crane Memorial Library, reading room hearth. *American Architect and Building News*, 20 August 1892.

**
*

As in all of Richardson's libraries, a great hearth, now set on the primary axis of the building, dominates the reading room (fig. 4.18). The overmantel of this fireplace is flanked by spiral columns and ornamented with panels depicting native trees and plants, such as oak, pine, and tupelo. While still inspired by the philosophy of the British aesthetic movement, the style of Quincy's "Windsor" reading chairs, or the long spindle-back settee that can be seen in an early photo in front of the delivery desk, now emerge more from American colonial sources than from Queen Anne. As Henry-Russell Hitchcock pointed out more than a half-century ago, an autograph sketch of the rear elevation of the Quincy library reveals how Richardson also expressed a more indigenous heritage on the exterior of the building (fig. 4.19). While translated into stone, the low horizontal profile and asymmetrical end gable of the projecting L depicted in this drawing all recall traditional New England saltbox houses of the seventeenth and eighteenth centuries, homes not unlike the Adams homesteads in Quincy or the old Converse house in Woburn (fig. 1.2).[28]

4.19
Rear perspective of the Crane Memorial Library. CLQ F1, Department of Printing and Graphic Arts, The Houghton Library, Harvard University.

As earlier, Richardson's specific relationship to the design of the Crane library's furnishings remains enigmatic. We do know that in January 1882, less than five months before the dedication of the building, the trustees, responding to an inquiry from the architect, agreed "that as he had large experience in matters of this kind, the board would prefer that he should take charge of the matter and select such furniture as his judgment should approve."[29] Whatever the source, the result manifests the most cohesive of the architect's designs to date. "Here at last is a whole in which all parts are so fused together that it is impossible to disassociate them in thought," enthused Van Rensselaer. The Quincy library "looks as though it had been conceived at a single inspiration, born by a single impulse. But this means of course that it was the result of patient constructive thought, of well-trained reasoning skill."[30] According to the *Quincy Patriot,* in fact, Richardson appears to have arrived at his final arrangement after considerable experimentation, much of which is documented in the Houghton Library at Harvard, where drawings representing five different designs (including the built version) for the building have been identified by L. Draper Hill and James F. O'Gorman.[31]

Featuring a prominent lecture hall, which occupies the left wing of the building, and "student alcoves" opening off the reading room, the first three schemes seem to reflect most closely Charles Francis Adams, Jr.'s, concept of the public library as an extension of the public school system, as well, perhaps, as Clarissa Crane's own interest in the continuing education of women (figs. 4.20, 4.21, 4.22). While the overall symmetry of the *parti* and the relative size of each of the primary spaces shifted somewhat from stage to stage during this early phase of the design process, the fundamental diagram remained the same. These plans all have been ordered by a simple cross-axial armature, with a central delivery area flanked by a lecture hall and reading room. As in the MIT student designs of 1875 (figs. 2.30, 2.31)—or several of the rejected designs for the Woburn Library—Richardson's book room extends from the rear of the building, directly behind the circulation desk. In what has been identified as scheme I for this building (fig. 4.20), a large central entryway appears to be flanked with symmetrically disposed porch arcades.

Most significantly, the gallery and alcove shelving system employed at Woburn has been replaced in all three of the earliest plans with a more compact system of book storage. Scheme I, for example, combines radiating shelving, reminiscent of Cummings and Sears's Woburn book room, with double-sided shelving set perpendicular to the side walls (figs. 4.20, 3.5, 3.7). Richardson subsequently changed this to the type of rectilinear "stack room" (a term even he applied to his third scheme) advocated by Justin Winsor, and proposed at Woburn by Peabody



**
*

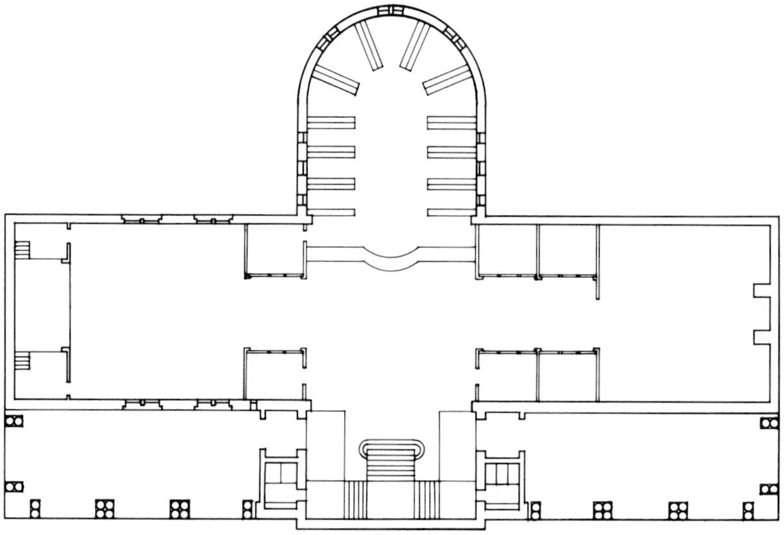

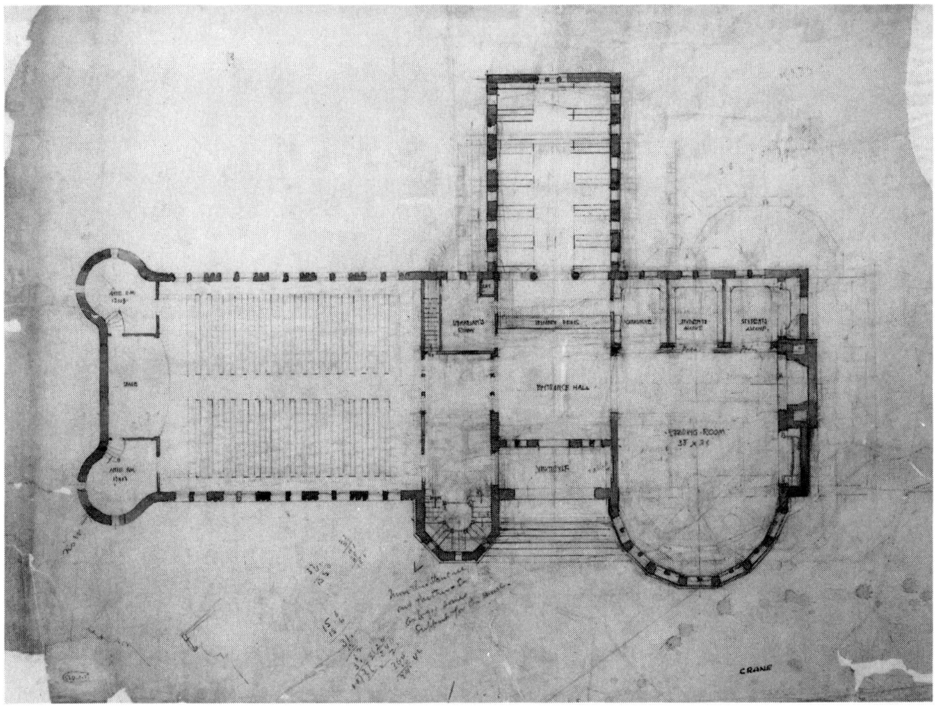
ENTRANCE HALL
CRANE

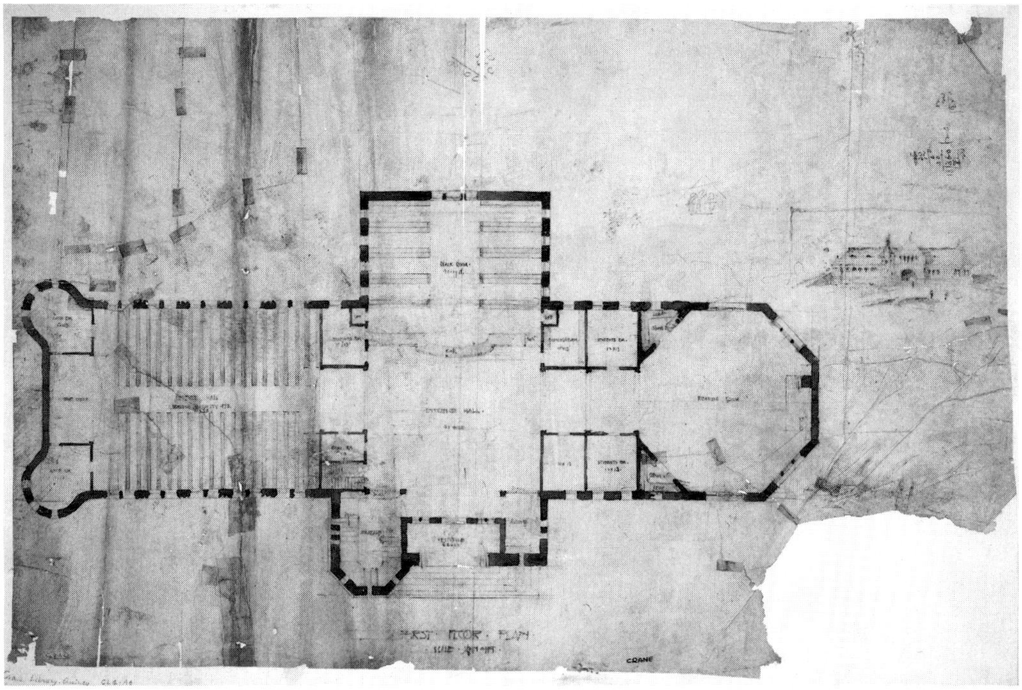


4.20
Crane Memorial Library, first-floor plan, scheme I. Drawing by Glenn Waguespack after a plan (CLQ A4) in the Department of Printing and Graphic Arts, The Houghton Library, Harvard University.

4.21
Crane Memorial Library, first-floor plan, scheme II. CLQ A5, Department of Printing and Graphic Arts, The Houghton Library, Harvard University.

4.22
Crane Memorial Library, first-floor plan, scheme III. CLQ A6, Department of Printing and Graphic Arts, The Houghton Library, Harvard University.



**
*

4.23
Crane Memorial Library, detail of elevation sketch in upper right corner of scheme III. CLQ A6, Department of Printing and Graphic Arts, The Houghton Library, Harvard University.

4.24
Crane Memorial Library, sketch plan and elevation for scheme IV on the architect's blue stationery. UNK F25, Department of Printing and Graphic Arts, The Houghton Library, Harvard University.

and Stearns (fig. 3.11). In schemes II and III Richardson attempted to differentiate the reading room wing from the lecture hall, first by expanding it forward from the block of the building, and then by incorporating it into an octagonal pavilion similar to the one he had employed at Woburn for the natural history museum, and would resurrect again in his design for the Billings Library at the University of Vermont (figs. 6.12, 6.13).

A tiny autograph sketch located in the upper right-hand corner of scheme III depicts the earliest extant elevation of the series (fig. 4.23). Here, a central, gabled pavilion is marked with a broad round arch and flanked by a small stair tower. To the left, the assembly hall appears to be illuminated with a narrow, horizontal strip of fenestration derived from the elevations of Richardson's earlier book wings at Woburn and North Easton. The different functions of the

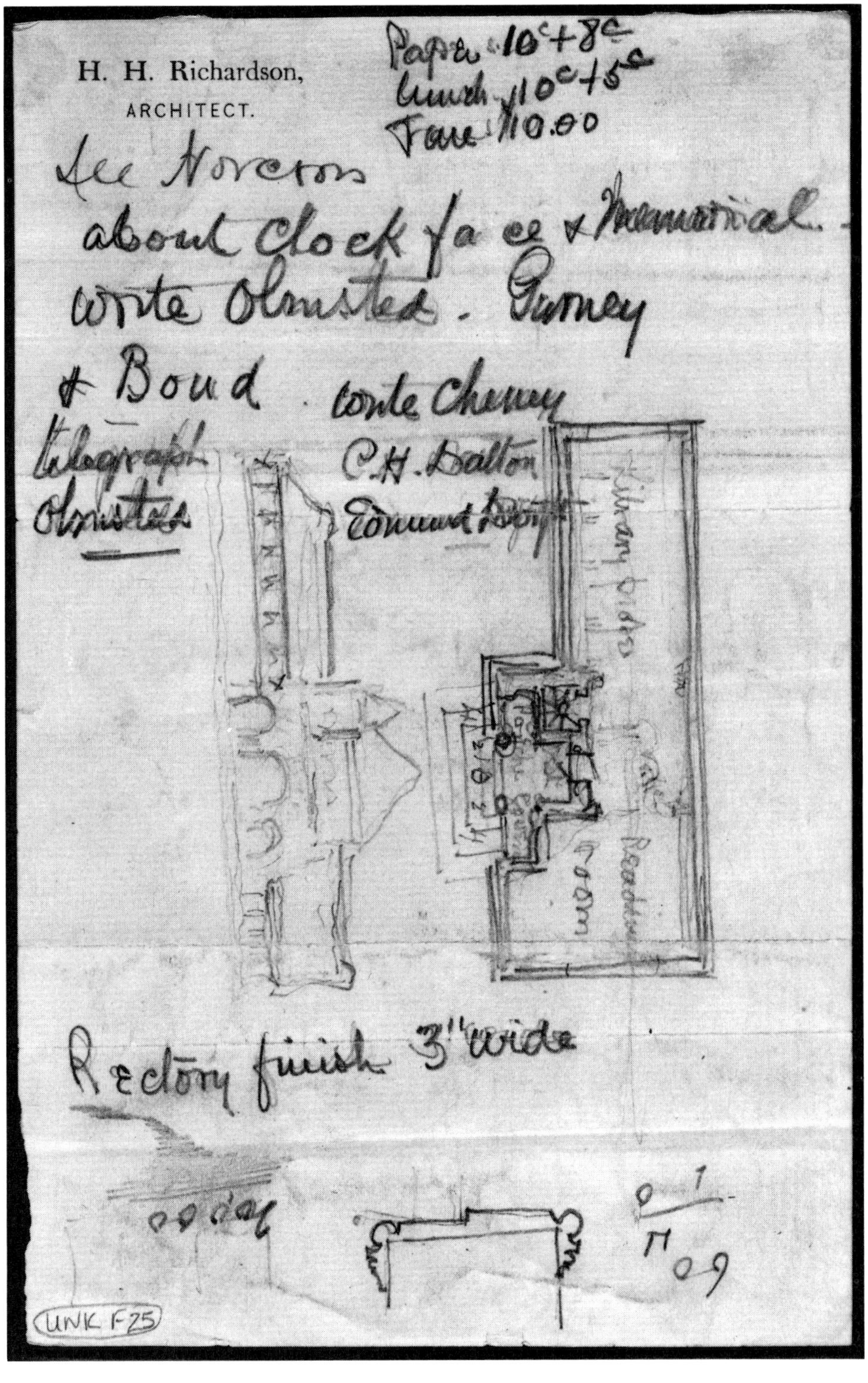
H. H. Richardson,
ARCHITECT.
Paper 10c+8c
Lunch 10c+5c
Fare 10.00
See Norcross
about clock face + memorial
write Olmsted - Gurney
+ Bond
write Cheney
telegraph
Olmsted
C.H. Dalton
Reading room
Rectory finish 3" wide
UNK F25

study alcoves and octagonal reading room have been distinguished with larger, more vertically oriented lights. The pyramidal roof of the reading area has been balanced at the opposite end of the building with corner turrets of the type Richardson would eventually employ as stair towers in Malden. In this Quincy scheme these form anterooms that flank the stage of the auditorium.

A fourth proposal, identified by O'Gorman and dated by him to 1880, can be found on a leaf of the architect's stationery amidst a series of hastily penned reminders to himself to contact Olmsted, Norcross, and others he was involved with at the time (fig. 4.24).[32] This scheme returns more closely in plan to Richardson's North Easton paradigm. Perhaps because of cost, the lecture hall has been eliminated and the book wing, which now appears to replace compact book storage with alcove shelving, has been shifted back to a position along the facade, opposite a reading room. While a more elaborate arcade and vestibule offer entry to the building, the overall concept is approaching the form of the final built project, which further simplified the plan and consolidated the elevation.

* * *

O'Gorman has observed that the evolution of Richardson's designs from Woburn to Quincy—from pastiche (thinking "in parts") to a more disciplined synthesis of elements—reflects, more than anything, his training at the Ecole des Beaux-Arts and his work in the ateliers of Jules André, Théodore Labrouste, and Jacques-Ignace Hittorf in Paris between 1860 and 1865. The surviving sketches for the Quincy library, in particular, reveal an extraordinary ability to transform an abstract program into a comprehensible and ordered composition, which was deeply indebted to the design method Richardson had been taught at the Ecole.[33] Indeed, the architect's accomplishment here, and in his subsequent and closely related designs for the Hoyt Library in East Saginaw, might be characterized by what A. E. Richardson, a later student at the Ecole, defined as "the epitome of design": a process by which "the tireless mind of the designer, . . . having obtained a great many ideas on his subject, melts these very ideas in the crucible of his imagination, refining them again and again until the minted metal gleams refulgent."[34]

A student's education at the Ecole des Beaux-Arts during the mid-nineteenth century consisted in large part of being led through a series of exercises staged as competitions, or *concours,* the most important of which were in architectural design.[35] In one form of these *concours,* the *projet rendu,* which was held six times a year, students were issued a written problem similar to the library program submitted to the MIT students in 1875. They were then given a specified period of time to transform this into a series of rapidly produced sketches, or *esquisses.* These had to be produced *en loge* (in cubicles at the school itself), without the aid of books or outside advice. Working from plan (*parti*), to section, to elevation, the participant in this process was asked to call upon a broad internalized knowledge of historical prototypes, related buildings, and solutions to similar programs produced by past students at the Ecole, to organize the elements of the problem at hand according to the classical rules of symmetry, proportion, and geometry that formed the foundation of the Beaux-Arts style. The *parti* of a successful *esquisse* ordered the basic components of a program according to the magnitude of their significance along major and minor axes similar to those evident in several of the MIT designs, or in the rotated *parti* of Richardson's plan for Woburn. The resulting scheme was then projected into section and elevation in a manner that reflected both the function and hierarchy of its fundamental parts and the most significant or appropriate historical and contemporary precedents for the typology being presented.

At the end of the time spent *en loge,* students submitted their preliminary sketches to the Ecole, returning with tracings of these *esquisses* to an atelier, where they had paid to study and work with an experienced architect, who acted as their tutor, or *patron.* In the atelier students were free to consult books, fellow students, and their *patron* in order to refine and enrich their initial conceptions, transforming over weeks or months their rapid sketches into the type of elaborate ink and watercolor wash renderings for which the Ecole was renowned. Upon completion of their final presentations, the students returned with them to the Ecole on a specified date, where a jury would compare them to the original *esquisses* and judge their overall success. If found to vary substantially from the initial conception, the student would be disqualified: declared *hors de concour.*

Because the finished, or presentation, drawings in a *projet rendu* were required to embody the fundamental arrangement and form of the *esquisse,* this final product was heavily dependent upon the ability of the student, while *en loge,* to mentally visualize and manipulate a building program. According to Van Rensselaer, Richardson believed that this "habit he had acquired in Paris of first designing in his head and then testing and elaborating upon paper" was "indispensable to an architect. The fact that it saved time was its smallest recommendation. Its greatest was that it fostered a sense of the relative value of chief and minor things;—for a man who begins his design in his head must begin by finding a conception and by arranging principal features; and even if he should try he could hardly begin with details."[36]

Richardson's own mastery of the first stage (the *esquisse*) of this French method of composition became an object of some wonder in America, and his ability to instantly translate a complex program into a series of rapidly executed sketches, often produced on whatever scrap of envelope or paper was nearest at hand, became the stuff of legend.[37] Several surviving drawings for the Quincy library, as well as an early conception for the Hoyt competition (fig. 6.10) in 1886, exemplify well this aspect of the Beaux-Arts design process, especially the small pencil sketch of a plan and elevation for the fourth scheme for the Crane building (fig. 4.24). While barely three inches in length, all of the primary elements of the program as ultimately embodied in the completed structure have been clearly delineated here: a book room; an entry/delivery area with arcade and tower; and off to the right, the reading room.

While most commonly noted for its classical bias, another significant result of the Beaux-Arts discipline was the development of an architectural system organized according to distinct and readily identifiable building typologies, especially during the latter half of the nineteenth century when Richardson was in attendance at the Ecole. This French approach to architectural design, argued Laurence Harvey, an English student at the school in 1870, "might be defined as *the art of arranging parts.*" It "of all the arts" was "the most likely to be swayed by the French spirit of centralization; so it occurs that a French building is, as a rule, the organic outgrowth of *one* idea. Every portion, every ornament in the building,—aye, the ground it stands on and the gardens which surround it,—subserve that idea or purpose. If a building be meant for a stable, the body of the building will be so suggestive of a stable, the most unpracticed eye could scarcely fail to recognize the purpose of the erection. The wings of the building and its minutest ornaments will all be in character with the main building."[38]

Richardson's fellow student and friend, Julien Guadet, later wrote along similar lines, that the "magnificent forms of a palace," for instance, "would appear ridiculous if applied to a prison and would be even more out of place on a school or an industrial building." Guadet himself identified the overall "architectural impression" that differentiated the typology of a building as *caractère,* or that quality of a design which derived from the unambiguous expression of a building's program, or the "idea" that had brought it into being.[39] Richardson's dependence on Labrouste's Bibliothèque Ste.-Geneviève for the generation of his own library book wing—the core "idea" of the institution—reflects his own fascination with the manipulation of typological paradigms. As Van Rensselaer so astutely observed, in language that, like the architect's own work, translates a French Beaux-Arts design vocabulary and method into English:



**
*

The chief thing which made Richardson's works alike among themselves and unlike the works of almost all of his contemporaries was his power to conceive a building as a whole, and to preserve the integrity of his conception no matter how various might be the features or how profuse the decoration he employed. Each of his best buildings is an organism, an entity, a coherent vital whole. Reduce it by a distance to a mere silhouette against the sky, or draw it down to a thumbnail size sketch, and it will still be the same, still be itself; yet the nearer we approach it the more individuality will be emphasized. This is because its character depends on no one feature, no one line, but upon a concord of all and the vigor of the impression which all together give. No feature is of dominant importance, but each is of the right relative importance from any given point of view, and all are vitally fused together;—the building seems to have grown, developed, expanded like a plant. . . . In each case a radically different idea was needed and in each case it came to him.

In each case, too, it came as a strikingly appropriate idea. While conceiving and developing a structure as a whole, he worked from the inside out, not from the outside in. The nature of the service it should render was his first thought, its plan his next; and these rule his exterior in its major and its minor features. . . . Here lies the true greatness of Richardson's works—in the fact that they are true conceptions, clearly expressing an idea as appropriate as vigorous. The great value of the Quincy Library, for instance, or the Pittsburgh Court-house, or—at the other end of the scale—of the Marion cottage, lies in the fact that it is a coherent vital entity and at the same time a speaking entity—unmistakably a library, a municipal palace, a gentleman's seaside home.[40]

* * *

One of the fascinating things about the evolution of Richardson's libraries, as O'Gorman has noted, is that it extends the Beaux-Arts method—the refinement of form and meaning from idea to final conception—through the development of a series of individual buildings; from Woburn to North Easton to Quincy. While the Woburn Public Library already presents the fundamental vocabulary of the subsequent libraries in its essential outline, its specific parts, as critics like Hitchcock have observed, "the porch, the tower, and the gable are each too individually designed; the octagonal art gallery [sic] at the right is like a strayed chapter house, quite unrelated to the rest of the building."[41] "One experiment," as Mrs. Van Rensselaer noted of the Woburn design, "was enough to show Richardson his mistake." Perhaps in recognition of this shortcoming, the architect appears to have brought an intensely mathematical discipline to bear on the composition of his second library in North Easton.[42] Here he returned to the kind of modular geometric and proportional devices that were not only sanctioned at the Ecole des Beaux-Arts, but that he himself had employed in his most successful commission to date, Trinity Church in Boston.

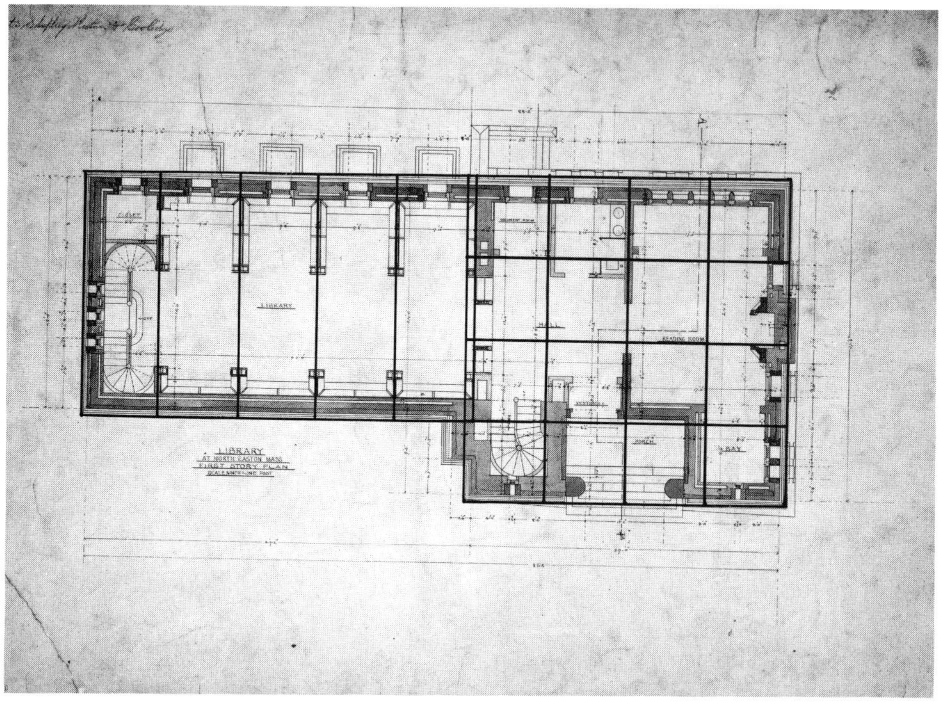

4.25
Ames Memorial Library, first-floor plan with a conjectural geometric and proportional system. ALNE A4, Department of Printing and Graphic Arts, The Houghton Library, Harvard University.

The exterior dimensions of the ground plan of the Ames Library, for example, generally appear to be derived from a square grid based on a 10-foot module (fig. 4.25). Following this module, the footprint of the main block of the building comes very near to forming a perfect square, 40 feet on each side, and has been divided laterally into two equal rectangles, which delineate the delivery and reading rooms. Likewise, the width of the alcoves in the book wing, which itself measures 50 feet by 30 feet, is 10 feet on center. If this grid system is projected into the elevation, the proportions of the book wing remain the same (50 feet in length by 30 feet high), while the upper edge of the vertical square of the reading room/delivery room block



**
*

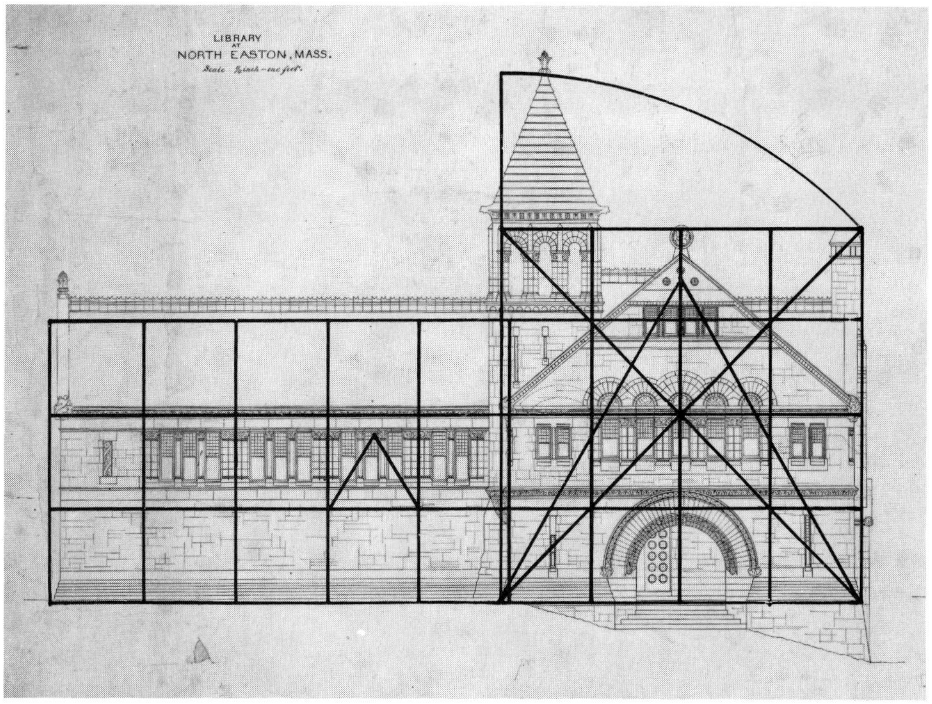


4.26
Ames Memorial Library, front elevation with a conjectural geometric and proportional system. ALNE B1, Department of Printing and Graphic Arts, The Houghton Library, Harvard University.

demarcates the cornice line of the stair tower (fig. 4.26). The diagonals of this same square not only intersect at the springing line of Richardson's second-story arcade, but are equal in length to the total height of the stair tower to the top of the steeple.

Numerous other major and minor elements in the elevation coincide with the 10-foot grid or regular subdivisions of it. The width of the arcade over the entryway is 20 feet, while the opening of the lower arch is exactly 10. The height of the base of the book wing also measures 10 feet from the top of the water table to the base of the fenestration, a bold horizontal that Richardson carries over into the gabled pavilion. In concordance with the dimensions of the

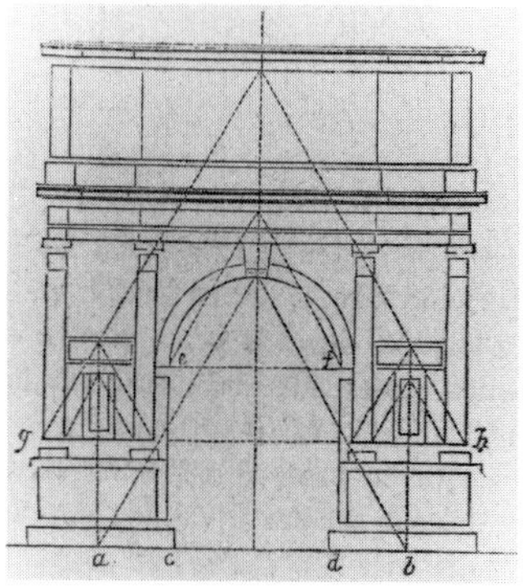


book room alcoves, the alternating rhythm of the single and bundled colonnettes in the window band of the book wing likewise conforms to this same 10-foot module (figs. 4.26, 4.13).

The distance from the base of the book wing windows to the top of the cornice, on the other hand, appears to have been determined by the altitude of an equilateral triangle generated from the 10-foot module of the alcoves. The height of the colonnettes and horizontal line of the window sash likewise conform to further subdivisions of this triangle in the second, window band module. As at Woburn, where Richardson appears to have applied a similar system, this sets up a complex proportional relationship between the horizontal rhythm of the colonnettes and their vertical dimensions, one that is played off against the regular cadence of the rectilinear ashlar blocks (each 2½ feet in length, or one-quarter of the 10-foot module) that frame the windows above and below. Significantly, this same proportional system governs the overall dimensions of the entry pavilion elevation, where the apex of an equilateral triangle projected along its base (hence 40 feet on each side) is commensurate with the top of the gable. The radius of the extrados of Richardson's great arch, moreover, is exactly one-quarter of this altitude.

While appearing complex and perhaps somewhat contrived, all of the operations needed to produce these proportional relationships can be easily and rapidly performed at the drafting table using only a compass and architect's triangle. As Ann Jensen Adams has pointed out, Richardson utilized an identical system to generate the dimensions of the west facade of Trinity Church, while he himself informs us that the plan of this building had been arrived at "in general" by employing the square formed by the crossing of the nave and transept as a "modulus."[43] According to O'Gorman, he also used a similar "modulus" to generate the proportions of the Ames Monument in Wyoming, a 60-foot-square granite pyramid, which he was commissioned to design in November 1879, just as he would have been completing work on the library in North Easton (fig. 1.11).[44] This type of geometric and proportional system was also commonplace in French architectural practice, at the Ecole des Beaux-Arts and elsewhere. In his *Entretiens sur l'architecture,* for example, Viollet-le-Duc contended that the proportions of many of the most important monuments of the past had likewise been generated from an equilateral triangle, for "no geometrical figure affords more satisfaction to the mind, and none fulfills

4.27
The Arch of Titus, Rome. Viollet-le-Duc, *Entretiens sur l'architecture,* 1863.

better those conditions that please the eye,—viz., regularity and stability."[45] To demonstrate this axiom, the French architect illustrated the facade of a basilica, as well as the elevation of the Arch of Titus (fig. 4.27), a Roman monument whose overall form—and perhaps meaning—is not dissimilar to that of the entry pavilion at North Easton. The French architect also describes how both the Egyptians and Greeks derived the intercolumniations and column proportions of their colonnades from this same modulus, a method that seems to parallel the articulation of Richardson's book wing fenestration.[46]

While some geometric modules recur in Richardson's earlier design for the library in Woburn (such as in the implied square of the delivery area, the dimensions of which reappear in the octagon of the museum, or in the proportions of the book wing colonnade), no unified mathematical system appears to regulate its more disparate assemblage of parts. Likewise at Quincy, the kind of rigid geometric composition that can be observed in the North Easton drawings is most evident in his earliest schemes for the building (figs. 4.20, 4.21), while his final design—although the plan is divided neatly in half between book room and reading and delivery areas—boldly integrates and asymmetrically balances its constituent elements, especially in the elevation. In contrast to the cold discipline, the much more schematic masses of the Ames library, *Harper's* magazine perceptively noted in 1883, at Quincy "there is nothing forced, no appearance of 'making architecture.'"

* * *

While certainly indebted heavily to rules of composition promulgated at the Ecole des Beaux-Arts, where he was first introduced to architecture, it seems likely that Richardson's evolution from the "pyrotechnique" drama of Woburn to the organic fusion of elements and "bigness" of forms found at Quincy was also spurred by his subsequent reading of John Ruskin, an author who had had a profound impact on American art and design during the 1860 and 1870s. In his description of the "Lamp of Power," for example, Ruskin argues that in the "memories of those works of architecture by which we have been most pleasurably impressed," two "broad classes" of building can be discerned: "one characterized by an exceeding preciousness and delicacy, to which we recur with a sense of affectionate admiration; the other by a severe, and, in many cases, mysterious, majesty, which we remember with an undiminished awe." To the second of these orders, observed Ruskin, belonged the Romanesque and the Egyptian, "whose interest is in their walls." In these traditions, as in the work of Richardson, "the wall is a confessed and honoured member, and the light is often allowed to fall on large areas of it, variously decorated." This is "pre-eminently the principle of power."[47]

This distinction between "preciousness" and "majesty" extended beyond the mere contrast between the beautiful and the sublime, however. According to Ruskin,

> It is, also, the difference between what is derivative and original in man's work; for what is in architecture fair and beautiful, is imitated from natural forms; and what is not so derived, but depends for its dignity upon arrangement and government received from human mind, becomes the expression of the power of that mind, and receives a sublimity high in proportion to the power expressed. All building, therefore, shows man either as gathering or governing; and the secrets of his success are his knowing what to gather, and how to rule. These are the two great intellectual Lamps of Architecture; the one consisting in a just and humble veneration for the works of God upon the earth, and the other in an understanding of the dominion over these works which has been vested in man.[48]

Richardson's maturation as a designer, as demonstrated by the development of his library designs, then, might be characterized as a transformation from a "gatherer" of architectural forms to a "governor."[49]

A similar transformation can be charted in Richardson's shift from the picturesque realism of Woburn to the stylized Byzantine ornament that begins to appear at North Easton. In contrast to the exuberance of Gothic naturalism, Ruskin felt that the essence of the more abstract Eastern forms lay in their "quality of pure gradation," an attribute "which nearly all natural objects possess, and the attainment of which is, in fact, the first and most palpable purpose in the natural arrangements of grand form."[50] In terms of Ruskin's scheme of historical evolution, Richardson can be seen moving backward in time from the naturalistic ornament of Gothic through the stylized medieval acanthus of Venice toward the origin of architectural decoration in Greece. Perhaps this is what Mrs. Van Rensselaer meant when she characterized Richardson's later Byzantine mode as "more modern, which also means a more classic spirit gradually possessed him" as he "gradually absorbed" its "delicate influence."[51]

Van Rensselaer similarly viewed Richardson's adaptation of the Romanesque style as lying somewhere between the Gothic and the Greek. Because the semicircular arch was "neither passive like the lintel" of Greek construction "nor soaring like the pointed arch," it represented "that balance between vertical and horizontal accentuations which means perfect repose."[52] Following his reading of the "Lamp of Power," it might be asserted that Richardson spent his later career slowly but inexorably absorbing its lessons. The result could be described in the same words Ruskin chose to conclude this important chapter in his *Seven Lamps of Architecture:* "that the relative majesty of buildings depends more on the weight and vigor of their masses than on any other attribute of their design: mass of everything, of bulk, of light, of darkness, of colour, not mere sum of any of these, but breadth of them."[53] Standing as they did as metaphors for the kind of New England traits said to have been exhibited by the men whose memory they enshrined, Richardson's buildings, with their craggy local granite and brownstone walls, embody the romantic imagery called for by Samuel Benjamin in 1864 in his early article on library buildings. This type of edifice, Benjamin averred, should always "be constructed on principles of permanence," with "no excess of tawdry decoration to lessen the effect of its majesty. . . . It should stand from age to age unscathed by the storms and wrecks of eras, a beacon to guide mankind in the course of duty, a shrine wherein shall be embalmed the glory of its founders, an oracle whither the generations shall come to seek wisdom."[54] Like their patrons, these monuments seemed to spring directly from the same "solid granitebase of character" that Richardson's close friend, the Reverend Phillips Brooks, viewed as the foundation of New England culture and virtue.

* * *

While most subsequent critics have come to agree with *Harper's* glowing assessment of Richardson's achievement, the immediate reaction in Quincy appears to have been somewhat less enthusiastic. What vexed local critics most was the idea that Richardson had used Quincy granite only for the foundation and not in the superstructure of his building: "For a Quincy library, in memory of a Quincy man, and, we might say, built and paid for by Quincy money, to be built of any granite but that of Quincy," complained one writer for the *Quincy Patriot Ledger* in 1882, "seems unnecessary and inexcusable."[55]

In addition to this perceived slight of one of Quincy's most important local industries, the same critic went on to observe that the entryway to the library was "too insignificant," and the windows "too small and prism-like either for dignity of design or for the practical admission of light." Predicting a shortcoming subsequently acknowledged even by Charles Francis Adams, Jr., this writer declared: "in years to come when the interior wood-work has grown dark with age, as it surely will, that lack of daylight will be a serious drawback." Again anticipating later criticisms of the library, the writer suggested that the plan should have included a vestibule and pointed out that, although "the effect of the grand hall would be in a measure lost," there should have been a greater separation between the reading room and the delivery area, so that readers would not be constantly disturbed by the activity in the latter, more public space. "A library," this critic somewhat sarcastically reminded the reader, "is for intellectual use, as well as for architectural effect."[56]

*five*

# Et in Arcadia Ego

It is in that golden stain of time, that we are to look for the real light, and colour, and preciousness of architecture; and it is not until a building has assumed this character, till it has been entrusted with the fame, and hallowed by the deeds of men, till its walls have been witnesses of suffering, and its pillars rise out of the shadows of death, that its existence, more lasting as it is than that of the natural objects of the world around it, can be gifted with even so much as these possess of language and life.

JOHN RUSKIN, *The Seven Lamps of Architecture,* 1849

According to Mariana Griswold Van Rensselaer, the commission for the Converse Memorial Building in Malden entered Richardson's office in August 1883, just five months after the long-delayed dedication of the Ames Free Library in North Easton. Although the contract for this building, which, like its predecessors, was awarded to the Norcross Brothers, was signed in December, the site was not chosen until the following month, when Richardson and Frederick Law Olmsted traveled together to Malden for this purpose. Ground was broken the following April.[1] Erected by Elisha Slade and Mary Diana Converse as a memorial to their son Frank, this building was dedicated on 1 October 1885; at a total cost of some $125,000, it was far and away the most expensive public library designed and built by Richardson.

While the exact motivation for the Converses' choice of architect is not known, Richardson's selection appears logical enough. Not only was he the preeminent architect in Boston by this date, but he was arguably the foremost designer of public library buildings. In February 1883, moreover, the First Baptist Church of Boston, for which Elisha's brother James W. Converse served as a deacon, had rededicated Richardson's Brattle Square Meeting House as their new sanctuary. According to the official history of this congregation, James had been "especially prominent in obtaining th[is] new house" for their use, a building that Richardson had originally designed as a Unitarian church in 1869 (fig. 5.10).[2] James W. Converse was likewise a contributor to the Malden Public Library, and Elisha and his wife were active members of the Malden Baptist Church, for which (as noted in chapter 1) they at one time intended to have Richardson design a new sanctuary (fig. 1.4). With Elisha Converse's ancestral home of Woburn located just five miles to the west of Malden, it seems more than likely that the family knew at least one of Richardson's libraries at first hand, a fact that may be corroborated by the number of similarities between the programs for the two buildings.[3]

As at Woburn (figs. 3.2, 3.3), the Converse Memorial Building houses a public library and art gallery, which have been arranged along a single axis flanked by areas set aside for reading rooms that open off either side of the delivery area (fig. 5.1, 5.2, 5.3). A massive fireplace

5.1
H. H. Richardson, Converse Memorial Building, Malden, book room, 1883–1885. Malden Public Library.

5.2
Converse Memorial Building, first-floor plan: *A,* book room; *B,* delivery area; *C,* reading room; *D,* memorial hall; *E,* art gallery; *F,* trustees' room; *G,* memorial porch. Drawing by Glenn Waguespack from a plan in the Department of Printing and Graphic Arts, The Houghton Library, Harvard University.

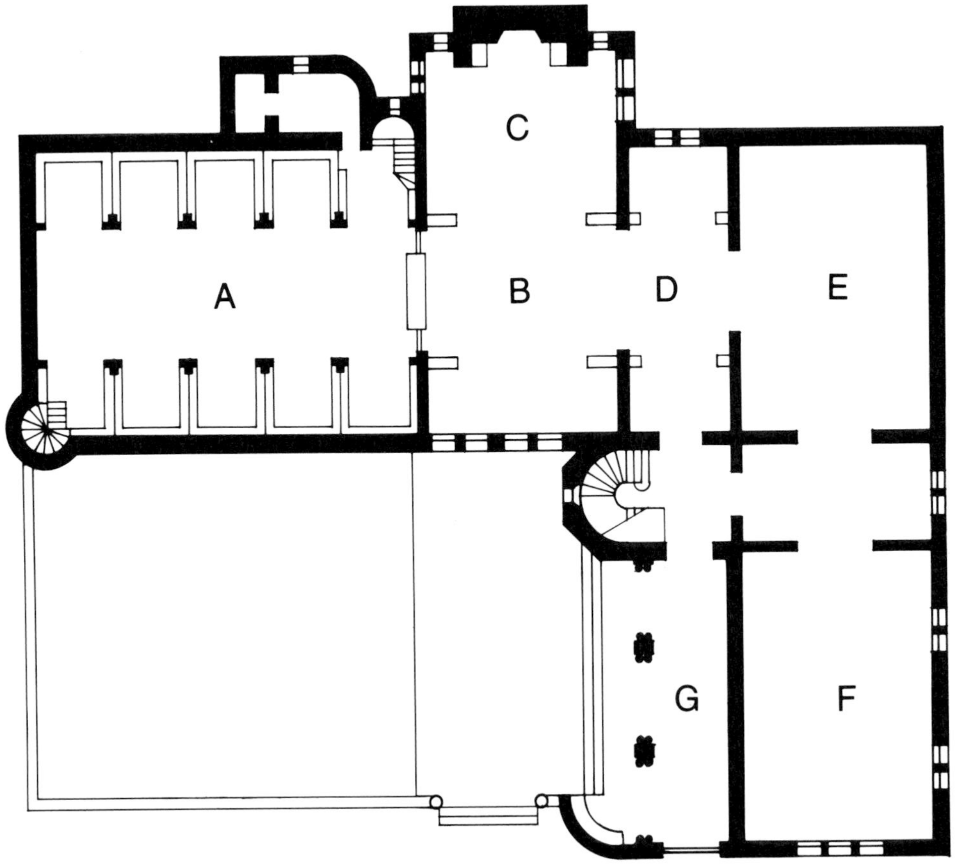




**
*

5.3
Converse Memorial Building, longitudinal section. MAL C1, Department of Printing and Graphic Arts, The Houghton Library, Harvard University.

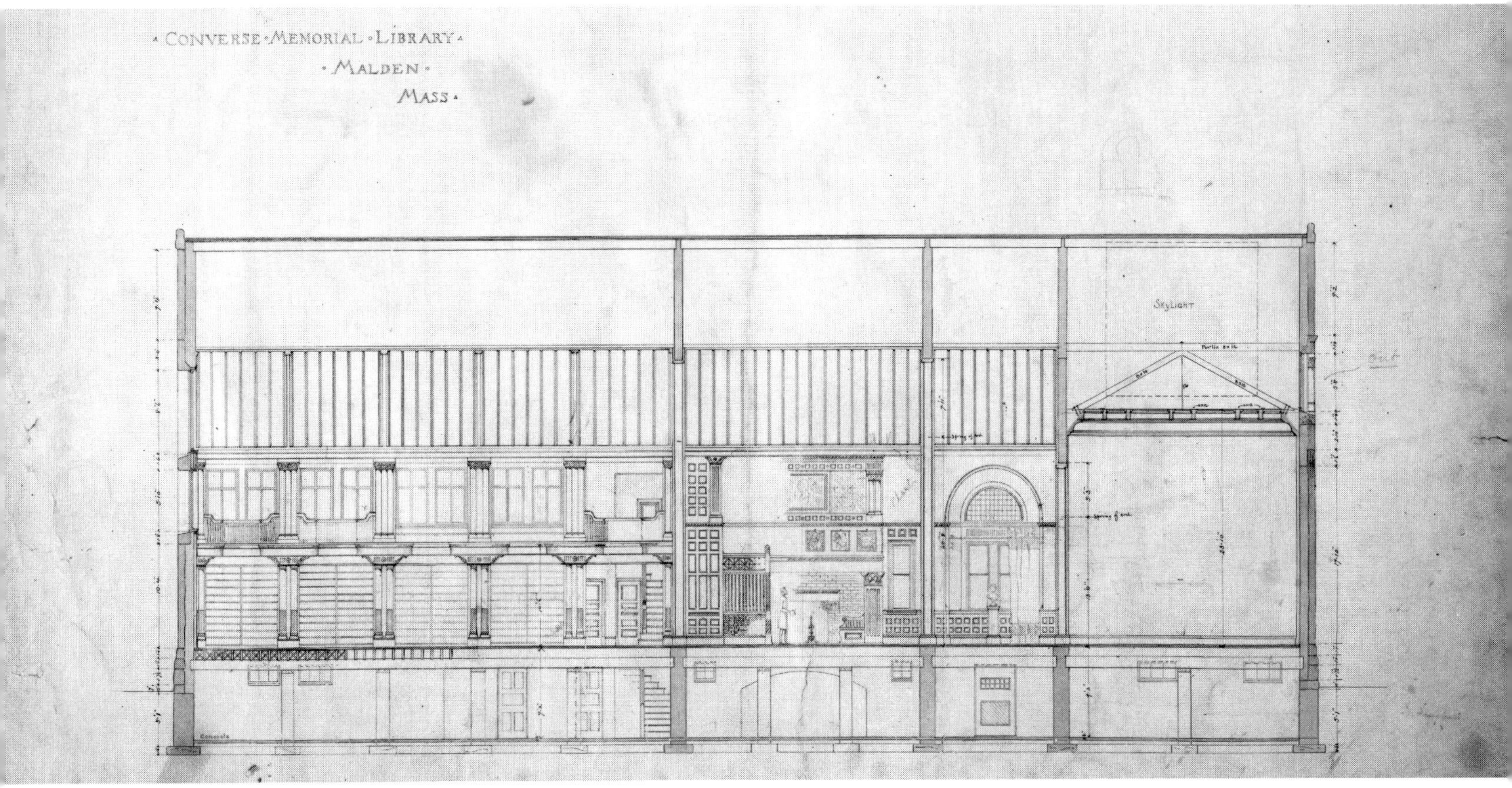

overlooks these public spaces, which were originally separated from the book room by an ornate delivery desk (figs. 5.4, 5.13). This book room, with five full alcoves arrayed to either side of a wide central aisle, had a projected capacity of 60,000 volumes. As at Woburn, gallery passages pass through the alcove partitions along the walls of this storage space, and undulate around the edges of each bay. Circular staircases in opposing corners of the room provide access to these galleries, which, as at Quincy, have no balcony connecting the two sides of this space. A light, wooden barrel vault constructed of narrow, beaded oak strips with molded ribs of the same material encloses this space, and its longitudinal elevation essentially reverses that of the Crane Library (fig. 4.17), with clustered columns set over fluted pilasters flanked by colonnettes. Similarly, the capitals, which Henry-Russell Hitchcock felt were "rather mechanical," have been ornamented with stylized, Byzanto-Romanesque acanthus.[4] Turned wooden balusters in the gallery follow the curve of the balconies and echo the vertical lines of the colonnettes, vault ribs, and the books themselves.

Opposite the book room at Malden, a "memorial hall" and art gallery complete the primary axis of the *parti,* while an entry porch, vestibule, "ante room," and trustees' room project forward to form an L, which encloses two sides of a courtyard. The second story of the front wing was originally intended to house the Middlesex Society, an association whose collection—perhaps in emulation of the museum at Woburn—was to be devoted to the study of natural history. The eastern end of this room opens onto a balustraded gallery that overlooks the two-story art museum. The lower walls throughout the interior were sheathed with paneled oak wainscoting, while above, a rough sand plaster finish was originally tinted in a panoply of colors, ranging from Pompeian red to subdued greens and yellows.[5] The furnishings throughout the building, which were manufactured by A. H. Davenport of Malden, are also of oak. The reading room chairs form an elegant hybrid between the Queen Anne and Windsor styles, with the same Byzanto-Romanesque motif that ornaments the architecture reappearing in the central splat (fig. 5.13). It has been suggested that this furniture may have been designed by Francis H. Bacon, who worked in Richardson's office in 1884 and 1885 and then for Davenport.[6] The reiteration of Byzantine ornament throughout the building, combined with the proliferation of polished oak in the architecture and furnishings, imparts a clear sense of unity to the overall design.

As at Quincy, the exterior elevation of the Converse book wing has been identified with a narrow horizontal strip of windows set over an unbroken base of rusticated stone, while the reading and delivery areas are illuminated with a two-story bank of lights that continues on

5.4
Converse Memorial Building, view of delivery desk and book room. Photograph by C. D. Shiloh, courtesy of the Society for the Preservation of New England Antiquities.

**
*

5.5
Converse Memorial Building. Photograph by Thomson and Thomson, courtesy of the Society for the Preservation of New England Antiquities.

5.6
Converse Memorial Building, presentation drawing, 1883? MAL B6, Department of Printing and Graphic Arts, The Houghton Library, Harvard University.

two levels the alternating pier and colonnette articulation of the book room fenestration (fig. 5.5). Two stair turrets, the larger marking the reentrant angle of the edifice and a second smaller tower at the far corner of the book room, bracket this library wing. In what appears to be an early presentation drawing of this elevation (fig. 5.6), Richardson had returned to the A-B-B-A rhythm of the North Easton window band (fig. 4.5), a triadic composition he repeated here in the reading room lights as well. The book wing, as completed, appears both more elegant and, with the addition of the corner turret, stronger.

To the right of this ensemble, a "cloister or porch,"[7] similar to the one that appeared in Richardson's *esquisse* for scheme IV at Quincy and seems to be indicated as a motif flanking both sides of the entryway in scheme I, shelters a memorial inscription and borders the enclosed courtyard like the cloister of a medieval monastery (figs. 5.7, 4.20, and 4.24). The clustered

5.7
Converse Memorial Building, porch. Courtesy of the Society for the Preservation of New England Antiquities.

5.8
Converse Memorial Building, sketch for porch arcade. MAL D11, Department of Printing and Graphic Arts, The Houghton Library, Harvard University.

capitals of this entry arcade, like the capitals in the book room, have been covered with a rich intertwine of abstracted vegetation and whimsical faces (fig. 5.8). In contrast to his earlier libraries, the exterior walls of the Converse building have been fabricated largely of Longmeadow brownstone, with trim and ornament of the same material. Only the tympanum of the trustees' wing, with green serpentine and white sandstone marquetry reminiscent of the art gallery gable at Woburn (a motif not apparent in the presentation drawing) and a great, curling dragon at the corner, strays—but then only cautiously—from the architect's increasing sense of quietude. The form of the Malden gable, with its allusions to the New England saltbox of the seventeenth and eighteenth centuries, recalls Richardson's sketch for the rear elevation of the library at Quincy as well as the form of the old Converse house that had been razed in Woburn in 1876 (figs. 4.19, 1.2). It is even possible that Elisha and Mary in some way intended the Converse Memorial as a replacement for this earlier family shrine.

* * *

While all of Richardson's libraries were erected as memorials to the dead, the marked gravity of the Malden building, in particular, may reflect the extreme seriousness of its commemorative function. "The artistic spirit and sympathetic thought of its design," noted the trustees in their 1885 report, "have given it the prime stamp and character of a memorial in all its parts; while, as well, it is a fitting and convenient habitation for an institution devoted to free education." Nor, they continued, was "there aught at variance in this; for while the first may dignify and endear the last, the latter may soften and deepen the other by bringing it within the wider range of the sympathies of a whole community."[8] As a "monument to parental affection worked out in generous good to the community," observed the *Malden City Press* in a special issue that appeared on the day of its dedication, this edifice

> stands as a memorial to the dead, but no less a tribute to the living. Not as a useless monumental pile which glorifies but the wealth of its builders, but in far-reaching beneficence. In an effort to uplift and ennoble the living as well as to build a remembrance to the dead, the stately structure stands a monument to unforgetting love and to wise and bountiful regard for the welfare of the people. . . .
>
> As one gets the first glimpse of its stately walls he is impressed with the two-fold character of the building. There is no glaring splendor about it. Its proportions are modest and simple. Were it to be alone a gift to the people, it might be more ornate. Were it to be alone a tribute to the dead, it might be more solemn. But it is a memorial as well as a gift, an expression of the generous giving as well as a tribute of sorrow. And so the lines are chaste, the dimensions elegant yet simple. There is the air of a church about it as well as that of a public resort. The stone is not more enduring than the love it typifies,

and the graceful architecture not more beautiful than the generosity which prompted it. The dead son lives in it and the living people are loved by it.[9]

As this eulogy implies, Christian metaphor pervades the Converse Memorial Building's form. Like Charles Garnier's Paris Opera, which was begun while Richardson was still a student at the Ecole des Beaux-Arts, the architect's design strategy should be understood not in terms of abstract architectural principles or even a stationary iconography but in the actual experience of its program. A complex narrative of associations and meanings unfolds like the parables in contemporary consolation literature; in the spirit of late nineteenth-century public mourning ritual, the visitor to the Malden library is consciously led along a picturesque architectural path, from the domain of nature, through the realm of death and commemoration, to the altars of intellect and culture. This was a ritual of mourning through which the "theater" of death was made to serve life.[10]

As was made clear by the *Malden City Press* in its description of this building, the moral and sentimental authority of the dead son's presence was implicit in the placement of his portrait at the far end of Richardson's ecclesiastical display of books (fig. 5.1). Not only was this a traditional position for the image of Christ in the Christian sanctuary, but from it the son gazed down the length of the building through a great window at his parent's church, which they once had contemplated having Richardson rebuild as a complement to the library (fig. 1.4).[11] Flanked by likenesses of his parents, this portrait, noted the paper, is "simple but forcible, since it [was] designed to 'carry' a long distance," indicating that it was likely to have been commissioned specifically for the prominent position in which it still hangs. In this painting Frank Converse has been pictured standing on an elevation overlooking a pastoral view of Malden. "The landscape," noted the same writer, "forms an impressive and appropriate setting for a portrait. . . . It is morning, in the spring, and a strong light falls on the figure, while the distant scene is veiled in shadow; so that it is evident the artist has associated the landscape with the subject, making it, in a remote sense, symbolic." As can be observed in historic photographs, the archway through which the image of the deceased boy and his parents look out over the library was once draped, as if in mourning, with a maroon "Moresque curtain."[12]

In addition to likenesses of Washington, Jefferson, and Madison (all copies after Gilbert Stuart originals) and a variety of other works of art, a large canvas depicting "Lincoln at Gettysburg" was prominently exhibited at the far end of the same gallery in which the Converse portraits were hung, executed—like the three family portraits—by Albion Harris Bicknell, a local artist who had himself attended the Ecole des Beaux-Arts in Paris between 1861 and 1864.[13] It is difficult to imagine that the parallel between the deaths of the young martyrs who had fallen on that great battlefield and the murder of Frank Converse could easily have escaped the staunchly Republican Elisha Converse, his wife, or the library's trustees. Lincoln had dedicated the Gettysburg battlefield and cemetery in 1863 to the cause of national unity just one month before the death of the Converse son, and only one year after the president had lost his own son, a child for whom many thought he was still in mourning the day he delivered his consecrating address.[14] Like the national cemetery at Gettysburg, as well as the American public libraries subsequently raised as Civil War memorials, the Converse building, observed John D. Long at its dedication, "will stand as a memorial of the pure, ingenious spirit of the noble boy it commemorates, and teach the young men of coming generations the lesson of a good example."[15]

The commemorative iconography at Malden, as at Richardson's other libraries, was not confined to a portrait of the deceased son. On entering the edifice, one comes first into a "memorial hall," which, as in Ware and Van Brunt's final configuration for Memorial Hall at Harvard (figs. 1.5, 1.6), cuts across the primary axis of the *parti.* It is from this room that one first glimpsed the effigy of Frank Converse through the curtain-draped arch that separated it from the art gallery. This memorial hall, moreover, is connected through a vestibule to a "memorial" porch, or "piazza," opening off the enclosed garden, that initially greets a visitor to the building (fig. 5.9). The donors' initials, E S and M D C (Elisha Slade and Mary Diana Converse), have been inscribed like medieval masons' marks on the right-hand capitals of the porch arcade, while a dedicatory plaque is set into its back wall. An empty stone bench—perhaps also intended to recall the memory of the absent son—has been placed at the far end of this "piazza," facing the entryway to the building. While medieval in spirit, the commemorative and triumphal intent of this porch is made clear by its three massive arches, which rest on clustered columns and Byzanto-Romanesque capitals. Like the entryways at North Easton and Quincy, this motif derives from the iconography of the Roman triumphal arch, but also mimics the form of a medieval cloister. This may have been intended to remind visitors of the historical role played by the Christian monastery in the preservation of Western literary traditions.[16] The form of this porch also carries with it the ecclesiastical, intellectual, and civic connotations of an Italian Renaissance loggia, or the facade of a Christian church, such as Richardson had designed for the Brattle Square Meeting House (fig. 5.10) or even Trinity Church in Boston. Like Leon Battista Alberti's Tempio Malatestiano in Rimini (c. 1450), it recalls the fame of its

5.9
Converse Memorial Building, porch arcade. Photograph by Soule Photograph Co., courtesy of the Society for the Preservation of New England Antiquities.

5.10
*Opposite:* H. H. Richardson, Brattle Square Church, Boston, entrance arcade, 1869–1873. Photograph by Soule Photograph Co., courtesy of the Society for the Preservation of New England Antiquities.

founders and their child. While not overtly labeled as such, the meaning of the adjacent garden is clearly conjoined with the meaning of this shrine. Originally intended to have been simply landscaped by Frederick Law Olmsted with bluestone pavers and a lawn bordered by rhododendrons, English boxwood, and azaleas, this precinct is enclosed with a stone wall that forms an extension of the building itself. Olmsted had, in fact, traveled with Richardson to Malden to help him choose a site for the building, and certainly he, if not Richardson himself, would have been well aware of the eighteenth-century English landscape tradition from which such elegiac associations ultimately evolved.[17] By August 1883, the month that the Converse commission entered Richardson's office, Olmsted had himself left New York for Boston, purchasing a house in Brookline very near the studio and home of the architect. Here, in the first library commission in which he appears to have participated in the design process from the beginning, we can witness the full integration of his ideas with Richardson's own experience and working method.

Like the sarcophagus discovered in Arcady by shepherds in Nicolas Poussin's *Et in Arcadia Ego* (c. 1635–1636), Richardson's memorial porch united with Olmsted's restrained display of nature to create a poignantly romantic commemoration of death. Erwin Panofsky and Richard Etlin have pointed out that during the eighteenth century the simple Latin inscription depicted by Poussin in this well-known painting became commonly mistranslated "And I was once an inhabitant in Arcadia." As a result, it came to signify the continued presence of the deceased within the precinct of nature.[18] This idea formed a signal inspiration for the continued association of English gardens with the romantic longing for the departed well into the twentieth century. It was to the contemplation of nature, as well as death, that the romantic tradition turned for the spiritual regeneration and redemption of the type Americans were yearning for in the years following the Civil War. This was the same type of salvation offered by memorial libraries, themselves buildings not only of culture but of death and, in the hands of Richardson, richly expressive of the natural world revered by the transcendentalists. These memorials united in one institution the Emersonian ideals of art and nature; like the rural cemetery, they represented "the awesome presence of nature and death conjoined."[19]

A half-century earlier, in Paris, Henri Labrouste had initially proposed erecting a garden as an entryway to the Bibliothèque Ste.-Geneviève (fig. 2.33). In 1852 in the *Revue générale de l'architecture* (in a description Richardson may very well have known), he explained that such an area "laid out in front of the building" would "shield it from the noise of the street outside" and "prepare those who come there for meditation. A beautiful garden would undoubtedly have been an appropriate introduction to a building devoted to study." Because the narrowness of the site in Paris did not allow for such an arrangement, Labrouste went on to describe how he had transformed his vestibule into a painted garden and memorial, with sculptural busts of French philosophers, scientists, and artists displayed beneath murals of trees, which represented their individual attributes.[20] Later, at the Bibliothèque Nationale, Labrouste filled the lunettes of the Salle des Imprimés with vistas of treetops, transforming his interior into an architectural garden (fig. 3.15). One enters this building, moreover, through a narrow vestibule, which opens off an enclosed courtyard. The attic over this entryway is marked with three massive glass-filled arches evocative of Richardson's own porch at Malden.

In proposing a garden for his first site in Paris, Labrouste may have known that during the late eighteenth century, when the neighboring church of Sainte-Geneviève was being converted into a pantheon to house the bodies of heroes of the French revolution, the eminent French architectural critic Quatremère de Quincy had suggested that a landscaped precinct, or Elysium, be planted around this memorial to similarly shelter it from the distractions of urban life. Quatremère believed that this display of nature, set in the presence of memorials to the dead, would serve to instill in visitors the kind of sentiments appropriate to such a shrine.[21] Coupled as it is with Richardson's memorial porch, Olmsted's garden at Malden should be given an analogous Arcadian reading. If recalling the form of a monastic cloister, this precinct might also be interpreted as a colonial churchyard or an Italian *campo santo.* In the latter respect, it could be related to yet another building in Paris that Richardson likely would have known, the Chapelle Expiatoire (1816–1826), a mortuary monument erected to house the exhumed remains of Louis XVI and Marie Antoinette, with an arcaded garden modeled on the Campo Santo in Pisa.[22]

The location of Richardson's library in Malden, which he chose in collaboration with Olmsted, was more fortuitous than the site of Labrouste's first library. Even though the edifice stood "close to the busy hum of trade and the pulsating life of a city," it still appeared to the *Malden City Press* "so retired and so surrounded with nature's decorations of turf and trees as to seem far removed." Sheltered from the chaotic world outside, Olmsted's garden offered a quiet respite, or, like a rural cemetery, a public "resort" for the visitor.[23] It furnished a transition from the world of industry and commerce to the protectively sheltered realm of culture. In the tradition of Plato's grove of Academe, or the grassy quadrangle of an English college, this precinct served as a natural counterpart to the lessons immured within. As an enclosed and carefully ordered domain of nature, its form recalls the medieval and Islamic origins of the garden as representation of paradise or the Garden of Eden. It acts as a sacred temenos through which one



**
*

enters a sanctuary of knowledge. Indeed, as Neil Harris has observed: "The approach to knowledge was once meant to possess, in itself, existential meaning. The encounter with the book, like the encounter with art, was supposedly distinguishable from commercial or industrial transactions. The cultural center, the art complex, was presented as an alternative world."[24]

If the garden and porch at Malden served to mark a separation of spheres, the moment of passage from the reality of the city into the sanctum of a crypto-religious shrine, the mysterious and cavernous openings of the libraries at North Easton and Quincy, in an even more sublime manner, articulated a parallel cleft in the boundary between the worlds of commerce and contemplation (figs. 4.3, 4.14). Opening into massive and somber walls of stone, and at Quincy sheltering an empty stone bench evocative of the absence of the commemorated, the thresholds of Richardson's memorials evoke the romantic rift between the sacred and the profane, historic time and immortality. They seem to hold out the awesome prospect of communication with the individuals they commemorate.[25] Clearly, too, the primordial forms and heavily rusticated masses of these edifices reflect the somber character of their function as memorials to the dead. Like the romantic funerary monuments that Henry Van Brunt singled out for special praise in his article "Greek Lines" in 1861, Richardson's libraries call forth associations appropriate for "the expression of those emotions to which we desire to give the immortality of stone in memory of departed friends . . . giving 'a local habitation and a name' to a thousand affections which hitherto have wandered unseen from heart to heart, or have been palpable only in words and gestures which disturb our sympathies and then die."[26]

* * *

Given the symbiotic relationship of garden and memorial at Malden, the contribution of Olmsted to Richardson's development of an iconography of death should not be overlooked. Their first known collaboration, in fact, appears to have occurred in 1868 when the landscape architect asked his new Staten Island neighbor to develop a design for a sepulchral monument to Alexander Dallas Bache, which was to be erected in the Congressional Cemetery in Washington, D.C. Subsequently the relationship between the two became extremely close. As Mrs. Van Rensselaer observed, the architect "was constantly turning to Olmsted for advice, even in cases where it seemed as though it could have little practical bearing upon his design."[27] According to James O'Gorman, it was during the formative years of this relationship in the late 1860s that Olmsted had begun to conceive of the post–Civil War American landscape as divisible into distinct urban and suburban zones, each of which demanded unique architectural forms to express its differing qualities. In this respect, all of Richardson's libraries as picturesque compositions belong to Olmsted's suburban aesthetic.[28] Although his work postdates the conception of the buildings themselves, Olmsted had developed landscape plans for both the Quincy library and the area surrounding the Ames Memorial in North Easton. He was, for example, commissioned to landscape the grounds of the Crane Memorial Library in November 1881, a year after Richardson had begun work on this edifice. While the full development of this project evolved over several decades, Olmsted subsequently designed a bucolic, parklike setting for the institution, placing it in the midst of a spacious lawn with gently curving paths and a handful of carefully sited trees (fig. I.3).[29]

At North Easton, where Olmsted does not appear to have become involved with the Ames family until some two years after the library building had been completed, the effect was radically different. Here he was brought in, perhaps at the suggestion of the architect, to develop the site for Ames Memorial Hall and a stone cairn to commemorate North Easton's Civil War casualties, both of which are contiguous with the library (figs. 2.36, 5.11). Through Olmsted and Richardson's artistry, the two buildings were conjoined into a single ensemble. "Nothing could be better than the way in which each building stands," observed Mrs. Van Rensselaer of the result: "The slighter swells and depressions of the ground beneath the library have been as carefully respected as the bold rocks that support the hall. Nature has been made to help the work of the architect in the only way which can effect a union fertile in true beauty. Her scheme has been accepted as the foundation for his, and all her suggestions have been emphasized yet harmonized by his treatment."[30]

In addition to manipulating the site of the memorial hall, Olmsted also erected a cairn of stones in front of it to commemorate North Easton's Civil War dead. These were piled atop a rustic arch, which imitates the memorial entryway to Richardson's library. Olmsted explained to Oakes Angier Ames (1831–1895) in April 1882 that monuments of this sort were among "the oldest and most enduring in the world," and in combination with "the beautiful plants that have become rooted in them and which spring out of their crannies or have grown over them," they "are far more interesting and pleasant to see than the greater number of those constructed of massive masonry and elaborate sculpture." Echoing Ruskin's notion that "the affectionate observation of the grace and outward character of vegetation is the sure sign of a more tranquil and gentle existence," the picturesque arrangement of "evergreens, vines, shrubs and blooming rock-plants" with which Olmsted proposed to soften the rugged grounds around this rocky "bastion" and the memorial hall was interpreted by the designer as an allegory of peace taming war.[31] While the landscape architect seems not to have officially collaborated with

5.11
The Rockery with Ames Memorial Hall and Library in background, North Easton. Easton Historical Society.

Richardson on his first library commission at Woburn, the profuse botanical forms with which the architect embellished that memorial betray a similar intent. The meaning implicit in the landscape, as in Richardson's designs for his memorial libraries—which were embellished with many of the same plant forms employed by Olmsted—was that of the victory of life over death.

It is in line with these romantic and picturesque themes that the ex-mayor of Malden, Jonathan Sleeper, upon first viewing Albion Bicknell's portrait of Frank Converse, was moved to compose a similarly evocative and Arcadian vision of the lost and "virtuous" youth, a sentimental reverie that he shared with the participants at the library's dedication. In this classic if somewhat hackneyed example of a late nineteenth-century consolatory elegy, Sleeper wanders out in early morning into the countryside of a surprisingly agrarian Malden,

O'er pastures green and fertile fields,—
Vine-clad ravines and limpid brooks,
*Where Nature still her magic wields!*

While resting upon a grassy slope, he is suddenly awakened from his musings upon the virtues of nature by the "startled scream" of a bird. "When looking to the crest of the hill, beyond," he spies "a Form, with manly mien, . . . Surveying, rapt, the enchanting scene."

His look was pure as angels' thought;
His eyes were brimming with delight,
As though the picture he had sought
Had burst upon his raptured sight!

"Startled" again by the sudden flash of lightning and the deafening crash of thunder, Sleeper starts toward the spot where the "stranger" had but a moment earlier stood;

But lo! *No man was there!* No sign,
Except the tracks, both deep and good,
And well defined in every line.

Following a chance encounter with the mourning parents in a cemetery, and an overheard prayer of the two through the open gateway of a garden, Sleeper recognizes the portrait of his "morning friend" in the library. Here again he communes with the dead boy's spirit, and, while he watches, the hall over which the commemorated youth's likeness silently gazes is transformed through time into a domain of domestic and heavenly virtue, as well as equality of classes, a blissful antidote to the grimly competitive industrial world outside its protective walls. In this place, Sleeper now

Saw rich and poor—who, now and then
  Their places changed! Heard, often, sung
In undertone, thanksgiving hymn!
  Noted when satisfaction beamed
From eyes and face! Saw visage grim
  Relax the sternness which had seemed
Part and parcel of itself, till
  A kindly sympathy was stirred,
And sweeter temper, governed will.[32]

Other speakers at the Converse Memorial's dedication envisioned the institution in similarly sentimental terms, carefully steering its mission away from the male arena of political and social reform into the more feminine realm of moral suasion. "Straight out of the busiest, most intense, hardest-headed and hardest-handed material concentration of industrial, manufacturing, money-making, labor employing forces and enterprise," noted John D. Long, for example, "springs this fair flower of the gentlest humanities, this grace of art, this fountain of letters, this frozen song of architecture!" Its commemorative function, in particular, carried with it memories of "that sweet domestic relation" of husband and wife through which it had been conceived, "stamping on this public act the tenderness of home itself."[33] This building not only stood as "an example of splendid business success," observed Governor George D. Robinson at this same ceremony, but spoke "of domestic unity. . . . It is also symbolic of parental love."[34]

"Feminine" and warm, in stark contrast to the cold and "masculine" persona of their exteriors, the interiors of Richardson's libraries seem to personify these sweet sentiments. Windsor-inspired chairs and settles, built-in benches, paneled walls, turned balusters, beamed ceilings, and cozy inglenooks everywhere extended notions of domesticity into the public realm. The imposing alcoves of books, likewise, project (if only symbolically) the intimacy of a private gentleman's library, much like those the architect designed for his houses or maintained in his own home and studio in Brookline (fig. 5.12), while the most commanding symbol of the domestication of this public institution was the "great generous fireplace, suggestive," as Long averred, "of the old time New England hospitality" (fig. 5.13).[35] As Gwendolyn Wright has observed, by this date the hearth, in particular, "had an even clearer symbolic meaning than

5.12

Library in the H. H. Richardson Studio, Brookline, Massachusetts. Courtesy of the Society for the Preservation of New England Antiquities.

5.13

Converse Memorial Building, reading room and hearth. Photograph by C. D. Shiloh, courtesy of the Society for the Preservation of New England Antiquities.

**
*

Et in Arcadia Ego



**
*

other architectural details of the time, for the widespread use of furnaces and stoves made fireplaces unnecessary for warmth. The appeal, then, was not functional but evocative. The image of the family gathered around the hearth was the most common way to call up the ideal of the home as a place of protection and communality."[36] Within the confines of a library, in fact, this anachronism had long been excoriated by librarians as a fire hazard. Enshrined beneath broad arches and combined with inglenooks, adorned with the bounty of nature, or displaying a relief of the patriarch, these monumental attributes of home life served, just the same, as the centerpieces of all of Richardson's reading rooms (figs. 1.10, 4.9, 4.18).

As noted earlier, this antimodern quest for authenticity celebrated the same preindustrial values promoted by Ruskin, Morris, and the British aesthetic movement, and the mythical sense of community believed to have existed in America's own past. "As an antidote to the present," as Mark Girouard put it, these men "recreated the past as an ideal world of preindustrial simplicity, at once homely and Arcadian."[37] Like the histories and genealogies that were recited endlessly at the dedications of the buildings, such associations were intended to serve as a reminder of the Anglo-Saxon roots of the country and of the men and women who endowed and controlled these institutions. In this sense, the rigorously disciplined eclecticism and insistence on the elegant refinement of form and materials that pervade Richardson's work finds a parallel in the Arnoldian literary prescriptions of the libraries' trustees and patrons. Like the representative examples of the "best" literature that the Western tradition had produced, the "moral and aesthetic power" of these forms stood as yet another lesson for the working men and women who were intended to frequent these rooms. "What the aesthetically awakened envisioned," argues David Huntington, "was a new vernacular that would at once discipline the arts, elevate popular taste, and unify the American people."[38]

* * *

Like the founding of public libraries themselves, it is evident that this strategy was fraught with contradictions. The sumptuousness of Richardson's libraries, for example, was unprecedented in earlier American public buildings. This was the kind of ostentatious display of wealth and pride previously eschewed by New England's elite, who typically preferred not so conspicuously or publicly to flaunt their affluence and power. The expense of this luxuriance, in fact, stands in jarring opposition to the simpler, preindustrial values that the colonial motifs were intended to imply and the dedication rhetoric so often explicated.[39] Yet, like the pious outpouring of grief that these libraries manifest, their function as instruments of mourning and tokens of public munificence seemed to sanction the extravagance, absolving their donors of the Puritan sin of pride. As Ann Douglas has argued within a literary context, the "sentimentalization of theological and secular culture" that these displays represented formed "an inevitable part of the self-evasion of a society committed to laissez-faire industrial expansion and disturbed by its consequences."[40] In Malden, as elsewhere, it was the success of this massive economic expansion that had made possible the erection of the Converse Memorial. And yet, it could be argued, it was the very ascendancy of this new capitalist order—largely driven by the industrial might of enterprises such as Elisha Converse's shoe factories—that had destroyed the bucolic agrarian villages so wistfully recalled by Adams in Quincy, or Sleeper in his revery at Malden. The same competitive system could perhaps be blamed for the greedy murder of Frank Converse in his father's bank.

Richardson's late embrace of Matthew Arnold's "sweetness and light," so evident in the growing proliferation of the more exotic antimodern gestures in his later work, is likewise indicative of the ambivalence with which these buildings could be viewed. The playful foxes, grimacing faces, fantastic curling dragons, cranes, and owls, fanciful stair turrets, as well as the Orientalism implicit in his growing preference for "Moresque" rinceau, all recall the escapism of many of the contemporary fables that filled the shelves of these institutions. In addition to acting as metonyms for the literary journeys that awaited prospective readers inside, Richardson's exotica also helped to soften the impact of his iconography of death. At the same time, the clear sense of humor evident in these motifs—one that has often been overlooked—seems to reflect his own jovial personality, and prefigures the postmodern whimsy of later admirers such as Charles Moore. In Richardson's journey from nature to history, the romantic spirituality of Ruskin and the American transcendentalists was ultimately tempered by the aesthetic "Hellenism" of Arnold, an evolution that might be viewed in consonance with the broader secularization of American culture that characterizes the arrival of the "modern" era.[41]



**
*

*six*

# Competition in East Saginaw

Why library architecture should have been yoked to ecclesiastical architecture, and the two have been made to walk down the ages *pari passu* is not obvious, unless it be that librarians in the past needed this stimulus to their religious emotions. The present state of piety in the profession renders the union no longer necessary and it is time that the bill was filed for a divorce. The same secular common sense and the same adaptation of means to ends which have built the modern grain elevator and reaper are needed for the reform of library construction.

William Frederick Poole, "The Construction of Library Buildings," 1881

Henry Hobson Richardson appears to have produced his final design for a small public library early in 1886 as an entry in a competition for a building that was to be constructed in East Saginaw, a lumber town in eastern Michigan. Money and a site for this endeavor derived from a bequest that had been made by Jesse Hoyt (1815–1882) of New York City. According to James B. Peter, the first secretary of the Hoyt Public Library board of trustees, the idea for this institution had initially arisen during a conference concerning the disposition of Hoyt's Michigan property that had been attended by his East Saginaw attorney, William L. Webber.[1]

While never a permanent resident of East Saginaw, Hoyt, in partnership with his father and Norman Little, had founded the town in 1850 as a speculative real estate venture and base for processing thousands of acres of timber that they controlled in the Saginaw River watershed. During subsequent decades, through Webber and other local agents, Hoyt and his brother Alfred continued to maintain a substantial investment in the community, expanding their milling enterprises, contributing to the establishment of a salt manufacturing industry, and building hotels, commercial blocks, banks, and roads. In rivalry with neighboring Saginaw City, and with West Bay City and Bay City which lay 12 miles downriver, the brothers promoted the Flint and Pere Marquette and other railroad lines over which to ship the products of their investments. Upon his death, Jesse Hoyt is said to have controlled an estate in Michigan valued at some two million dollars.[2] Of this, Hoyt directed in his will, which was executed in June 1882, that four lots and $100,000 be conveyed to the city of East Saginaw for a public "Consulting and Reference Library." Half of this amount was to be devoted to the erection of a building, and the balance used for the purchase of books and the maintenance of the library. Hoyt's trust deed further stipulated that the "building and the library . . . be known and designated as the 'Hoyt Public Library,'" and that this "name shall never be changed or altered."[3] These wishes were to be carried out, and the institution governed, by a self-electing board of five trustees. As initially constituted in 1883 by Webber, the executor and trustee of Jesse Hoyt's Michigan property, members of this board included Henry C. Potter, Jr., secretary of the Flint and Pere Marquette Railroad, his father, Henry C. Potter, Sr., Joseph C. Jones, Timothy E. Tarsney, and Webber's son-in-law, James B. Peter. When Jones resigned the following year, Webber, who himself had been a director of Hoyt's Flint and Pere Marquette Railroad since 1864, took his place.[4] In spite of their economic ties to the donor, these men were far removed from both the Hoyt family and the genteel aspirations and fears of Richardson's New England patrons and friends.

With his action Jesse Hoyt, of course, was following in the footsteps of a fellow New Yorker and earlier Michigan entrepreneur, John Jacob Astor, who in 1848 had left a bequest of $400,000 to found and support a noncirculating library in New York City (fig. 2.11). Of the more than 50 public library buildings constructed through similar gifts and bequests during the next three decades, almost all had been established instead for circulating libraries on the model of the Boston Public Library, which had opened in 1859. Three of Richardson's widely acclaimed library buildings had been completed by the date Hoyt executed his will; the Crane Library in Quincy, a gift of another New York family, had in fact been dedicated only one month previous to this act. Whether or not Hoyt was cognizant of this gift is not known. It is very likely, however, that by this date, his attorney, William Webber, would have been aware of Henry Sage's intention to erect a public library building in the rival lumber town of West Bay City, Michigan. This plan had apparently taken "definite shape in 1881, when [Sage] expressed his purpose to some of the citizens" of this community, and was publicly announced in April of the following year. Sage was a resident of Ithaca, New York, who had likewise accumulated a fortune in Michigan lumber and real estate. His new library building, which was erected at a cost of $25,000, would be dedicated in January 1884.[5] With $50,000 to expend on their own building, the Hoyt trustees, who apparently did come to know the Crane Library, quickly became interested in raising an edifice that would rival if not surpass both the Crane and Sage libraries in cost and form. And architects across the country seem immediately to have become aware of this aspiration.

On 26 January 1883, for example, even before Hoyt's bequest had been legally conveyed to the town, Elijah E. Myers, whose office was then in Detroit, descended upon the community, bringing with him designs for a "proposed building, for submission to those interested." These called for "a structure of strictly classical (Ionic) style of proportions," which was to be executed in the form of a Greek cross.[6] Although Myers's drawings were examined by several members of the newly constituted board of trustees in May 1883, no substantive action appears to have been taken by this body until early the following year, when Peter wrote to William Frederick Poole, who was then serving as the director of the Chicago Public Library, asking if he would be willing to travel to East Saginaw to act as a consultant to this board.[7]

* * *

William Poole (1821–1894) was a man of wide-ranging experience in library management and design. After graduating from Yale in 1849, he had served as librarian of the Boston Mercantile Library, first as assistant and then as librarian at the Boston Athenaeum, and in 1870 had become director of the newly opened public library in Cincinnati. He was the author of *Poole's Guide to Periodical Literature,* precursor to the well-known *Readers Guide,* and in 1876 had been one of the founding members of the American Library Association (ALA), an organization that he would serve as president in 1886–1887 (years in which he also was elected president of the American Historical Association). As a result of his leading role in the struggle to professionalize the administration, organization, and design of the American public library, he, along with Justin Winsor, has been identified as one of the founders of the modern library movement in the United States.[8]

Like Winsor, Poole was a staunch advocate of utilitarian principles of planning. "In all cases," he argued at the annual conference of the American Library Association in 1879, "architectural effect" should be held "subsidiary to the practical uses of the library—in other words, [I] would build around my books." In this respect Poole—also like Winsor—believed that all earlier library buildings, especially the type of hall library he had administered in Cincinnati, had failed, and he made this more than clear when he announced at the same meeting that he knew "of no better rule to be observed, in library architecture of the future, than this: 'Avoid everything that pertains to the plan and arrangement of the conventional American library building.'"[9]

Poole's unequivocal indictment of American library design, and by implication of the architectural profession, did not pass unnoticed. Just three weeks after his pronouncement appeared in the *Library Journal,* the editors of *American Architect and Building News* responded with a lengthy rebuttal, touching off a debate between librarians and architects that would last well into the next century. Particularly vexing to the architectural profession was what they saw as an increasingly common tendency to undervalue their services. "This prejudice," they noted, "found fair expression in the discussion to which we have alluded, where one librarian of eminence gave utterance to a remark which apparently found acceptance among most of his brethren, that in the building of the ideal library it is necessary to forget all that architects have hitherto done for them, and to begin anew on what might be called a practical basis, without any embarrassments from the traditions of architectural practise; as if ideas of beauty and style, which seemed to be considered the whole stock in trade of architecture, could only be expressed at the expense of some practical requirement of convenience and necessity." Of course, they added, this was not the case, for it was the "fundamental basis of all sound building" to combine the two so as to obtain "beauty without any unnecessary sacrifice of fitness and economy."[10]



**
*

6.1
James H. McLaughlin, Cincinnati Public Library, 1868–1874.
The Public Library of Cincinnati and Hamilton County.



**
*

Undeterred, Poole continued to lead forays against the architectural profession at annual meetings of the ALA throughout the early 1880s. Here he reiterated his earlier objections to "conventional" library buildings such as the Astor in New York (fig. 2.11), the first Boston Public Library (fig. 2.16), or the Cincinnati Public Library (fig. 6.1), with their "immense hall[s], fifty or sixty feet high, surrounded with tiers, galleries where the bindings perish with heat, and to which attendants must climb for books which ought to be within reach on the working floors."[11] Additionally, a book hall arrangement was difficult to enlarge. "Shall it be extended heavenward," asked Poole sarcastically, "and more galleries be piled on these, with more wasted space in the nave, greater difficulty of access to books, and more extravagance in the heating? Shall the transepts and chancel be built, so that the plan will represent the true ecclesiastical cross? However pious these improvements and gratifying to the taste of the refined architect, they are expensive, they involve demolishing much that has already been constructed, and they will give but little additional room."[12]

This problem, continued Poole at the 1883 ALA conference,

> is not a difficult one to solve if we will abandon conventional and medieval ideas, and apply the same common-sense, practical judgment and good taste which is used in the construction of houses to live in, stores to do business in, and hotels to accommodate transient visitors in. We want buildings for doing the work of a library in; for giving readers the best facilities for study; for storing books in the most convenient manner, where they will be secure from fire, and for doing everything which pertains to the administration of a library. The architect is not qualified to decide what the requirements of a library are, for he knows nothing about the details of its administration. The librarian should study out and design the original plan, and the architect should take these practical suggestions, harmonize them, and give to the structure an artistic effect. It will be well if librarians gave more attention to library construction. If left to architects alone, the business will run in the old ruts.[13]

In place of galleries and alcoves, Poole proposed the construction of multiple stories of small subject-oriented rooms grouped around a central courtyard. Each of these rooms, as Poole would describe in detail many times during the 1880s, should be 16 feet in height with free-standing wooden bookcases no taller than the reach of the average person, the 10 feet of open space between the top of the shelves and the ceiling serving to dissipate excess heat and dry air. And while many librarians did not agree with this solution—Winsor, for example, favored metal stacks—their general frustration was expressed in a resolution that was unanimously adopted by the association in 1881: "That, in the opinion of the Association, the time has come

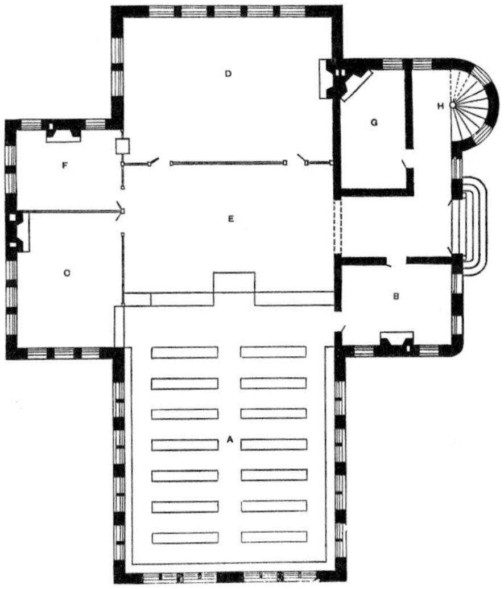


6.2
William F. Poole, plan for a small library building: *A,* book room; *B,* librarian's office; *C,* general reference room; *D,* periodical reading room; *E,* delivery room; *F,* ladies' reference room; *G,* director's room; *H,* stair tower. *The Library Journal,* 1885.

for a radical modification of the prevailing typical style of library building, and the adoption of a style of construction better suited to economy and practical utility."[14]

The request in March 1884 that he assist the Hoyt Library board in developing a program for their new building, and a subsequent meeting with them in June, appear to have spurred Poole to shift his attention to the arrangement of smaller public libraries of the type that the East Saginaw trustees wished to erect. At the board's request, in fact, the librarian asked the Chicago architect William LeBaron Jenney to prepare plans based on ideas he had discussed with them. Jenney's response was forwarded by Poole to James Peter the following September. These drawings, noted the secretary in a return letter to the librarian, had "impressed the members of the Board more favorably than anything already submitted, but of course in this case as in all others" the trustees had "suggestions of some changes which should better be obtained by a personal interview with Mr. Jenney."[15] While this consultation appears never to have occurred, Jenney's plans, which have not survived, may have served as the basis for the plan of a model library building that Poole described at the annual meeting of the ALA in July 1885. Two months later this description and scheme were published in the *Library Journal* (fig. 6.2).

In this article, entitled "Small Library Buildings," Poole observed that since the founding of the librarians' association in 1876, the discussion of library design had "been directed almost wholly to the requirements of large libraries," when, for every library of "the larger class" that had been erected in America, "a hundred" small buildings were in fact needed.[16] To fill this gap, his program called for a structure that, like the Hoyt, would cost in the neighborhood of $50,000 and would be capable of storing up to 30,000 books, but he maintained that the general principles of this plan could "be modified to almost any extent in their application to other libraries where the conditions are different." Not surprisingly, Poole's scheme was arranged and divided according to function. The entry, for example, led directly into either the director's room, librarian's office, or delivery room. In "immediate connection" with the delivery area were the general reference room, a ladies' reference room ("if such a room be thought desirable by the directors"), a reading room for periodicals and newspapers, and "a room for the storage of books *without alcoves or galleries*." If desired, a lecture hall and trustees' room could be placed on the second story, with work rooms for the librarians in the basement. The book room, as Poole had prescribed in his earlier discussions of larger libraries, was to be 15 or 16 feet in height, with eight-foot-high wall cases around its periphery and parallel rows of freestanding, double-sided wooden shelves set in the center of the space. Extending as it did from the rear block of the building, this room should be illuminated by long rows of windows set above the wall cases, and was capable, with minor modifications, of being expanded in any of three directions.[17]

Whatever the specific scheme, what was most important was that all designs reflect what Poole deemed to be the "correct principles of construction." All library buildings, large or small, he argued, "should be constructed with some reference to common-sense, utility, economy, the safety of the books, the convenience of the public in using them, and of the custodians of the library in doing their work. Every other class of structures—dwelling houses, stores, workshops, factories—are planned and built with reference to the purpose for which they are to be used; and in these latter days the principle has begun to be applied to library buildings."[18]

The fundamental requirements in this new type of structure were "sufficient light, proper drainage, safe heating and healthful ventilation." Thus, whenever possible, "a location should be selected where light and air will be accessible on every side," or, at the very least, the building



***

should be sited on a corner, "where light may be taken in on three sides." In Poole's estimation it was "not possible to have too much light in a library, provided it be side-light," not "sky-light," which should be avoided unless no other alternative presented itself. "The north light is the most desirable; hence the reading-rooms should be placed, if possible, so as to use that light." Finally, it was essential that a library building should be made "practically fireproof . . . by the use of porous terra-cotta in ceilings and partitions, and laying floors over a bed of mortar." For this reason stone was always the preferable material for exterior walls. "Undressed and laid in irregular rubble-work," this type of construction could be "very tasteful, and is not expensive." While Poole insinuated that he did have an opinion "as to the style of the exterior elevation," he chose not to divulge it in this article. He did note, however, that the cruciform plan that he published along with his article, "in the breaking of lines in the facade," would "commend itself to any tasteful architect."[19]

During the discussion that followed the presentation of these ideas at the librarians' conference, Poole noted that in addition to their having been "accepted by . . . [a] Western library," the city of Dayton, Ohio, was also in the process of erecting a building that had been based upon them (fig. 6.3).[20] A diagram of this building, which was designed by the Dayton firm of Peters and Burns, had, in fact, been published four months earlier in the *Dayton Daily Democrat.* Both this sketch plan and the final plan, which was published in *American Architect and Building News* in February 1886, as well as Dayton's freestanding shelving system, bear a close resemblance to Poole's *Library Journal* proposal (fig. 6.4).[21] Even though the Hoyt trustees had yet to choose an architect for their building, it is clear from Peter's correspondence that the board, while perhaps undecided as to details, was rapidly moving forward with the project by this date. It thus seems likely that Poole's "Western library" was the East Saginaw building.

* * *

In September 1884 the trustees in Michigan had ordered all of the back issues of the *Library Journal,* and in early June of the following year they received, perhaps at their own request, plans and photos of the Nevins Memorial Library in Methuen, Massachusetts.[22] This building, which was designed by the Boston architect Samuel F. J. Thayer, had been described at length in the *Library Journal* the previous April and was published in *American Architect and Building News* in June 1884. In sharp contrast to Poole's scheme, the book room of this structure, which ran perpendicular to one side of the main block, had been modeled on Richardson's Woburn space, with a barrel-vaulted hall enclosing two-story alcoves with galleries. This room was awkwardly appended onto a brick variation on the same architect's Ames Memorial Hall in

**
*

6.3

Peters and Burns, Dayton Public Library, Dayton, Ohio, 1885–1888. Dayton and Montgomery County Public Library.

6.4

Dayton Public Library, book room. Dayton and Montgomery County Public Library.

North Easton. Within this block Thayer arranged a warren of smaller rooms for the librarians and trustees, the delivery of books, and reading.

In November 1885, even as the Dayton trustees were breaking ground for their new building, and just two months after the publication of Poole's article, Peter informed Jesse Hoyt's brother, Alfred M. Hoyt, that the trustees had finally "agreed upon a form of invitation to architects to prepare plans for the proposed building," and that they wished him to choose one of five architectural firms that they intended to invite to submit designs to this competition. While the East Saginaw trustees asked E. E. Myers, Henry Hobson Richardson, Peabody and Stearns, and Van Brunt and Howe to compete, Hoyt chose to invite McKim, Mead and White, a firm that in 1881 had designed his summer house on Long Island and was just then completing his new townhouse in New York City.[23] Perhaps not coincidentally, three of the board's choices had participated in the Woburn library competition in 1876, after which the designs of Gambrill and Richardson and of Peabody and Stearns, along with those of Cummings and Sears, were published in *American Architect and Building News.*[24] Myers, of course, had offered the village of East Saginaw an unsolicited plan for the Hoyt Library in 1883. On 30 November 1885 a printed *Invitation to Architects* was forwarded to all of these firms (McKim, Mead and White's was sent by way of Alfred Hoyt), with Van Brunt and Howe receiving a special plea from Peter to submit plans to the trustees: "I am personally, especially anxious that you should do so, as your Mr. Howe has been here, and we have had the pleasure of a meeting with him."[25]

Following Jesse Hoyt's instructions, the total cost of the building that the trustees intended to erect in East Saginaw, "including architect's compensation, superintendence, excavation, plumbing, gas fittings, and heating, was limited to a sum not exceeding fifty thousand dollars." Like the model library Poole described in the September issue of the *Library Journal,* this structure was to include a lecture hall and trustees' room on the second floor, while the first floor, which it was suggested should be entered from the west, was to accommodate reading and delivery rooms, work space and offices for the librarians, and "a fire-proof book room, abundantly lighted, equally warmed, and ventilated in all its parts, containing in the most compact manner consistent with accessibility and classification, thirty thousand or more volumes. This room to be so devised as to be capable of extension, and of addition thereto of further administrative or book storage rooms, without injury to the architectural character and usefulness of the building, and may have fire-proof isolation from the administrative part of the structure without detriment to or convenient service of the library." It was further stipulated that the trustees were specifically "committed to the system of book storage advocated by Mr. Poole, librarian of the Chicago Public Library, which contemplates a storage room of sixteen feet or thereabouts in height from the floor, distributed over the floor so that the librarian can have quick and easy access thereto."[26]

All of the architects were to be paid $100 for their designs, which were to be in the hands of the trustees no later than 1 February 1886, "the sketches and designs thus submitted to be the property of the Board," which reserved "the right to modify and change any of the plans and designs as in their judgment may be expedient."[27] While Myers, Van Brunt and Howe, and Peabody and Stearns immediately agreed to these conditions (as presumably did McKim, Mead and White, who were in correspondence with Hoyt), Richardson, as was his policy, insisted in a return letter to Peter that he be allowed to retain his drawings, and, if chosen, that they be used without substantial modification. He also required that his firm be allowed to supervise the construction of the library, for which, upon completion of the work, he would charge a commission equal to 10 percent of the overall cost of the building, inclusive of all supervision and design work. Since, as Peter was to note in a letter of 14 December, it was by then too late to change the rules of the competition, Richardson declined to compete for this commission.[28] His negative response, however, did not deter the board secretary from further pursuing the famous architect, for on the same day he wrote to a J. L. Lockwood in Boston asking him to try to persuade Richardson to change his mind.[29] When the architect still refused to take part in the competition, the board acquiesced to his demands. In early January, Peter informed Richardson of this decision and also that the deadline for receipt of submissions was to be extended to 1 March 1886 so that he would have sufficient time to prepare his entry. On 13 January Richardson accepted these terms.[30]

In the meantime, as word of the competition spread, the East Saginaw trustees were besieged with requests from other architects for copies of their *Invitation.* These included inquiries from the firms of William LeBaron Jenney; Palliser and Palliser of Bridgeport, Connecticut; L. J. Hall of Columbus, Ohio; J. L. Faxon of Boston; and Patton and Fisher of Chicago, which forwarded a copy of its design for the Scoville Institute, a library then under construction in Oak Park, Illinois (1884–1888; fig. 6.5). Although the arrangement of this building was somewhat awkward—with a delivery room and reading room opening off two different sides of the book room—the books were shelved, as Poole suggested, in freestanding wooden cases with a capacity of 30,000 to 40,000 volumes.[31]

In his reply to all of these architects, however, Peter made it clear that they had not been invited to participate in the competition and thus would be entitled to no guarantees of equal

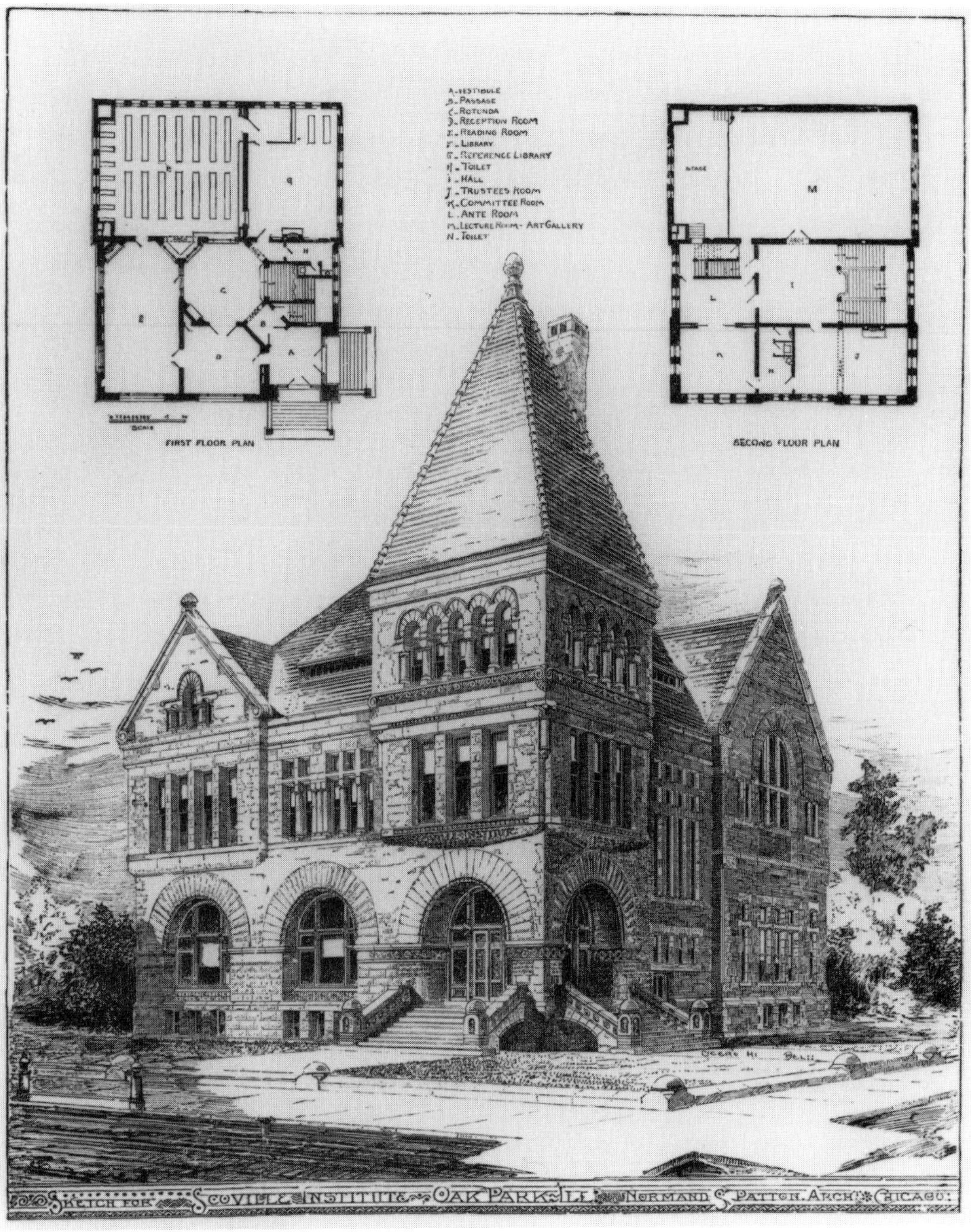


6.5
Patton and Fisher, Scoville Institute, Oak Park, Illinois, 1884–1888. *Inland Architect and Builder,* February 1885.

consideration or recompense for any designs that they might wish to submit to the board. Jenney, even though he had already prepared a plan developed in collaboration with Poole, was informed that it had unfortunately not met with the board's favor.[32] In spite of these caveats, Hall and Patton and Fisher persisted, the latter firm declaring in early January of 1886 that it still intended to forward a proposal to the board. Perhaps because Richardson at this date had not yet agreed to enter the competition and Patton and Fisher's plan for the Scoville Institute met a number of Poole's requirements, that firm did not receive an entirely unfavorable response from Peter, who in a letter of 11 January suggested that it might be given the Boston architect's place.[33] Two days later, however, Richardson agreed to submit his own entry to the competition.

When, by the new 1 March deadline, E. E. Myers failed to offer the board a proposal, Patton and Fisher suggested to Peter that this architect had now "forfeited altogether his claim to a place in the competition, and that it would be within the province of the trustees, if they should see fit, to appoint some other architect" in his place. Of course "this is a matter which is altogether at the option of the trustees, and in which we hope you will pardon our boldness for even making a suggestion." Still, it would improve their chances, they added, if the board was to deem theirs "the best of the voluntary contributions," and if they were to be paid Myers' stipend, this would "defray a part of [their] expenses" in the case that their plans were not adopted. "We are in the field as library specialists," they announced, and although "we have spent more time on the designs for your building than we would have done with this single building in view . . . the study we have put upon the plans, and the sketches themselves will be of some value to us in the future, and may enable us to secure other work without competition."[34]

Though it is not clear from the surviving correspondence whether or not the Hoyt trustees accepted Patton and Fisher's entire argument, their plans were ultimately entered into the competition. Early in March, in fact, Peter wrote to Poole offering to pay his expenses to East Saginaw in order to help the trustees judge proposals that had been submitted to them by six firms: Patton and Fisher, Henry Hobson Richardson, Van Brunt and Howe, Peabody and Stearns, McKim, Mead and White, and L. J. Hall.[35]

* * *

While Patton and Fisher's original design has not survived, a group of alternate sketches for a somewhat reduced version of their entry, "embodying changes suggested by Mr. Patton during his visit to Saginaw," have (figs. 6.6, 6.7).[36] In this scheme and an accompanying description

6.6
Patton and Fisher, alternate design for the Hoyt Public Library, East Saginaw, Michigan, 1886. Hoyt Public Library.

6.7
Patton and Fisher, alternate design for the Hoyt Public Library, first-floor plan. Hoyt Public Library.

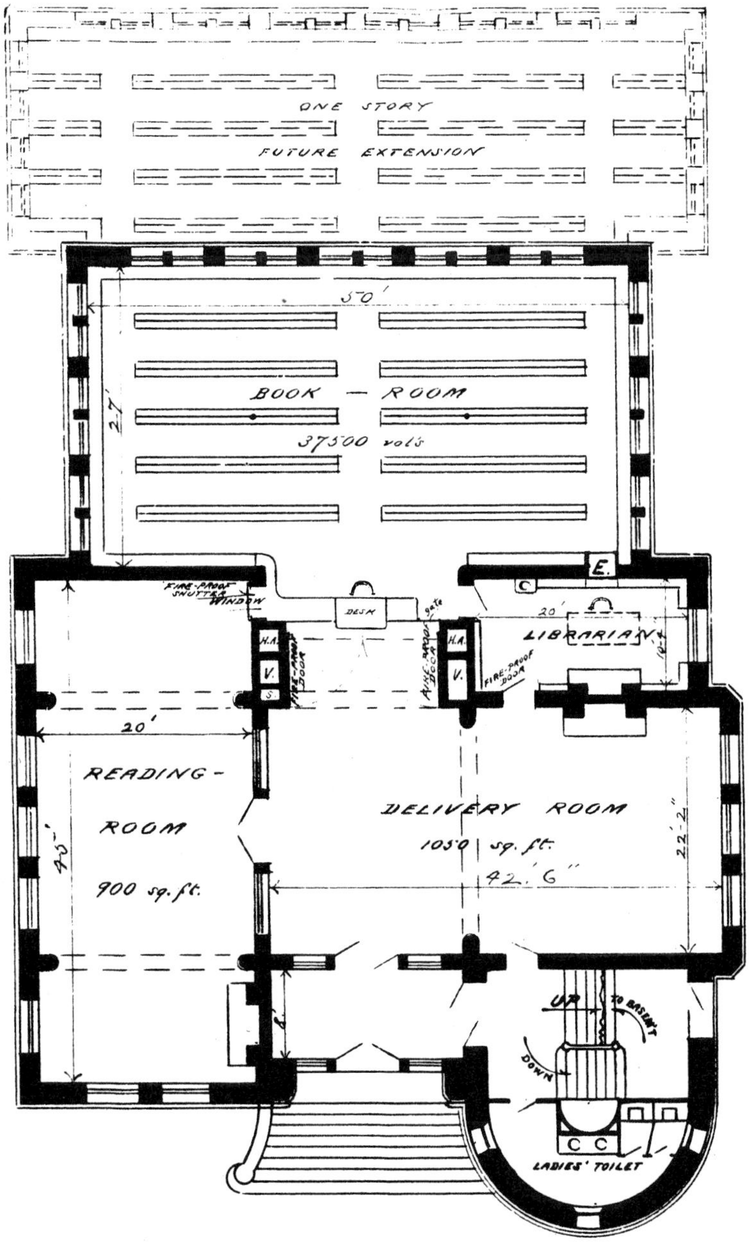


Competition in East Saginaw



**
*

6.8
McKim, Mead and White, Manchester Memorial Hall, Manchester-by-the-Sea, Massachusetts, 1886. Reproduced courtesy of the Trustees of the Boston Public Library.

6.9
*Opposite:* Manchester Memorial Hall, book room. Reproduced courtesy of the Trustees of the Boston Public Library.

**
*

that was sent to Peter in April 1886, the architects proposed a cruciform arrangement that is remarkably similar to Poole's published plan of 1885 (fig. 6.2), only reversed. The book room, which extends from the rear of the building, would have housed 37,500 books in freestanding shelves set in the center of this space, over which was to have been placed the lecture hall. In the basement were rooms for a museum and a "library shop." Like Van Brunt and Howe's completed building, the Romanesque style of Patton and Fisher's building, with its multiple arcades, massive entry arch, and prominent corner stair tower, was heavily indebted to Richardson.

What McKim, Mead and White proposed for East Saginaw, on the other hand, can only be surmised from an almost contemporary library that Charles McKim designed in Manchester, Massachusetts (1886; fig. 6.8). Although planned to hold only half as many books and to cost half as much as the Hoyt library, its interior arrangement, which even McKim characterized as "mediaeval," would surely have met with the disapprobation of Poole and the trustees, especially the ill-lit and tiny book room, which in no way reflected modern library planning theory (fig. 6.9). One of the firm's most Richardsonian of designs, it was described by its architect as "a building dependent for its ourward effect upon massive wall construction, designed intentionally upon the simplest lines, and roofed with rough slate, under a system of ridge and gable common to many buildings on the French side of the channel."[37] It is even more difficult to know what Peabody and Stearns and L. J. Hall might have suggested, as there is no record of their designs.[38]

Richardson's own proposal for the Hoyt Library appears to be represented by a group of nine graphite and watercolor drawings on manila paper in the Houghton Library at Harvard, all of which conform to the directives laid out in the trustees' *Invitation to Architects,* as well as a printed booklet of specifications that can be found in the same collection.[39] Although they were subsequently trimmed, eyelets in the upper corners of one of the plans (fig. 6.16) seem to indicate that they were once bound together in two booklets, one measuring approximately 35 by 55 cm and the other 25 by 20 cm. In addition, a small *esquisse,* which has been quickly produced in iron gall ink directly over a pencil delineation of a plan on Richardson's Brookline stationery, may represent the architect's initial concept for the building (fig. 6.10). The elevation for this charming little edifice reverses (as does the plan) the arch, gable, and stair tower ensemble of the Crane Library and replaces its reading room window with a polygonal hall crowned by elaborate dormer windows. Some half a dozen variations on this elevation, often no more than quick sketches on tracing paper by unidentified members of the office, can also be found among the Hoyt drawings. These studies are accompanied by an assortment of plans and

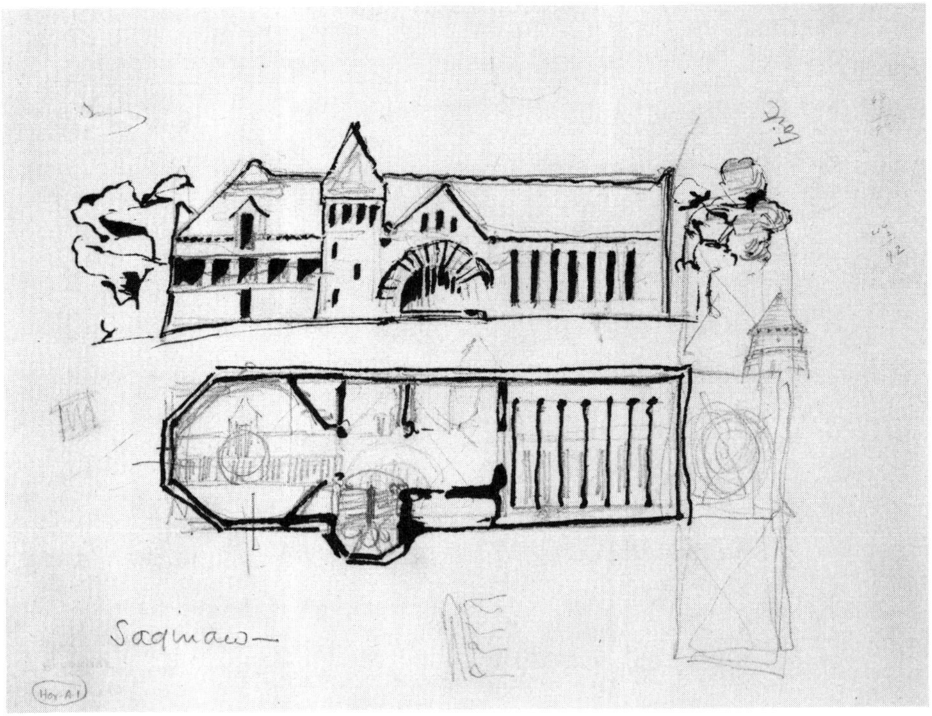


6.10
H. H. Richardson, sketch plan and elevation for the Hoyt Public Library, East Saginaw, 1886. HOY A1, Department of Printing and Graphic Arts, The Houghton Library, Harvard University.

6.11
H. H. Richardson, Billings Memorial Library, University of Vermont, 1883–1886. *The Billings Library, the Gift to the University of Vermont of Frederick Billings, H. H. Richardson, Architect,* [c. 1888], courtesy of the Print Department, Boston Public Library.

sections and a handful of miscellaneous details of fenestration, the entry portal, and a dedicatory inscription. An additional series of ten sketches (all on tracing paper by various hands) represent a variety of proposals for the eastern end elevation of the book wing.

In plan, both the *esquisse* and the more finished proposals reveal a strong debt to several of Richardson's early schemes for the Quincy library, as well as the architect's subsequent arrangement of the Billings Memorial Library at the University of Vermont in Burlington (1883–1886; fig. 6.11). Although it had been dedicated in June 1885, construction on this building was still in progress at the time of the Hoyt competition.[40] As completed, the Billings Library, like several of the Crane Library *partis,* had a polygonal reading room balanced along the primary axis by the book wing (fig. 6.12). At Burlington the reading room was covered with an open-timber roof and encircled, along the panoptic principles of Benjamin Delessert (fig. 2.10), with two stories of shallow, radiating alcoves (fig. 6.13). This space was intended to house some 12,000 volumes, which the building's donor, Frederick Billings (1823–1890; U. Vt. '44), had purchased for the university from the estate of George Perkins Marsh (1801–1882). The remainder of the school's library was stored in a linear book room that was very similar in configuration, as well as articulation and ornamentation, to Richardson's nearly contemporaneous book wing at Malden (figs. 6.14, 5.4), but now with a flat beamed ceiling like the one he had employed at Quincy (fig. 4.15). Because the buildings in Burlington and Malden had been under development in the office at the same time, the architect seems to have used various motifs interchangeably. Besides sharing similar designs for furniture and fixtures, for example,

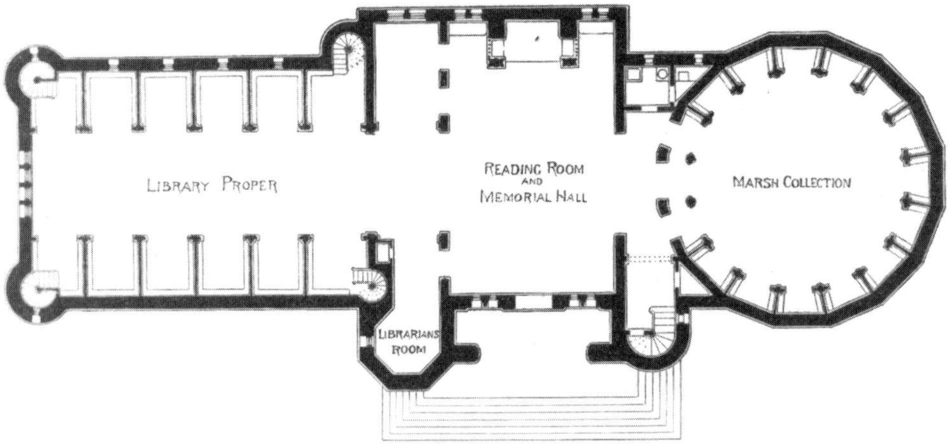


PLAN OF LIBRARY, BURLINGTON.

6.12
Billings Memorial Library, plan. Van Rensselaer, *Henry Hobson Richardson and His Works,* 1888.

6.13
Billings Memorial Library, reading room. *The Billings Library, the Gift to the University of Vermont of Frederick Billings, H. H. Richardson, Architect,* [c. 1888], courtesy of the Print Department, Boston Public Library.

6.14

Billings Memorial Library book room. *The Billings Library, the Gift to the University of Vermont of Frederick Billings, H. H. Richardson, Architect,* [c. 1888], courtesy of the Print Department, Boston Public Library.

the elevations of the book room alcoves in the two buildings essentially reverse the articulation of one another's first and second stories.

As it had previously, Richardson's office appears to have used these current commissions and the earlier sequence of schemes it had developed at Woburn, North Easton, and Quincy as the basis for its Hoyt design. According to the drawings Richardson submitted to the East Saginaw competition, one would have entered directly into the delivery area through a broad arch set into the south face of the building (figs. 6.15, 6.16). To the right stood the delivery desk and book room, while to the left was located a narrow anteroom, with a staircase leading up to study alcoves. A lecture hall was situated at the west end of the upper floor, while a trustees' room was placed opposite it. A polygonal reading room was located on the first floor beneath the stage area of the auditorium. Perhaps confusing this space with its counterpart at Burlington, the architect's specifications indicate that this reading room "extends up through two stories with an open timbered ceiling. The windows are so arranged as to give light either from the sides or above through the dormers, so that on the dullest day the best possible light for reading can be obtained." As in all of Richardson's previous libraries, "a great monumental fireplace" was to be located in this space, "afford[ing] a proper and dignified ending to the long vista through the library." In contrast to his earlier designs, this space was now "removed from the rest of the building, so as to be as far as possible from the noise and bustle of the crowd."[41]

If the Houghton *esquisse* plan does indeed represent an early idea for this building, it would appear to indicate that Richardson intended from the outset to replace his alcove book room with freestanding shelving similar to the type advocated by William Poole. According to the specifications, and as is evident in section, this space was to be 14 feet in height, with two rows of iron book racks that supported oak shelves (fig. 6.17). In contrast to the high bands of fenestration that illuminated the architect's earlier book wings, this area was to be "abundantly lighted by a great line of windows extending to the ceiling, which are so placed as to throw a flood of light down the aisles between book-cases." "The Plan of the building," noted Richardson, "is strictly utilitarian, the aim being to obtain the greatest practicable advantages for its distinctive purposes that can be had within reasonable limits of outlay."[42]

Despite these concessions to the board's preference for compact book storage and utilitarian planning, as well as the trustees' earlier acquiescence to the architect's demands for changes in the competition, Richardson's proposal did not meet with their approval. Besides inaccuracies in the specifications—including the discrepancy between the description of the reading room as two stories in height and its representation as one story in section and plan, and the

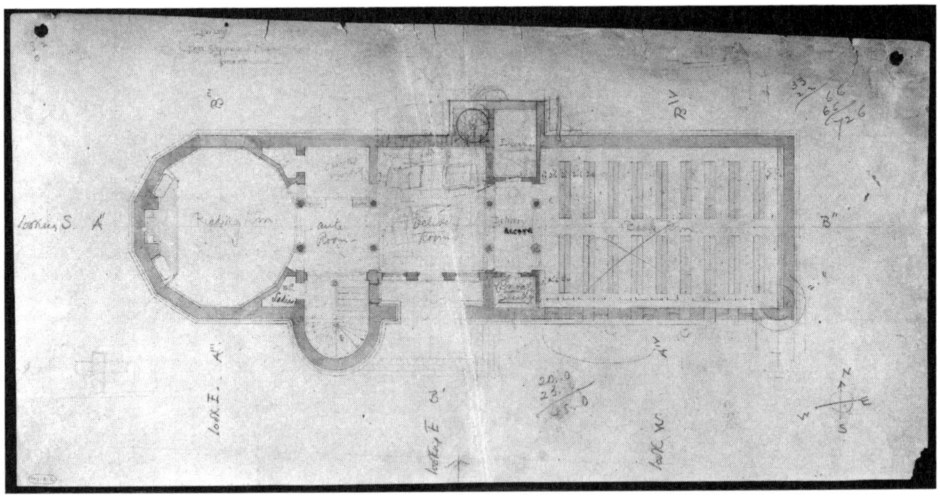

6.15
H. H. Richardson, design for the Hoyt Public Library, principal facade, 1886. HOY B5, Department of Printing and Graphic Arts, The Houghton Library, Harvard University.

6.16
H. H. Richardson, design for the Hoyt Public Library, first-floor plan, 1886. HOY A2, Department of Printing and Graphic Arts, The Houghton Library, Harvard University.

6.17
*Opposite:* H. H. Richardson, design for the Hoyt Public Library, section through book room, 1886. HOY C2, Department of Printing and Graphic Arts, The Houghton Library, Harvard University.

mention of the "Middlesex Society Room," a room in the Converse Memorial Library that had been completed the previous September—the architect had faced his building south despite the *Invitation* directive that it face west.[43] Given the rapidity with which the proposal had to be prepared, and the fact that it was being produced at a time when the architect was increasingly incapacitated by the illness that would lead to his untimely death in April, this lack of focus—a condition the Hoyt trustees also may have recognized—is understandable. The sense of disarray in the office at the time is clearly conveyed by a note Richardson penned to his assistant, George Shepley, on 6 March, when the misunderstanding over the orientation of the building seems first to have become apparent: "I am annoyed that I did not read the proofs of Saginaw specifications & that such a slip should have been made as the mention of the 'Middlesex Society Room' but after all it is not surprising that we should now & then mix up libraries when we are building so many. Your letters have given me a very clear idea of the state of things and the longer they delay decision the better for us. You had better see Poole if you can, *not* in Chicago but in Saginaw—I am right about placing & facing the building—the southern sun on the porch & steps alone, all things considered, is enough to decide it. Stand solid on position as it is. I thought all their recommendations were suggestions."[44]

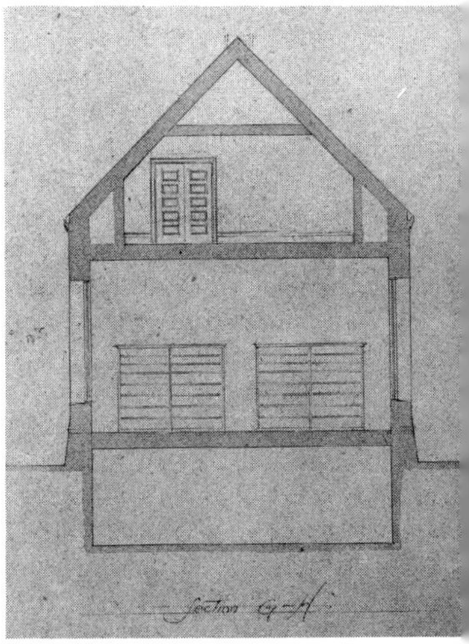

Even though Poole was unable to make this trip, and Shepley was advised by Peter not to return to East Saginaw at that time ("I do not think it would do any good for you to come here again at present and would advise against it"),[45] Richardson's assistant did pay a visit to the town in late March. Upon Shepley's return to Boston, Richardson again wrote to Peter concerning the board's "very detailed objections to placing the entrance of the building on William St.," and the fact that they "considered it as one of the conditions of the competition that the entrance" should face west, not south. "I certainly did not consider it so, but only as a suggestion, not thinking that you attached any great importance to it, or I certainly would have accepted the condition and made my design accordingly," he noted. "We supposed it was clearly understood," replied the secretary, "that our wishes regarding the entrance was a condition as to the form in which the sketches should be submitted."[46]

On 6 April, just three weeks before the architect's death, Peter returned Richardson's submission to his office, as well as those of L. J. Hall and Peabody and Stearns. "I am especially sorry that your plan should have shown a frontage which we did not desire," noted Peter in a letter which accompanied Richardson's returned entry. "That fact, and the general great length and lowness of the building, with the further fact that the other plans submitted gave us additional and more convenient library facilities were the grounds upon which the trustees have based their present action."[47] The same day, the secretary informed Poole that the board still had come to no final decision concerning the competition, and that it had requested Peter to forward two sets of plans each by Van Brunt and Howe and Patton and Fisher and one by McKim, Mead and White to the librarian for his comments. "Confidentially," added the secretary, "the Board lean strongly towards the Van Brunt and Howe plan with some modification as to internal arrangement. We think that it comes nearer to your view of what a library should be than anything we have seen."[48]

* * *

Although no record exists of Poole's reaction to these designs, it is not surprising, given Peter's early bias toward Van Brunt and Howe—as well as that firm's own record of cooperation with librarians—that early in May 1886 the Hoyt board chose them to design the new library building. Still, even at this date a number of questions concerning the final form of the structure appear to have remained unresolved. Van Brunt and Howe, for example, in opposition to Poole's preference, were pressing the trustees to accept a stack system of book storage similar to what Van Brunt, his former partner William Ware, and the librarian Justin Winsor had earlier erected at Gore Hall, Harvard (fig. 2.25).[49] In 1881, moreover, Van Brunt and Ware had designed a similar five-story book stack for the library of the University of Michigan in Ann Arbor. As completed in 1883, this was reduced to three floors of shelving with a capacity of 100,000 volumes. In June 1886, Peter reported that, at the request of the architects, four of the five Hoyt trustees had visited this library to examine its arrangement, but that they remained steadfast in their advocacy of Poole's system: "one floor for the storage of books, the Bookroom to be 16 feet high in the clear with one tier of windows on each side at least 5 feet from the floor." They therefore opted to accept Van Brunt and Howe's "alternative plan," a scheme that employed this type of arrangement. "We are aware that we have changed your idea respecting the Bookroom," wrote Peter to them on 3 June, "but our library is not likely to grow for many years to such an extent that we shall require more than one floor of books."[50]

In addition to conforming to Poole's insistence upon freestanding wooden shelving, Van Brunt and Howe's accepted design followed the librarian's and the trustees' directives in several other significant ways. Their reading room, in conformance with Poole's own preference, was placed on the north side of the building and their entry porch on the west (figs. 6.18, 6.20). Most tellingly, perhaps, like Patton and Fisher's entry, the original cross-axial configuration of the Hoyt Library is almost a mirror image of the model plan the Chicago librarian had published in the *Library Journal* in 1885 (fig. 6.2), the only major deviations being a shifting around

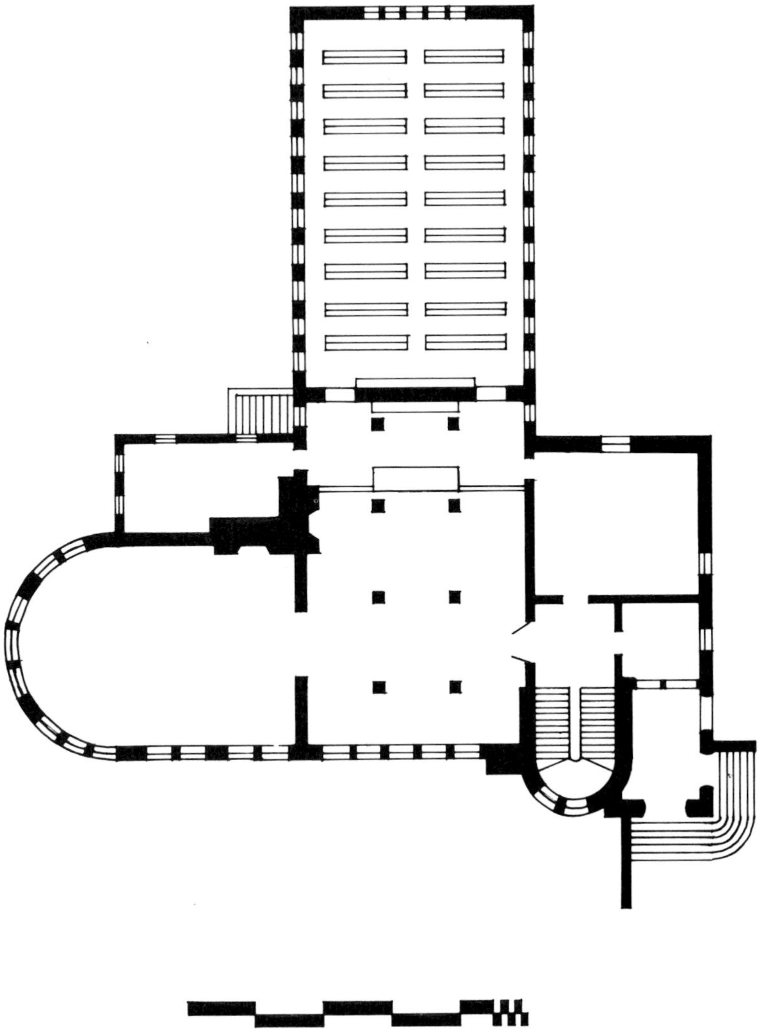

6.18
Van Brunt and Howe, Hoyt Public Library, East Saginaw, 1886–1890, first-floor plan. Drawing by Glenn Waguespack.

6.19
Hoyt Public Library, delivery room and desk. Hoyt Public Library.

6.20
Hoyt Public Library, view from southwest. Hoyt Public Library.

**
*

Competition in East Saginaw



**
*

of the tower and entry porch and the substitution of an apsidal reading room for Poole's reference and ladies' reference rooms. The architects also separated their book room from the body of the library with a thick fire wall and pine doors of double thickness sheathed in tin, a precaution against the spread of fire not called for by Poole but suggested as a possible feature by the trustees in their *Invitation* (fig. 6.19). Van Brunt had recommended a similar fireproof division between the book wing and main body of the library as early as 1879 in a paper he delivered at the annual conference of the American Library Association.[51]

Following Poole's suggestion, as well as the example of Richardson's earlier library designs, Van Brunt and Howe's exterior massing was derived directly from their plan (figs. 6.20, 6.21). The prominent corner entry porch, stair tower, and reading and book room wings all were intended to be expressive of their functions, with variations in fenestration marking differences

6.21
Hoyt Public Library, book wing from southeast. Hoyt Public Library.

in use. A narrow band of windows with alternating colonnettes and rusticated piers, similar to those employed by Richardson on his North Easton book wing, now wrapped around the reading room and delivery areas, while Van Brunt and Howe's book room was lighted with an expanded variation on the Crane Library's reading room window. As was often the case with Van Brunt's designs, the massing of this building is finicky and awkward.[52] As required by the board, it was constructed of bluish gray Bay Port limestone with red Lake Superior sandstone trim, further imparting an effect that, in contrast to Richardson's impression of horizontality and stability, is thin and pebbly, and unpleasantly vertical in orientation.

Since its founding at midcentury, East Saginaw had been in competition with neighboring municipalities for economic and cultural hegemony in the Saginaw River Valley, and in their *Invitation to Architects* the board had clearly stated that "the library property is distant south from one of the main business centers of the city only about two squares, and is in full view therefrom."[53] Both Patton and Fisher's and Van Brunt and Howe's schemes, with their prominent corner towers, would have been much more visible from East Saginaw's commercial hub than "the general great length and lowness" of Richardson's design. In this light, Van Brunt and Howe's grand staircase and erect corner tower may indeed have been more appropriate than Richardson's lower and more somber design. Given their own roles as aggressive, professional entrepreneurs and community leaders, it seems likely that the trustees of the Hoyt Library wanted a modern monument to civic pride and stability more than a family memorial steeped in the iconography of tradition and death.

While Richardson's entry also failed to meet several of the key requirements of the Hoyt program, it seems likely that the firm's carelessness and what may have been perceived as a rather cavalier—if not elitist—eastern attitude also helped convince the trustees to accept the proposal of the newly transplanted, midwestern firm of Van Brunt and Howe. The Boston architect's initial refusal to participate in the competition and ultimate insistence on a 10 percent commission, even if it did include construction supervision, may have served to reinforce this interpretation, especially since the trustees were aware that Richardson charged only 8 percent on the East Coast.[54]

* * *

The "sawdust city" of East Saginaw was a far different place from the much older "island communities" in which Richardson's earlier libraries had been raised. In stark contrast to the perceived disintegration of order bemoaned by men such as Charles Francis Adams, Jr., in their eastern communities, this rough and tumble lumber town truly was plagued with violence, prostitution, and labor unrest during the years the Hoyt board was contemplating the erection of their new building. In 1881 alone there had been 15 murders in the city, which had a population in 1880 of just over 19,000, and the summer of 1885 had witnessed a tense and protracted strike by the largely Polish and French Canadian mill workers over the ten-hour work day.[55] It was in the immediate wake of this turmoil that the board issued their *Invitation to Architects.* Although Jesse Hoyt had been a staunch Republican, board members Timothy Tarsney and William Webber were both prominent Democrats, Webber serving as mayor of East Saginaw in 1873 and in the state senate the following year, while Tarsney, the son of Irish immigrants, was elected to the 49th Congress in 1884. They may thus have found themselves in a rather ambivalent mood when the Republican governor, Russell A. Alger, mobilized the state militia and armed Pinkerton guards to intimidate the striking mill workers, members of their own political constituency.[56] While these trustees, like their eastern counterparts, may still have envisioned the library as a supporter of social and political stability, they would have interpreted this charge within the parameters of their own experience.

As members of the newly empowered professional middle class identified by scholars such as Neil Harris and Robert Wiebe, the Hoyt trustees' relationship to traditional centers of power was ambiguous at best.[57] Although surely moved to defend their own interests, these interests were not as clearly embedded in tradition and history as those of the eastern elite. In building their new institution, these midwestern businessmen turned instead to more modern notions of efficiency and progress in place of sentiment and moral suasion. As Thomas W. Palmer would note at the dedication of the Hackley Library (1888–1890; fig. 7.4) in the cross-state lumbertown of Muskegon, a public library should be viewed like any other corporate venture. "When a proposition is made to a business man to induce him to invest his money, the first question to the exploiter and to himself is, What per cent. will it pay? The parable of the talents is nothing more than the application by the Great Teacher of mankind of an economic truth to spiritual things. . . . The rich have wealth, which, if rightly applied, encourages virtue, promotes reforms, rewards industry and concentrates ten thousand hands at a given point, at a given time, for a given purpose, which otherwise might have slept undeveloped and unaccomplished."[58]

In search of a fiscally responsible institution, the Hoyt trustees had turned naturally to Chicago, to William Frederick Poole, director of the Chicago Public Library, and to the engineer William LeBaron Jenney for advice. Chicago was the economic and cultural nexus for the midwestern region, the primary market for Michigan and Wisconsin timber, and the focus of a railroad and merchandizing network that physically tied it to its hinterlands. It also laid claim to the most modern architecture in the world. It was here that men such as Jenney, who had taught architecture at the University of Michigan, and John Wellborn Root were struggling to create other new building types, "adapted solely to the present, and of which twenty years ago no man could have dreamed."[59] It was also in Chicago that architects like Peter Bonnett Wight were evolving and promoting new methods of fireproof construction of the type advocated by Poole and specified by the trustees in their *Invitation to Architects.*[60] It was in this spirit that Poole, who despite his own eastern roots felt very much at home in the hard-nosed world of Chicago businessmen, first envisioned his own proposal for a small public library, a design that would "apply the same common-sense, practical judgment and good taste which is used in the construction of houses to live in, stores to do business in, and hotels to accommodate transient visitors in."[61]

Poole's claim to expertise in the field of library design, likewise, reflects the struggle of librarians to establish their own professional identity at the end of the nineteenth century, an effort that found itself in conflict with the parallel struggle for recognition being waged by American architects. Their advocacy of "scientific" methods of administration and "modern" planning is indicative of a broader "search for order," which Wiebe associates with the professionalization of the middle class in general during this period. According to Harris this growing emphasis on modernization resulted, among other things, in "a secularizing insistence upon rationality and bureaucratic efficiency rather than sentiment or religion as the source of social reform and the basis of human relationships."[62] While motivated by many of the same tensions that alarmed Charles Francis Adams, Jr., in Quincy, these new technocrats were turning to different solutions to assuage their fears. Applying modern technologies to the storage and distribution of books not only held forth a potential to reach a wider audience, but increased the significance of the public library and its librarians within a modern capitalist system.[63]

By the late nineteenth century, observes Neil Harris, the public library in particular "combined in volatile quantities the modern era's capacity to gather, organize, and manipulate experience in the interest of modernity, and the same era's infatuation with the simpler verities of an earlier day." In East Saginaw, Van Brunt and Howe's building, ungainly as it may be, seems to have supplied "the arresting combinations of internal efficiency and external archaicism" that "such a division of loyalties" often engendered, a division that Richardson's paradigm appears to have been ultimately unable to accommodate.[64]



**
*

*seven*

# Epilogue

An architect sat in an office so high,
Genius lighted his forehead, ambition his eye;
"Oh, I'm planning a library wondrous to see,
And its praises shall ring all the world round," quoth he.
Then he flourished his pencil, and quickly up grew
A building the public all hastened to view. . . .
There were nice little corners to lounge in at ease,
And dusky recesses the aesthetes to please,
And corridors quaint, where the shaded light fell
Upon dados and friezes too lovely to tell.
There were bookcases? Yes, I was going to say
These were hid in odd corners quite out of the way,
So that nobody heeded, except to exclaim
At the wonderful carving of bracket and frame.
And the public remarked, as in rapture they gazed:
"Too highly this architect cannot be praised!"

Y^E^ Architect and Y^E^ Librarian

*Library Journal,* 1888

While almost nothing of the important confrontation between Richardson, McKim, Mead and White, Van Brunt and Howe, and William Frederick Poole in East Saginaw reached the professional or popular press, the controversy that surfaced here did not die with the selection of the Kansas City firm by the Hoyt trustees. Richardson's rejected plans, in fact, were to resurface almost immediately in New Orleans, in the guise of the slightly larger Howard Memorial Library, which would be opened in March 1889 (fig. 7.1). While several contemporary accounts suggest that Richardson himself had begun preliminary work on a scheme for this building in 1885, it appears fairly certain that his successor firm, Shepley, Rutan and Coolidge—which actually oversaw the construction of the building after the architect's death on 27 April 1886—partially reused his Hoyt designs for this structure. As James O'Gorman has pointed out, the perspective rendering that appeared in both *Harper's Weekly* and the *Library Journal* in 1888 is almost identical to a rendering for the Hoyt Library now in the Houghton Collection at Harvard.[1] The first-floor plan for the Hoyt competition (fig. 6.16), likewise, has been overlaid in pencil with the addition of a corner stair turret, and the shelving in this plan has been lightly Xed out, both of which would be appropriate alterations for the two-story alcove system that Shepley, Rutan and Coolidge reintroduced at New Orleans (figs. 7.2, 7.3).

When the plans and elevations for the New Orleans library were exhibited at the annual conference of the American Library Association in late September 1888, a number of the issues that appear to have decided the Saginaw contest attained a national audience. As might be expected by this date, the architects' decision to employ a traditional gallery-and-alcove book room only served to fuel the librarians' growing discontent with architects. According to a report in *The Nation,* they "riddled" these designs "with objections." From "the library point of view," reported the magazine, the association now pronounced "all of Richardson's designs for libraries . . . failures," and further wondered "whether the famous architect ever gave any thought to the object for which his buildings of this sort were intended." In the librarians' opinion "there is little indication that he did in any of them," appearing "to have been satisfied if he drew a beautiful design, and to have left it to some draftsman to fit in the books and the service. . . . Looking at such plans as this of the Howard Library (where, for instance, an attendant must go 320 feet to get a book within 10 feet of the delivery desk), and scores of others like it, . . . one may say, as did the President of the Association, 'The architect is the natural enemy of the librarian.'"[2]



**
*

"The Convention of the American Library Association," returned the editors in *American Architect and Building News* in October, "amused itself, as usual, by falling foul of the architects, over whose prostrate forms every scientific hobby is made to prance." Especially irritated by the librarians' criticism of their recently deceased and highly revered colleague, the architects then went on the offensive:

Considering that no two librarians appear to be agreed as to "where book-shelves and reading-halls and work-rooms ought to go for the highest efficiency," and that any plan advocated by one is generally laughed to scorn by the rest, it is not surprising that architects have not yet invented an arrangement which suits everybody. . . . In point of fact, Richardson, although he liked to draw "beautiful designs" for libraries, and generally succeeded in doing so, was very far from careless as to the object to which his building was to be put. As in all his work, the requirements of the case, so far as he could understand them, dictated the plan, and this suggested the rest, and to improve the arrangement he never tired of studying methods of lighting, heights and widths of shelves, ease of access to the several portions, quiet for the reading-rooms, and space for the movement of the public. . . . Although we speak modestly of

7.1
Shepley, Rutan and Coolidge, Howard Memorial Library, New Orleans, 1887–1889. Postcard view.

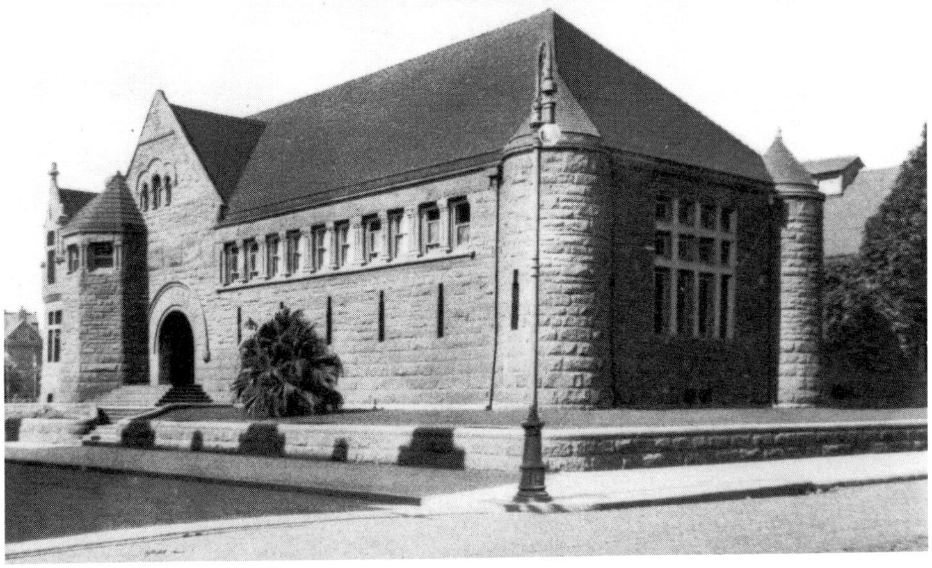



**
*

arrangement of book-shelves, as a matter about which we profess little knowledge, does the Richardsonian plan of successive alcoves, with no shelves beyond reach of the floor, each brightly lighted by a window, and all communicating by convenient doors through the shelving, seem utterly bad in comparison with that adopted in libraries that have not been molested by architects?[3]

In reality, replied the *Library Journal* in its November issue, the "Richardsonian plan of successive alcoves," was not even an invention of the architect, but had been in use in the United States for decades. What then, they asked rhetorically, is really Richardsonian about them? "Is it the 'no shelves beyond the reach from the floor'? His library at Woburn has shelves 9 ft. from the floor, and worse than that, the top shelf in the gallery is 9 ft. high and must be reached by getting on steps in a gallery only 2½ ft. wide, protected by a railing only 2 ft. 7 in. high (knee high?). 'Each brightly lighted from a window'? The alcoves in his Howard Library at New Orleans are ten or twelve feet square and are lighted, we are told, by a window 18 inches wide, pierced through a wall 3 feet thick, and indeed 4 ft. thick if the book-shelves at the side of the window are taken into account. This does not strike us as brilliant illumination."[4]

Librarians who had to use these buildings every day, they continued, were in perfect agreement that this was not the type of arrangement they wanted to see in their libraries. These

7.2
Howard Memorial Library, plan. *Library Journal,* 1888.

7.3
Howard Memorial Library, book room. Courtesy of Shepley Bulfinch Richardson and Abbott, Architects.

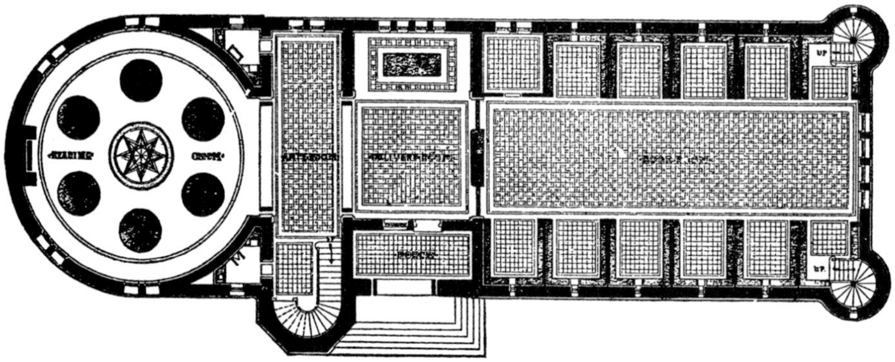

**
*

men and women were tired of having the delivery desk placed in the darkest part of the building, "as is done in several libraries, among others one of Richardson's," and likewise of "bookshelves on the walls by the side windows, where a strong light shines into the eyes and no light on the books." They were also almost unanimous in their condemnation of galleries, "where superheated air dries the bindings to powder," and especially of the type that had no convenient means of access: "Do not, as is done in one of Richardson's libraries, put the only staircase at the end of the book-room farthest from the delivery desk, so that to get a book which is just over one's head one must travel 50 yards." While members of the ALA might disagree on some points, "all librarians are perfectly agreed," they concluded, when they say that "they want plenty of fresh air, plenty of light, warmth in the winter, coolness in the summer, compact storage, easy access to their books: and these things the architects ought to know how to give them. These things they have often not given them, furnishing them instead with a handsome or an imposing or a charming elevation. . . . The fact that different librarians prefer different forms of building, some alcoves, some separate rooms, some stacks, is no excuse for architects if they make bad alcoves, rooms, and stacks."[5]

While it was undeniably true that many American public library buildings failed to meet the requirements of a modern lending institution, not all librarians were ready to place the full blame on the shoulders of Henry Hobson Richardson and the architectural profession. William I. Fletcher, the librarian at Amherst College, for example, adopted a much more conciliatory tone in a letter he directed in October 1888 to the editors of the *American Architect and Buildings News.* "As a librarian of perhaps a little more than ordinary experience with, and observation of, library buildings of different styles," he maintained, "I feel inclined to attempt to explain this appearance of conflict and say a word for peace and coöperation." While "satisfied that no librarian, who could be quoted as authority in the profession, would express approval of the main features of Mr. Richardson's library buildings in so far as the interior is concerned or affected," he noted, these inadequacies had arisen primarily because the architect had not had the opportunity to work directly with librarians, but had been in the employ of trustees and building committees. "I have the best reason for believing that had he lived but a few years longer, he would have come to build libraries no less beautiful and appropriate in general effect than those he left, but far better fitted to meet the wants of the modern public library. For while there may be more or less conflict between 'art and use,' in this department as elsewhere, I do not believe that any man of genius, alive to the real needs of such an institution, will fail in the attempt to meet those necessities, while still responding to the aesthetic requirements peculiar to this class of work. Fortunately examples of success with this problem are multiplying, and many librarians are ready to point to their architects as friends, not 'natural enemies.'"[6]

* * *

As if to underscore this point, Normand S. Patton, partner in the firm of Patton and Fisher and architect of the newly designed Hackley Public Library in Muskegon, Michigan (fig. 7.4), was invited to exhibit plans for this building and to speak before the National Conference of Librarians in 1889, the first architect to be so honored since Henry Van Brunt's appearance a decade earlier. Because it had "been planned with special reference to the ideas advanced by members of this Association," noted Patton at this meeting, "it is a matter of no small interest to the designers to know how far the arrangement meets with your approval."[7] While no record survives of the association's reaction to the architect's presentation that year, the editors of the *Library Journal* did note several years later, in reaction to the opening of the building, that "Mr. Patten [sic], the architect, has the true theory of library construction; he thinks that the shell

7.4
Patton and Fisher, Hackley Public Library, Muskegon, Michigan, 1888–1890. Postcard view.

7.5
George Keller, sketch for the Ansonia Memorial Library, Ansonia, Connecticut, 1891–1892. Reproduced courtesy of the Trustees of the Boston Public Library.

7.6
A. H. Vinal, Calais Free Public Library, Calais, Maine, 1892–1894. Reproduced courtesy of the Trustees of the Boston Public Library.

7.7
J. W. Northrop, Taylor Memorial Library, Milford, Connecticut, 1893–1894. Prints and Photographs Division, Library of Congress.

**
*

should be fashioned to accommodate the animal, not that the animal should be squeezed into the shell."[8] Indeed, both the plan and the freestanding wooden shelving system exhibited by the Hackley building follow closely the notions of William Poole as they had been evolved by the firm for the Hoyt competition in 1886 (figs. 6.5, 6.6).

The heavy romanesque revival "shell" of the Hackley Public Library, on the other hand, owes no small debt to the work of Richardson, a score that Patton acknowledged at the dedication of the building in 1890: "You would not need the inscription over the entrance to tell you it is a library. If no other feature should give the clue, the high windows on the sides of the rear wing would hardly be adapted to any apartment except one for book storage." The tower, likewise, served as "an appropriate expression of" the main staircase, as well "as a beacon to guide [the public] by day or night" to "the prominent and inviting" entrance arch. "In like manner the smaller tower indicates the private stairs and entrance."[9]

By the end of the century this vocabulary had percolated deep into the American consciousness, with dozens of public library buildings paying similar, if not more direct, homage to Richardson's work. In addition to buildings such as McKim, Mead and White's Manchester Memorial Hall (fig. 6.8) or the Dayton Public Library (fig. 6.3), these include subsequent libraries by Shepley, Rutan and Coolidge (fig. 7.9), Van Brunt and Howe (figs. 7.11, 7.12), Patton and Fisher, and many others (figs. 7.5, 7.6, 7.7).[10] If imitation is the highest form of flattery, no greater compliment could be paid to this architect's power of invention. One might argue, in fact, that in his progression from the more discursive forms of Woburn to the economy and power of language exhibited at Quincy, Richardson accomplished for American architecture what Lincoln achieved for American political rhetoric in his Gettysburg Address. Like Lincoln, to borrow Garry Wills's masterful description of the president's speech, Richardson appears to have "sensed, from his own developed artistry, the demands that bring forth classic art—compression, grasp of the essential, balance, ideality, an awareness of the deeper polarities in the situation (life for the city coming from the death of its citizens)."[11] The result was a new, powerful and identifiable building typology. As Henry Van Brunt observed in an obituary that appeared in *Atlantic Monthly* some months after the architect's death, "the general idea of his buildings is patent to all. The beholder is flattered to find that here, at last, is a fine building which he can understand. His eye is not distracted by detail; that is to say, the detail remains subordinated to the general conception, and only presents itself to the mind subsequently as a confirmation of the first impression. He may like or dislike the design, but he does not forget it."[12]

* * *

Even as these new Richardsonian libraries were appearing in the American countryside, however, his style was already being challenged by a renewed taste for the classical, heavily driven by the ideas of men such as Matthew Arnold as well as the growing influence of the Ecole des Beaux-Arts in Paris. Prefigured by the MIT student designs of 1875 (figs. 2.30, 2.31), this new fashion had also been spurred by the example of McKim, Mead and White's new Boston Public Library (1887–1895; fig. 7.8) and the spectacular success of the Columbian Exposition in 1893. Even Shepley, Rutan and Coolidge, whose early fealty to their mentor is manifest at New Orleans and later in Springfield, Ohio (1889–1890), and New London, Connecticut (1889–1891; fig. 7.9), rapidly succumbed to this growing classical movement; a shift in allegiance that is

7.8
McKim, Mead and White, Boston Public Library, Copley Square, 1887–1895. Courtesy of the Print Department, Boston Public Library.

more than apparent in their design for the Field Memorial Library, a building erected by the Chicago merchandising magnate Marshall Field in his home village of Conway, Massachusetts (fig. 7.10), at the turn of the century. The shift away from the Romanesque revival, in fact, was as rapid as its ascension. Of 67 library designs published in a special issue of the *Architectural Review* in 1902, for example, 57 were classically inspired and only five reflected the style of Richardson.[13]

As might more likely be expected, Richardson's alcove book rooms were equally rapidly abandoned for more modern methods of book storage. Van Brunt and Howe, for example, employed stack systems in their public libraries at Dedham and Cambridge, Massachusetts (figs. 7.11, 7.12), and even Shepley, Rutan and Coolidge turned to metal stack book storage in their subsequent libraries at Springfield, New London, and Conway.[14] In 1896, when it was found that Richardson's library in Malden had already outgrown its shelf space, this same firm extended a metal stack room from the rear of this building.[15] During the 1890s and the first decade of this century, as free access to shelves became a commonly accepted policy, Poole's advocacy of freestanding shelving in an attached and expandable book wing, combined with an open approach to planning, became even more common features of the American public library.[16]

By 1905 even Charles Francis Adams, Jr., came to admit the shortcomings of Richardson's work. After a visit to Quincy in May of that year, he wrote to Albert Crane that "after looking over the library building" he had to "acknowledge to a sense of disappointment and a certain degree of self-reproach." While he still greatly admired the exterior of the edifice, the interior arrangement he declared a "failure." "It is now twenty-four years since the library was built," he concluded, "and it was designed during the early days of construction of this character, when the requirements of a public library were not understood." At a time when the collection had grown from 12,000 to 26,000 volumes, Adams was particularly critical of the architect's alcove system of shelving, "which now no architect or builder would adopt." It was "dark, inconvenient and supplies a minimum of shelf room"; even more seriously, it did not allow for a convenient means of expansion. Although he confessed to being "very largely responsible for what was done . . . for one thing," Adams wrote, "I was not responsible; that is, for the wretchedly inadequate lighting. I well remember telling Mr. Richardson that I thought the supply of light was inadequate. He over-ruled me, insisting that, if anything, there was too much light. Architect's are apt to be wrong on this head. The result is that, whereas the interior of a library should be bright and cheerful, in that case it is murky and dismal."[17]

7.9
*Opposite:* Shepley, Rutan and Coolidge, New London Public Library, New London, Connecticut, 1889–1891. Author.

7.10
Shepley, Rutan and Coolidge, Field Memorial Library, Conway, Massachusetts, 1900–1901. Prints and Photographs Division, Library of Congress.

Two years later, in 1907, Crane, at Adams's behest, donated $64,000 to the Quincy Public Library for the construction of a metal stack book wing. This was designed by Richardson's former clerk of the works, William Martin Aiken. Upon receipt of the money for this addition Adams again wrote to Crane, thanking him for his long-standing patronage of this institution, especially this last gift, with which he was "particularly gratified." In spite of his reservations concerning the interior arrangement of the building and his growing disenchantment with his native village, noted Adams, he still viewed Richardson's library and his own involvement in its conception with considerable pride. "When I go to Quincy," he confessed, "the library, with the work you have done there, is about the only satisfactory feature of the place. . . . Every time I go there that strikes me as a species of oasis in a somewhat dreary desert."[18]

7.11
Van Brunt and Howe, Dedham Public Library, Dedham, Massachusetts, 1886. Prints and Photographs Division, Library of Congress.

7.12
Van Brunt and Howe, Rindge Memorial Library, Cambridge, Massachusetts, 1888–1889. Prints and Photographs Division, Library of Congress.

# NOTES

* *
*

The following abbreviations have been used in the notes:

*AABN* — *American Architect and Building News*

FPLM — Free Public Library Commission of Massachusetts, *The Free Public Libraries of Massachusetts: Ninth Report of the Free Public Library Commission of Massachusetts,* Henry S. Nourse, comp. (Boston, 1899)

HPL — Hoyt Public Library, Saginaw, Michigan

*JSAH* — *Journal of the Society of Architectural Historians*

*LJ* — *Library Journal*

Ruskin — *The Works of John Ruskin,* ed. E. T. Cook and Alexander Wedderburn, 39 vols. (London, 1903–1912)

## PREFACE

1. Neil Harris, "Cultural Institutions and American Modernization," *Journal of Library History* 16 (1981): 43.

2. Compare, for example the "affectionate mood" of Dr. Wentworth's haphazardly arranged books with those in Parson Buell's study, which in spite of the formality of its order was still "picturesque." Henry Ward Beecher, *Norwood; or, Village Life in New England* (New York, 1868), 71, 245–246. See also William J. Gilmore, *Reading Becomes a Necessity of Life: Material and Cultural Life in Rural New England, 1780–1835* (Knoxville, Tenn., 1989); and Ann Douglas, *The Feminization of American Culture* (New York, 1977).

## INTRODUCTION

1. Richardson to Olmsted, 26 November and 15 December 1876, "Henry Hobson Richardson Collection," Shepley Bulfinch Richardson and Abbott, Reel 643, Archives of American Art, Smithsonian Institution. See also James F. O'Gorman, *H. H. Richardson and His Office: Selected Drawings* (Boston, 1974), 156. A number of authors have discussed this period; see, for example, Mariana Griswold (Mrs. Schuyler) Van Rensselaer, *Henry Hobson Richardson and His Works* (Boston, 1888), 67–86; Henry-Russell Hitchcock, *The Architecture of H. H. Richardson and His Times* (New York, 1936; reprint, Cambridge, Mass., 1966), 109–73; and James F. O'Gorman, *H. H. Richardson: Architectural Forms for an American Society* (Chicago, 1987), 35–45. For Richardson's recently completed projects and the New York State Capitol, see Jeffrey Karl Ochsner, *H. H. Richardson: Complete Architectural Works* (Cambridge, Mass., 1982), 133–167.

2. O'Gorman, *Drawings,* 156–159; and Ochsner, *Richardson,* 174–179.

3. "Accepted Design for the Town Library, Woburn, Mass.," *AABN* 2 (3 March 1877); and Van Rensselaer, *Richardson,* 67–68; Hitchcock, *Richardson,* 172; and O'Gorman, *Architectural Forms,* 44–47. O'Gorman is the least critical, but views the Woburn building as the first in a design evolution that culminated at Quincy.

4. *Harper's Weekly* 27 (1883): 251. For the other libraries see Ochsner, *Richardson,* 183–187, 226–231, 313–317.

5. For the sources and early history of the public library movement in the United States see Jesse H. Shera, *Foundations of the Public Library* (Chicago, 1949); Sidney Ditzion, *Arsenals of a Democratic Culture: A Social History of the American Library Movement in New England and the Middle States, 1850–1900* (Chicago, 1947); Samuel S. Green, *The Public Library Movement in the United States, 1852–1893* (Boston, 1913); and Rosemary Ruhig Dumont, *Reform and Reaction: The Big City Public Library in American Life* (Westport, Conn., 1977). For earlier accounts of the beginning of this movement see Joseph Leroy Harrison, "The Public Library Movement in the United States," *New England Magazine,* n.s. 10 (1894): 709–722; and Henry Nourse, "The Public Libraries of Massachusetts," *New England Magazine,* n.s. 5 (1891–1892): 139–159.

6. *Report of the Trustees of the Public Library of the City of Boston, July, 1852,* as quoted in Walter Muir Whitehill, *Boston Public Library: A Centennial History* (Cambridge, Mass., 1956), 32. See also Dee Garrison, *Apostles of Culture: The Public Librarian and American Society, 1876–1920* (New York, 1979), 36–63.

7. Quoted in Michael B. Katz, *The Irony of Early School Reform: Educational Innovation in Mid-Nineteenth Century Massachusetts* (Cambridge, Mass., 1968), 41.

8. Ibid., 124.

9. Whitehill, *Boston Public Library,* 22–23. See also Ditzion, *Arsenals,* 53–54; and John Y. Cole, "Storehouses and Workshops: American Libraries and the Uses of Knowledge," in *The Organization of Knowledge in Modern America, 1860–1920,* ed. Alexandra Oleson and John Voss (Baltimore, 1976), 365–366. Although Theodore Parker called Ticknor "the arch devil of the aristocracy," he also was Smith Professor of Modern Languages at Harvard (1819–1835) and authored a massive treatise on Spanish literature. See Robert F. Dalzell, Jr., *Enterprising Elite: Boston Associates and the World They Made* (Cambridge, Mass., 1987), 152–155.

10. Whitehill, *Boston Public Library,* 27–30. For the Astor Library see Ditzion, *Arsenals,* 142–147; Elizabeth Stone, *American Library Development 1600–1899* (New York, 1977), 150–151; Harry Lydenberg, *History of the New York Public Library* (New York, 1923), 1–25; and Frederick K. Saunders, "The Astor Library," *New England Magazine,* n.s. 2 (1890–1891): 48–59.

11. Horace G. Wadlin, *The Public Library of the City of Boston: A History* (Boston, 1911), 28; and Michael H. Harris, "The Purpose of the American Public Library: A Revisionist Interpretation of History," *LJ* 98 (15 September 1973): 2510–11. Between 1840 and 1850 the Irish-born population of Boston alone had grown from fewer than 4,000 to 35,000, or more than one quarter of the city's inhabitants. Dalzell, *Enterprising Elite,* 140; Oscar Hamlin, *Boston's Immigrants* (Cambridge, Mass., 1941), passim.

12. Whitehill, *Boston Public Library,* 29, 32.

13. Shera, *Foundations,* 175. For the early years of the Boston Public Library, ibid., 170–181; and Whitehill, *Boston Public Library,* 1–42.

14. Shera, *Foundations,* table 19 and pp. 185–188.

15. Ibid., 189–199; Harrison, "Public Library Movement," 712–713; Nourse, "Libraries of Massachusetts," 35–59; and Haynes McMullen, "Prevalence of Libraries in the Northeastern States before 1876," *Journal of Library History* 22 (1987): 321–326.

16. "Hints upon Library Buildings," *Norton's Literary Gazette and Publishers' Circular* 3 (15 January 1853): 1.

17. FPLM, 421–423; Christina M. DiNapoli, *Woburn Public Library 1856, 1879–1979* (Woburn, Mass., 1979), 4–5; and Woburn Public Library, *Report of the Library Committee of the Town of Woburn, March 1, 1874* (Woburn, Mass., 1874), 6.

18. L. Draper Hill, Jr., *The Crane Library* (Quincy, Mass., 1962), 11–14; and "Report of the Committee on the Adams Academy and Public Library May 2, 1871," in *Records of the Proceedings of the Trustees of the Thomas Crane Public Library and the Quincy Public Library: May 11, 1871–June 2, 1886* (handwritten copy in the Crane Public Library). Charles Francis Adams, Jr., a trustee of both the library and the Adams Academy, reported on the need for more space for the school as early as July 1873. See the minutes for the meetings of 16 July 1873, 1 April 1874, and 30 March 1874. For the Adams Academy see William John Hennessey, "The Architectural Works of Henry Van Brunt," Ph.D. diss., Columbia University, 1979, 110–111; and "The Adams Academy, Quincy, Mass.," *AABN* 1 (30 December 1876): 421.

19. Malden Public Library, *Fourth Annual Report of the Trustees of the Malden Public Library for the Year Ending December 31, 1881* (Boston, 1882), 2.

20. Malden Public Library, *Fifth Annual Report of the Trustees of the Malden Public Library for the Year Ending December 31, 1882* (Cambridge, Mass., 1883), 10.

21. FPLM, 421–423; William R. Cutter, "A Model Village Library," *New England Magazine,* n.s. 1 (1889–1890): 617–625; and DiNapoli, *Woburn Public Library,* 4–5. See also O'Gorman, *Drawings,* 156–159; and Ochsner, *Richardson,* 174–179. For Jonathan Winn's obituary see *Woburn Advertiser,* 19 December 1873.

22. Woburn Public Library, *Report of the Library Committee, 1874,* 4–6.

23. Woburn Public Library, *Report of the Library Committee of the Town of Woburn, March 1, 1875* (Woburn, Mass., 1875), 54. For the will of Charles Bowers Winn see the *Woburn Journal,* 25 December 1875.



**
*

24. Quincy Public Library, *Annual Report of the Public Library of Quincy for 1878* (Boston, 1879), 5; and Hill, *Crane Library,* 11–14.

25. Quincy Public Library, *Annual Report for 1878,* 6.

26. City of Boston, *A Memorial of Joshua Bates from the City of Boston* (Boston, 1865), 30; Whitehill, *Boston Public Library,* 26–38; Wadlin, *Public Library of the City of Boston,* 41–68; and Shera, *Foundations,* 170–181.

27. Whitehill, *Boston Public Library,* 66; and *Memorial of Joshua Bates,* 40.

28. Phebe A. Hanaford, *The Life of George Peabody* (Boston, 1870), 80–82. Of the $20,000 that Peabody initially offered to the community, he directed that a sum "not exceeding seven thousand dollars" should be allocated for the erection of "a suitable building for the use of this lyceum." He soon added $10,000 to this offer, making $17,000 available for a building and site, $3,000 for books, and $10,000 for investment in a permanent fund. The cornerstone of the Peabody Institute was laid in August 1853, and it was dedicated on 29 September of the following year. The architect of this building is unknown. For the history and a description of the building, which has been heavily remodeled inside, see ibid., 80–101, and FPLM, 289–291; also Franklin Parker, *George Peabody: A Biography* (Nashville, 1971), 40–41, 57–60.

29. Hanaford, *Peabody,* passim; and FPLM, 93–95, 136–138.

30. This building, which was designed by the Syracuse firm of Hughs and Rhodes, appears to have opened in July 1857. See "History," in *Minutes of the Trustees of the Oswego City Library, 19 September 1892.* The building was restored in 1979.

31. FPLM, 38–39, 250–253, 347–348, 352; New Bedford Free Public Library, *Proceedings on the Occasion of the Laying of the Corner-Stone of the Library Edifice for the Free Public Library of the City of New Bedford: August 28, 1856* (New Bedford, Mass., 1856), and *Exercises at the Opening of the New Library Building of the Free Public Library* (New Bedford, Mass., 1910); Paul Sherman, "The First Hundred Years: A History of the Cornell Public Library, Ithaca, New York and the Cornell Library Association 1864–1964" (typescript in the Tompkins County Public Library, Ithaca, New York, [1964?]), 9–11; Cornell Library Association, *Dedication of the Cornell Library Building, Ithaca, New York, December 20, 1866* (Ithaca, N.Y., 1867); and Morrisson-Reeves Library, *The Seventy-Fifth Anniversary of the Founding of the Morrisson-Reeves Library: 1864–1939* (Richmond, Ind., 1939). For philanthropy in general during this period see Robert H. Bremner, *The Public Good: Philanthropy and Welfare in the Civil War Era* (New York, 1980).

32. These figures compare to approximately $100,000 in private moneys that had been expended on nine public library buildings constructed between 1850 and 1865. These ranged in cost from $2,000 for the Cushman Library in Bernardston, Massachusetts, to almost $60,000 for the Cornell Library in Ithaca, New York. The 1865–1875 figures exclude the Lennox Library in New York (1869–1876) the Cincinnati Public Library (1868–1874), which cost more than $500,000 and $300,000 respectively.

33. For 1876, for example, I count 43 public library buildings among the 457 institutions reported by McMullen in "Prevalence of Libraries," 321–326.

34. Kenneth A. Breisch, "Small Public Libraries in America 1850–1890: The Invention of a Building Type," Ph.D. diss, University of Michigan, 1982, passim; and Garrison, *Apostles,* 3–6.

35. Abigail A. Van Slyck, "Free to All: Carnegie Libraries and the Transformation of American Culture, 1886–1917," Ph.D. diss., University of California at Berkeley, 1989; and George Bobinski, *Carnegie Libraries: Their History and Impact on American Public Library Development* (Chicago, 1969).

36. O'Gorman, *Drawings,* 172.

37. Garrison, *Apostles,* 62.

38. Kenneth L. Kusmer, "The Social History of Cultural Institutions: The Upper-Class Connection," *Journal of Interdisciplinary History* 10 (Summer 1979): 146.

39. David Van Zanten, *Designing Paris: The Architecture of Duban, Labrouste, Duc, and Vaudoyer* (Cambridge, Mass., 1987), 225.

40. O'Gorman, *Architectural Forms,* 53. For a slight revision of Olmsted's vision of the American landscape see also James F. O'Gorman, *Three American Architects: Richardson, Sullivan, and Wright, 1865–1915* (Chicago, 1991), 33–34.

41. Kenneth A. Breisch, "William Frederick Poole and Modern Library Architecture," *Modern Architecture in America: Visions and Revisions,* ed. R. G. Wilson and S. K. Robinson (Ames, Iowa, 1990), 52–72.

## CHAPTER ONE

1. Charles Francis Adams, Jr., *Three Episodes of Massachusetts History,* 2 vols. (Boston, 1893), 2: 922–930, 946–947. For Adams see Edward C. Kirkland, *Charles Francis Adams, Jr., 1835–1915: The Patrician at Bay* (Cambridge, Mass., 1965); and Charles Francis Adams, Jr., *Autobiography* (Boston, 1916). The literature on industrialization, culture, and philanthropy in the late nineteenth century is vast. A sampling on which I have relied most heavily includes Howard Mumford Jones, *The Age of Energy: Varieties of American Experience, 1865–1915* (New York, 1970); George M. Frederickson, *The Inner Civil War: Northern Intellectuals and the Crisis of Union* (New York, 1965); Paul Boyer, *Urban Masses and Moral Order in America: 1820–1920* (Cambridge, Mass., 1978); T. J. Jackson Lears, *No Place for Grace: Antimodernism and the Transformation of American Culture, 1880–1920* (Chicago, 1991); Helen Lefkowitz Horowitz, *Culture and the City; Cultural Philanthropy in Chicago from the 1880s to 1917* (Lexington, Ken., 1976); Lawrence Levine, *Highbrow/Lowbrow: The Emergence of Cultural Hierarchy in America* (Cambridge, Mass., 1988); Ann Douglas, *The Feminization of American Culture* (New York, 1977); and Nell Irvin Painter, *Standing at Armageddon: The United States 1877–1919* (New York, 1987).

2. Adams, *Three Episodes,* 2: 984–986. In reality, of a population of 12,145 (1885), there were 1,565 Irish and 142 French Canadians living in Quincy. Carroll D. Wright, *The Census of Massachusetts, 1885,* 2 vols. (Boston, 1887), 1: 26–27, 302–305.

3. Adams, *Three Episodes,* 2: 928; Kirkland, *Adams,* 155–156.

4. Adams, *Three Episodes,* 2: 986, 948.

5. Letter from Charles Francis Adams, Jr., to Albert Crane, 22 July 1907, Albert Crane Collection, Massachusetts Historical Society. Reproduced with permission of the Massachusetts Historical Society. See also Kirkland, *Adams,* 150–152. For another childhood report, see Henry Adams, *The Education of Henry Adams: An Autobiography* (Boston, 1918), 3–22.

6. *Woburn: An Historical and Descriptive Sketch of the Town, with an Outline of Its Industrial Interests* (Woburn, Mass., 1885), 29.

7. For the leather and shoe industry in Woburn, see *Woburn Advertiser,* 30 December 1875; *Woburn: An Historical and Descriptive Sketch,* 33; and Wright, *Census of Massachusetts,* 2: 24–25, 282–283.

8. George M. Champney, "Diary of George M. Champney, 1876–1877," 16 August 1876, typescript copy in the Woburn Public Library. I would like to thank Mr. Edwin Champney for permission to reproduced material from this diary. See also *Woburn Advertiser,* 17 August 1876; and *Woburn Journal,* 19 August 1876.

9. *Malden Mirror,* 1 October 1885; and *Malden City Press,* 1 October 1885, 7. The population of Malden continued to grow rapidly. By 1886, it had reached 17,236. See *Malden, Maplewood, Wakefield, Reading, Stoneham, Medford and West Medford: Their Representative Business Men and Points of Interest* (New York, 1893), 8. For Elisha S. Converse see *The National Cyclopedia of American Biography* (New York, 1909), 10: 120; City of Malden, *In Memory of Elisha Slade Converse* (Malden, 1905); and *Malden Mirror,* 11 June 1904. See also Deloraine P. Corey, "Two and a Half Centuries in Malden," *New England Magazine,* n.s. 20 (1899): 357–378; B. G. Underwood, "Manufacture of Rubber Shoes," *Scientific American* 67 (10 December 1892): 367, 374–375; and Wright, *Census of Massachusetts,* 2: 20–21, 246–249.

10. City of Malden, *Converse,* 8.

11. "The incorporation of Woburn as a city was looked upon as an event of the near future" as early as 1872, according to D. Hamilton Hurd, comp., *History of Middlesex County, Massachusetts,* 3 vols. (Philadelphia, 1890), 1: 365–366.

12. These factories had been established in North Easton by their father, Oliver Ames, Sr., in 1803. In 1844, the management of this shop was turned over to Oliver, Jr., and his brother Oakes and reorganized as Oliver Ames and Sons. See *The National Cyclopedia of American Biography* (New York, 1917), 14: 201–202; *Dictionary of American Biography,* ed. Allen Johnson (New York, 1964), 1: 251–254; Charles Edgar Ames, *Pioneering the Union Pacific: A Reappraisal of the Builders of the Railroad* (New York, 1969), 62–76; George M. Miller, "The Development of an Industrial Village in the Nineteenth Century: North Easton, Massachusetts" (typescript pamphlet published by the Easton Historical Society, North Easton, Mass., 1977), 45–50; "A Day with the Shovel-Makers," *Atlantic Monthly* 26 (September 1870), 367–374; and Wright, *Census of Massachusetts,* 1: 84–85.

13. Ronald Story, *The Forging of an Aristocracy: Harvard and the Boston Upper Class, 1800–1870* (Middletown, Conn., 1980), 180–181.

14. *Quincy Daily Ledger,* 3 May 1895; and *Malden Mirror,* 11 June 1904.

15. Wage estimates for shoe and leather workers are based on those in Lynn, Massachusetts, during the same period. See Alan Dawley, *Class and Community: The Industrial Revolution in Lynn,* Harvard Studies in Urban History (Cambridge, Mass., 1976), 156–159; and Henry F. Bedford, ed. and intro., *Their Lives and Numbers: The Condition of Working People in Massachusetts, 1870–1900* (Ithaca, N.Y., 1995), [48–75]. In 1886, the Knights of Labor in Woburn demanded wage hikes of up to $16 per week for mill stuffers and to between $10 to $12 per week for other leather workers, as well as a reduction of working hours from 60 per week to 59. *Woburn Advertiser,* 11 March 1886.

16. See the annual budgets in *Records of the Proceedings of the Trustees of the Thomas Crane Public Library and the Quincy Public Library: May 11, 1871–June 2, 1886;* and Ames Free Library of Easton, Inc., *The First Century: A Centennial History of the Ames Free Library of Easton, Inc., 1883–1983* (North Easton, Mass., [1983]), [5]. By this date the Ames family was one of the wealthiest in New England.

17. Robert V. Bruce, *1877: Year of Violence* (Indianapolis, 1959); Dawley, *Class and Community,* 184–193; John R. Commons et al., *History of Labour in the United States,* 2 vols. (New York, 1936), 2: 185–189; Boyer, *Urban Masses,* 121–131; and Painter, *Armageddon,* 15–31.

18. *Woburn Journal,* 23 December 1898; *Woburn News,* 22 January 1909; *Eighth Annual Report of the Directors of the Boston and Albany Railroad Co. to the Stockholders, January, 1876* (Springfield, 1876); and *Twenty-Second Report of the Directors of the Boston and Albany Railroad Co. to the Stockholders, January, 1889* (Boston, 1889). In his article on Richardson's later commissions for this railroad, Ochsner points to the influence of two other directors, John Sprague Sargent and Charles Augustus Rumrill, in obtaining these. Cummings and Hayden should probably be added to this list. See Jeffrey Karl Ochsner, "Architecture for the Boston and Albany Railroad: 1881–1894," *JSAH* 47 (1988): 109–131.

19. Adams, who had been appointed to the Massachusetts Railroad Commission in 1869, reacted to the 1877 strike in a predictably genteel manner by calling for "an enlightened public opinion" to avoid such stoppages in the future. Kirkland, *Adams,* 54–55; C. F. Adams, *Autobiography,* 174–175; and Bruce, *Year of Violence,* 35–37. At the time of his death in 1877, Oliver Ames II controlled some 10 percent of the Union Pacific stock, an interest then inherited by his son Frederick Lothrop Ames. Adams himself, following nearly a decade of speculation in railroads in Michigan and the West, began to invest in Union Pacific stock during the late 1870s, after serving for one year as a government director of the line. In 1884 he assumed its presidency, a position he held until forced to resign in 1890. Arthur M. Johnson and Barry E. Supple, *Boston Capitalists and Western Railroads: A Study in the Nineteenth-Century Railroad Investment Process,* Harvard Studies in Business History XXIII (Cambridge, Mass., 1967), 203–221, 251–261; and Kirkland, *Adams,* 67–129. For Oliver Ames II's principal positions on the boards of other western railroads at the time of his death, see C. E. Ames, *Union Pacific,* 529–530.

20. James W. Scoville, "Address," *A Brief History of the Organization, Building and Dedication of Scoville Institute, Oak Park, Cook County, Illinois* (Chicago, 1888), 20. See also Dee Garrison, *Apostles of Culture: The Public Librarian and American Society, 1876–1920* (New York, 1979), 42–50; Neil Harris, "Cultural Institutions and American Modernization," *Journal of Library History* 16 (1981): 37; and Lears, *No Place for Grace,* 31–32. For the impact of the 1877 strike on the building of armories, see Robert M. Fogelson, *America's Armories: Architecture, Society, and Public Order* (Cambridge, Mass., 1989), 13–47; and Painter, *Armageddon,* 22. For an interesting parallel reaction of Richardson and others of his clients, John and Frances Glessner, to the railroad strike and the later Haymarket riots in Chicago, see Thomas C. Hubka, "H. H. Richardson's Glessner House: A Garden in the Machine," *Winterthur Portfolio* 24 (1989): 221–222.

21. John Hay, *The Bread-Winners: A Social Study* (New York, 1883). Although he never formed his own militia in Quincy, there may be some parallel here to Charles Francis Adams, Jr., who was also a calvary officer during the war. Hay was a very close friend of the Adams family, especially Charles's brother Henry, with whom he commissioned a house in Washington, D.C., from Richardson in 1884. Jeffrey Karl Ochsner, *H. H. Richardson: Complete Architectural Works* (Cambridge, Mass., 1982), 344–349; and Ernst Scheyer, *The Circle of Henry Adams: Art and Artists* (Detroit, 1970), 164–171.

22. See, for example, *Life, Character, and Career of Edward W. Green, Postmaster of Malden: The Murderer of Frank Converse* (Boston, 1864); *Middlesex Journal,* 10 December 1863; or as late as 1940, a fictionalized version by Lowell Ames Norris, "Clue of the Cripple's Boot," in *Master Detective* (23 December 1940):

40–45, 79–80. See also *Encyclopedia of World Crime, Criminal Justice, Criminology, and Law Enforcement,* 3 vols. (Wilmette, Ill., 1990), 3: 1373.

23. *Malden City Press,* 1 October 1885, 8.

24. Charles Francis Adams, Jr., "The Public Library and the Public Schools," in *The Public Library and the Common Schools: Three Papers on Educational Reform* (Boston, 1879), 5, 15. Everett had married Charlotte Brooks, sister of Adams's mother.

25. Adams worked closely with educational reformer Francis W. Parker; in 1880 he was appointed to the State Board of Education. Kirkland, *Adams,* 144–152; Garrison, *Apostles,* 50–60; and Michael B. Katz, *Class, Bureaucracy and Schools: The Illusion of Educational Change in America* (New York, 1971), 75–85.

26. Adams, "Fiction in Public Libraries and Educational Catalogues," in *The Public Library and the Common Schools: Three Papers on Educational Reform* (Boston, 1879), 5, 21.

27. Ames Free Library, *First Century,* [1–2]; Miller, "Industrial Village," 52–57; and Larry J. Homolka, "Henry Hobson Richardson and the 'Ames Memorial Buildings,'" Ph.D. diss., Harvard University, 1976, 41–48.

28. Woburn Public Library, *Report of the Library Committee of the Town of Woburn, March 1, 1874* (Woburn, Mass., 1874), 5.

29. Malden Public Library, *Fourth Annual Report of the Trustees of the Malden Public Library for the Year Ending December 31, 1881* (Boston, 1882), 8. This passage, as the Malden report notes, was taken from the twenty-ninth annual report of the Boston Public Library.

30. Malden Public Library, *Fifth Annual Report of the Trustees of the Malden Public Library for the Year Ending December 31, 1882* (Cambridge, Mass., 1883), 7–8; and *Malden City Press,* 1 October 1885, 8.

31. Matthew Arnold, *Culture and Anarchy,* ed. Samuel Lipman (London, 1869; New Haven, 1994), 5, 55.

32. Horowitz, *Culture and the City,* 1–26; Michael W. Brooks, "New England Gothic: Charles Eliot Norton, Charles H. Moore, and Henry Adams," in *The Architectural Historian in America,* ed. E. B. MacDougall (Hanover, N.H., 1990), 113–116; and Lears, *No Place for Grace,* 243–247.

33. Likewise at Woburn, "the fiction, . . . under [the board's] supervision, [was] read by a committee of intelligent persons, before it [was] added to the library, to avoid the admission of vicious, unworthy, and uninteresting books." See *Woburn News,* 27 October 1900, 4. Also Malden Public Library, *Fourth Annual Report,* 8; and *Fifth Annual Report,* 7. The question of what types of books might be appropriate in a public library and how they were to function had a long history and would continue to be debated well into the twentieth century. See Garrison, *Apostles,* 60–101; John Y. Cole, "Storehouses and Workshops: American Libraries and the Uses of Knowledge," in *The Organization of Knowledge in Modern America, 1860–1920,* ed. Alexandra Oleson and John Voss (Baltimore, 1976), 368–369; and Michael Harris, "The Purpose of the American Public Library: A Revisionist Interpretation of History," *LJ* 98 (15 September 1973): 2511.

34. Champney, "Diary," 8 October 1876.

35. *Woburn Advertiser,* 23 January 1879. This may very well have been by Champney as well, a man who contributed frequently to this paper.

36. Malden Public Library, *Tenth Annual Report of the Trustees of the Malden Public Library for the Year*

*Ending December 31, 1887* (Boston, 1888), 9. For a description of the collection see *Malden City Press,* 1 October 1885, 2–3.

37. Malden Public Library, *Twenty-Sixth Annual Report of the Trustees of the Malden Public Library for the Year Ending December 31, 1903* (Boston, 1904), 12–13; and *Twenty-Seventh Annual Report of the Trustees of the Malden Public Library for the Year Ending December 31, 1904* (Boston, 1905), 11–12. Recently the Millet and some of the other paintings acquired with this fund were auctioned to raise money for a new building campaign. See *New York Times,* 20 March 1992, B:9.

38. Charles Francis Adams, Jr., Elisha Converse, Frederick Lothrop Ames, and Edward D. Hayden were influential men who, with the exception of Adams, all held office as members of the Republican party during this period: F. L. Ames as a member of the State Senate in 1872–1873; Converse in the Massachusetts House of Representatives in 1878 and 1879 and the State Senate the following two years; and Hayden as a member of the Massachusetts House of Representatives in 1881 and 1882 and the United States Congress between 1885 and 1889. See "Elisha S. Converse," *National Cyclopedia,* 10:120; "Frederick Lothrop Ames," *Dictionary of American Biography,* 1: 246–247; and "Edward Daniel Hayden," in John C. Rand, comp., *One of a Thousand: A Series of Biographical Sketches of One Thousand Representative Men Resident in the Commonwealth of Massachusetts: A.D. 1888–89* (Boston, 1890), 293–294; *New York Times,* 16 November 1908, 9: 5. This was the typical profile of a library trustee at the time. See Harris, "Purpose of the American Public Library," 2511; and Garrison, *Apostles,* 50.

39. Geoffrey Blodgett, "Landscape Design as Conservative Reform," in Bruce Kelly et al., *Art of the Olmsted Landscape* (New York, 1981), 111.

40. Robert F. Dalzell, Jr., *Enterprising Elite: The Boston Associates and the World They Made* (Cambridge, Mass., 1987), 160.

41. *Malden Mirror,* 18 July 1885; City of Malden, *Converse,* 5–6; and A Citizen of Malden, "The Malden Muddle: Looking a Gift Horse in the Mouth," *LJ* 10 (1885): 155–156. As one correspondent complained, this battle appears to have pitted the town's Democrats against its Republicans. According to this person, all nine of the library's trustees were Republicans, and the library's new Charter, under which this board was to operate, had passed the state legislature "along strict party lines." *Malden City Press,* 11 July 1885, 1.

42. Deloraine P. Corey served as president for 32 years, from 1878 until his own death in 1910. Of the trustees in place in 1885, seven of nine were still on the board in 1900. See Malden Public Library, *Annual Reports* for the years 1878–1910.

43. Kirkland, *Adams,* 150–151. For his interest in the public schools see 144–148.

44. See the letters from Charles Francis Adams, Jr., to Albert Crane in the Albert Crane Correspondence, Massachusetts Historical Society, dated 7 December 1891, 30 July 1903, 27 June 1904, and 22 July 1907.

45. Hayden had been married to Charles Bowers Winn's sister Marcia Ann, who died in 1862, and Cummings to Jonathan B. Winn's sister Nancy. See Christina M. DiNapoli, *Woburn Public Library 1856, 1879–1979* (Woburn, Mass., 1979), 4; Edward D. Hayden's obituary, *New York Times,* 16 November 1908, 9: 5. For Cummings, see Hurd, *Middlesex County,* 455–456; *Woburn Journal,* 23 December 1898; and *Woburn News,* 24 December 1898.



**
*

46. *Boston Evening Transcript,* 16 November 1908, 2.

47. A further conflict of interest was created when Oliver Ames II specified in his will that $15,000 of his bequest be invested as a permanent library fund in stock of the Old Colony Railroad Company, an enterprise otherwise entirely owned by his heirs and their cousins. William L. Chaffin, *History of the Town of Easton, Massachusetts* (Cambridge, Mass., 1886), 378–379.

48. *Address of Charles Francis Adams, Jr. and Proceedings at the Dedication of the Crane Memorial Hall at Quincy, Mass., May 30, 1882* (Cambridge, Mass., 1883), 1–5.

49. E. Digby Baltzell, *The Protestant Establishment: Aristocracy and Caste in America* (New York, 1964), 109–121. For another example, see David Ames, *Some Notes on the Ames Family of Easton: Their Ancestry and Their Varied Interests* [Easton, Mass., 1970].

50. *Henry Crane of Milton, Mass., 1654, and Some of His Descendents,* compiled for Mr. Albert Crane by Emily W. Leavitt (New York, 1893), 26. According to the Woburn librarian William R. Cutter, the Winn family had likewise "been promient in the annals of the town from the time of its first settlement, and the first-born child recorded in Woburn was Increase Winn, born 5 December 1641." See William R. Cutter, "A Model Village Library," *New England Magazine,* n.s. 1 (1889–1890): 618.

51. *Malden City Press,* 1 October 1885, 8.

52. Champney, "Diary," 16 August 1876; *Woburn Advertiser,* 17 August 1876; and *Woburn Journal,* 19 August 1876.

53. *Woburn Advertiser,* 6 January 1881; Hurd, *Middlesex County,* 1: 408–409; and Rodris Roth, "The New England, or 'Olde Tyme,' Kitchen Exhibit at Nineteenth-Century Fairs," in *The Colonial Revival in America,* ed. Alan Axelrod (New York, 1985), 173–178. Charles B. Winn's uncle John Cummings, whose natural history collection was placed in the Woburn library, had himself been a judge at the Centennial Exposition. See Hurd, *Middlesex County,* 455–456.

54. William B. Rhoads, "The Colonial Revival and the Americanization of Immigrants," in *The Colonial Revival in America,* 341–361; and Brenda K. Shelton, *Reformers in Search of Yesterday: Buffalo in the 1890s* (Albany, N.Y., 1976).

55. *Records of the Proceedings of the Trustees of the Thomas Crane Public Library and the Quincy Public Library: May 11, 1871–June 2, 1886,* 22 May 1882; and *Records of the Proceedings of the Trustees of the Thomas Crane Public Library and the Quincy Public Library: June 7, 1886–June 7, 1900,* 1 December 1886 and 25 November 1893.

56. *Woburn News,* 22 January 1909.

57. *Address of Charles Francis Adams, Jr.,* 6.

58. Cutter, "Model Village Library," 618; and C. E. Ames, *Union Pacific,* 65.

59. *Presentation of the Bust of Hon. Elisha Slade Converse. Exercises at the Converse Memorial Building, Malden, Monday, May 26, 1890* (Malden, Mass., 1890), 14.

60. Andrew Carnegie, "Wealth," *North American Review* 48 (1889): 663. See also Carnegie, "Best Fields for Philanthropy," *North American Review* 48 (1889): 682–698; J. F. Wall, *Andrew Carnegie* (New York, 1970), 805–827; and Abigail A. Van Slyck, "'The Utmost Amount of Effectiv (sic) Accommodation': Andrew Carnegie and the Reform of the American Library," *JSAH* 50 (1991): 364–365.

61. At the same time, acknowledged Choate, it was also true that the educated worker often earned more money and rose "faster" and "higher, from the lower to the more advanced positions of his employment, than the uneducated operative." *Proceedings at the Reception and Dinner in Honor of George Peabody, Esq., of London, by the Citizens of the Old Town of Danvers, October 9, 1856* (Boston, 1856), 179.

62. *Life, Character, and Career of Edward W. Green,* 11. For a contemporary reference to Elisha's own temperance crusading in Malden, see *Malden Mirror,* 19 April 1884. See also Sidney Ditzion, *Arsenals of a Democratic Culture: A Social History of the American Library Movement in New England and the Middle States, 1850–1900* (Chicago, 1947), 104–107; Adams, *Three Episodes,* 2: 975–979; Ames Free Library, *First Century,* [2]; and Hurd, *Middlesex County,* 529.

63. From an address given by Carnegie at the opening of the public library in Jedburgh, Scotland, on 4 October 1894. Quoted in Wall, *Carnegie,* 821. See also Lears, *No Place for Grace,* 20–23.

64. Van Slyck, "'Utmost Amount of Effectiv (sic) Accommodation,'" 369. For Carnegie libraries in general, see Abigail A. Van Slyck, "Free to All: Carnegie Libraries and the Transformation of American Culture, 1886–1917," Ph.D. diss., University of California at Berkeley, 1989; and George Bobinski, *Carnegie Libraries: Their History and Impact on American Public Library Development* (Chicago, 1969).

65. Levine, *Highbrow/Lowbrow,* 206; and Boston Athenaeum, *The Athenaeum Centenary: The Influence and History of the Boston Athenaeum from 1807 to 1907* (Boston, 1907), 132, 136, 159, 167. This was a debate played out in relation to the foundation of the Boston Public Library when it was suggested by George Ticknor that the Boston Athenaeum merge its collections with the new public library, a suggestion soundly rejected by the proprietors of the Athenaeum. See Dalzell, *Enterprising Elite,* 152–156; and Whitehill, *Boston Public Library,* 38–40.

66. Harris, "Cultural Institutions," 40; and also Story, *Forging of an Aristocracy,* 167–169.

67. Mary Antin, *The Promised Land* (Boston, 1911), 342–343.

68. Kenneth L. Kusmer, "The Social History of Cultural Institutions: The Upper-Class Connection," *Journal of Interdisciplinary History* 10 (Summer 1979): 143; and Harris, "Cultural Institutions," 37–39.

69. Levine, *Highbrow/Lowbrow,* 206.

70. Johnson and Supple, *Boston Capitalists,* 203–221; C. E. Ames, *Union Pacific,* 488ff.; Robert William Fogel, *The Union Pacific Railroad* (Baltimore, 1960), passim; and *Oakes Ames: A Memoir with an Account of the Dedication of the Oakes Ames Memorial Hall at North Easton* (Cambridge, Mass., 1883).

71. Dalzell, *Enterprising Elite,* 158. For Carnegie and Bertram's new corporate structure of philanthropy, see Van Slyck, "'The Utmost Amount of Effectiv (sic) Accommodation,'" 369–372.

72. *Malden City Press,* 1 October 1885, 8.

73. *Woburn Journal,* 25 December 1875.

74. *National Cyclopedia of American Biography* (New York, 1909), 10: 120; *Malden Mirror,* 19 December 1903 and 11 June 1904.

75. *Quincy Daily Ledger,* 3 May 1895.

76. *Address of Charles Francis Adams, Jr.,* 21. Greeley was also a member of the same congregation as Thomas Crane. The Universalist Church believed in a "progressive" interpretation of Christianity united by a single belief in Christ. Peter W. Williams, "Unitarianism and Universalism," in *Encyclopedia*



**
*

*of the American Religious Experience: Studies of Traditions and Movements,* 2 vols., ed. Charles H. Lippy and Peter W. Williams (New York, 1988), 1: 579–593. See also "Edwin Hubbell Chapin," *National Cyclopedia of American Biography* (New York, 1929), 6: 89; Sumner Ellis, *Life of Edwin Hubbell Chapin* (Boston, 1882); Edwin Hubbell Chapin, *The Church of the Living God and Other Sermons* (New York, 1881); and Boyer, *Urban Masses,* 67–75.

77. This was on the condition that other members of the church contribute an equal amount. Hurd, *Middlesex County,* 515–516; and Ochsner, *Richardson,* 313–314.

78. Lears, *No Place for Grace,* 24; Phillips Brooks, *Twenty Sermons,* 4th series (New York, 1887). See also Douglas, *Feminization of American Culture,* 103; and Boyer, *Urban Masses,* 121.

79. Lears, *No Place for Grace,* 16.

80. Douglas, *Feminization of American Culture,* 60.

81. Quoted in Kathleen D. McCarthy, *Women's Culture: American Philanthropy and Art, 1830–1930* (Chicago, 1991), 44. See also Rev. Charles H. Eaton, "Address at the Funeral of Mrs. Thomas Crane," in *The Starkeys of New England and Allied Families,* Emily Wilder Leavit, comp. (n.p., 1910), xii; and the *Quincy Daily Ledger,* 3 May 1895. The Sororis Club was founded in New York City in 1868; among its more prominent members was Phebe C. Hanaford, author of *The Life of George Peabody* (Boston, 1870). For Sarah Ames see FPLM, 112.

82. Malden Historical Society, *One Hundredth Anniversary of the Malden Public Library 1879–1979* (Malden, Mass., 1979), frontispiece. This photograph now appears to be lost.

83. Douglas, *Feminization of American Culture,* 52. See also Ann Douglas, "Heaven Our Home: Consolation Literature in the Northern United States, 1830–1880," in *Death in America,* ed. David E. Stannard (Philadelphia, 1975), 53–56.

84. *In Memoriam: Mary Diana Converse March 3, 1825–December 16, 1903* (Boston, [1904?]), n.p.

85. Levine, *Highbrow/Lowbrow,* 85–168.

86. Joseph Story, *An Address Delivered at the Dedication of the Cemetery at Mount Auburn* (Boston, 1831), 13. See also Neil Harris, *The Artist in American Society: The Formative Years, 1790–1860* (New York, 1966), 207–211; Stanley French, "The Cemetery as Cultural Institution," in *Death in America,* 69–91; and Blanche Linden-Ward, *Silent City on a Hill: Landscapes of Memory and Boston's Mount Auburn Cemetery* (Columbus, Ohio, 1989), 191–196. The dedication of Mount Auburn Cemetery established the ritual for the dedication ceremonies of future rural cemeteries as well as memorial libraries (the procession of dignitaries, the opening prayer, an ode for the occasion, the formal address, the formula of dedication, a closing prayer, and the recessional). See Gary Wills, *Lincoln at Gettysburg: The Words That Remade America* (New York, 1992), 69.

87. John Claudius Loudon, *On the Laying Out, Planting, and Managing of Cemeteries* (London, 1843), 12–13.

88. Other early Civil War memorial libraries were erected in Foxboro (1868) and Framingham (1873), Massachusetts. FPLM, 16–18, 128–130, 179–181, 262–268; and *Report of the Committee on Soldiers' Monument* (Foxboro, Mass., 1867). At Foxboro, the edifice took the form of an octagonal cenotaph or chapel, atop which stood a statue of a Union sentry. In 1871 the building's uses were expanded to include a public library, a function that appears to have been intended from the beginning. Bookcases were ar-

ranged along the walls alternating with plaques inscribed with the names of the town's war dead.

89. Robert B. Shaffer, "Ruskin, Norton, and Memorial Hall," *Harvard Library Bulletin* 3 (Spring 1949): 215; see Bainbridge Bunting, *Harvard: An Architectural History,* completed and edited by Margaret Henderson Floyd (Cambridge, Mass., 1985), 86–92; and Moses King, *Harvard and Its Surroundings,* fourth subscription edition (Cambridge, Mass., 1882), 41–43.

90. *Alumni Hall: An Appeal to the Alumni and Friends of Harvard College* (Cambridge, Mass., 1866); and Shaffer, "Ruskin, Norton," 215–218.

91. George E. Ellis, *Memoir of Nathaniel Thayer* (Cambridge, Mass., 1885), 24–31; King, *Harvard,* 30; and Abijah P. Marvin, *History of the Town of Lancaster, Massachusetts: From the First Settlement to the Present Time, 1643–1879* (Lancaster, Mass., 1879), 554. Frederick L. Ames also donated $2,000 toward the cost of Memorial Hall. See *Final Reports of the Building Committee and of the Treasurer of the Harvard College Memorial Fund to the Committee of Fifty, 26 June 1878* (Cambridge, Mass., 1878), 36, 40. For Thayer and his railroad interests see Johnson and Supple, *Boston Capitalists,* passim; and also Kirkland, *Adams,* 65–80.

92. Lancaster Town Library, *Address Delivered at the Dedication of Memorial Hall, Lancaster, June 17, 1868. By Christopher T. Thayer; and Ode, by H. F. Buswell* (Boston, 1868), 68, 70. The Reverend Bartol, minister of the Congregational Church, had served as chairman of the Lancaster library's building committee.

93. Lancaster Town Library, *Address Delivered at the Dedication of Memorial Hall,* 38–39.

94. Phillips Brooks, *An Address Delivered May 30, 1873 at the Dedication of the Memorial Hall, Andover, Massachusetts* (Andover, Mass., 1873), 23.

95. Ibid.

96. While about a quarter of the public library buildings erected by American philanthropists before 1875, such as the Peabody Library in Peabody (1853–1854) or the Thayer Public Library in Braintree (1873–1874), were named for their founders, very few of them took on the ceremonial trappings of a private memorial.

97. Champney, "Diary," 11 August 1876; Woburn Public Library, *Bulletin of Accessions to the Woburn Public Library for the Year Ending March 1, 1884* (Woburn, Mass., [1884]), 1*–13*; and *Woburn Advertiser,* 20 January 1881.

98. John H. Dryfhout, *The Work of Augustus Saint-Gaudens* (Hanover, N.H., 1982), 124. In North Easton, the Unitarian Church, which was built with Ames money, became the more overt family shrine, with numerous memorials to members of the family. See Mary Ames Frothingham, *History of Unity Church, North Easton: 1875–1935* ([Easton, Mass.], n.d.), 11–15.

99. James F. O'Gorman, *H. H. Richardson and His Office: Selected Drawings* (Boston, 1974), 160; and *Quincy Patriot,* 28 August 1880.

100. *Presentation of the Bust of Hon. Elisha Slade Converse;* and *Malden Mirror,* 19 December 1903.

101. Bobinski, *Carnegie Libraries,* 3.

102. Henry Nourse, "The Public Libraries of Massachusetts," *New England Magazine,* n.s. 5 (1891–1892): 155.

103. James F. O'Gorman, "Man-Made Mountain: 'Gathering and Governing' in H. H. Richardson's Design for the Ames Monument in Wyoming," in *The Railroad in American Art: Representation of Technologi-*

*cal Change,* ed. Susan Danly and Leo Marx (Cambridge, Mass., 1987), 113–126; and *H. H. Richardson: Architectural Forms for an American Society* (Chicago, 1987), 95–104.

104. Edward W. Said, *Culture and Imperialism* (New York, 1993), passim.

## CHAPTER TWO

1. For a general introduction to American library architecture before 1850 see Donald Oehlerts, "The Development of American Public Library Architecture form 1850 to 1940," Ph.D. diss., Indiana University, 1974, 26–33; Elizabeth Stone, *American Library Development 1600–1899* (New York, 1977), 300–309; Kenneth A. Breisch, "Small Public Libraries in America 1850–1890: The Invention and Evolution of a Building Type," Ph.D. diss., University of Michigan, 1982, 48–115; and John Boll, "Library Architecture 1800–1875: A Comparison of Theory and Buildings with an Emphasis on New England College Libraries," Ph.D. diss., University of Illinois, 1961. For the Loganian Library in particular, see United States Department of Interior, Bureau of Education, *Public Libraries in the United States of America: Their History, Condition and Management,* 3 pt. 1 (Washington, D.C., 1876), 5–9, illus. opp. 7. Information on the Walterboro Society Library comes from the HABS archives in the Library of Congress. See "LIBRARY, Walterboro, Colleton County, South Carolina" (HABS No. SC-2), 1.

2. Information on the Redwood Library, which possessed some 1,200 volumes, can be found in Antoinette Downing and Vincent Scully, *The Architectural Heritage of Newport, Rhode Island: 1640–1915* (New York, 1951), 80–83; Carl Bridenbaugh, *Peter Harrison, First American Architect* (Chapel Hill, N.C., 1949), 45–49; William H. Pierson, Jr., *American Buildings and Their Architects: The Colonial and Neo-Classical Styles* (New York, 1970), 143–145; and David King, *A Historical Sketch of the Redwood Library and Athenaeum* (Boston, 1860), iv–v. For the Providence Athenaeum, see William H. Jordy and Christopher P. Monkhouse, *Buildings on Paper: Rhode Island Architectural Drawings 1825–1945* (Providence, 1982), 155–157.

3. Arnold Nicholson, "Dr. Thornton, Who Practised Everything but Medicine," *Smithsonian* 2 (April 1971), 69–70; Oehlerts, "American Public Library," 28.

4. For a good introduction to the literature on the development of library architecture in Europe see Dennis M. Gromly, "A Bibliographic Essay of Western Library Architecture to the Mid-Twentieth Century," *Journal of Library History* 9 (1974): 4–24. The primary sources for this topic include John W. Clark, *The Care of Books: An Essay on the Development of Libraries and Their Fittings, from the Earliest Times to the End of the Eighteenth Century* (Cambridge, Eng., 1909); Georg Leyh, "Das Haus und seine Einrichtung," *Handbuch der Bibliothekswissenschaft,* ed. F. Milkau, 3 vols. (Leipzig, 1933–1940), 2: 1–38; and Nikolaus Pevsner, *A History of Building Types* (Washington, D.C., 1976), 91–110. For the influence of these European buildings on early American libraries, see Breisch, "Small Public Libraries," 48–115.

5. Clark, *Care of Books,* 270 and fig. 123.

6. Pevsner, *Building Types,* 97–108.

7. Pierson, *Colonial and Neo-Classical,* 316–334; William H. Adams, ed., *The Eye of Jefferson* (Washington, 1976), 295–297, illus. 506; Paul Venable Turner, *Campus: An American Planning Tradition* (Cambridge, Mass., 1984), 76–87; and Harry Clemons, *The University of Virginia Library 1825–1950* (Charlottesville, 1954).

8. Pevsner, *Building Types,* 102–103, 151–152, 163–164; James Gibbs, *Bibliotheca Radcliviana, or a Description of the Radcliffe Library, Oxford* (Oxford, 1747); John Summerson, *Architecture in Britain 1530 to 1830* (Harmondsworth, Eng., 1953; first paperback edition, 1970), 355–357; and Bryan Little, *The Life and Works of James Gibbs* (London, 1959), 128–137.

9. The construction of a second library room of similar configuration in 1820 doubled Harvard's shelving capacity. The tradition of placing libraries in academic buildings with multiple functions continued until well after midcentury. When the University of North Carolina found itself in need of new library facilities in the 1840s, for instance, it commissioned Alexander Jackson Davis to design a combination library and ballroom. See John V. Allcott, "Scholarly Books and Frolicsome Blades: A. J. Davis Designs a Library Ballroom," *JSAH* 33 (1974): 145–154; Boll, "Library Architecture," 50–56, 114–115, 167–173 and table 2, 16; and, more generally, Louis Shores, *Origins of the American College Library: 1638–1800* (Nashville, 1934).

10. Although it has not survived, the earliest library to demonstrate this more complex form of arrangement in a coherent fashion seems to have been installed at Magdalen College, Oxford, about 1480. Clark, *Care of Books,* 126–172 and 166–179, figs. 71, 82, and 83; Pevsner, *Building Types,* 91–93; Burnett Hillman Streeter, *The Chained Library: A Survey of Four Centuries in the Evolution of the English Library* (London, 1931); Alfred A. Franklin, *Les anciennes bibliothèques de Paris; églises, monastères, collèges . . . ,* 3 vols. (Paris, 1867–1870), 1: 221–317; and James F. O'Gorman, *The Architecture of the Monastic Libraries in Italy, 1300–1600* (New York, 1972). An interesting variation on this arrangement, which anticipates the modern library with its compact grouping of tall, upright shelves, is recorded in an early seventeenth-century view of the University of Leiden library, reproduced in Clark, *Care of Books,* 164.

11. A plan and elevation of the Guildhall Library, which was designed by Horace Jones, was published in *The Builder* 29 (27 August 1870): 686–687; and again in *The Architect* 9 (November 1872): 263. For this and other contemporary libraries in London, see Alan W. Ball, *The Public Libraries of Greater London: A Pictorial History 1856–1940* (London, 1977), 57–83. For the evolution of this type see Pevsner, *Building Types,* 100–102; Edward Sekler, *Wren and His Place in European Architecture* (New York, 1956), 148–150, pls. 57A–58B; and Philip Gaskell and Robert Robson, *The Library of Trinity College Cambridge: A Short History* (Cambridge, Eng., 1971), 13–22, illus. 4–11. The library at Trinity College, Dublin, was finished in 1724 but not opened until 1734. It was designed by Thomas Burgh. The barrel vault that now covers the book room of this library was proposed in January 1858 by Benjamin Woodward and constructed between 1860 and 1862 as part of a renovation and expansion of the old building. See John Ingram, *The Library of Trinity College Dublin* (London, 1886); Boll, "Library Architecture," 44–45; Margaret Burton, *Famous Libraries of the World* (London, 1937), 66–68; and Eve Blau, *Ruskinian Gothic: The Architecture of Deane and Woodward 1845–1861* (Princeton, 1982), 153–154. For another example of a nineteenth-century alcove library, erected at Edinburgh University (1831–1834) only a few years before Bond designed Gore Hall, see Pevsner, *Building Types,* 104, illus 7.35; and Boll, "Library Architecture," 44–45.

12. Josiah Quincy, *The History of Harvard University,* 2 vols. (Cambridge, Mass., 1840), 2: 599–600. The designs for Gore Hall would seem to date to 1835, when a June entry in the university treasurer's report shows a payment to "Rogers and Bond on account of their Bill for drawings, plans, elevations, &c

of a New Library Building 200.00." The identity of Rogers remains unclear, although he may be the well-known Boston architect Isaiah Rogers; he was in New York at this time working on the Astor House, which would explain his absence during the construction of Gore Hall after 1835. Little is known of the career of Richard Bond, so that a brief collaboration with Rogers is entirely possible. See Boll, "Library Architecture," 126–148; and *Gore Hall: The Library of Harvard College 1838–1913* (Cambridge, Mass., 1917); Walter Kilham, *Boston after Bulfinch: An Account of Its Architecture 1800–1900* (Cambridge, Mass., 1946), 35–36, 45; and Henry and Elsie R. Withey, *Biographical Dictionary of American Architects* (Los Angeles, 1956), 65.

13. Quincy, *Harvard University,* 2: 599–600.

14. John William Tebbel, *A History of Book Publishing in the United States,* vol. 1, *The Creation of an Industry, 1630–1865* (New York, 1972), 257–262; and vol. 2, *The Expansion of an Industry, 1865–1919* (New York, 1975), 23–24.

15. Boll, "Library Architecture," 173–198, 358–366. Boll attributes the design for the Yale Library to Austin, whereas Roger Hail Newton (*Town and Davis, Architects* [New York, 1942], 238–240) believes that Austin, along with an Englishman, Henry Flockton, only supervised the construction of a Town and Davis design. See also the HABS Archives, The Library of Congress, "The Library of the University of South Carolina, Columbia, Richland County, South Carolina" (HABS SC-40-COLUM 2), 1.

16. "The Boston Athenaeum," *Norton's Literary Gazette and Publishers' Circular* 2 (15 May 1852); and Josiah Quincy, *The History of the Boston Athenaeum, with Biographical Notices of Its Deceased Founders* (Cambridge, Mass., 1851), 240–241. The third story of this new building was devoted to exhibitions of painting and was divided into six galleries, all of which were illuminated with skylights.

17. Boll, "Library Architecture," 73–80; Leopold August Constantin Hesse, *Bibliothéconomie; où, Nouveau manuel complet pour l'arrangement, la conservation, et l'administration des bibliothèques* (Paris, 1839); and J. A. F. Schmidt, *Handbuch der Bibliothekwissenschaft, der Literatur- und Bücherkunde* (Weimar, 1840).

18. Hesse, *Bibliothéconomie,* 75–76. In the 1841 edition of his book, Hesse added a plate for a second type of book room disposition in which the volumes are stored in a single, double-faced shelf running down the center of a long hall. He preferred the alcove system, however, and this second arrangement seems rarely to have been utilized. Boll ("Library Architecture," 76, fig. 4) mistakenly calls this the first edition. For Hesse see ibid., 82–86; Leyh, "Haus," 32–35; and Pevsner, *Building Types,* 10, illus. 7.40. See also Edward Edwards, *Memoirs of Libraries, Including a Handbook of Library Economy,* 2 vols. (London, 1859), 2: 715–717. Leopoldo della Santa first suggested the division of functions. See *Della costruzione e del regolamento di una pubblica universale biblioteca con la pianta dimostrativa* (Florence, 1816).

19. Boll, "Library Architecture," 27–28; Breisch, "Small Public Libraries," 23–32; David A. Brenneman, "Innovations in American Library Design," in *Thomas Alexander Tefft: American Architecture in Transition, 1845–1860* (Providence, 1988), 62; Martin Schrettinger, *Versuch eines vollständigen Lehrbuchs der Bibliothek-Wissenschaft; oder, Anleitung zur Volkommenen Geschäftführung eines Bibliothekars, in wissenschaftlicher Form abgefasst,* 2 vols. (Munich, 1810–1829), and *Handbuch der Bibliothek-Wissenschaft, besonders zum Gebrauche der Nicht-Bibliothekare, welche ihre Privat-Büchersammlungen selbst einrichten wollen* (Vienna, 1834); and Benjamin Delessert, *Mémoire sur la Bibliothèque Royale, où l'on indique les mesures à prendre pour la transférer dans un bâtiment circulaire, d'une forme nouvelle* (Paris, 1835). Charles Coffin Jewett, one of the leading Ameri-

can librarians of the era, was the librarian at Brown from 1841 until 1848, when he left to take the position of librarian of the Smithsonian Institution. See Joseph A. Borome, *Charles Coffin Jewett* (Chicago, 1951); and Michael H. Harris, intro. and ed., *The Age of Jewett: Charles Coffin Jewett and American Librarianship, 1841–1868* (Littleton, Col., 1975).

20. Cabot was assisted in his work by Dexter, who in 1845 had actually been awarded the commission for the new building. When the Athenaeum building committee decided to change the location of their proposed structure in 1846, they put Cabot in charge. Although the interior was not yet finished, the Athenaeum was occupied in July 1849. Quincy, *Boston Athenaeum,* 152–241; "Boston Athenaeum," *Norton's Literary Gazette;* and Boston Athenaeum, *Change and Continuity: A Pictorial History of the Boston Athenaeum* (Boston, 1985).

21. "Williams College Library," *Norton's Literary Gazette and Publishers' Circular* 3 (13 March 1853); Charles Coffin Jewett, *Notices of Public Libraries in the United States of America. Appendix to the 4th Annual Report of the Smithsonian Institution* (Washington, D.C., 1851), 42; Boll, "Library Architecture," 199–235; R. E. Malmstrom, "Lawrence Hall at Williams College," *Studies in the History of Art* 2 (Williamstown, Mass., 1979); and Brenneman, "Innovations," 63–67, 180–181. For Thomas Tefft see E. M. Stone, *The Architect and Monetarian: A Brief Memoir of Thomas Alexander Tefft* (Providence, 1869); Barbara Wriston, "The Architecture of Thomas Tefft," *Bulletin of the Museum of Art of the Rhode Island School of Design, Providence* 28 (November 1940): 37–45; and Jordy and Monkhouse, *Buildings on Paper,* 234–235.

22. Jewett, *Notices,* 42.

23. Edward Everett Hale, "Report of the Council," *Proceedings of the American Antiquarian Society* (27 April 1853): 7–8; and Malmstrom, "Lawrence Hall," 9–10.

24. Delessert, *Mémoire,* 10–11. Delessert himself notes that circular plans had been suggested since the time of Claude Perrault in the seventeenth century and mentions an 1810 design by M. Baltard and the Halle aux Blés (1808–1813) in Paris as precedents for his concept for the Bibliothèque Royale. The Radcliffe Camera at Oxford was also much admired by the French in the early nineteenth century. Quatremère de Quincy, for instance, praised it highly in his *Dictionnaire d'Architecture* in 1832, just three years before Delessert published his own centralized plan. César Daly reproduced Delessert's plan for the Bibliothèque Royale and, likewise, praised it and the Radcliffe Camera in "Des bibliothèques publiques," *Revue générale de l'architecture et des travaux publics* 8 (1850), col. 421, and pl. 40. For an opposite assessment of the Camera see Edwards, *Memoirs,* 2: 681–682. See also Jeremy Bentham, *Panopticon* (London, 1791); Michel Foucault, *Discipline and Punish: The Birth of the Prison,* trans. A. Sheridan (New York, 1979), 195–228, and "The Eye of Power: A Conversation with Jean-Pierre Barou and Michele Perrot," *Power/Knowledge: Selected Interviews and Other Writings: 1972–1977,* ed. and trans. C. Gordon (New York, 1980), 146–165.

25. Hale, "Report," 7–8.

26. Astor had written this bequest into his will in 1838 at the urging of his secretary, Joseph Green Cogswell, who would become the first librarian of the library. See Sidney Ditzion, *Arsenals of a Democratic Culture: A Social History of the American Library Movement in New England and the Middle States, 1850–1900* (Chicago, 1947), 142–147; and Stone, *Library Development, 150–151.* For a history of events leading up to this bequest and of the Astor building see Harry Lydenberg, *History of the New York Public Library* (New

York, 1923), 1–25; Frederick K. Saunders, "The Astor Library," *New England Magazine,* n.s. 2 (1890–1891): 48–59; and the description in *Literary World,* 22 September 1849, as reprinted in Jewett, *Notices,* 91–92.

27. Montgomery Schuyler, "The Romanesque Revival in New York," *Architectural Record* 1 (1891–1892): 11–12. For the Munich Staatsbibliothek see Leyh, "Das Haus," 35–36; Arnim Graesel, *Grundzüge der Bibliothekslehre* (Leipzig, 1890), 9–53; and Oswald Hederer, *Friedrich von Gärtner 1792–1847: Leben, Werk, Schüller* (Munich, 1976), 112–125. For two mid-nineteenth-century views on the Munich library building see Daly, "Bibliothèques publiques," col. 421; and Edwards, *Memoirs,* 2: 692–694. In spite of this major commission, surprisingly little seems to be known about Saeltzer himself. Jewett (*Notices,* 91–92) says that he was "from Berlin [and] a pupil of the celebrated Schinkel." He apparently arrived in this country in 1842 and continued to practice into the 1850s. See Ellen W. Kramer, "Contemporary Descriptions of New York and Its Public Architecture ca. 1850," *JSAH* 27 (1968): 273. For similar designs in the Florentine *Rundbogenstil,* executed by other students of Schinkel, see Eva Borsch-Supan, *Berliner Baukunst nach Schinkel: 1840–1870* (Munich, 1977), 142–143 and pls. 473–475; especially pl. 474, which is a design of 1843 for an apartment building by Ferdinand Wilhelm Holz based on the Strozzi Palace.

28. Quoted in Ditzion, *Arsenals,* 144.

29. Jewett, *Notices,* 91–92. Within a year of opening to the public, it was recognized that the Astor Library's book hall was already nearly filled to capacity and allowed no room for future expansion. A second book hall was consequently erected immediately adjacent to the north wall of the original building. This was begun in 1856 and opened on 1 September 1859. A third hall was added to the north of this addition twenty-five years later. These parallel book rooms made it similar in disposition to the Munich Staatsbibliothek. Lydenberg, *New York Public Library,* 24–25, 43–44, 70–71.

30. Quoted in Ditzion, *Arsenals,* 145.

31. "Hints upon Library Buildings," *Norton's Literary Gazette and Publishers' Circular* 3 (15 January 1853): 1.

32. Ibid. The alcove disposition may have been adopted from the arrangement of the book room of the American Antiquarian Society, which was just being completed in Worcester, Massachusetts. This was designed by Thomas Tefft in collaboration with Edward Everett Hale. "Worcester Antiquarian Society," *Norton's Literary Gazette and Publishers' Circular* 3 (15 November 1852): 1; and Brenneman, "Innovations," 68–70.

33. "Hints upon Library Buildings."

34. "Bibliothèque Ste.-Geneviève," *Norton's Literary Gazette and Publishers' Circular* 3 (15 October 1853): 1.

35. Walter Muir Whitehill, *Boston Public Library: A Centennial History* (Cambridge, Mass., 1956), 46–47; City of Boston, *Proceedings at the Dedication of the Building for the Public Library of the City of Boston, January 1, 1858* (Boston, 1858), 138–141; and *Proceedings on the Occasion of the Laying of the Corner-Stone of the Public Library of the City of Boston, 17 September 1855* (Boston, 1855).

36. Whitehill, *Boston Public Library,* 34–47. Described in the dedication booklet as being in the "Roman Italian Style," the new Boston Public Library had "circular-headed" windows and doors and was

constructed of red brick with Connecticut sandstone trim. The following description of the building is based upon that found in *Proceedings at the Dedication of the Building,* 163–170. See also City of Boston, *Specifications for a Building for the Public Library* (Boston, 1855).

37. Nathaniel B. Shurtleff, *A Decimal System for the Arrangement and Administration of Libraries* (Boston, 1856), 3; and Boll, "Library Architecture," 34–35, 97–101.

38. Shurtleff, *Decimal System,* 64–66.

39. Ibid., 66–67.

40. Ibid., 27; and Whitehill, *Boston Public Library,* 37. Sandwiched between the two main floors was "an entresol, or half story," which accommodated storerooms and a work room for librarians. This level could be accessed from the upper gallery of the circulating library or by means of iron staircases that rose to the reference room. The 200,000 books that this room was intended to accommodate were arranged according to a "decimal system" that had been devised by Shurtleff. Following this system, each of the library's twenty alcoves contained ten ranges of shelves consisting of ten shelves each. By cataloguing a book with the number of the alcove, range, and shelf in which it was housed, its location in the library could be immediately determined by the library staff.

41. Shurtleff, *Decimal System,* 67.

42. The Springfield Public Library was designed by George Hathorne of New York. The book room, which measured some 50 feet in height, was surrounded by tiers of alcoves set beneath a glass dome and located on the second floor. It had a capacity of about 80,000 volumes. *Annual Report of the City Library Association of the City of Springfield for the Year Ending May 6, 1872* (Springfield, Mass., 1872); and *The New-York Sketch-Book of Architecture* no. 6 (June 1874), plate XXIII. The architect of the Cincinnati Library was James McLaughlin. The book hall was appended onto a remodeled opera house that had been purchased by the board of managers of the public library in 1868. This room measured 105 by 75 feet and was 55 feet in height. "Report of the Board of Managers," Public Library of Cincinnati, *Annual Reports: 1869* (Cincinnati, 1869), 8–11. In Detroit, the plans of Brush and Smith were accepted in 1874 after the library committee had inspected—among others—the libraries in Boston and Cincinnati. Frank B. Woodford, *Parnassus on Main Street: A History of the Detroit Public Library* (Detroit, 1965), 93–106, illus. on 61 and 65. Of all of these book rooms, only that in the Peabody Institute in Baltimore has survived. A visit to this impressive space serves to convey something of the powerful impression created by these hybrid American *Saalbibliotheken.* Although the first part of the building was erected in 1859–1861, the Peabody Library hall was not built until 1875–1878. It was designed by E. G. Lind of Philadelphia. See Rosann Kahn, *A History of the Peabody Institute Library, Baltimore, Maryland 1857–1916* (Rochester, N.Y., 1954).

43. William Rhees, *Manual of Public Libraries, Institutions, and Societies in the United States and British Provinces of North America* (Philadelphia, 1859), vi–vii; and Edwards, *Memoirs,* 2: 730–731.

44. Ibid., 2: 669–727.

45. S. G. W. [Samuel Greene Wheeler] Benjamin, "Libraries," *Harper's New Monthly Magazine* 29 (September 1864): 487, 488. Benjamin, an artist and illustrator, was at the time an assistant in the New York State Library in Albany. *Dictionary of American Biography,* ed. Allen Johnson (New York, 1964), 1: 189.

46. *Address Delivered at the Dedication of Memorial Hall, Lancaster, June 17, 1868. By Christopher T. Thayer; and Ode, by H. F. Buswell* (Boston, 1868); and FPLM, 179–180.



**
*

47. Concord Free Public Library, *Dedication of the New Building for the Free Public Library of Concord, Massachusetts, . . . October 1, 1873* (Boston, 1873), 11–15; Allen French, "A Review of the History of the Concord Free Public Library," in Concord Free Public Library, *A History of the Concord Free Public Library* (Concord, Mass., 1973), 3–6; and FPLM, 87–89.

48. See for example the letter to E. R. Hoar, dated 18 May 1869, in the Concord Free Public Library, where Munroe states that he has not yet decided whether to build a single large hall or use the two-story model of the Boston Public Library for his scheme.

49. Margaret Sidney [Harriet Mulford Lothrop], *Old Concord: Her Highways and Byways,* revised and enlarged edition (Boston, 1893), 88. Not surprisingly, Lothrop is only echoing the ideas of Ralph Waldo Emerson, who spoke at the dedication of the building in 1873. See "Address," *Concord Free Public Library, Dedication,* 37–45. "Now if you can kindle the imagination by a new thought, by heroic histories, by uplifting poetry, instantly you expand,—are cheered, inspired, and become wise, and even prophetic" (42).

50. Miss H. R. Hudson, "Concord Books," *Harper's New Monthly Magazine* 51 (June-November 1875): 20.

51. The Brookline Library has been demolished, but the interior arrangement of its book room can be reconstructed from contemporary accounts and surviving photographs. See FPLM, 62–63; Brookline Public Library, *Special Report of the Board of Trustees of the Brookline Public Library, upon the Library Lot and Building, March 29, 1867* (Boston, 1867), 4–10, and *Thirteenth Report of the Board of Trustees of the Public Library* (Brookline, Mass., 1864), 3–7. The Thayer Public Library in Braintree has been converted to city offices and its interior remodeled. A personal investigation of the building and a typescript description by Mabel S. Sawyer (1936) in the Braintree Historical Society allow for this conjectural reconstruction of the original interior disposition. See also FPLM, 54–55, and James F. O'Gorman, "H. and J. E. Billings of Boston: From Classicism to the Picturesque," *JSAH* 42 (1983): 69–70.

52. Justin Winsor, "Report of the Superintendent," Boston Public Library, *Twentieth Annual Report of the Trustees of the Public Library, 1872* (Boston, 1872), 14. As early as 1867, as chairman of the library's examining committee, Winsor had already begun to condemn the poor quality of light found in the alcoves of Boston's upper hall, as well as the lack of good ventilation throughout the structure as a whole. Boston Public Library, "Report of the Examining Committee," *Fifteenth Annual Report of the Trustees of the Public Library, 1867* (Boston, 1867), 11–14. For a discussion of the general controversy during these years see Whitehill, *Boston Public Library,* 76–81, and the "Report of the Examining Committee," *Eighteenth Annual Report of the Trustees of the Public Library, 1870* (Boston, 1870), 12–13. In 1876, Winsor was elected the first President of the American Library Association, and the following year accepted a new position as librarian at Harvard University. For Winsor's life and work, see Joseph A. Borome, "The Life and Letters of Justin Winsor," Ph.D. diss., Columbia University, 1950; and W. F. Yust, *A Bibliography of Justin Winsor* (Cambridge, Mass., 1902).

53. Winsor, "Report of the Superintendent," 1872, 15.

54. Justin Winsor, "Library Buildings," in United States Department of Interior, Bureau of Education, *Public Libraries in the United States of America: Their History, Condition and Management,* 3, pt. 1 (Washington, D.C., 1876), 466.

55. Ibid., 465.

56. Ibid., 466. For a description of this building see Boston Public Library, "Description and Plans," *Twentieth Annual Report of the Trustees of the Public Library, 1872* (Boston, 1872), 84–85. According to the dedication booklet, "the general plan of the interior [was] due to the Superintendent of the Public Library, as modified by the large experience of the accomplished architects." See Boston Public Library, *Dedication Services of the Fellowes Athenaeum and the Roxbury Branch of the Boston Public Library, July 9, 1873* (Boston, 1873), 7.

57. Winsor, "Report of the Superintendent," in Boston Public Library, *Twenty-First Annual Report of the Trustees of the Public Library, 1873* (Boston, 1873), 14.

58. *The Nation* 15 (3 October 1872): 216.

59. Both of these buildings were widely published in French, British, and American literature, and would have been well known to Winsor as well as other Americans. See, for example, César Daly, "Bibliothèque Sainte-Geneviève," *Revue générale de l'architecture et des travaux publics* 10 (1852), cols. 379–381, pls. 21–27, and 11 (1853), cols. 392–393, pls. 30–32; Edwards, *Memoirs,* 2: 473–476; "Bibliothèque Sainte-Geneviève," *Norton's Literary Gazette* (15 October 1853); and P. Planat, *Encyclopédie de l'architecture et de la construction,* vol. 2, pt. 2 (Paris, [1888]), 330–339. The stacks at the Bibliothèque Nationale had been based upon earlier metal shelving at the British Museum (1854–1856), which also would have been known in the United States. Pevsner, *Building Types,* 108.

60. Henry Van Brunt, "Library Buildings," *LJ* 4 (1879): 296. For Gore Hall see also *AABN* 3 (1878): 173–174; William H. Jordy, *American Buildings and Their Architects: Progressive and Academic Ideals at the Turn of the Century* (New York, 1976), 326–327; Kenneth A. Breisch, "William Frederick Poole and Modern Library Architecture," in *Modern Architecture in America: Visions and Revisions,* ed. R. G. Wilson and S. K. Robinson (Ames, Iowa, 1991), 56–57; and *Gore Hall: The Library of Harvard College.*

61. The first example of a metal stack system in a public library seems to have been the two-story metal stack in Ware and Van Brunt's Topeka, Kansas, Free Public Library (1881–1883). See William J. Hennessey, "The Architectural Works of Henry Van Brunt," Ph.D. diss., Columbia University, 1979, 140–144.

62. J. A. E. Smith, *The History of Pittsfield, Massachusetts: 1800–1876,* 2 vols. (Springfield, Mass., 1876), 2: 643–649; *Berkshire County Eagle,* 28 September 1876; FPLM, 295–300; and Sarah Bradford Landau, *Edward T. and William A. Potter: American Victorian Architects* (New York, 1979), 263–265. Potter's design for the Athenaeum was published in A. J. Bicknell, *Wooden and Brick Buildings with Details* (New York, 1875).

63. *Northampton Courier,* 26 September 1871; and FPLM, 263–266. This building was erected for $80,000, part of which was contributed by the town of Northampton and the remainder raised through public subscription.

64. Breisch, "William Frederick Poole," 53–68; and "Report of the Board of Managers," in Public Library of Cincinnati, *Annual Reports: 1869,* 8–11. Like Winsor, Poole would argue, at the first annual conference of the American Library Association in 1876, that galleries were "a radical defect . . . in the construction of nearly all our libraries." As in the Northampton arrangement, he felt that the "model library building of the future" would have book storage rooms no more than 14 to 16 feet high, with freestanding double-faced book cases set at right angles to "and free from the wall." See *LJ* 1 (1876): 125.

65. "Problem XVI.—A Memorial Library," *The Architectural Sketch Book* 2 (1875), plates XLIV–XLVI.

66. The program itself specified that "pointed arches and medieval details not to be used" (ibid.). Ware had been introduced to the Beaux-Arts tradition during the late 1850s in the atelier of Richard Morris Hunt in New York City. See J. A. Chewning, "William Robert Ware at MIT and Columbia," *Journal of Architectural Education* 33 (1979): 25–29; and William Coles, "Richard Morris Hunt and His Library as Revealed in the Studio Sketchbooks of Henry Van Brunt," *Art Quarterly* 30 (1967): 224–238. This French bias was further reinforced the following year when Ware hired Francis W. Chandler, a young American student whom he had met at the Ecole des Beaux-Arts, to teach at the school; and again in 1872 when Eugène Letang, a former French student at the Paris school, was brought to Boston to act as instructor of architectural design.

67. [Charles Ammi Cutter], *The Nation* 29 (1879): 126.

68. "Tribunal de 1ère instance," *Croquis d'architecture* 1, no. 11 (June 1866): 2–3. This publication appears to have been well known in Boston by this date. I, for example, am in possession of the first four volumes (1866–1870), which were presented by the Boston Society of Architects to William W. Woolett for the best work in the class of construction at MIT in 1870. For more on the French notion of *caractère,* see chapter 4, note 39.

69. "Ce catalogue monumental est la principale décoration de la façade, comme les livres eux-mêmes sont le plus bel ornament de l'intérieur." Henri Labrouste, "A. M. le Directeur de la Revue d'Architecture," *Revue générale de l'architecture et des travaux publics* 10 (1852), col. 383. For recent discussions of the Bibliothèque Ste.-Geneviève see David Van Zanten, *Designing Paris: The Architecture of Duban, Labrouste, Duc and Vaudoyer* (Cambridge, Mass., 1987), 83–98; and Neil Levine, "The Romantic Idea of Architectural Legibility: Henri Labrouste and the Neo-Grec," in *The Architecture of the Ecole des Beaux-Arts,* ed. Arthur Drexler (New York, 1977), 325–416, and "The Book and the Building: Hugo's Theory of Architecture and Labrouste's Bibliothèque Ste.-Geneviève," in *The Beaux-Arts and Nineteenth-Century French Architecture,* ed. Robin Middleton (Cambridge, Mass., 1982), 139–173.

70. Henry Van Brunt, "Greek Lines," *Atlantic Monthly* 8 (1861): 86.

71. See for example *Croquis d'architecture* 2, no. 8 (December 1867), no. 10 (February 1868), or 3, no. 4 (August 1868); and the *Encyclopédie d'architecture* (1874), pls. 169–170, 175, 224, 249, 253, 279. See also Julien Guadet, *Eléments et théorie de l'architecture,* 4 vols. (Paris, 1901–1904), 2: 392–393; and Louis Hautecoeur, *Histoire de l'architecture classique en France,* 7 vols. (Paris, 1943–1957), 7: 140–142.

72. "Monument funéraire commémoratif du combat du Nuits," *Revue générale de l'architecture et des travaux publics* 31 (1874), pl. 20 and cols. 54–55; and "Concours pour les pierres commémoratives des combats sous Paris," *Croquis d'architecture* 6, no. 10 (October 1872): 2–6. Similar memorials for a "Concours pour un monument commemoratif de la défense de Dijon" had appeared in the August issue. See no. 8 (August 1872): 6. See also *Croquis d'architecture* 1, no. 3 (July 1866): 1; and no. 11 (March 1867): 2. Henry Van Brunt had himself praised a similar monument, the tomb of Admiral Dumont d'Urville, which had been illustrated in *Revue générale de l'architecture et des travaux publics* 8 (1850): 438: "This structure contains in its outlines a symbolic expression of human life, death, and immortality, and in its details an architectural version of the character and public services of the distinguished deceased. The finest and



**
*

most eloquent resources of color and the chisel are brought to bear on the work; and the whole, combined by a very sensitive and delicate feeling of proportion, thus embodies one of the most expressive elegies ever written" (Van Brunt, "Greek Lines," 86–87). For American examples, see the Bunker Hill Monument or the ubiquitous obelisks that mark grave sites and commemorate heroes and men of letters in garden cemeteries such as Mount Auburn. Illustrated in Blanche Linden-Ward, *Silent City on a Hill: Landscapes of Memory and Boston's Mount Auburn Cemetery* (Columbus, Ohio, 1989), 215–255.

73. See, for example, "Une chapelle rurale," *Croquis d'architecture* 2, no. 2. (June 1867): 3, and no. 3 (July 1868): 5; "Une chapelle jardinale" by Mr. Degré and Mr. Vinceneux, ibid. 5, no. 3 (July 1871): 6; or the *esquisse* of the first class, by M. Roussi for a gate to a cemetery, ibid. 9, no. 8 (August 1875): 4.

74. For Richardson's Civil War memorials see Jeffrey Karl Ochsner, *H. H. Richardson: Complete Architectural Works* (Cambridge, Mass., 1982), 50–52, 43–146; and James F. O'Gorman, *H. H. Richardson and His Office: Selected Drawings* (Boston, 1974), 188–190.

75. *AABN* 11 (1882), 6; and FPLM, 56–57. The T-shaped *parti* of this latter building is also similar to both Atkinson's and Stickney's *Architectural Sketch Book* designs (figs. 2.30, 2.31). George Tilden had worked in the office of Ware and Van Brunt before forming his partnership with Rotch in Boston in 1880. See Richard Herndon, comp., *Boston of Today* (Boston, 1892), 375, 423.

## CHAPTER THREE

1. For the history of the Woburn library, see FPLM, 421–423; William R. Cutter, "A Model Village Library," *New England Magazine,* n.s. 1 (1889–1890): 617–625; Christina M. DiNapoli, *Woburn Public Library 1856, 1879–1979* (Woburn, Mass., 1979), 4–5; James F. O'Gorman, *H. H. Richardson and His Office: Selected Drawings* (Boston, 1974), 156–159; and Jeffrey Karl Ochsner, *H. H. Richardson: Complete Architectural Works* (Cambridge, Mass., 1982), 174–179. For Jonathan Winn's obituary see *Woburn Advertiser,* 19 December 1873.

2. *Woburn Advertiser,* 25 December 1875; and Cutter, "Model Village Library," 620–621.

3. Donald Oehlerts, "The Development of American Public Library Architecture from 1850 to 1940," Ph.D. diss., Indiana University, 1974, 34, table 3. The cost of the buildings alone ranged from $347,000 for the Peabody Library to $850,000 for the Ridgeway.

4. FPLM, 16–18, 87–89; *Boston Globe,* 2 October 1873, 5; *Andover Advertiser,* 15 March 1872; Mary Byers Smith, *The Founding of the Memorial Hall Library, Andover* ([Andover, Mass.], n.d.); Phillips Brooks, *An Address Delivered May 30, 1873, at the Dedication of the Memorial Hall, Andover, Massachusetts* (Andover, Mass., 1873); Ralph Waldo Emerson, "Address," Concord Free Public Library, *Dedication of the New Building for the Free Public Library of Concord, Massachusetts, . . . October 1, 1873* (Boston, 1873), 37–45.

5. *Woburn Journal,* 25 December 1875.

6. Ibid.

7. DiNapoli, *Woburn Public Library,* 6; and *Woburn Journal,* 23 December 1876. For an overview of the Boston architectural scene at the time, see Douglas Shand Tucci, *Built in Boston: City and Suburb 1800–1950* (Boston, 1978), 46–64.

8. *The Architectural Sketch Book* 1 (1873), pl. XIX; Wheaton A. Holden, "Robert Swain Peabody of Peabody and Stearns in Boston: The Early Years (1870–1886)," Ph.D. diss., Boston University, 1969, 35–37, 48–49; and FPLM, 308–309, 429–430.

9. Hayden had married C. B. Winn's sister, Marcia Ann Winn, in 1860; she died in 1862. "Edward Daniel Hayden," in John C. Rand, comp., *One of a Thousand: A Series of Biographical Sketches of One Thousand Representative Men Resident in the Commonwealth of Massachusetts: A.D. 1888–'89* (Boston, 1890), 293–294; and his obituaries in the *New York Times,* 16 November 1908, 9: 5; and the *Boston Evening Transcript,* 16 November 1908, 2. See also Ronald Story, *The Forging of an Aristocracy: Harvard and the Boston Upper Class, 1800–1870* (Middletown, Conn., 1980), passim.

10. William J. Hennessey, "The Architectural Works of Henry Van Brunt," Ph.D. diss., Columbia University, 1979, 1–47, 116–119; J. A. Chewning, "William Robert Ware at MIT and Columbia," *Journal of Architectural Education* 33 (1979): 25–29; and obituary for John Cummings, *Woburn News,* 24 December 1898.

11. Ochsner, *Richardson,* 196–199, 246–247.

12. Wheaton A. Holden, "The Peabody Touch: Peabody and Stearns of Boston," *JSAH* 32 (1973): 114–131.

13. Henry F. and Elise Rathburn Withey, *Biographical Dictionary of American Architects* (Los Angeles, 1970), 152–153, 544–555, 563. For George Snell's obituary see the *AABN* 39 (4 March 1893): 129–130.

14. George M. Champney, "Diary of George M. Champney, 1876–1877," typescript copy in the Woburn Public Library, entries for 15 June 1876 and 21 June 1876.

15. Champney, "Diary," 7 July 1876 and 18 November 1876. See also Helene Barbara Weinberg, "John LaFarge and the Decoration of Trinity Church, Boston," *JSAH* 33 (1974): 329. Letter from Edwin A. Champney to author, July 1996.

16. Champney, "Diary," 20 June 1876. Champney became librarian in 1879, a post he held until his death three years later. The Haverhill library building, which was designed by Josiah M. Littlefield of that town, no longer stands; its arrangement can only be partially surmised from contemporary descriptions and photographs. See Haverhill Public Library, "Report of the Building Committee," *Proceedings at the Dedication of the Haverhill Public Library, November 11th, 1875,* and *Report of the Trustees to the City of Haverhill January 1, 1876* (Haverhill, 1876), 25; and FPLM, 159–160. In 1873, several members of the newly appointed board of trustees of this library, in preparation for a competition to choose an architect for their new building, had inspected the Roxbury Branch and main building of the Boston Public Library and libraries in Concord, Brookline, and Worcester. The interior disposition of the Haverhill building seems to have reflected the two Boston structures and the ideas of Nathaniel Shurtleff and Justin Winsor. On the ground floor was located an entry hall with a delivery counter, behind which was set the librarian's room. To the left of the entrance was a stair hall and the circulating library, while a galleried reference hall to the right extended through both floors of the building. A reading room occupied the space above the circulating library.

17. Champney, "Diary," 7 August 1876.

18. Ibid., 11 August 1876. A copy of the survey (Drawing WML F1) can be found in the Richardson drawings in the Houghton Library at Harvard. It is signed and dated "J. R. Carter, C.E./Sept. 1876." See also John W. Johnson, "An Abstract of the Title of Land in Woburn now Occupied by the Public Library," in the *Bulletin of Accessions to the Woburn Public Library for the Year Ending March 1, 1884* (Woburn, Mass., [1884]), 1*–13*.

19. Champney, "Diary," 28 October 1876 and 13 November 1876. Dewey was the first managing editor of the *Library Journal.* Dee Garrison, *Apostles of Culture: The Public Librarian and American Society, 1876–1920* (New York, 1979), 105–125; and Wayne A. Wiegand, "Melvil Dewey and the American Library Association, 1876–1907," in *Melvil Dewey: The Man and the Classification,* ed. G. Stevenson and J. Kramer-Greene (Albany, N.Y., 1983), 102–107.

20. Champney, "Diary," 14 November 1876.

21. Ibid., 15 and 16 November 1876.

22. Ibid., 22 December 1876. It is clear from this entry and others that Winn's ex-brother-in-law Edward Hayden was the man who ultimately made the decisions.

23. Ibid., 16 January 1877. For the announcement of the winner see the *Boston Globe,* 25 January 1877; and the *Woburn Advertiser,* 25 January 1877. A memorial tribute written by the trustees at the time of Hayden's death states: "It is chiefly to his fine taste and liberal spirit that we owe the beautiful library building whose graceful form was his delight." See Woburn Public Library, "In Memoriam. Hon. Edward D. Hayden," *Report of the Trustees of the Public Library, March 1, 1909* (Woburn, Mass., 1909), 138. E. D. Hayden was the son of Ezekial and Elizabeth Hayden of Cambridge; he may have been very distantly related to Richardson's father-in-law, John Cole Hayden (1801–1864), but I have not been able to determine this. For Richardson's wife Julia Hayden's genealogy, see "Henry Hobson Richardson Collection," Reel 1184, Archives of American Art/Smithsonian Institution.

24. *Woburn Advertiser,* 24 May 1877; Woburn Public Library, *Report of the Library Committee of the Town of Woburn, March 1, 1881* (Woburn, Mass., 1881), 84–85; and Cutter, "Model Village Library," 625. For their close relationship to Richardson see James F. O'Gorman, "O. W. Norcross: Richardson's Master Builder," *JSAH* 32 (1973): 104–113.

25. *AABN* 2 (3, 10, and 31 March 1877). The Houghton drawings include the original plan and elevation reproduced in the *AABN* (WML A2 and WML B1), as well as two later drawings for the dedicatory plaque and bench (WML D6 and WML D7), which were not placed in the porch until January 1881 (*Woburn Advertiser,* 20 January 1881). See also O'Gorman, *Drawings,* 156–159.

26. Mariana Griswold (Mrs. Schuyler) Van Rensselaer, *Henry Hobson Richardson and His Works* (Boston, 1888; reprint, New York, 1969), 114.

27. Henry Hobson Richardson, *A Description of Trinity Church by the Architect Henry Hobson Richardson,* reprinted by Trinity Church, Boston (Boston, n.d.), 14.

28. Sarah Bradford Landau, *Edward T. and William A. Potter: American Victorian Architects* (New York, 1979), 263–265.

29. *AABN* 1 (22 July 1876). As this Grand Rapids design indicates, Potter was one of the earliest American architects to appropriate Richardson's Romanesque-derived motifs in his own work. See Landau, *Potter,* 305, 471; and Lawrence Wodehouse, "William Appleton Potter, Principal Pasticheur of Henry Hobson Richardson," *JSAH* 31 (1973): 175–192.

30. See *The Architectural Sketch Book* 1 (November 1873), pl. XIX.

31. A plan and elevation of the Guildhall Library had been published in *The Builder* 29 (27 August 1870): 686–687, and again in *The Architect* 9 (November 1872): 263. For Richardson's visits to London and Dublin see Richard Chafee, "Richardson's Record at the Ecole des Beaux-Arts," *JSAH* 36 (1977): 175.

32. For Trinity College Library, Dublin, see Eve Blau, *Ruskinian Gothic: The Architecture of Deane and Woodward, 1845–1861* (Princeton, 1982), 153–154.

33. Eugène-Emmanuel Viollet-le-Duc, *Dictionnaire raisonné de l'architecture française du XIe au XVIe siècle,* 10 vols. (Paris, 1854–1868), 7: 74. Richardson owned both the *Dictionnaire* and Viollet-le-Duc's *Entretiens sur l'architecture,* 2 vols. (Paris, 1863 and 1872). See James F. O'Gorman, "Documentation: An 1886 Inventory of H. H. Richardson's Library, and Other Gleanings from Probate," *JSAH* 41 (1982): 155.

34. Boullée's proposal had been reproduced in Edward Edwards, *Memoirs of Libraries, Including a Handbook of Library Economy,* 2 vols. (London, 1859), 2: 714.

35. David Van Zanten, *Designing Paris: The Architecture of Duban, Labrouste, Duc, and Vaudoyer* (Cambridge, Mass., 1987), 93.

36. Published in the *Building News* 25 (5 September 1873). See Andrew Saint, *Richard Norman Shaw* (New Haven, 1976), 133–137.

37. Dee Garrison (*Apostles,* 36–40) argues, in fact, that many early librarians drew a strong parallel between their own responsibility toward the moral state of their patrons and that of the ministry, which some viewed as ineffective by this date. See also Neil Harris, "Cultural Institutions and American Modernization," *Journal of Library History* 16 (1981): 44.

38. These chairs were not unique to the Winn Library, which probably means they were not designed specifically for this building. Richardson used them again at both North Easton and Quincy, as well as in the James B. Goodwin House in Hartford, Connecticut. Another example can be identified in a photograph of his own parlor library. See Detroit Institute of the Arts, *The Quest for Unity: American Art between World's Fairs, 1876–1893* (Detroit, 1983), 195–196. See also Charles H. Eastlake, *Hints on Household Taste in Furniture, Upholstery, and Other Details* (London, 1868; first American edition, Boston, 1872), 60–61, 78–80, 150–151.

39. Ann Gilkerson, "The Public Libraries of H. H. Richardson," senior honors thesis, Smith College, 1978, 124–125. According to the *Report of the Library Committee of the Town of Woburn, March 1, 1881,* 84, the furniture, lamps, sconces, and other hardware were all supplied by the building's contractors, the Norcross Brothers, who may have subcontracted the woodworking and carving to John Evans and Co. Evans was paid $50 for carving the clock face in the reading room, while the Norcross Brothers received nearly $2,000 for the furnishings. The tables, chairs, and benches, like the woodwork in the library, were all of natural oak.

40. "Georgian Homes of New England," *AABN* 2 (1877): 338. Peabody signed himself "Georgian." See Vincent J. Scully, *The Shingle Style and the Stick Style: Architectural Theory and Design from Downing to the Origins of Wright,* rev. ed. (New Haven, 1971), 19–53. See also Richard Guy Wilson, "American Architecture and the Search for a National Style in the 1870s," *Nineteenth Century* 3 (Autumn 1877): 74–80; David C. Huntington, "The Quest for Unity: American Art between World's Fairs, 1876–1893," in Detroit Institute of the Arts, *The Quest for Unity,* 30; and Martha Crabill McClaugherty, "Household Art: Creating the Artistic Home, 1863–1893," *Winterthur Portfolio* 18 (1983): 1–26.

41. Jeffrey Karl Ochsner and Thomas C. Hubka, "H. H. Richardson: The Design of the William Watts Sherman House," *JSAH* 51 (1992), 136–145; and Mark Girouard, *Sweetness and Light: The "Queen Anne" Movement, 1860–1900* (Oxford, 1977; paperback edition, New Haven, 1984), 208–209.

42. Gilkerson, "The Public Libraries of H. H. Richardson," 88–89; Viollet-le-Duc, *Dictionnaire,* 6: 224; and Ochsner and Hubka, "William Watts Sherman House," 136–145. The facade of a second townhouse illustrated by Viollet-le-Duc (*Dictionnaire,* 4: 210) may have supplied the inspiration for the segmental arch.

43. *AABN* 2 (3 March 1877). Henry Antoine Révoil, in *Architecture romane du Midi de la France,* 3 vols. (Paris, 1867–1873), 3: pl. XXIV, illustrates a similar alternation of pilasters and single colonnettes above the entry portal to the church of Ste.-Marthe at Tarascon.

44. Van Zanten, *Designing Paris,* 236–246, and "Ornament," *VIA: The Journal of the Graduate School of Fine Arts of the University of Pennsylvania* 3 (1977): 52.

45. Eastlake, *Household Taste,* ix.

46. Ruskin, 10: 215. All told, Richardson owned no fewer than a dozen works by Ruskin, including his major architectural and critical treatises *The Seven Lamps of Architecture* (1849), *Modern Painters,* 5 vols. (1849–1860), *The Stones of Venice,* 2 vols. (1851, 1853), and *Lectures on Architecture and Painting* (1854). O'Gorman, "Documentation," 154.

47. James F. O'Gorman, *H. H. Richardson: Architectural Forms for an American Society* (Chicago, 1987), 91–95. See also Ochsner, *Richardson,* 48–49; Lauren S. Weingarten, "Naturalized Nationalism: A Ruskinian Discourse on the Search for an American Style of Architecture," *Winterthur Portfolio* 24 (1989): 55, n. 22; Roger Stein, *John Ruskin and Aesthetic Thought in America, 1840–1900* (Cambridge, Mass., 1967), 101–105; and Henry-Russell Hitchcock, "Ruskin and American Architecture, or Regeneration Long Delayed," in *Concerning Architecture: Essays on Architectural Writers and Writing Presented to Nikolaus Pevsner,* ed. John Summerson (Baltimore, 1968), 169–176.

48. Quoted in Cynthia Zaitzevsky, *Frederick Law Olmsted and the Boston Park System* (Cambridge, Mass., 1982), 62. See also S. D. Sutton, *Charles Sprague Sargent and the Arnold Arboretum* (Cambridge, Mass., 1970), 22–57; and Alexander von Hoffman, *Local Attachments: The Making of an American Urban Neighborhood, 1850 to 1920* (Baltimore, 1994), 76–85.

49. A copy of this book, currently in the collection of the University of California at Los Angeles, has Olmsted's New York City address inscribed on the title page, along with the later stamp of his son Frederick Law Olmsted, Jr. Emerson's work would only be supplanted by the publication of Sargent's own monumental study, *Silva of North America,* 14 vols. (Boston, 1891–1902), in which he employed similar illustrations. Emerson was Arnold's brother-in-law and one of the first trustees of the Arnold Arboretum. Zaitzevsky, *Boston Park System,* 58–63. While Richardson may not have owned a copy of his report, he could have become familiar with it through Sargent or Olmsted. There are also similar presentations of "leaves and flowers from nature" illustrated at the back of Owen Jones's *Grammar of Ornament* (London, 1856), a book that the architect had in his own library. Jones advocated using plant forms as the basis for a more abstracted ornament, "based upon a geometrical construction" but still "sufficiently suggestive to convey the intended image to the mind, without destroying the unity of the object they are employed to decorate." See *Grammar of Ornament,* 5–6, plates 91–100; and O'Gorman, "Documentation," 153.

50. Henry Acland, *The Oxford Museum* (London, 1859); Blau, *Ruskinian Gothic,* 67–77; Michael W. Brooks, *John Ruskin and Victorian Architecture* (New Brunswick, N.J., 1987), 117–134; George Hersey, *High Victorian Gothic: A Study in Associationism* (Baltimore, 1972), 191–199; and Chafee, "Richardson's Record," 184.

51. Ruskin, 10: 237.

52. Theodore Minot Clark, *Building Superintendence: A Manual for Young Architects, Students and Others Interested in Building Operations as Carried On at the Present Day* (Boston, 1883), 7.

53. Van Rensselaer, *Richardson,* 68–69; and O'Gorman, "O. W. Norcross," 104–113.

54. Ruskin, 8: 113–114.

55. Charles Eliot Norton, "The Harvard and Yale Memorial Buildings," *The Nation* 5 (11 July 1867): 35; Robert B. Shaffer, "Ruskin, Norton, and Memorial Hall," *Harvard Library Bulletin* 3 (Spring 1949): 213–231; Hennessey, "Van Brunt," 29–47; and, for the National Academy, Sarah Bradford Landau, *P. B. Wight: Architect, Contractor, and Critic, 1838–1925* (Chicago, 1981), 16–20.

56. Ruskin, 8: 102–103. For more on the geological analogy and a detailed description of the structure of the Alps and the relationship of geology to the "wall veil" of buildings, see *Stones of Venice* in Ruskin, 9: 85–90.

57. Ruskin, 8: 114–115. This is from the *The Seven Lamps of Architecture.* In *Modern Painters* (Ruskin, 4: 137) Ruskin opposes the rustication of the Pitti. See also *Stones of Venice,* vol. 1 (Ruskin, 9: 350–351), where he also opposes the use of rustication in general.

58. John Bascom, *Aesthetics; or, the Science of Beauty* (New York, 1877), 190.

59. Ruskin, 9: 82–84; Viollet-le-Duc, *Entretiens,* 1: 296; and Révoil, *Architecture romane,* 3: pl. II. See also Gilkerson, "Public Libraries of H. H. Richardson," 88–89.

60. Ruskin, 9: 347.

61. Ibid., 9: 85–90.

62. For the impact of Ruskin's geological imagery on American painters, see Virginia L. Wagner, "John Ruskin and Artistical Geology in America," *Winterthur Portfolio* 23 (1988): 151–167.

63. Barbara Novak, *Nature and Culture: American Landscape and Painting 1825–1875* (New York, 1980), 49. Ruskin referred to the "vital truth" of geology, that is, its ability to simultaneously convey the past, present, and future in its makeup. See Wagner, "Artistical Geology," 153.

64. Henry Van Brunt, "Greek Lines," *Atlantic Monthly* 8 (1861): 86.

65. Henri Labrouste, "A M. le Directeur de la Revue d'Architecture," *Revue générale de l'architecture et des travaux publics* 10 (1852), col. 383.

66. Van Zanten, *Designing Paris,* 225. For the notion of the wall veil as metaphor see Van Zanten, "Ornament," 49–54.

67. Viollet-le-Duc, *Dictionnaire,* 3: 409.

68. The inscription reads, "This building was erected in memory of Jonathan B. Winn from funds bequeathed by his son for the use, benefit and improvement of the people of Woburn." Cutter, "Model Village Library," 622; *Woburn Journal,* 25 December 1875.

69. Van Rensselaer, *Richardson,* 67, 81.

70. Henry-Russell Hitchcock, *The Architecture of H. H. Richardson and His Times* (New York, 1936; reprint, Cambridge, Mass., 1966), 172.

71. With a reading room in one of its "transepts," the basilican form of the Harvard library—still one of the largest and most impressive in this country—may also have influenced Richardson's choice of a cruciform plan at Woburn. Although it is not clear how Richardson might have known it, one of Eden Nesfield's farm buildings at Shipley Hall (1860–1861) likewise betrays a remarkably similar massing,

with a central tower and segmentally arched entryway flanked by a two-story gable and octagonal pavilion. See Saint, *Shaw,* fig. 30.

72. Richardson, *Trinity Church,* 14.

73. O'Gorman, *Architectural Forms,* 30–35; and Jack Quinan, "H. H. Richardson and the Boston Granite Tradition," *Little Journal of the S. A. H. Western New York Chapter* 3 (February 1979): 20–29.

74. See, for example, Baltard's St.-Augustin (1860–1868) or Vaudremer's St.-Pierre de Montrouge (1864–1872). Hitchcock, *Richardson,* 30–31. For Marseilles see Van Zanten, *Designing Paris,* 138–175.

75. O'Gorman, *Architectural Forms,* 95–104.

76. Andrew Jackson Downing, *The Architecture of Country Houses* (New York, 1850), 264; O'Gorman, *Architectural Forms,* 91–93; and Weingarten, "Naturalized Nationalism," 43–48.

77. Henry Van Brunt, "John Wellborn Root," *Inland Architect and News Record* 16 (January 1891): 86. Van Rensselaer observed that Richardson "was never a theorist about himself except in retrospect" (*Richardson,* 57).

78. Van Rensselaer, *Richardson,* 114.

79. Van Zanten, *Designing Paris,* 5–17, and "Architecture," in *The Second Empire, 1852–1870: Art in France under Napoleon III* (Philadelphia, 1978), 35–40; Neil Levine, "The Romantic Idea of Architectural Legibility: Henri Labrouste and the Neo-Grec," in *The Architecture of the Ecole des Beaux-Arts,* ed. Arthur Drexler (New York, 1977), 360–393; Robin Middleton and Davis Watkin, *Neoclassical and 19th Century Architecture* (New York, 1980), 217–238; Robin Middleton, "Vive l'Ecole," *A.D. Profiles 17: The Beaux-Arts* (London, n.d.), 38–47; and Richard A. Moore, "Academic Dessin Theory in France after the Reorganization of 1863," *JSAH* 36 (1977): 145–174.

80. Van Zanten, *Designing Paris,* 13. For an extensive discussion of Labrouste's work at Paestum see Levine, "Romantic Idea," 357–393.

81. Both Taine and Viollet-le-Duc lectured at the Ecole during the years that Richardson was a student there. See Viollet-le-Duc, *Entretiens,* 2: passim; Barry Bergdoll, introduction to Eugène-Emmanuel Viollet-le-Duc, *The Foundations of Architecture: Selections from the Dictionnaire raisonné,* trans. Kenneth D. Whitehead (New York, 1990), 1–31; and Hanno-Walter Kruft, *A History of Architectural Theory from Vitruvius to the Present* (New York, 1994), 279–286. See also Henry Van Brunt, "Translator's Introduction to the Discourses of Eugène-Emmanuel Viollet-le-Duc," reprinted in *Architecture and Society: Selected Essays of Henry Van Brunt,* ed. William A. Coles (Cambridge, Mass., 1969), 97–110. Although he later came to own many of his books, Richardson had a rather ambiguous relationship to Viollet-le-Duc. As a student, for example, he had protested the Frenchman's appointment as a lecturer at the Ecole des Beaux-Arts. While he appears to have relied on Viollet-le-Duc's books for motifs, he never made it completely clear what he thought of his theories. Certainly he was never the structural rationalist that Viollet-le-Duc claimed to be. See Edward R. Ford, *The Details of Modern Architecture* (Cambridge, Mass., 1990), 19–21; Van Rensselaer, *Richardson,* 15–16; and A. Boime, "The Teaching Reforms of 1863 and the Origins of Modernism in France," *Art Quarterly* 1 (1977): 15.

82. T. M. Clark, "H. H. Richardson," *The Nation* 47 (1888): 151.

83. Ellen W. Kramer, "Detlef Lienau, an Architect of the Brown Decades," *JSAH* 14 (1955): 18–25; Richard Chafee, "Hunt in Paris," and Sarah Bradford Landau, "Richard Morris Hunt: Architectural Inno-

vator and Father of a 'Distinctive' American School," both in *The Architecture of Richard Morris Hunt,* ed. Susan R. Stein (Chicago, 1986), 13–49; and William A. Coles, introduction to Van Brunt, *Architecture and Society,* 10–16, and "Richard Morris Hunt and His Library as Revealed by the Studio Sketchbooks of Henry Van Brunt," *Art Quarterly* 30 (1967): 224–238.

84. Detlef Lienau, "On Romantic and Classical Architecture," *The Crayon* 5 (1858): 168.

85. Van Brunt, "Greek Lines," 86.

86. Lienau, "On Romantic and Classical Architecture," 168.

87. *Boston Globe,* 25 January 1877; and *Woburn Journal,* 27 January 1877.

88. *LJ* 1 (1877): 235.

89. Cutter, "Model Village Library," 618.

## CHAPTER FOUR

1. Montgomery Schuyler, "The Romanesque Revival in America," *Architectural Record,* 1 (1891–1892): 161–163.

2. Ames Free Library of Easton, Inc., *The First Century: A Centennial History of the Ames Free Library of Easton, Inc. 1883–1983* (North Easton, Massachusetts, [1983]), [3]. See also FPLM, 111–112; Henry-Russell Hitchcock, *The Architecture of H. H. Richardson and His Times* (New York, 1936; reprint, Cambridge, Mass., 1966), 185–188; Jeffrey Karl Ochsner, *H. H. Richardson: Complete Architectural Works* (Cambridge, Mass., 1982), 183–187; "The Ames Memorial Building, North Easton, Mass.," *Monographs of American Architecture,* no. 3 (Boston, 1886); "The Ames Memorial Library, North Easton, Mass.," *AABN* 13 (30 June 1883): 307; Larry J. Homolka, "Henry Hobson Richardson and the 'Ames Memorial Buildings,'" Ph.D. diss., Harvard University, 1976, 57–96; and Robert F. Brown, "The Aesthetic Transformation of an Industrial Community," *Winterthur Portfolio* 12 (1977): 35–41.

3. FPLM, 54–55, 308–309; *The Architectural Sketch Book* 1 (1873), pl. XIX; and Homolka, "'Ames Memorial Buildings,'" 48.

4. The final cost of the building is noted in the archives of Shepley Bulfinch Richardson and Abbott in the "Ames Library" file. F. L. Ames, for example, increased the endowment from $15,000 to $40,000. William L. Chaffin, *History of the Town of Easton, Massachusetts* (Cambridge, Mass., 1886), 378–379.

5. See for example Ochsner, *Richardson,* 183; or Ann Gilkerson, "The Public Libraries of H. H. Richardson," senior honors thesis, Smith College, 1978, 27–28. Other commissions due to Richardson's Harvard acquaintances include Unity Church (1867–1869), the Western Railroad Offices (1867), and the Agawam Bank (1869) in Springfield, Massachusetts, and quite possibly Trinity Church, Boston (1872–1877). Jeffrey Karl Ochsner, "Architecture for the Boston and Albany Railroad: 1881–1894," *JSAH* 47 (1988): 112; and Ochsner, *Richardson,* 24–27, 32–33, 64, 114–123.

6. F. L. Ames also became a liberal supporter of the Arnold Arboretum. "Frederick L. Ames," *The National Cyclopedia of American Biography* (New York, 1917), 14: 202–203. For Olmsted and Richardson see James F. O'Gorman, *H. H. Richardson and His Office: Selected Drawings* (Boston, 1974), 29–30; and Gilkerson, "Public Libraries of H. H. Richardson," 27. For Sargent see S. D. Sutton, *Charles Sprague Sargent and the Arnold Arboretum* (Cambridge, Mass., 1970).


**
*

7. Brown, "Industrial Community," 44–48; and Frederick Law Olmsted, Jr., and Theodora Kimball, eds. *Frederick Law Olmsted: Landscape Architect, 1822–1903,* 2 vols. (New York, 1928) 2: 27.

8. Henry quite likely had introduced Charles to the architect by this date. Edward Chase Kirkland, *Charles Francis Adams, Jr., 1835–1915: The Patrician at Bay* (Cambridge, Mass., 1965), 74, 83–84; and Ernst Scheyer, *The Circle of Henry Adams* (Detroit, 1970), 147–172.

9. *Quincy Patriot Ledger,* 7 January 1937, 6. See also FPLM, 305–308; Hitchcock, *Richardson,* 210–213; O'Gorman, *Drawings,* 160–161; Ochsner, *Richardson,* 226–231; L. Draper Hill, Jr., *The Crane Library* (Quincy, Mass., 1962); *Address of Charles Francis Adams, Jr. and Proceedings at the Dedication of the Crane Memorial Hall at Quincy, Mass., May 30, 1882* (Cambridge, Mass., 1883); *Harper's Weekly* 27 (1883): 251; and "The Crane Library, Quincy, Mass.," *AABN* 13 (30 June 1883): 306–307.

10. *Quincy Patriot Ledger,* 7 January 1937, 6.

11. Quincy Public Library, *Annual Report of the Public Library of Quincy for 1880* (Boston, 1881), 4; and Thomas Crane's obituary, *Quincy Patriot Ledger,* 4 October 1875, 2.

12. See, for example, the *Stamford Advocate,* 19 December 1879, 23 January and 27 February 1880; and Lynn Winfield Wilson, *History of Fairfield County, Connecticut: 1639–1928,* 3 vols. (Chicago and Hartford, 1929), 3: 65–66. While no building was erected in Stamford until 1910, the public library was incorporated on 12 March 1880.

13. Quoted in the *Quincy Patriot Ledger,* 7 January 1937, 6. Charles Francis Adams, Jr., *Autobiography* (Boston, 1916; reprint, New York, 1983), 178–179, *Three Episodes of Massachusetts History,* 2 vols. (Boston, 1893), 2: 933–940, and "The Public Library and the Public Schools," in *The Public Library and the Common Schools: Three Papers on Educational Reform* (Boston, 1879), 5–15.

14. Hill, *Crane Library,* 25–26; and letters from C. F. Adams, Jr., to Albert Crane in the Albert Crane Correspondence in the collections of the Massachusetts Historical Society dated 7 December 1891, 30 July 1903, 27 June 1904, and 22 July 1907.

15. *Records of the Proceedings of the Trustees of the Thomas Crane Public Library and the Quincy Public Library: May 11, 1871–June 2, 1886,* 12 April 1880. It is interesting to note that Albert Crane was required to provide a bond that guaranteed that within two years he would erect "a Memorial library building at the expense of not less than $25,000 in accordance with the terms of 19 February 1880 letter." This was witnessed in New York by William Dean. See ibid., 30 April 1880.

16. *Quincy Patriot,* 28 August 1880; Quincy Public Library, *Annual Report of the Public Library of Quincy for 1880,* 2; Hill, *Crane Library,* 21–23; and O'Gorman, *Drawings,* 161.

17. Mariana Griswold (Mrs. Schuyler) Van Rensselaer, *Henry Hobson Richardson and His Works* (Boston, 1888; reprint, New York, 1969), 68. Henry-Russell Hitchcock (*Richardson,* 84–86) suggested that the architect derived the form of this new entryway from the arches of early Christian churches in Syria.

18. Eugène-Emmanuel Viollet-le-Duc, *Dictionnaire raisonné de l'architecture française du XIe au XVIe siècle,* 10 vols. (Paris, 1868), 3: 344.

19. Van Rensselaer, *Richardson,* 68.

20. Edward R. Ford, *The Details of Modern Architecture* (Cambridge, Mass., 1990), 29. The walls are actually constructed of load-bearing brick, with a stone veneer on the exterior and plaster inside.

21. Clarence Cook, *The House Beautiful: Essays on Beds and Tables, Stools and Candlesticks* (New York,

1877); Arthur Little, *Early New England Interiors Sketched by Arthur Little* (Swampscott, Mass., 1877); and Eileen Boris, *Art and Labor: Ruskin, Morris, and the Craftsman Ideal in America* (Philadelphia, 1986), 54–58. The contractors again included the Norcross Brothers and John Evans and Company. See also Ford, *Modern Architecture,* 25–27.

22. The relief of Ames was originally executed in stone, then replaced with bronze. Gilkerson, "Public Libraries of H. H. Richardson," 32–33.

23. Hitchcock, *Richardson,* 210; and Schuyler, "Romanesque Revival," 163.

24. Ford, *Modern Architecture,* 31.

25. H. H. Richardson, *The Hoyt Public Library, East Saginaw, Michigan* (Boston, [1886]), 4, 9. There is a copy of this in the Houghton Library, Harvard University.

26. *Harper's Weekly* 27 (1883): 251.

27. Van Rensselaer, *Richardson,* 79; description in the *Quincy Patriot Ledger,* 27 May 1882; and Lauren S. Weingarten, "Naturalized Nationalism: A Ruskinian Discourse on the Search for an American Style of Architecture," *Winterthur Portfolio* 24 (1989): 45–50.

28. Hitchcock, *Richardson,* 211–212. Richardson similarly mixed medieval and colonial allusions, including the saltbox gable, in the contemporary designs for the Glessner House in Chicago. See Thomas C. Hubka, "H. H. Richardson's Glessner House: A Garden in the Machine," *Winterthur Portfolio* 24 (1989): 209–229.

29. *Records of the Proceedings of the Trustees of the Thomas Crane Public Library and the Quincy Public Library: May 11, 1871–June 2, 1886,* 23 January 1882.

30. Van Rensselaer, *Richardson,* 78–79.

31. Hill, *Crane Library,* 20–24; and O'Gorman, *Drawings,* 160–161.

32. O'Gorman, *Drawings,* 161.

33. James F. O'Gorman, *Three American Architects: Richardson, Sullivan, and Wright, 1865–1915* (Chicago, 1991), 41; and Van Rensselaer, *Richardson,* 128, 141.

34. Quoted in Robin Middleton and David Watkin, *Neoclassical and 19th Century Architecture* (New York, 1980), 230. The original appeared in *Architectural Review* (July 1911): 28.

35. For a good summary of the Beaux-Arts teaching method at the time Richardson attended, see Richard Chafee, "Richardson's Record at the Ecole des Beaux-Arts," *JSAH* 36 (1977): 175–188, and "The Teaching of Architecture at the Ecole des Beaux-Arts," in *The Architecture of the Ecole des Beaux-Arts,* ed. Arthur Drexler (New York, 1977), 61–110; Jean Paul Carlhian, "The Ecole des Beaux-Arts: Modes and Manners," *Journal of Architectural Education* 33 (1979): 7–17; and David Van Zanten, "Architectural Composition at the Ecole des Beaux-Arts from Charles Percier to Charles Garnier," in Drexler, ed., *Architecture of the Ecole des Beaux-Arts,* 111–290, and "Le Système des Beaux-Arts," *A. D. Profiles 17: The Beaux-Arts* (London, n.d.), 68–79. The following discussion is heavily indebted to these authors, as well as to O'Gorman, *Drawings,* 16–27.

36. Van Rensselaer, *Richardson,* 128.

37. As, for example, with the design of the Glessner House in Chicago in 1885. O'Gorman, *Drawings,* 87.

38. "The French Mind," *The Builder* 28 (9 April 1870): 280.

39. Julien Guadet, *Eléments et théorie de l'architecture,* 4 vols. (Paris, 1901–1904) 1: 132. Although Guadet, who won the Prix de Rome in 1864, did not actually record his ideas until 1901, they represent notions he learned in the 1850s as a student of Henri Labrouste, and during the following decade, along with Richardson, in the atelier of Jules André. Guadet defined *caractère* as the "identité entre l'impression architecturale et l'impression morale du programme." This concept was central to his whole treatise, which was essentially concerned with the analysis of different building typologies. Egbert identifies this as *type* character, and differentiates it from general and specific character. The former, he notes, was "the one most easily taught, and therefore, appropriately, the one that eventually was most emphasized" at the Ecole des Beaux-Arts. Donald Drew Egbert, *The Beaux-Arts Tradition in French Architecture Illustrated by the Grands Prix de Rome,* ed. David Van Zanten (Princeton, 1980), 136. For more on the evolution and definition of *caractère* and type in France, see Hanno-Walter Kruft, *A History of Architectural Theory from Vitruvius to the Present* (New York, 1994), 144–165; and Anthony Vidler, "The Idea of Type: The Transformation of the Academic Ideal, 1750–1830," *Oppositions* 8 (1977): 95–115, and *The Writing of the Walls: Architectural Theory in the Late Enlightenment* (Princeton, 1987), 147–164.

40. Van Rensselaer, *Richardson,* 112–113. Terms such as "conception," "character," and "idea" all seem to come directly from a French design vocabulary.

41. Hitchcock, *Richardson,* 172.

42. Van Rensselaer, *Richardson,* 68.

43. Ann Jenson Adams, "The Birth of a Style: Henry Hobson Richardson and the Competition Drawings for Trinity Church, Boston," *Art Bulletin* 62 (1980): 420; and Henry Hobson Richardson, *A Description of Trinity Church, reprinted by Trinity Church* (Boston, n.d.), 11–12.

44. This monument was also described at the time as being 65 by 65 and 60 by 65 feet. See James F. O'Gorman, "Man-Made Mountain: 'Gathering and Governing' in H. H. Richardson's Design for the Ames Monument in Wyoming," in *The Railroad in American Art: Representation of Technological Change,* ed. Susan Danly and Leo Marx (Cambridge, Mass., 1987), 126, n. 35, and *H. H. Richardson: Architectural Forms for an American Society* (Chicago, 1987), 95–104.

45. Viollet-Le-Duc, *Lectures on Architecture,* 2 vols., trans. Benjamin Bucknel (London, 1877), 1: 392–393.

46. Eugène-Emmanuel Viollet-le-Duc, *Entretiens sur l'architecture,* 2 vols. (Paris, 1863 and 1872), 1: 397–403.

47. Ruskin, 8: 108–109.

48. Ibid., 8: 100–102. For parallel notions in *The Stones of Venice* see Ruskin, 10: 213.

49. O'Gorman ("Man-Made Mountain," 120–121) makes the case for Richardson as both gatherer and governor in the design for the Ames Monument, viewing "governing" as the application of mathematical principles to nature. I read "governing" in Ruskin's text as more a result of the powerful emotional will of the architect over natural form; thus at Quincy, Richardson uses this principle to move beyond the mathematical precision of North Easton.

50. Ruskin, 8: 119–120.

51. Van Rensselaer, *Richardson,* 122.

52. Ibid., 114, n. 1.

53. Ruskin, 8: 134.

54. S. G. W. [Samuel Green Wheeler] Benjamin, "Libraries," *Harper's New Monthly Magazine* 29 (September 1864): 488.

55. *Quincy Patriot Ledger,* 27 May 1882. This author might have noted, as well, that Thomas Crane had himself been a dealer in this same building material. As O'Gorman ("O. W. Norcross," 104–113) has noted, however, by this date the Norcross Brothers, contractors upon whom Richardson had come to rely more and more, had opened their own quarries specifically to supply the architect with the type of stone he most preferred, and this did not include a source of Quincy granite.

56. *Quincy Patriot Ledger,* 27 May 1882. For Adams's view see chapter 7 below, and the letter of C. F. Adams, Jr., to Albert Crane after a visit to the library in May 1905, quoted in Hill, *Crane Library,* 25–26.

## CHAPTER FIVE

1. According to Olmsted, he was responsible for the choice of a site next to the Baptist Church. F. L. Olmsted to Mr. Baxter, 29 January 1884, Olmsted Papers, General Correspondence, Library of Congress, Container 44, Reel 39; and Frederick Law Olmsted, Jr., and Theodora Kimball, eds., *Frederick Law Olmsted: Landscape Architect, 1822–1903,* 2 vols. (New York, 1928), 2: 27. See also *Family Records of Deacons James W. Converse and Elisha S. Converse,* comp. William G. Hill (Malden, Mass., 1887), 177; Malden Historical Society, *One Hundredth Anniversary of the Malden Public Library 1879–1979* (Malden, Mass., 1979); FPLM, 212–217; *Malden City Press,* 10 May 1884 and 1 October 1885; Mariana Griswold (Mrs. Schuyler) Van Rensselaer, *Henry Hobson Richardson and His Works* (Boston, 1888; reprint, New York, 1969), 140; James F. O'Gorman, *H. H. Richardson and His Office: Selected Drawings* (Boston, 1974), 156–159; and Jeffrey Karl Ochsner, *H. H. Richardson: Complete Architectural Works* (Cambridge, Mass., 1982), 313–317.

2. Nathan E. Wood, *The History of the First Baptist Church of Boston (1665–1899)* (Philadelphia, 1899), 345, 369; Ochsner, *Richardson,* 73–77.

3. Firm records indicate that "scale drawings" for the Woburn Library were forwarded to Mr. Converse in October 1884, the same month elevations for the Converse building were sent to the Norcross Brothers. "Woburn Library," however, has been written in ink over the words "Converse Library." These transactions, moreover, would make more sense in October 1883, before the contract for the building was let to the Norcross firm. Perhaps there is an inaccuracy in these entries, which remain interesting, just the same. See Drawings List, Book No. 5: 1884–1894, 5, 6, "Henry Hobson Richardson and Shepley, Rutan and Coolidge Collection," Shepley Bulfinch Richardson and Abbott, roll 676, Archives of American Art, Smithsonian Institution. I would like to thank Robert Roche of that firm for kindly allowing me to see the original.

4. Hitchcock, *Richardson,* 257.

5. *AABN* 28 (3 October 1885): 163. For the Middlesex Society, which appears never to have occupied its second-story space, see *Malden City Press,* 4 July 1885, 2. I would like to thank Joel Thiele, Research Librarian at the Malden Public Library, for clarifying the function of this society.

6. Much of this furniture survives in the current trustee's room, which now is on the second story of the forward wing of the building. See Anne Farnam, "H. H. Richardson and A. H. Davenport: Architecture and Furniture as Big Business in America's Gilded Age," in *Tools and Technologies: America's Wooden Age,* ed. Paul B. Kebabian and William C. Lipke (Burlington, Vt., 1979), 81, 84; Wendy Kaplan, ed., *The*

*Art That Is Life: The Arts and Crafts Movement in America, 1875–1920* (Boston, 1987), 75; and O'Gorman, *Drawings,* 204.

7. *Malden Mirror,* 10 May 1884. This porch is also labeled "piazza" in the small plan that appears in *AABN* 22 (3 October 1885).

8. Trustees of the Malden Public Library, *Eighth Annual Report of the Trustees of the Malden Public Library for the Year Ending December 31, 1885* (Boston, 1886), 10.

9. *Malden City Press,* 1 October 1885, 8.

10. Consolation literature included obituary poems and memoirs, mourners' manuals, prayer guidebooks, hymns, and books about heaven. According to Ann Douglas, these writings "sponsored elaborate methods of burial and commemoration, communications with the next world, and microscopic viewings of a sentimentalized afterlife." See Ann Douglas, *The Feminization of American Culture* (New York, 1977), 201–202, and also "Heaven Our Home: Consolation Literature in the Northern United States, 1830–1880," in *Death in America,* ed. David E. Stannard (Philadelphia, 1975), 49–68. For an interpretation of Garnier's intent at the Opera, see David Van Zanten, *Designing Paris: The Architecture of Duban, Labrouste, Duc, and Vaudoyer* (Cambridge, Mass., 1987), 231–234, and "Architectural Composition at the Ecole des Beaux-Arts from Charles Percier to Charles Garnier," in *The Architecture of the Ecole des Beaux-Arts,* ed. Arthur Drexler (New York, 1977), 163, 185; also Charles Garnier, *Le Théatre* (Paris, 1871); and *Le Nouvel Opéra de Paris,* 2 vols. and atlas (Paris, 1878–1881).

11. Ochsner, *Richardson,* 313–314.

12. *Malden City Press,* 1 October 1885, 2.

13. Bicknell studied with Thomas Couture. Whether he may have known Richardson at this time is not certain, although it is quite possible. For Bicknell see John C. Rand, comp., *One of a Thousand: A Series of Biographical Sketches of One Thousand Representative Men Resident in the Commonwealth of Massachusetts: A.D. 1888-'89* (Boston, 1890), 53.

14. Garry Wills, *Lincoln at Gettysburg: The Words That Remade America* (New York, 1992), 76.

15. *Malden City Press,* 1 October 1885, 8.

16. Richardson himself collected dozens of photographs of monastic cloisters, especially St.-Trophime in Arles. See, for example, the album Richardson 104, vol. (1) in the Frances Loeb Library, Harvard. See also Eugène-Emmanuel Viollet-le-Duc, *Dictionnaire raisonné de l'architecture française du XIe au XVIe siècle,* 10 vols. (Paris, 1854–1868), 3: 409.

17. Five drawings for this courtyard survive in the Olmsted Archives at the Frederick Law Olmsted National Historic Site in Brookline (Olmsted job #292). Two of these are dated 25 April 1885, the same day they were sent to E. S. Converse. See also the letters from F. L. Olmsted to E. S. Converse, 25 April 1885; E. S. Converse to F. L. Olmsted, 15 April 1885; and F. L. Olmsted to Mr. Baxter, 29 January 1884 (concerning his site visit with Richardson), in the Olmsted Papers, General Correspondence, Library of Congress, Container 44, Reel 39; *Malden City Press,* 1 October 1885, 8; and Olmsted and Kimball, *Olmsted,* 2: 27.

18. Erwin Panofsky, "*Et in Arcadia Ego:* Poussin and the Elegiac Tradition," in *Meaning in the Visual Arts: Papers in Art History* (Garden City, N.Y., 1955), 295–320; Richard A. Etlin, *The Architecture of Death: The Transformation of the Cemetery in Eighteenth-Century Paris* (Cambridge, Mass., 1984), 179–184; and



**
*

Blanche Linden-Ward, *Silent City on a Hill: Landscapes of Memory and Boston's Mount Auburn Cemetery* (Columbus, Ohio, 1989), 35–64.

19. Wills, *Lincoln,* 47.

20. Henri Labrouste, "A M. le Directeur de la Revue d'Architecture," *Revue générale de l'architecture et des travaux publics* 10 (1852), col. 382; and Van Zanten, *Designing Paris,* 236–238.

21. Etlin, *Architecture of Death,* 233–236.

22. *The Architecture of the Ecole des Beaux-Arts,* ed. Arthur Drexler (New York, 1977), 418–419; and Howard Colvin, *Architecture and the After-Life* (New Haven, 1991), 364–366.

23. *Malden City Press,* 1 October 1885, 8. In Chicago, Richardson turned this notion inside out at the Glessner House (1885–1887), where in this more urban context he designed the home around a garden. Thomas C. Hubka, "H. H. Richardson's Glessner House: A Garden in the Machine," *Winterthur Portfolio* 24 (1989): 228–229. For rural cemeteries as places of public "resort," see Douglas, *Feminization of American Culture,* 210–211.

24. Neil Harris, "Cultural Institutions and American Modernization," *Journal of Library History* 16 (1981): 43.

25. Mircea Eliade, *The Sacred and the Profane: The Nature of Religion,* trans. Willard R. Trask (New York, 1959; paperback edition, San Diego, 1987), 20–65. In an age of spiritualism and the seance, the idea of communication with the departed was a common theme. See, for example, Douglas, *Feminization of American Culture,* 200–226. Richardson's arches are evocative of a variety of eighteenth- and nineteenth-century romantic, neoclassical, and néo-grec cenotaphs, sepulchers, and memorials with which the architect would have been familiar, such as the funerary designs of Etienne-Louis Boullée and others in Etlin, *Architecture of Death,* 115–129, and Richard A. Etlin, *Symbolic Space: French Enlightenment Architecture and Its Legacy* (Chicago, 1994), figs. 12, 54, 81, 93; or the student designs for votive monuments of 1851 in *Architecture of the Ecole des Beaux-Arts,* 412–413.

26. Henry Van Brunt, "Greek Lines," *Atlantic Monthly* 8 (1861): 86.

27. Quoted in O'Gorman, *Drawings,* 29–30. For the Bache monument see Ochsner, *Richardson,* 48–49; and Francis R. Kowsky, "The William Dorsheimer House: A Reflection of French Suburban Architecture in the Early Work of H. H. Richardson," *Art Bulletin* 62 (1980): 136–137.

28. O'Gorman, *Three American Architects: Richardson, Sullivan, and Wright, 1865–1915* (Chicago, 1991), 33–34, and also *H. H. Richardson: Architectural Forms for an American Society* (Chicago, 1987), 91–95.

29. Albert Crane, at Charles Francis Adams, Jr.'s, behest, continued to purchase adjacent property well into the twentieth century in order to create the spacious grounds that exist today. See L. Draper Hill, Jr., *The Crane Library* (Quincy, Mass., 1962), 27–31.

30. Van Rensselaer, *Richardson,* 71; and Robert F. Brown, "The Aesthetic Transformation of an Industrial Community," *Winterthur Portfolio* 12 (1977): 41–48.

31. F. L. Olmsted to Oakes Angier Ames, 10 April 1882, Olmsted Associates Letter Book, vol. 1, 16 June 1884–9 September 1889, Olmsted Papers, Container 20, Reel 19. Reproduced from the collections of the Manuscript Division, Library of Congress. See also Francis R. Kowsky, "H. H. Richardson's Ames Gate Lodge and the Romantic Landscape Tradition," *JSAH* 50 (1991): 186; and Ruskin, 10: 237.

32. *Malden City Press,* 1 October 1885, 8.

33. Ibid.

34. Ibid., 5.

35. Ibid., 8.

36. Gwendolyn Wright, *Moralism and the Model Home* (Chicago, 1980), 31–32.

37. Mark Girouard, *Sweetness and Light: The "Queen Anne" Movement, 1860–1900* (Oxford, 1977; paperback edition, New Haven, 1984), 5; also Eileen Boris, *Art and Labor: Ruskin, Morris, and the Craftsman Ideal in America* (Philadelphia, 1986), 3–12; and T. J. Jackson Lears, *No Place for Grace: Antimodernism and the Transformation of American Culture, 1880–1920* (Chicago, 1991), passim.

38. David C. Huntington, "The Quest for Unity: American Art between World's Fairs, 1876–1893," in Detroit Institute of the Arts, *The Quest for Unity: American Art between World's Fairs, 1876–1893* (Detroit, 1983), 25. Charles Eliot Norton was spreading this same gospel from his classroom at Harvard. See Michael W. Brooks, "New England Gothic: Charles Eliot Norton, Charles H. Moore, and Henry Adams," in *The Architectural Historian in America,* ed. E. B. MacDougall (Hanover, N.H., 1990), 113–116; and Ronald Story, *The Forging of an Aristocracy: Harvard and the Boston Upper Class, 1800–1870* (Middletown, Conn., 1980), 124–134.

39. See, for example, the social proscriptions against ostentation at Mount Auburn: Linden-Ward, *Silent City,* 219; and also Robert F. Dalzell, Jr., *Enterprising Elite: Boston Associates and the World They Made* (Cambridge, Mass., 1987), 121–123.

40. Douglas, *Feminization of American Culture,* 12.

41. Huntington views this as a defining phenomenon in American arts and literature during the late nineteenth century ("The Quest for Unity," 11–46); also Lears, *No Place for Grace,* 41–42; Steven Marcus, "Culture and Anarchy Today," in Matthew Arnold, *Culture and Anarchy,* ed. Samuel Lipman (London, 1869; New Haven, 1994), 165–169; and Neil Harris, "Cultural Institutions," 38.

## CHAPTER SIX

1. James B. Peter, "The Hoyt Public Library," in *History of Saginaw and Saginaw County, Michigan,* ed. James Cooke Mills, 2 vols. (Saginaw, Mich., 1918), 1: 304. See also William J. Hennessey, "The Architectural Works of Henry Van Brunt," Ph.D. diss., Columbia University, 1979, 158–163; T. F. Trombley, "Invitation to Architects: The Competition to Design the Hoyt Library," *Saginaw County Historian* 1 (1983): 129–135; G. Blakely, "The Libraries of Saginaw 1855–1971," *Eddy Historical Series,* no. 3 (typescript in Hoyt Public Library), 19–23; James F. O'Gorman, *H. H. Richardson and His Office: Selected Drawings* (Boston, 1974), 171–174; and Jeffrey Karl Ochsner, *H. H. Richardson: Complete Architectural Works* (Cambridge, Mass., 1982), 174–179, 430–431.

2. Mills, *History of Saginaw,* 2: 244–247; Jeremy W. Kilar, *Michigan's Lumbertowns: Lumbermen and Laborers in Saginaw, Bay City, and Muskegon, 1870–1905* (Detroit, 1990), 30–33; obituary for Jesse Hoyt, *New York Times,* 15 August 1882, 5: 1. Like those of Ames and C. F. Adams, Jr., Hoyt's railroad interests ranged widely—suggesting a possible connection with one or both of these men. In addition to the Flint and Pere Marquette, for example, he and his brother Alfred were among the builders and owners of the Milwaukee and Northern Railroad. See [Lyman Horace Weeks], "Alfred Miller Hoyt," *Prominent Families of New York* (New York, 1897), 294.

3. *Hoyt Public Library of East Saginaw, Michigan: Trust Deed from William L. Webber* (East Saginaw, Mich., 1883).

4. Mills, *History of Saginaw,* 1: 302–303; M. A. Lucson, *History of Saginaw County, Michigan* (Chicago, 1881), 587–589; and *American Biographical Index,* ed. Laureen Baille (London, 1993), fiches 1297: 130, 1578: 248, 1702: 25–28. East Saginaw already had a small circulating library, which had been founded in 1859. In 1882 it had 4,720 books and an annual circulation of 3,500 volumes.

5. Sage Public Library, *Dedication of the Sage Public Library of West Bay City, Michigan* [West Bay City, Mich., 1884], 1, 10. This structure was designed by Pratt and Koppe of West Bay City. After the Detroit Public Library (1874–1877), it was the second public library building to be erected in Michigan. For the intense rivalry between these towns see Kilar, *Michigan's Lumbertowns,* 98–99, and "A Comparative Study of Lumber Barons as Community Leaders in Saginaw, Muskegon and Bay City," *Michigan History* 74 (July/August 1990): 35–42. Sage, who was a close friend of Ezra Cornell, eventually gave over $1,175,000 to Cornell University and another $266,000 to Sage Women's College. Cornell had himself founded the Cornell Public Library in Ithaca in 1866.

6. *Saginaw Evening News,* 18 January 1883, 2; and James L. Peter to E. E. Myers, HPL Letter Book, 25 May 1883. The Letter Book contains letters from Peter in his capacity as secretary of the board of trustees to various correspondents concerning the business of the library between 1883 and 1888. The *Saginaw Evening News* curiously reports that work on Myers's design was to begin "as soon as the frost is out of the ground." Peter's letter to Myers, however, gives no indication that the board had ever intended to move forward with such efficiency, or at all, with this architect's proposal.

7. J. L. Peter to W. F. Poole, HPL Letter Book, 15 March 1884. This was just two months after the dedication of the Sage Public Library in West Bay City.

8. For more on Poole see William Landram Williamson, *William Frederick Poole and the Modern Library Movement* (New York, 1963); and Kenneth A. Breisch, "William Frederick Poole and Modern Library Architecture," in *Modern Architecture in America: Visions and Revisions,* ed. R. G. Wilson and S. K. Robinson (Ames, Iowa, 1991), 52–72. While noting his break with the eastern establishment, Dee Garrison still considers Poole more conservative and traditional than the next generation of librarians. See *Apostles of Culture: The Public Librarian and American Society, 1876–1920* (New York, 1979), 27–31.

9. *LJ* 4 (1879): 293–294; and Breisch, "Poole," 57–58.

10. *AABN* 3 (1879): 25. The librarians answered this editorial with one of their own, which was published by Charles Ammi Cutter in *The Nation* 29 (1879): 125–126.

11. *LJ* 8 (1883): 270–271. Poole himself had been director of the Cincinnati Public Library from 1870 to 1873 but was not responsible for the design of this building, which he latter criticized.

12. William Frederick Poole, "The Construction of Library Buildings," *AABN* 10 (1881): 131. This paper was also published in *LJ* 6 (1881): 69–77; and reprinted as U.S. Bureau of Education, *Circular of Information,* no. 1 (Washington, D.C., 1881). It had been surprisingly well received by the editors of *AABN* 9 (1881): 85–86, who probably invited him to publish it in their journal.

13. *LJ* 4 (1879): 294.

14. This was noted the following year by Poole in his report, "Progress of Library Architecture," *LJ* 7 (1882): 131.

15. J. L. Peter to W. F. Poole, HPL Letter Book, 15 March, 14 June, and 25 September 1884.

16. William Frederick Poole, "Small Library Buildings," *LJ* 10 (1885): 250.

17. Ibid., 252–256.

18. Ibid., 250.

19. Ibid., 250–252.

20. *LJ* 10 (1885): 328.

21. *Dayton Daily Democrat,* 7 March 1885; and *AABN* 19 (1886): 66. According to another local account, "the interior arrangement" of this building "was adopted upon the recommendation of Mr. William F. Poole, of the Chicago Public Library, who was consulted by our Library Committee upon the best method of library construction." See Dayton Public Library, *The Dedication of the Dayton Public Library Building, January 24, 1888* (Dayton, Ohio, 1888), 7–13. It is difficult to determine what, if any, impact these events may have had on the thinking of the Hoyt Library trustees. No reference to the Dayton Library is made in any of the surviving Hoyt correspondence during this period.

22. J. L. Peter to S. J. F. Thayer, HPL Letter Book, 2 June 1885. The Nevins Memorial Library was designed in 1882 and dedicated 11 June 1884. See *AABN* 15 (1884): 294; and *LJ* 9 (1884): 77–78. See also J. L. Peter, letter of 25 September 1885, in HPL Letter Book.

23. J. L. Peter to A. M. Hoyt, HPL Letter Book, 30 November 1885. Alfred M. Hoyt's choice was to remain confidential until the close of the competition. All communication with the firm, in fact, appears to have been through Hoyt, so there remains little record of McKim, Mead and White's participation in this event. On McKim, Mead and White's other work for Alfred Hoyt, see Leland M. Roth, *McKim, Mead and White: Architects* (New York, 1983), 77, 95.

24. *AABN* 2 (3, 10, and 31 March 1877).

25. J. L. Peter to E. E. Myers, H. H. Richardson, Peabody and Stearns, and Van Brunt and Howe, HPL Letter Book, 30 November 1885.

26. Hoyt Public Library of East Saginaw, Michigan, Board of Trustees, *Invitation to Architects* ([East Saginaw, Mich.], 1885), [2–3].

27. Ibid., [3].

28. J. L. Peter to A. M. Hoyt and H. H. Richardson, HPL Letter Book, 14 December 1885, and to H. H. Richardson, HPL Letter Book, 7 January 1886. There is also a printed copy of Richardson's standard conditions in the HPL Collection, which states that the architect's commission is 8 percent. This has been crossed out by the architect, who had added at the bottom: "For work as far distant as East Saginaw my charge is 10% including everything." Richardson explained in a circular that he distributed to prospective clients that it had been his practice to charge 5 percent of the cost of the building, plus expenses for supervision of the work. Over time he had found that 8 percent typically covered all of these costs. Mariana Griswold (Mrs. Schuyler) Van Rensselaer, *Henry Hobson Richardson and His Works* (Boston, 1888; reprint, New York, 1969), 147.

29. J. L. Peter to J. L. Lockwood, HPL Letter Book, 14 December 1885. See also an earlier letter in which Peter thanks Lockwood for having sent him both Peabody and Stearns's and Richardson's addresses and also urges him to put in a good word to them on behalf of the board. J. L. Peter to J. L. Lockwood, HPL Letter Book, 9 December 1885. To date, I have been unable to determine the identity of J. L. Lockwood.

30. J. L. Peter to H. H. Richardson, HPL Letter Book, 7 January and 16 January 1886.



**
*

31. J. L. Peter to L. J. Hall and E. J. Jenison, HPL Letter Book, 30 November 1885; to George Keister, Palliser and Palliser, William M. Coots, E. M. Buell and J. L. Faxon, HPL Letter Book, 30 December 1885; to Patton and Fisher, HPL Letter Book, 6 January 1886; and to W. L. B. Jenney, HPL Letter Book, 18 January 1886; and Normand S. Patton, "Architects and Librarians," *LJ* 14 (1889): 160–161. A copy of the Scoville Institute design can still be found in the HPL Collection. This is an offprint from *The Inland Architect and Builder* 5 (February 1885). The building was designed in 1884 but would not be completed until October 1888. See *LJ* 12 (1887): 391–392; and Scoville Institute, *A Brief History of the Organization, Building and Dedication of Scoville Institute, Oak Park, Cook County, Illinois* (Chicago, 1888).

32. J. L. Peter to W. L. B. Jenney, HPL Letter Book, 18 January 1886.

33. J. L. Peter to Patton and Fisher, HPL Letter Book, 11 January 1886.

34. Letter from Patton and Fisher to J. L. Peter, April 1886, in HPL Collection; and J. L. Peter to W. F. Poole, HPL Letter Book, 4 March 1886. E. E. Myers, who earlier had asked for an extension and still had not submitted drawings, was disqualified at this time.

35. J. L. Peter to W. F. Poole, HPL Letter Book, 4 March 1886.

36. Letter from Patton and Fisher to J. L. Peter, April 1886, in HPL Collection.

37. According to the architect, the arrangement of the book room, which in no way reflected Poole's ideas, had been "suggested by the twelfth-century library at Merton College, Oxford." See Manchester Memorial Library, *Dedication Services of the Memorial Library and Grand Army Hall at Manchester-by-the-Sea, Massachusetts, October 13, 1887* (Boston, 1888), 4. Whatever its configuration, the firm's proposal was no doubt included as a finalist because it had been submitted by the one firm chosen by the Hoyt family. See also Roth, *McKim, Mead and White,* 111–112.

38. Peabody and Stearns did design a small library in Easthampton, Massachusetts, which was dedicated in February 1881. Like Richardson's earlier libraries, it employed two-story alcove shelving in the book room. See Wheaton A. Holden, "Robert Swain Peabody of Peabody and Stearns in Boston: The Early Years (1870–1886)," Ph.D. diss., Boston University, 1969, 124–128, 352–353, ills. 156–160; and *AABN* 2 (1877): 100.

39. The Hoyt Public Library's *Invitation to Architects* specified that each architect submit "three elevations with basement, first and second floor plans, drawn to the scale of one eighth inch to the foot, together with such sections to the same scale, or such additional drawings to a larger scale, as may be absolutely necessary to the full understanding of the design submitted. A perspective study is also admissable but not required. These drawings to be studies in pencil." The Hoyt drawings at Harvard that conform to these directives include three plans (HOY A2, HOY A5, HOY A7), principal (HOY B5), rear (HOY B9), and east (HOY B22) elevations, and three sections (HOY C1, HOY C2, HOY C8). A longitudinal section, which would have been labeled A-B, appears to be missing. Richardson's specifications state that several perspective drawings were also submitted. These may be among those that survive at Harvard (HOY B1–8). See also O'Gorman, *Drawings,* 171–174; and Henry Hobson Richardson, *The Hoyt Public Library, East Saginaw, Michigan* (Boston, [1886]).

40. The commission for the Billings Library had entered the office in April 1883, four months before the Converse work had begun. Ochsner, *Richardson,* 300–305; O'Gorman, *Drawings,* 162–165; and University of Vermont, *The Billings Library, the Gift to the University of Vermont of Frederick Billings, H. H. Richardson Architect* (Boston, [c. 1888]).

41. Richardson, *Hoyt Public Library,* 6–7.

42. Ibid., 4, 6, 37.

43. Ibid., 19.

44. "Henry Hobson Richardson Collection," Shepley Bulfinch Richardson and Abbott, Reel 643, Archives of American Art, Smithsonian Institution; and O'Gorman, *Drawings,* 171. In a 31 March letter to Peter, Richardson maintained that he had faced his building south in order to keep it dry and free from snow and ice during the harsh Michigan winters, but it also seems likely that he intentionally oriented it away from the northern edge of the lot because this adjoined a parcel owned by the city upon which the trustees noted it was "expected that a city hall will be erected." The other three sides of the library property opened onto city avenues. Letter from H. H. Richardson to J. L. Peter, 31 March 1886, in HPL Collection; and Hoyt Public Library, *Invitation to Architects,* [2]. Richardson by this date appears to have been in very poor health, a condition that often confined him to his bed. See Van Rensselaer, *Richardson,* 35–36, 118–119.

45. J. L. Peter to G. F. Shepley, HPL Letter Book, 9 March 1886.

46. Letter from H. H. Richardson to J. L. Peter, 31 March 1886, in HPL Collection; and J. L. Peter to H. H. Richardson, HPL Letter Book, 3 April 1886.

47. J. L. Peter to H. H. Richardson, Peabody and Stearns, and L. J. Hall, HPL Letter Book, 6 April 1886.

48. J. L. Peter to Van Brunt and Howe, HPL Letter Book, 6 April 1886. Peter, however, was still apparently skeptical that Van Brunt and Howe's entry could be built for $50,000. See J. L. Peter to Van Brunt and Howe, HPL Letter Book, 24 March 1886. This skepticism was apparently based on a visit that the Detroit architect Gordon Lloyd had made to East Saginaw in mid-March to inspect all of the plans. J. L. Peter to Gordon Lloyd, HPL Letter Book, 24 March 1886. On 19 April Peter announced that he was coming to Chicago to confer with Poole. J. L. Peter to W. F. Poole, HPL Letter Book, 19 April 1886.

49. J. L. Peter to Van Brunt and Howe, HPL Letter Book, 10 May and 3 June 1886.

50. J. L. Peter to Van Brunt and Howe, HPL Letter Book, 3 June 1886. According to J. L. Larned, the issue of whether to employ Poole's system or stacks still had not been resolved as late as 1887. See his "Report on Library Architecture" given at the 1887 ALA conference, *LJ* 12 (1887): 387. In spite of Peter's optimism, the library had to be greatly expanded in 1921 by Edward L. Tilton of New York. At this time Van Brunt and Howe's original book room was converted into further reading space and a metal stack addition was appended onto the north side of this wing, while a new entry porch was constructed on the south side of the library. This led directly into what was originally the book room wing. See Blakely, "The Libraries of Saginaw," 19–23. For the University of Michigan Library see Hennessey, "Henry Van Brunt," 144–158. Copies of the basement and second-floor plans of Van Brunt and Howe's library, signed by James L. Whitney and dated 24 August 1888, can be found in the Boston Public Library (#6190a85). These have been used to reconstruct the original configuration of the building.

51. Henry Van Brunt, "Library Buildings," *LJ* 4 (1879): 294–297.

52. For the sources of Van Brunt's aesthetic philosophy—and relative lack of design facility—see Mary N. Woods, "Henry Van Brunt: 'The Historic Styles, Modern Architecture,'" in *American Public Architecture: European Roots and Native Expressions,* ed. Craig Zabel and Susan Scott Munshower Papers in Art History from Pennsylvania State University, vol. 5 (University Park, Pa., 1989), 89–90.

53. Hoyt Public Library, *Invitation to Architects,* [2].

54. See above, note 28; and Richardson, *Hoyt Public Library,* 19.

55. Kilar, *Michigan's Lumbertowns,* passim.

56. Ibid., 237–249.

57. Robert Wiebe, *The Search for Order, 1877–1920* (New York, 1967), 11–23; Neil Harris, "Cultural Institutions and American Modernization," *Journal of Library History* 16 (1981), 35–44; and Garrison, *Apostles,* 8–9.

58. Thomas W. Palmer, "What Per Cent," *The Hackley Public Library of Muskegon, Michigan, Dedication, October 15, 1890* (Chicago, 1891), 48.

59. John Wellborn Root, "A Great Architectural Problem," in *The Meanings of Architecture: Buildings and Writings by John Wellborn Root,* ed. Donald Hoffman (New York, 1967), 133. This article, which dealt with the problem of designing tall commercial buildings, first appeared in *The Inland Architect and News Record* 15 (1890): 67–71. For Chicago's dominant position in the Midwest see William Cronon, *Nature's Metropolis: Chicago and the Great West* (New York, 1991). There were especially strong economic and transportation connections between Chicago and its surrounding lumber communities (ibid., 148–206).

60. In Poole, "Small Library Buildings," 250–251, the librarian suggests using "porous terra-cotta in ceilings and partitions, and laying floors over a bed of mortar." See also Hoyt Public Library, *Invitation to Architects* [2]. For fireproof construction in Chicago in the late 1870s and early 1880s see Sarah Bradford Landau, *P. B. Wight: Architect, Contractor, and Critic, 1838–1925* (Chicago, 1981), 44–50.

61. *LJ* 4 (1879): 294. For Poole's affinity with Chicago see Garrison, *Apostles,* 27–31.

62. Harris, "Cultural Institutions," 38; and Wiebe, *Search for Order,* 111–112.

63. By 1896, the librarian John Cotton Dana would be comparing book selection to shopping. This trend would ultimately reduce the role of the librarian from that of steward of community morals to that of a clerk. See Abigail A. Van Slyck, "'The Utmost Amount of Effectiv (sic) Accommodation': Andrew Carnegie and the Reform of the American Library," *JSAH* 50 (1991): 371–383; also Neil Harris, "Shopping—Chicago Style," in *Chicago Architecture 1872–1922: Birth of a Metropolis,* ed. John Zarkowsky (Munich, 1987), 137–155.

64. Harris, "Cultural Institutions," 41.

## CHAPTER SEVEN

1. As a tribute to him, Richardson's monogram was carved on a capital of the entryway, and the New Orleans *Times-Democrat,* 22 January 1888, attributes the "architectural design" to him, but the actual chronology of events and issue of authorship is confused and may never be resolved. See James F. O'Gorman, *H. H. Richardson and His Office: Selected Drawings* (Boston, 1974), 172–174. An announcement for the building appears in the *Library Notes* 1 (December 1886): 226; and according to Shepley, Rutan, and Coolidge's Drawings List, Book No. 2: 1885–1888, a set of plans for this building was first forwarded to the Norcross Brothers on 8 March 1887 and "Mr. Howard" the following April. (Howard is probably Frank T. Howard, son of Charles Howard, to whom the building was dedicated. He and his sister, Annie T. Howard, were the project's patrons.) Howard made his first payment for this commission in September 1887, and the final one is recorded 6 July 1889. Shepley, Rutan and Coolidge Account Book, "Henry

Hobson Richardson and Shepley, Rutan and Coolidge Collection," Shepley Bulfinch Richardson and Abbott, roll 676, Archives of American Art, Smithsonian Institution. See also *LJ* 8 (1888): 316–318; "Howard Library: An Important Addition to the City's Architecture," *Times-Democrat,* 13 January 1889; and Kenneth A. Breisch, "William Frederick Poole and Modern Library Architecture," in *Modern Architecture in America: Visions and Revisions,* ed. R. G. Wilson and S. K. Robinson (Ames, Iowa, 1991), 64–66. Surprisingly, there is no mention of this important commission in Richardson's New Orleans obituary in the *Daily Picayune,* 29 April 1886, which might lead one to believe that the commission, if established, was not far along at this date.

2. *The Nation* 47 (1888): 272.

3. *AABN* 24 (1888): 165. Reprinted in *LJ* 13 (1888): 339–340.

4. *LJ* 13 (1888): 331.

5. Ibid., 331–332.

6. William I. Fletcher, "Architects and Librarians: An Eirenicon," *AABN* 24 (1888): 198. Reprinted in *LJ* 13 (1888): 338–339. See also William I. Fletcher, "Library Buildings," *AABN* 24 (1888): 252–253, where he was invited by the editors to develop his ideas further.

7. Normand S. Patton, "Architects and Librarians," *LJ* 14 (1889): 160.

8. *LJ* 16 (1891): 4.

9. Hackley Public Library, *The Hackley Public Library of Muskegon, Michigan, Dedication, October 15, 1890* (Chicago, 1891), 42–43.

10. See, for example, Kenneth A. Breisch, "Small Public Libraries in America 1850–1890: The Invention and Evolution of a Building Type," Ph.D. diss., University of Michigan, 1982, 280–291. For Ansonia, Connecticut, see *LJ* 27 (1892): 209–210; *AABN* 32 (13 June 1891); and David R. Ransom, *George Keller, Architect* (Hartford, Conn., 1978), 196–99. For Calais, Maine, see Maine Library Commission, *Second Report of the Library Commission of Maine* (Augusta, Maine, 1901), 20–21. For Milford, Connecticut, see *LJ* 31 (May 1896): 244–245; and *AABN* 46 (20 October 1894).

11. Garry Wills, *Lincoln at Gettysburg: The Words That Remade America* (New York, 1992), 52.

12. Henry Van Brunt, "Henry Hobson Richardson, Architect," reprinted in *Architecture and Society: Selected Essays of Henry Van Brunt,* ed. William A. Coles (Cambridge, Mass., 1969), 176.

13. *Architectural Review* 9 (1902): 1–60. For Conway, Massachusetts, see *AABN* 74 (5 April 1902): 131.

14. Dedham's seems to be only the second small public library in the country, after Van Brunt's Topeka, Kansas, Free Public Library (1881–1883), to employ a metal stack system. See William J. Hennessey, "The Architectural Works of Henry Van Brunt," Ph.D. diss., Columbia University, 1979, 163–166; Dedham Public Library, *Seventeenth Annual Report of the Trustees of the Dedham Public Library* (Dedham, Mass., 1889); *LJ* 12 (1887): 550–552; and FPLM, 65–68, 98–102. For the work of Shepley, Rutan and Coolidge in Springfield and New London, see *LJ* 15 (1890): 113–114, and 18 (1893): 153–154; and *AABN* 33 (26 September 1891).

15. FPLM, 215–216.

16. See, for example, Abigail A. Van Slyck, "'The Utmost Amount of Effectiv (sic) Accommodation': Andrew Carnegie and the Reform of the American Library," *JSAH* 50 (1991): 373–383; or Joseph

L. Wheeler and Alfred Morton Githens, *The American Public Library Building: Its Planning and Design with Special Reference to Its Administration and Service* (New York, 1941), 1–14.

17. Letter from C. F. Adams, Jr., to Albert Crane after a visit to the library in May 1905. Quoted in L. Draper Hill, Jr., *The Crane Library* (Quincy, Mass., 1962), 25–26. In 1890, K. A. Linderfelt, a close friend of William Frederick Poole and the director of the Milwaukee Public Library, who visited both the Quincy and Woburn libraries in anticipation of erecting a new building for his institution, similarly had complained about the level of light in the Crane book room, as well as the configuration of its alcoves and galleries. K. A. Linderfelt and Adolph Meinecke, "Notes on Library Buildings, Visited November 3–26, 1890," *Reports of the Proposed Library and Museum Building for the City of Milwaukee,* Appendix I (Milwaukee, 1890), 44.

18. Charles Francis Adams, Jr., to Albert Crane, 22 July 1907, Albert Crane Correspondence, Massachusetts Historical Society. Reproduced with permission of the Massachusetts Historical Society.


**
*

# BIBLIOGRAPHY

* *
*

In addition to the publications and manuscripts listed below, sources for this study include the Richardson drawings and papers in the Houghton Library, Harvard, his library and collection of photographs in the Loeb Library at the Harvard Graduate School of Design, the papers of Richardson, Shepley, Rutan, and Coolidge, which belong to the architectural firm of Shepley Bulfinch Richardson and Abbott and are available in the Archives of American Art, as well as the Frederick Law Olmsted papers in the Library of Congress and papers and drawings housed in the Olmsted Archives at the Frederick Law Olmsted National Historic Site in Brookline.

The following abbreviations have been used in the bibliography.

*JSAH* *Journal of the Society of Architectural Historians*
*LJ* *Library Journal*
*AABN* *American Architect and Building News*

## LIBRARY PROJECTS

### Sources Related to the Woburn Public Library, Woburn

"Accepted Design for the Town Library, Woburn, Mass." *AABN* 2 (3 March 1877).

Champney, George M. "Diary of George M. Champney, 1876–1877." Typescript copy in the Woburn Public Library.

Cutter, William R. "A Model Village Library." *New England Magazine,* n.s. 1 (1889–1890): 617–625.

DiNapoli, Christina M. *Woburn Public Library 1856, 1879–1979.* Woburn, Mass., 1979.

Johnson, John W. "An Abstract of the Title of Land in Woburn Now Occupied by the Public Library." In *Bulletin of Accessions to the Woburn Public Library for the Year Ending March 1, 1884.* Woburn, Mass., [1884].

"The Public Library, Woburn, Mass." *AABN* 19 (1 May 1886).

Woburn Public Library. *Annual Report of the Library Committee of the Town of Woburn.* Woburn, Mass., 1874–1895.

Woburn Public Library. *Bulletin of Accessions to the Woburn Public Library.* Woburn, 1880–1884.

Woburn Public Library. "In Memoriam. Hon. Edward D. Hayden." In *Report of the Trustees of the Public Library, March 1, 1909.* Woburn, Mass., 1909.

*Woburn: An Historical and Descriptive Sketch of the Town, with an Outline of Its Industrial Interests.* Woburn, Mass., 1885.

### Sources Related to the Ames Free Library, North Easton

Ames, Charles Edgar. *Pioneering the Union Pacific: A Reappraisal of the Builders of the Railroad.* New York, 1969.

Ames, David. *Some Notes on the Ames Family of Easton: Their Ancestry and Their Varied Interests.* [Easton, Mass., 1970].

Ames Free Library of Easton, Inc. *The First Century: A Centennial History of the Ames Free Library of Easton, Inc. 1883–1983.* North Easton, Mass., [1983].

"The Ames Memorial Building, North Easton, Mass." *Monographs of American Architecture* 3. Boston, 1886.

"The Ames Memorial Library, North Easton, Mass." *AABN* 13 (30 June 1883).

Brown, Robert F. "The Aesthetic Transformation of an Industrial Community." *Winterthur Portfolio* 12 (1977): 35–64.

Chaffin, William L. *History of the Town of Easton, Massachusetts.* Cambridge, Mass., 1886.

"A Day with the Shovel-Makers." *Atlantic Monthly* 26 (September 1870): 367–374.

Frothingham, Mary Ames. *History of Unity Church, North Easton: 1875–1935.* [Easton, Mass.], n.d.

Homolka, Larry J. "Henry Hobson Richardson and the 'Ames Memorial Buildings.'" Ph.D. diss., Harvard University, 1976.

Homolka, Larry J. "Richardson's North Easton." *Architectural Forum* 124 (May 1966): 72–77.

Miller, George M. "The Development of an Industrial Village in the Nineteenth Century: North Easton, Massachusetts." Typescript pamphlet published by the Easton Historical Society, North Easton, Mass., 1977.

*Oakes Ames: A Memoir with an Account of the Dedication of the Oakes Ames Memorial Hall at North Easton, Mass., November 17, 1881.* Cambridge, Mass., 1883.

"Sketch for Public Library at Easton, Mass." *AABN* 2 (3 November 1877).



**
*

### Sources Related to the Crane Memorial Library, Quincy

Adams, Charles Francis, Jr. *Autobiography.* Boston, 1916.

Adams, Charles Francis, Jr. *The Public Library and the Common Schools: Three Papers on Educational Reform.* Boston, 1879.

Adams, Charles Francis, Jr. *Three Episodes of Massachusetts History.* 2 vols. Boston, 1893.

*Address of Charles Francis Adams, Jr. and Proceedings at the Dedication of the Crane Memorial Hall at Quincy, Mass., May 30, 1882.* Cambridge, Mass., 1883.

"The Crane Library." *Harper's Weekly* 27 (1883): 251–252.

"The Crane Public Library, Quincy, Mass." *AABN* 13 (13 June 1883).

Eaton, Rev. Charles H. "Address at the Funeral of Mrs. Thomas Crane." In *The Starkeys of New England and Allied Families,* comp. Emily Wilder Leavitt. N.p., 1910, ix–xv.

Hill, L. Draper, Jr. *The Crane Library.* Quincy, Mass., 1962.

Kirkland, Edward Chase. *Charles Francis Adams, Jr., 1835–1915: The Patrician at Bay.* Cambridge, Mass., 1965.

Leavitt, Emily W., comp. *Henry Crane of Milton, Mass., 1654, and Some of His Descendents.* New York, 1893.

Quincy Public Library and Thomas Crane Public Library. *Annual Report of the Public Library.* Quincy, Mass., 1872–1910.

*Records of the Proceedings of the Trustees of the Thomas Crane Public Library and the Quincy Public Library: May 11, 1871–June 2, 1886.*

*Records of the Proceedings of the Trustees of the Thomas Crane Public Library and the Quincy Public Library: July 7, 1886–July 7, 1900.*

### Sources Related to the Converse Memorial Library, Malden

A Citizen of Malden. "The Malden Muddle: Looking a Gift Horse in the Mouth." *LJ* 10 (1885): 155–156.

City of Malden. *In Memory of Elisha Slade Converse.* Malden, 1905.

Converse Memorial Library. *Dedication of the Converse Memorial Library Building October 1, 1885.* Boston, 1886.

"The Converse Memorial Library, Malden, Mass." *AABN* 18 (3 October 1885).

"The Converse Memorial Library, Malden, Mass." *AABN* 20 (6 November 1886).

Corey, Deloraine P. *Arthur Deloraine Corey 1866–1891: A Memorial.* Cambridge, Mass., 1892.

Corey, Deloraine P. "Two and a Half Centuries in Malden." *New England Magazine,* n.s. 20 (May 1899): 357–378.

"Entrance to Converse Memorial Library, Malden, Mass." *AABN* 24 (22 September 1888).

Hill, William G., comp. *Family Records of Deacons James W. Converse and Elisha S. Converse.* Malden, 1887.

*In Memoriam: Mary Diana Converse March 3, 1825—December 16, 1903.* Boston, [1904?].

*Life, Character, and Career of Edward W. Green, Postmaster of Malden: The Murderer of Frank Converse.* Boston, 1864.

*Malden, Maplewood, Wakefield, Reading, Stoneham, Medford and West Medford: Their Representative Business Men and Points of Interest.* New York, 1893.

Malden Public Library. *Annual Report of the Trustees of the Malden Public Library.* 1878–1910.

Malden Public Library. *One Hundredth Anniversary of the Malden Public Library 1879–1979.* Malden, Mass., 1979.

Norris, Lowell Ames. "Clue of the Cripple's Boot." *Master Detective* 23 (December 1940): 40–45, 179–180.

*Presentation of the Bust of Hon. Elisha Slade Converse. Exercises at the Converse Memorial Building, Malden, Monday, May 26, 1890.* Malden, Mass., 1890.

Underwood, B. G. "Manufacture of Rubber Shoes." *Scientific American* 67 (10 December 1892): 367, 374–375.

**Sources Related to the Hoyt Public Library, East Saginaw**

Blakely, G. "The Libraries of Saginaw 1855–1971." *Eddy Historical Series,* no. 3. Typescript in Hoyt Public Library.

Hoyt Public Library of East Saginaw, Michigan, Board of Trustees. *Invitation to Architects.* East Saginaw, Mich., 1885.

*Hoyt Public Library of East Saginaw, Michigan: Trust Deed from William L. Webber.* East Saginaw, Mich., 1883.

Kilar, Jeremy W. "A Comparative Study of Lumber Barons as Community Leaders in Saginaw, Muskegon and Bay City." *Michigan History* 74 (July/August 1990): 35–42.

Kilar, Jeremy W. *Michigan's Lumbertowns: Lumbermen and Laborers in Saginaw, Bay City, and Muskegon, 1870–1905.* Detroit, 1990.

Lucson, M. A. *History of Saginaw County, Michigan.* Chicago, 1881.

Mills, James Cooke, ed. *History of Saginaw and Saginaw County, Michigan.* 2 vols. Saginaw, Mich., 1918.

Peter, James B. Hoyt Public Library Letter Book. Correspondence of the Trustees of the Hoyt Public Library, 1883–1888.

Richardson, Henry Hobson. *The Hoyt Public Library, East Saginaw, Michigan.* Boston, [1886].

Trombley, T. F. "Invitation to Architects: The Competition to Design the Hoyt Library." *Saginaw County Historian* 1 (1983): 129–135.

Van Brunt and Howe. *Specifications for the Construction of the Hoyt Public Library in the City of East Saginaw, Mich.* East Saginaw, Mich., 1886.

## OTHER WORKS ON HENRY HOBSON RICHARDSON


Adams, Ann Jenson. "The Birth of a Style: Henry Hobson Richardson and the Competition Drawings for Trinity Church, Boston." *Art Bulletin* 62 (1980): 409–433.

Bonk, Sharon C. "Temples of Knowledge: A Study of H. H. Richardson and His Times and Small Public Library Architecture in Massachusetts 1865–1890." In *Milestones to the Present: Papers from the Library History Seminar* 5, ed. Harold Goldstein. Syracuse, N.Y., 1978, 53–72.

Chafee, Richard. "Richardson's Record at the Ecole des Beaux-Arts." *JSAH* 36 (1977): 175–188.

Clark, T. M. "H. H. Richardson." *The Nation* 47 (1888): 151.

Farnam, Anne. "H. H. Richardson and A. H. Davenport: Architecture and Furniture as Big Business in America's Gilded Age." In *Tools and Technologies: America's Wooden Age,* ed. Paul B. Kebabian and William C. Lipke. Burlington, Vt., 1979.

Gilkerson, Ann. "The Public Libraries of H. H. Richardson." Honors thesis, Smith College, 1978.

Hale, Edward. "H. H. Richardson and His Work." *New England Magazine,* n.s. 11 (1894–1895): 513–533.

"Henry Hobson Richardson and Shepley, Rutan and Coolidge Collection." Shepley Bulfinch Richardson and Abbott, roll 676, Archives of American Art, Smithsonian Institution.

Hitchcock, Henry-Russell. *The Architecture of H. H. Richardson and His Times.* New York, 1936; reprint, Cambridge, Mass., 1966.

Hubka, Thomas C. "H. H. Richardson's Glessner House: A Garden in the Machine." *Winterthur Portfolio* 24 (1989): 209–229.

Kowsky, Francis R. "H. H. Richardson's Ames Gate Lodge and the Romantic Landscape Tradition." *JSAH* 50 (June 1991): 181–188.

Kowsky, Francis R. "H. H. Richardson's Project for the Young Men's Association in Buffalo." *Niagara Frontier: Journal of the Buffalo and Erie County Historical Society* 35 (1978): 29–35.

Kowsky, Francis R. "The William Dorsheimer House: A Reflection of French Suburban Architecture in the Early Work of H. H. Richardson." *Art Bulletin* 62 (March 1980): 134–147.

Ochsner, Jeffrey Karl. "Architecture for the Boston and Albany Railroad: 1881–1894." *JSAH* 47 (1988): 109–131.

Ochsner, Jeffrey Karl. *H. H. Richardson: Complete Architectural Works.* Cambridge, Mass., 1982.

Ochsner, Jeffrey Karl, and Thomas C. Hubka. "H. H. Richardson: The Design of the William Watts Sherman House." *JSAH* 51 (1992): 136–145.

O'Gorman, James F. "Documentation: An 1886 Inventory of H. H. Richardson's Library, and Other Gleanings from Probate." *JSAH* 41 (May 1982): 150–155.

O'Gorman, James F. *H. H. Richardson and His Office: Selected Drawings.* Boston, 1974.

O'Gorman, James F. *H. H. Richardson: Architectural Forms for an American Society.* Chicago, 1987.

O'Gorman, James F. "Man-Made Mountain: 'Gathering and Governing' in H. H. Richardson's Design for the Ames Monument in Wyoming." In *The Railroad in American Art: Representation of Technological Change,* ed. Susan Danly and Leo Marx. Cambridge, Mass., 1987, 113–126.

O'Gorman, James F. "O. W. Norcross: Richardson's Master Builder." *JSAH* 32 (1973): 104–113.

O'Gorman, James F. *Three American Architects: Richardson, Sullivan, and Wright, 1865–1915.* Chicago. 1991.

Quinan, Jack. "H. H. Richardson and the Boston Granite Tradition." *Little Journal of the S. A. H. Western New York Chapter* 3 (February 1979): 20–29.

Richardson, Henry Hobson. *A Description of Trinity Church by the Architect Henry Hobson Richardson.* Reprint, Boston, n.d.

University of Vermont. *The Billings Library, the Gift to the University of Vermont of Frederick Billings, H. H. Richardson, Architect.* Boston, [c. 1888].

Van Rensselaer, Mariana Griswold (Mrs. Schuyler). *Henry Hobson Richardson and His Works.* Boston, 1888; reprint, New York, 1969.

Weinberg, Helene Barbara. "John LaFarge and the Decoration of Trinity Church, Boston." *JSAH* 33 (1974): 323–353.

## OTHER PRIMARY SOURCES

Acland, Henry. *The Oxford Museum.* London, 1859.

Adams, Henry. *The Education of Henry Adams: An Autobiography.* Boston, 1918.

*Alumni Hall: An Appeal to the Alumni and Friends of Harvard College.* Cambridge, Mass., 1866.

Antin, Mary. *The Promised Land.* Boston, 1911.

Arnold, Matthew. *Culture and Anarchy.* Ed. Samuel Lipman. London, 1869; reprint, New Haven, 1994.

Bascom, John. *Aesthetics; or, the Science of Beauty.* New York, 1877.

Benjamin, S. G. W. [Samuel Greene Wheeler]. "Libraries." *Harper's New Monthly Magazine* 29 (September 1864): 483–488.

Bentham, Jeremy. *Panopticon.* London, 1791.

"Bibliothèque Ste.-Geneviève." *Norton's Literary Gazette and Publishers' Circular* 3 (15 October 1853): 169.

Bicknell, A. J. *Wooden and Brick Buildings with Details.* New York, 1875.

Boston and Albany Railroad Co. *Annual Report of the Directors of the Boston and Albany Railroad Co. to the Stockholders.* Boston, 1868–1890.

Boston Athenaeum. *The Athenaeum Centenary: The Influence and History of the Boston Athenaeum from 1807 to 1907.* Boston, 1907.

"The Boston Athenaeum." *Norton's Literary Gazette and Publishers' Circular* 2 (15 May 1852): 83.

Brookline Public Library. *Special Report of the Board of Trustees of the Brookline Public Library, upon the Library Lot and Building, March 29, 1867.* Boston, 1867.

Brookline Public Library. *Thirteenth Report of the Board of Trustees of the Public Library.* Brookline, 1864.

Brooks, Phillips. *An Address Delivered May 30, 1873 at the Dedication of the Memorial Hall, Andover, Massachusetts.* Andover, Mass., 1873.

Brooks, Phillips. *Twenty Sermons.* 4th series. New York, 1887.

Carnegie, Andrew. "Best Fields for Philanthropy." *North American Review* 48 (1889): 682–698.

Carnegie, Andrew. "Wealth." *North American Review* 48 (1889): 653–664.

Chapin, Edwin Hubbell. *The Church of the Living God and Other Sermons.* New York, 1881.

Chapin, Edwin Hubbell. *Lessons of Faith and Life.* New York, 1877.

City of Boston, *Annual Report of the Trustees of the Public Library.* Boston, 1855–1880.

City of Boston. *Dedication Services of the Fellowes Athenaeum and the Roxbury Branch of th Boston Public Library, July 9, 1873.* Boston, 1873.

City of Boston. "Description and Plans [for the Roxbury Branch of the Boston Public Library]." In *Twentieth Annual Report of the Trustees of the Public Library, 1872.* Boston, 1872, 84–85.

City of Boston. *A Memorial of Joshua Bates from the City of Boston.* Boston, 1865.

City of Boston. *Proceedings at the Dedication of the Building for the Public Library of the City of Boston, January 1, 1858.* Boston, 1858.

City of Boston. *Proceedings on the Occasion of the Laying of the Corner-Stone of the Public Library of the City of Boston, 17 September 1855.* Boston, 1855.

City of Boston. *Specifications for a Building for the Public Library.* Boston, 1855.

Clark, Theodore Minot. *Building Superintendence: A Manual for Young Architects, Students and Others Interested in Building Operations as Carried On at the Present Day.* Boston, 1883.

Concord Free Public Library. *Dedication of the New Building for the Free Public Library of Concord, Massachusetts. . . . October 1, 1873.* Boston, 1873.

Connecticut Public Library Committee. "Report of the Connecticut Public Library Committee: 1893–94." *Connecticut Public Library Document* 1. Hartford, Conn., 1895.

Connecticut Public Library Committee. "Report of Connecticut Public Library Committee: 1897–1900." *Connecticut Public Library Document* 8. Hartford, Conn., 1901.

Cook, Clarence. *The House Beautiful: Essays on Beds and Tables, Stools and Candlesticks.* New York, 1877.

Cornell Library Association. *Dedication of the Cornell Library Building, Ithaca, New York, December 20, 1866.* Ithaca, N.Y., 1867.

Daly, César. "Bibliothèque Sainte-Geneviève." *Revue générale de l'architecture et des travaux publics* 10 (1852), cols. 379–381.

Daly, César. "Des bibliothèques publiques." *Revue générale de l'architecture et des travaux publics* 8 (1850), cols. 415–438.

Dayton Public Library. *The Dedication of the Dayton Public Library Building, January 24, 1888.* Dayton, Ohio, 1888.

Dedham Public Library. *Seventeenth Annual Report of the Trustees of the Dedham Public Library.* Dedham, Mass., 1889.

Delessert, Benjamin. *Mémoire sur la Bibliothèque Royale, où l'on indique les mesures à prendre pour la transférer dans un bâtiment circulaire, d'une forme nouvelle.* Paris, 1835.

Della Santa, Leopoldo. *Della costruzione e del regolamento di una pubblica universale biblioteca con la pianta dimostrativa.* Florence, 1816.

Downing, Andrew Jackson. *The Architecture of Country Houses.* New York, 1850.

Eastlake, Charles H. *Hints on Household Taste in Furniture, Upholstery, and Other Details.* London, 1868; reprint, Boston, 1872.

Edwards, Edward. *Memoirs of Libraries, Including a Handbook of Library Economy.* 2 vols. London, 1859.

Ellis, George E. *Memoir of Nathaniel Thayer.* Cambridge, Mass., 1885.

Ellis, Sumner. *Life of Edwin Hubbell Chapin.* Boston, 1882.

Emerson, George B. *Report on the Trees and Shrubs Growing Naturally in the Forests of Massachusetts.* Boston, 1850.

*Final Reports of the Building Committee and of the Treasurer of the Harvard College Memorial Fund to the Committee of Fifty, 26 June 1878.* Cambridge, Mass., 1878.

Fletcher, William I. "Architects and Librarians: An Eirenicon." *AABN* 24 (1888): 198.

Fletcher, William I. "Library Buildings." *AABN* 24 (1888): 252–253.

Franklin, Alfred A. *Les anciennes bibliothèques de Paris; églises, monastères, collèges.* 3 vols. Paris, 1867–1870.

Garnier, Charles. *Le nouvel Opéra de Paris.* 2 vols. and atlas. Paris, 1878–1881.

Garnier, Charles. *Le théâtre.* Paris, 1871.

"Georgian [George Swain Peabody]." "Georgian Homes of New England." *AABN* 2 (1877): 338.

Gibbs, James. *Bibliotheca Radcliviana, or a Description of the Radcliffe Library, Oxford.* Oxford, 1747.

Graesel, Arnim. *Grundzüge der Bibliothekslehre.* Leipzig, 1890.

Guadet, Julien. *Eléments et théorie de l'architecture.* 4 vols. Paris, 1901–1904.

Gwilt, Joseph. *An Encyclopedia of Architecture.* London, 1867.

Hackley Public Library. *The Hackley Public Library of Muskegon, Michigan, Dedication, October 15, 1890.* Chicago, 1891.

Hanaford, Phebe A. *The Life of George Peabody.* Boston, 1870.

Harrison, Joseph Leroy. "The Public Library Movement in the United States." *New England Magazine,* n.s. 10 (1894): 709–722.

Harvey, Laurence. "The French Mind." *The Builder* 28 (9 April 1870): 280.

Haverhill Public Library. *Proceedings at the Dedication of the Haverhill Public Library, November 11th, 1875, and Report of the Trustees to the City of Haverhill January 1, 1876.* Haverhill, Mass., 1876.

Hay, John. *The Bread Winners: A Social Study.* New York, 1883.

Hermant, Achille. "La Bibliothèque Sainte-Geneviève." *L'Artiste,* 5th series 7 (1 December 1851): 129–131.



**
*

Herndon, Richard, comp. *Boston of Today.* Boston, 1892.

Hesse, Leopold August Constantin. *Bibliothéconomie; ou, Nouveau manuel complet pour l'arrangement, la conservation, et l'administration des bibliothèques.* Paris, 1839.

"Hints upon Library Buildings." *Norton's Literary Gazette and Publishers' Circular* 3 (15 January 1853): 1.

Hudson, Miss H. R. "Concord Books." *Harper's New Monthly Magazine* 51 (June-November, 1875): 18–32.

Hugo, Victor. *Notre-Dame de Paris, 1482.* Paris, 1831.

Hurd, D. Hamilton, comp. *History of Middlesex County, Massachusetts.* 3 vols. Philadelphia, 1890.

Ingram, John. *The Library of Trinity College Dublin.* London, 1886.

Jewett, Charles Coffin. *Notices of Public Libraries in the United States of America. Appendix to the 4th Annual Report of the Smithsonian Institution.* Washington, D.C., 1851.

Jones, Owen. *The Grammar of Ornament.* London, 1856.

King, David. *A Historical Sketch of the Redwood Library and Athenaeum.* Boston, 1860.

King, Moses. *Harvard and Its Surroundings.* 4th subscription edition. Cambridge, Mass., 1882.

King, Moses. *King's Handbook of Boston.* Cambridge, Mass., 1878.

Labrouste, Henri. "A M. le Directeur de la *Revue d'Architecture.*" *Revue générale de l'architecture et des travaux publics* 10 (1852), cols. 381–383.

Labrouste, M. A. "Bibliothèque Nationale." *Revue générale de l'architecture et des travaux publics* 35 (1878), cols. 143–152.

Lampue, P. *Programmes des concours d'architecture pour le Grand Prix de Rome.* Paris, 1881.

Lancaster Town Library. *Address Delivered at the Dedication of Memorial Hall, Lancaster, June 17, 1868. By Christopher T. Thayer; and Ode, by H. F. Buswell.* Boston, 1868.

Larned, J. L. "Report on Library Architecture." *LJ* 12 (1887): 377–395.

Lenoir, Albert. "De l'architecture byzantine." *Revue générale de l'architecture et des travaux publics* 1 (1840), cols. 7–17, 65–76, 257–263, 321–327, 449–456, 585–590.

Lienau, Detlef. "On Romantic and Classic Architecture." *The Crayon* 5 (1858): 168–169.

Linderfelt, K. A., and Adolph Meinecke. "Notes on Library Buildings, Visited November 3–26, 1890." *Reports of the Proposed Library and Museum Building for the City of Milwaukee,* Appendix I. Milwaukee, 1890.

Little, Bryan. *The Life and Works of James Gibbs.* London, 1959.

Loudon, John Claudius. *On the Laying Out, Planting, and Managing of Cemeteries.* London, 1843.

Manchester Memorial Library. *Dedication Services of the Memorial Library and Grand Army Hall at Manchester-by-the-Sea, Massachusetts, October 13, 1887.* Boston, 1888.

Marvin, Abijah P. *History of the Town of Lancaster, Massachusetts: From the First Settlement to the Present Time, 1643–1879.* Lancaster, Mass., 1879.

Massachusetts Public Library Commission. *First Report: Free Public Libraries of Massachusetts, 1891.* Public Document no. 44. Boston, 1891.

Massachusetts Public Library Commission. *Ninth Report: Free Public Libraries of Massachusetts, 1899.* Public Document no. 44. Boston, 1899.

"Monument Funéraire Commémoratif du combat du Nuits." *Revue générale de l'architecture et des travaux publics* 31 (1874), pl. 20 and cols. 54–55.

New Bedford Free Public Library. *Exercises at the Opening of the New Library Building of the Free Public Library.* New Bedford, Mass., 1910.

New Bedford Free Public Library. *Proceedings on the Occasion of the Laying of the Corner-Stone of the Library Edifice for the Free Public Library of the City of New Bedford: August 28, 1856.* New Bedford, Mass., 1856.

Norton, Charles Eliot. "The Harvard and Yale Memorial Buildings." *The Nation* 5 (11 July 1867): 34–35.

Nourse, Henry. "The Public Libraries of Massachusetts." *New England Magazine,* n.s. 5 (1891–1892): 139–159.

Oswego City Library. "History." Minutes of the Trustees of the Oswego City Library, 19 September 1892.

Patton, Normand S. "Architects and Librarians." *LJ* 14 (1889): 159–161.

Planat, P. *Encyclopédie de l'architecture et de la construction.* 7 vols. Paris, [1888].

Poole, William Frederick. "The Construction of Library Buildings." *AABN* 10 (1881): 131–134.

Poole, William Frederick. "Progress of Library Architecture." *LJ* 7 (1882): 130–136.

Poole, William Frederick. "Small Library Buildings." *LJ* 10 (1885): 250–256.

"Problem XVI.—A Memorial Library." *The Architectural Sketch Book* 2 (1875), plates XLIV–XLVI.

*Proceedings at the Reception and Dinner in Honor of George Peabody, Esq., of London, by the Citizens of the Old Town of Danvers, October 9, 1856.* Boston, 1856.

Public Library of Cincinnati. "Report of the Board of Managers." In *Public Library of Cincinnati, Annual Report: 1869.* Cincinnati, Ohio, 1869, 8–11.

Quatremère de Quincy, A. C. *Encyclopédie méthodique: Architecture.* 3 vols. Paris, 1788–1825.

Quincy, Josiah. *The History of Harvard University.* 2 vols. Cambridge, Mass., 1840.

Quincy, Josiah. *The History of the Boston Athenaeum, with Biographical Notices of Its Deceased Founders.* Cambridge, Mass., 1851.

Rand, John C., comp. *One of a Thousand: A Series of Biographical Sketches of One Thousand Representative Men Resident in the Commonwealth of Massachusetts A.D. 1888–89.* Boston, 1890.

*Report of the Committee on Soldiers' Monument.* Foxboro, Mass., 1867.

Révoil, Henry Antoine. *Architecture romane du Midi de la France.* 3 vols. Paris, 1867–1873.

Reynaud, Léonce. *Traité d'architecture.* 2 vols. with atlas. Paris, 1850–1858.

Rhees, William. *Manual of Public Libraries, Institutions, and Societies in the United States and British Provinces of North America.* Philadelphia, 1859.

Root, John Wellborn. "A Great Architectural Problem." *Inland Architect and News Record* 15 (1890): 67–71.

Ruskin, John. *The Works of John Ruskin.* Ed. E. T. Cook and Alexander Wedderburn. 39 vols. London, 1903–1912.

Sage Public Library. *Dedication of the Sage Public Library of West Bay City, Michigan.* [West Bay City, Mich., 1884].

Sargent, Charles Sprague. *Silva of North America.* 14 vols. Boston, 1891–1902.

Saunders, Frederick K. "The Astor Library." *New England Magazine,* n.s. 2 (1890): 148–159.

Schmidt, J. A. F. *Handbuch der Bibliothekwissenschaft, der Literatur- und Bücherkunde.* Weimar, 1840.

Schrettinger, Martin. *Handbuch der Bibliothek-Wissenschaft, besonders zum Gebrauche der Nicht-Bibliothekare, welche ihre Privat-Büchersammlungen selbst einrichten wollen.* Vienna, 1834.

Schrettinger, Martin. *Versuch eines vollständigen Lehrbuchs der Bibliothek-Wissenschaft; oder, Anleitung zur vollkommenen Geschäftführung eines Bibliothekars, in wissenschaftlicher Form abgefasst.* 2 vols. Munich, 1810–1829.

Schuyler, Montgomery. "The Romanesque Revival in America." *Architectural Record* 1 (1891–1892): 151–198.

Schuyler, Montgomery. "The Romanesque Revival in New York." *Architectural Record* 1 (1891–1892): 7–38.

Scoville Institute. *A Brief History of the Organization, Building and Dedication of Scoville Institute, Oak Park, Cook County, Illinois.* Chicago, 1888.

Shurtleff, Nathaniel B. *A Decimal System for the Arrangement and Administration of Libraries.* Boston, 1856.

Sidney, Margaret [Harriet Mulford Lothrop]. *Old Concord: Her Highways and Byways.* Revised and enlarged edition. Boston, 1893.

Smith, J. A. E. *The History of Pittsfield, Massachusetts: 1800–1876.* 2 vols. Springfield, Mass., 1876.

Smith, Mary Byers. *The Founding of the Memorial Hall Library, Andover.* [Andover, Mass.], n.d.

Stone, E. M. *The Architect and Monetarian: A Brief Memoir of Thomas Alexander Tefft.* Providence, 1869.

Story, Joseph. *An Address Delivered at the Dedication of the Cemetery at Mount Auburn.* Boston, 1831.

Sumner, William Graham. *What Social Classes Owe Each Other.* New York, 1883.

Talbert, Bruce. *Gothic Forms Applied to Furniture, Metalwork and Decoration for Domestic Purposes.* Birmingham and London, 1876.

Thayer, Christopher T. "Address." In *Address Delivered at the Dedication of Memorial Hall, Lancaster, June 17, 1868. By Christopher T. Thayer; and Ode, by H. F. Buswell.* Boston, 1868.

"Tribunal de 1ère instance." *Croquis d'architecture* 1, no. 11 (June 1866): 2–3.

United States Bureau of Education. *Statistics of Public, Society and School Libraries.* Washington, D.C., 1900.

United States Department of Interior, Bureau of Education. *Public Libraries in the United States of America: Their History, Condition and Management.* 3 pts. 1. Washington, D.C., 1876.

Van Brunt, Henry. *Architecture and Society: Selected Essays of Henry Van Brunt.* Ed. and intro. William A. Coles. Cambridge, Mass., 1969.

Van Brunt, Henry. "Greek Lines." *Atlantic Monthly* 7 (June 1861): 654–667; 8 (July 1861): 76–88.

Van Brunt, Henry. "John Wellborn Root." *Inland Architect and News Record* 16 (January 1891): 85–88.

Van Brunt, Henry. "Library Buildings." *LJ* 4 (1879): 294–297.

Van Rensselaer, Mariana Griswold. "Recent Architecture in America." *Century Magazine* 28 (1884): 48–67.

Viollet-le-Duc, Eugène-Emmanuel. *Dictionnaire raisonné de l'architecture française du XIe au XVIe siècle.* 10 vols. Paris, 1854–1868.

Viollet-le-Duc, Eugène-Emmanuel. *Entretiens sur l'architecture.* 2 vols. and atlas. Paris, 1863, 1872.

Viollet-le-Duc, Eugène-Emmanuel. *Lectures on Architecture.* Trans. Benjamin Bucknell. 2 vols. London, 1881.

"Williams College Library." *Norton's Literary Gazette and Publishers' Circular* 3 (March 13, 1853): 1.

Winsor, Justin. "Libraries in Boston." In *The Memorial History of Boston Including Suffolk County, Massachusetts: 1630–1880.* Boston, 1881, 279–294.

Winsor, Justin. "Library Buildings." United States Department of Interior, Bureau of Education. *Public Libraries in the United States of America: Their History, Condition and Management.* Washington, D.C., 1876, 465–475.

Wood, Nathan E. *The History of the First Baptist Church of Boston (1665–1899).* Philadelphia, 1899.

"Worcester Antiquarian Society." *Norton's Literary Gazette and Publishers' Circular* 3 (15 November 1852): 1.

Wright, Carroll D. *The Census of Massachusetts, 1875.* 2 vols. Boston, 1876.

Wright, Carroll D. *The Census of Massachusetts, 1885.* 2 vols. Boston, 1887.

## OTHER SECONDARY SOURCES

Adams, William H., ed. *The Eye of Jefferson.* Washington, D.C., 1976.

Adriani, Gert. *Die Klosterbibliotheken des Spätbarock in Österreich und Suddeutschland; ein Beitrag zur Bau- und Kunstgeschichte des 17. und 18. Jahrhunderts.* Graz, 1935.

Allcott, John V. "Scholarly Books and Frolicsome Blades: A. J. Davis Designs a Library Ballroom." *JSAH* 33 (1974): 145–154.

Baille, Laureen, ed. *American Biographical Index.* London, 1993.

Ball, Alan W. *The Public Libraries of Greater London: A Pictorial History 1856–1940.* London, 1977.

Baltzell, E. Digby. *The Protestant Establishment: Aristocracy and Caste in America.* New York, 1964.

Bedford, Henry F., ed. and intro. *Their Lives and Numbers: The Condition of Working People in Massachusetts, 1870–1900.* Ithaca, N.Y., 1995.

Bender, Thomas. *Toward an Urban Vision: Ideas and Institutions in Nineteenth Century America.* Baltimore and London, 1975.

Blau, Eve. *Ruskinian Gothic: The Architecture of Deane and Woodward, 1845–1861.* Princeton, 1982.

Blodgett, Geoffrey. "Landscape Design as Conservative Reform." In *Art of the Olmsted Landscape,* ed. Bruce Kelly et al. New York, 1981, 111–122.

Bobinski, George. *Carnegie Libraries: Their History and Impact on American Public Library Development.* Chicago, 1969.

Boime, A. "The Teaching Reforms of 1863 and the Origins of Modernism in France." *Art Quarterly* 1 (Autumn, 1979): 1–39.

Boll, John. "Library Architecture 1800–1875: A Comparison of Theory and Buildings with an Emphasis on New England College Libraries." Ph.D. diss., University of Illinois, 1961.

Boris, Eileen. *Art and Labor: Ruskin, Morris, and the Craftsman Ideal in America.* Philadelphia, 1986.

Borome, Joseph A. *Charles Coffin Jewett.* Chicago, 1951.

Borome, Joseph A. "The Life and Letters of Justin Winsor." Ph.D. diss., Columbia University, 1950.

Borsch-Supan, Eva. *Berliner Baukunst nach Schinkel: 1840–1870.* Munich, 1977.

Boston Athenaeum. *Change and Continuity: A Pictorial History of the Boston Athenaeum.* Boston, 1985.

Boyer, Paul. *Urban Masses and Moral Order in America: 1820–1920.* Cambridge, Mass., 1978.

Breisch, Kenneth A. "The Hackley Public Library of Muskegon, Michigan: Its Evolution, Design and Place in Late Nineteenth-Century America." Master's thesis, University of Michigan, 1976.

Breisch, Kenneth A. "Small Public Libraries in America 1850–1890: The Invention of a Building Type." Ph.D. diss., University of Michigan, 1982.

Breisch, Kenneth A. "William Frederick Poole and Modern Library Architecture." In *Modern Architecture in America: Visions and Revisions,* ed. R. G. Wilson and S. K. Robinson. Ames, Iowa, 1991, 52–72.

Bremner, Robert H. *The Public Good: Philanthropy and Welfare in the Civil War Era.* New York, 1980.

Brenneman, David A. "Innovations in American Library Design." In *Thomas Alexander Tefft: American Architecture in Transition, 1845–1860.* Providence, 1988, 61–76.

Bridenbaugh, Carl. *Peter Harrison, First American Architect.* Chapel Hill, N.C., 1949.

Brooks, Michael W. *John Ruskin and Victorian Architecture.* New Brunswick, N.J., 1987.

Brooks, Michael W. "New England Gothic: Charles Eliot Norton, Charles H. Moore, and Henry Adams." In *The Architectural Historian in America,* ed. E. B. MacDougall. Hanover, N.H., 1990, 113–125.

Bruce, V. Robert. *1877, Year of Violence.* Indianapolis, 1959.

Buchowiecki, Walther. *Der Barockbau der ehemalgen Hofbibliothek in Wien, ein Werk J. B. Fischers von Erlach.* Vienna, 1957.

Bunting, Bainbridge. *Harvard: An Architectural History.* Completed and edited by Margaret Henderson Floyd. Cambridge, Mass., 1985.

Burton, Margaret. *Famous Libraries of the World.* London, 1937.

Carlhian, Jean-Paul. "The Ecole des Beaux-Arts: Modes and Manners." *Journal of Architectural Education* 33 (1979): 7–17.



**
*

Chafee, Richard. "Hunt in Paris." In *The Architecture of Richard Morris Hunt,* ed. Susan R. Stein. Chicago, 1986, 13–45.

Chafee, Richard. "The Teaching of Architecture at the Ecole des Beaux-Arts." In *The Architecture of the Ecole des Beaux-Arts,* ed. Arthur Drexler. New York, 1977, 61–110.

Chewning, J. A. "William Robert Ware at MIT and Columbia." *Journal of Architectural Education* 33 (1979): 25–29.

Clark, John W. *The Care of Books, an Essay on the Development of Libraries and Their Fittings, from the Earliest Times to the End of the Eighteenth Century.* Cambridge, Eng., 1909.

Clemons, Harry. *The University of Virginia Library 1825–1950.* Charlottesville, Va., 1954.

Cole, John Y. "Storehouses and Workshops: American Libraries and the Uses of Knowledge." In *The Organization of Knowledge in Modern America, 1860–1920,* ed. Alexandra Oleson and John Voss. Baltimore, 1976, 364–385.

Coles, William A. "Richard Morris Hunt and His Library as Revealed by the Studio Sketchbooks of Henry Van Brunt." *Art Quarterly* 30 (1967): 224–238.

Colvin, Howard. *Architecture and the After-Life.* New Haven, 1991.

Commons, John R., et al. *History of Labour in the United States.* 2 vols. New York, 1936.

Concord Free Public Library. *A History of the Concord Free Public Library.* Concord, Mass., 1973.

Cronon, William. *Nature's Metropolis: Chicago and the Great West.* New York, 1991.

Dalzell, Robert F., Jr. *Enterprising Elite: The Boston Associates and the World They Made.* Cambridge, Mass., 1987.

Davies, David William. *Public Libraries as Culture and Social Centers: The Origin of the Concept.* Metuchen, N.J., 1974.

Dawley, Alan. *Class and Community: The Industrial Revolution in Lynn.* Harvard Studies in Urban History. Cambridge, Mass., 1976.

Detroit Institute of the Arts. *The Quest for Unity: American Art between World's Fairs, 1876–1893.* Detroit, 1983.

Ditzion, Sidney. *Arsenals of a Democratic Culture: A Social History of the American Library Movement in New England and the Middle States, 1850–1900.* Chicago, 1947.

Douglas, Ann. *The Feminization of American Culture.* New York, 1977.

Douglas, Ann. "Heaven Our Home: Consolation Literature in the Northern United States, 1830–1880." In *Death in America,* ed. David E. Stannard. Philadelphia, 1975, 49–68.

Downing, Antoinette, and Vincent Scully. *The Architectural Heritage of Newport, Rhode Island: 1640–1915.* New York, 1951.

Doyle, Edward G., ed. *A Commemorative History of the Cambridge Public Library.* Cambridge, Mass., 1989.

Drexler, Arthur, ed. *The Architecture of the Ecole des Beaux-Arts.* New York, 1977.

Dryfhout, John H. *The Work of Augustus Saint-Gaudens.* Hanover, N.H., 1982.

Dumont, Rosemary Ruhig. *Reform and Reaction: The Big City Public Library in American Life.* Westport, Conn., 1977.

Egbert, Donald Drew. *The Beaux-Arts Tradition in French Architecture Illustrated by the Grands Prix de Rome.* Ed. David Van Zanten. Princeton, N.J., 1980.

Eliade, Mircea. *The Sacred and the Profane: The Nature of Religion.* Trans. Willard R. Trask. New York, 1959; reprint, San Diego, 1987.

Etlin, Richard A. *The Architecture of Death: The Transformation of the Cemetery in Eighteenth-Century Paris.* Cambridge, Mass., 1984.

Etlin, Richard A. *Symbolic Space: French Enlightenment Architecture and Its Legacy.* Chicago, 1994.

Fernstein, Estelle F. "Stamford, Connecticut, 1868–1893: A Study of Small Town Politics in the Gilded Age." Ph.D. diss., Columbia University, 1970.

Fogel, Robert William. *The Union Pacific Railroad.* Baltimore, 1960.

Fogelson, Robert M. *America's Armories: Architecture, Society, and Public Order.* Cambridge, Mass., 1989.

Forbes, J. D. "Shepley, Bulfinch, Richardson & Abbott: An Introduction." *JSAH* 18 (1959): 19–21.

Ford, Edward R. *The Details of Modern Architecture.* Cambridge, Mass., 1990.

Foucault, Michel. *Discipline and Punish: The Birth of the Prison.* Trans. A. Sheridan. New York, 1979.

Foucault, Michel. *Power/Knowledge: Selected Interviews and Other Writings: 1972–1977.* Ed. and trans. C. Gordon. New York, 1980.

Frederickson, George M. *The Inner Civil War: Northern Intellectuals and the Crisis of Union.* New York, 1965.

French, Stanley. "The Cemetery as Cultural Institution." In *Death in America,* ed. David E. Stannard. Philadelphia, 1975, 69–91.

Garrison, Dee. *Apostles of Culture: The Public Librarian and American Society, 1876–1920.* New York, 1979.

Gaskell, Philip, and Robert Robson. *The Library of Trinity College Cambridge: A Short History.* Cambridge, Eng., 1971.

Gilmore, William J. *Reading Becomes a Necessity of Life: Material and Cultural Life in Rural New England, 1780–1835.* Knoxville, Tenn., 1989.

Girouard, Mark. *Sweetness and Light: The "Queen Anne" Movement, 1860–1900.* Oxford, 1977; reprint, New Haven, 1984.

*Gore Hall: The Library of Harvard College, 1838–1913.* Cambridge, Mass., 1917.

Green, Martin. *The Problem of Boston: Some Readings in Cultural History.* New York, 1966.

Green, Samuel S. *The Public Library Movement in the United States, 1852–1893.* Boston, 1913.

Gromly, Dennis M. "A Bibliographic Essay of Western Library Architecture to the Mid-Twentieth Century." *Journal of Library History* 9 (January 1974): 4–24.

Hamlin, Oscar. *Boston's Immigrants.* Cambridge, Mass., 1941.

Harris, Michael H., intro. and ed. *The Age of Jewett: Charles Coffin Jewett and American Librarianship, 1841–1868.* Littleton, Col., 1975.

Harris, Michael H. "The Purpose of the American Public Library: A Revisionist Interpretation of History." *LJ* 98 (15 September 1973): 2509–2514.

Harris, Neil. *The Artist in American Society: The Formative Years, 1790–1860.* New York, 1966.

Harris, Neil. "Cultural Institutions and American Modernization." *Journal of Library History* 16 (1981): 28–47.

Harris, Neil. "Shopping—Chicago Style." In *Chicago Architecture 1872–1922: Birth of a Metropolis,* ed. John Zarkowsky. Munich, 1987, 137–155.

Hautecoeur, Louis. *Histoire de l'architecture classique en France.* 7 vols. Paris, 1943–1957.

Hederer, Oswald. *Friedrich von Gärtner 1792–1847: Leben, Werk, Schüller.* Munich, 1976.

Hennessey, William J. "The Architectural Works of Henry Van Brunt." Ph.D. diss., Columbia University, 1979.

Hersey, George. *High Victorian Gothic: A Study in Associationism.* Baltimore, 1972.

Hitchcock, Henry-Russell. *Architecture: Nineteenth and Twentieth Centuries.* Harmondsworth, Eng., 1958.

Hitchcock, Henry-Russell. *Early Victorian Architecture.* 2 vols. New Haven, 1954.

Hitchcock, Henry-Russell. "Ruskin and American Architecture, or Regeneration Long Delayed." In *Concerning Architecture: Essays on Architectural Writers and Writing Presented to Nikolaus Pevsner,* ed. John Summerson. Baltimore, 1968, 166–208.

Hoffman, Donald, ed. *The Meanings of Architecture: Buildings and Writings by John Wellborn Root.* New York, 1967.

Holden, Wheaton A. "The Peabody Touch: Peabody and Stearns of Boston." *JSAH* 32 (1973): 114–131.

Holden, Wheaton A. "Robert Swain Peabody of Peabody and Stearns in Boston: The Early Years (1870–1886)." Ph.D. diss., Boston University, 1969.

Horowitz, Helen Lefkowitz. *Culture and the City: Cultural Philanthropy in Chicago from the 1880s to 1917.* Lexington, Ky., 1976.

Huntington, David C. "The Quest for Unity: American Art between World's Fairs, 1876–1893." In *The Quest for Unity: American Art between World's Fairs, 1876–1893.* Detroit, 1983, 11–46.

Hutton, S. B. *Charles Sprague Sargent and the Arnold Arboretum.* Cambridge, Mass., 1970.

Johnson, Arthur M., and Barry E. Supple. *Boston Capitalists and Western Railroads: A Study in the Nineteenth-Century Railroad Investment Process.* Harvard Studies in Business History XXIII. Cambridge, Mass., 1967.

Jones, Howard Mumford. *The Age of Energy: Varieties of American Experience, 1865–1915.* New York, 1970.

Jordy, William H. *American Buildings and Their Architects: Progressive and Academic Ideals at the Turn of the Century.* New York, 1976.

Jordy, William H., and Christopher P. Monkhouse. *Buildings on Paper: Rhode Island Architectural Drawings 1825–1945.* Providence, 1982.

Kahn, Rosann. *A History of the Peabody Institute Library, Baltimore, Maryland 1857–1916.* Rochester, N.Y., 1954.

Kaplan, Wendy, ed. *The Art That Is Life: The Arts and Crafts Movement in America, 1875–1920.* Boston, 1987.

Katz, Michael B. *Class, Bureaucracy and Schools: The Illusion of Educational Change in America.* New York, 1971.

Katz, Michael B. *The Irony of Early School Reform: Educational Innovation in Mid-Nineteenth Century Massachusetts.* Cambridge, Mass., 1968.

Kilham, Walter. *Boston after Bulfinch: An Account of Its Architecture 1800–1900.* Cambridge, Mass., 1946.

Kramer, Ellen W. "Contemporary Descriptions of New York and Its Public Architecture ca. 1850." *JSAH* 27 (1968): 264–280.

Kramer, Ellen W. "Detlef Lienau, an Architect of the Brown Decades." *JSAH* 14 (1955): 18–25.

Kruft, Hanno-Walter. *A History of Architectural Theory from Vitruvius to the Present.* New York, 1994.

Kusmer, Kenneth L. "The Social History of Cultural Institutions: The Upper-Class Connection." *Journal of Interdisciplinary History* 10 (Summer 1979): 137–146.

Landau, Sarah Bradford. *Edward T. and William A. Potter: American Victorian Architects.* New York, 1979.

Landau, Sarah Bradford. *P. B. Wight: Architect, Contractor, and Critic, 1838–1925.* Chicago, 1981.

Landau, Sarah Bradford. "Richard Morris Hunt: Architectural Innovator and Father of a 'Distinctive' American School." In *The Architecture of Richard Morris Hunt,* ed. Susan R. Stein. Chicago, 1986, 47–77.

Larson, Paul Clifford, ed. *The Spirit of H. H. Richardson on the Midland Prairies: Regional Transformations of an Architectural Style.* Ames, Iowa, 1988.

Lears, T. J. Jackson. *No Place for Grace: Antimodernism and the Transformation of American Culture, 1880–1920.* Chicago, 1991.

Levine, Lawrence. *Highbrow/Lowbrow: The Emergence of Cultural Hierarchy in America.* Cambridge, Mass., 1988.

Levine, Neil. "The Book and the Building: Hugo's Theory of Architecture and Labrouste's Bibliothèque Ste. Geneviève." In *The Beaux-Arts and Nineteenth-Century French Architecture,* ed. Robin Middleton. Cambridge, Mass., 1982, 139–173.

Levine, Neil. "The Competition for the Grand Prix in 1824." In *The Beaux-Arts and Nineteenth-Century French Architecture,* ed. Robin Middleton. Cambridge, Mass., 1982, 66–123.

Levine, Neil. "The Romantic Idea of Architectural Legibility: Henri Labrouste and the Neo-Grec." In *The Architecture of the Ecole des Beaux-Arts,* ed. Arthur Drexler. New York, 1977, 325–416.

Leyh, Georg. "Das Haus und seine Einrichtung." In *Handbuch der Bibliothekswissenschaft,* ed. F. Milkau. 3 vols. Leipzig, 1933–1940, 2: 1–38.

Linden-Ward, Blanche. *Silent City on a Hill: Landscapes of Memory and Boston's Mount Auburn Cemetery.* Columbus, Ohio, 1989.

Lippy, Charles H., and Peter W. Williams, eds. *Encyclopedia of the American Religious Experience: Studies of Traditions and Movements.* 2 vols. New York, 1988.

Lydenberg, Harry. *History of the New York Public Library.* New York, 1923.

Malmstrom, R. E. "Lawrence Hall at Williams College." *Studies in the History of Art* 2. Williamstown, Mass., 1979.

Martin, Theodora Penny. *The Sound of Our Own Voices: Womens's Study Clubs 1860–1910.* Boston, 1987.

McCarthy, Kathleen D. *Noblesse Oblige: Charity and Cultural Philanthropy in Chicago, 1849–1929.* Chicago, 1982.

McCarthy, Kathleen D. *Women's Culture: American Philanthropy and Art, 1830–1930.* Chicago, 1991.

McClaughtery, Martha Crabill. "Household Art: Creating the Artistic Home, 1863–1893." *Winterthur Portfolio* 18 (1983): 1–26.

McMullen, Haynes. "Prevalence of Libraries in the Northeastern States before 1876." *Journal of Library History* 22 (1987): 321–326.

Middleton, Robin, ed. *The Beaux-Arts and Nineteenth-Century French Architecture.* Cambridge, Mass., 1982.

Middleton, Robin, "Vive l'Ecole." In *A.D. Profiles 17: The Beaux-Arts.* London, n.d., 38–47.

Middleton, Robin, and David Watkin. *Neoclassical and 19th Century Architecture.* New York, 1980.

Moore, Richard A. "Academic *Dessin* Theory in France after the Reorganization of 1863." *JSAH* 36 (1977): 145–174.

Morrisson-Reeves Library. *The Seventy-Fifth Anniversary of the Founding of the Morrisson-Reeves Library: 1864–1939.* Richmond, Ind., 1939.

Mumford, Lewis. *The Brown Decades.* New York, 1931.

Mumford, Lewis. *Sticks and Stones.* New York, 1924; revised ed., 1955.

Nash, Jay Robert. *Encyclopedia of World Crime, Criminal Justice, Criminology, and Law Enforcement.* 3 vols. Wilmette, Ill., 1990.

New Hampshire State Library. "Histories of Public Libraries." *Reports of the Trustees of the State Library and the State Librarian for the Period Beginning June 1, 1904 and Ending May 31, 1906,* vol. 8, pt. 6. Concord, N.H., 1906, 365–497.

Newton, Roger Hail. *Town and Davis, Architects.* New York, 1942.

Nicholson, Arnold. "Dr. Thornton, Who Practised Everything but Medicine." *Smithsonian* 2 (April 1971): 66–75.

Novak, Barbara. *Nature and Culture: American Landscape and Painting 1825–1875.* New York, 1980.

Oehlerts, Donald. "The Development of American Public Library Architecture from 1850 to 1940." Ph.D. diss., Indiana University, 1974.

O'Gorman, James F. *The Architecture of the Monastic Libraries in Italy, 1300–1600.* New York, 1972.

O'Gorman, James F. "H. and J. E. Billings of Boston: From Classicism to the Picturesque." *JSAH* 42 (1983): 54–73.

Olmsted, F. L., Jr., and Theodora Kimball, eds. *Frederick Law Olmsted: Landscape Architect, 1822–1903.* 2 vols. New York, 1928.

Painter, Nell Irvin. *Standing at Armageddon: The United States 1877–1919.* New York, 1987.

Panofsky, Erwin. "*Et in Arcadia Ego:* Poussin and the Elegiac Tradition." In *Meaning in the Visual Arts: Papers in Art History.* New York, 1955, 295–320.

*Paris, Rome, Athènes: le voyage en Grèce des architectes français au XIXe et XXe siècles.* Paris, 1982.

Parker, Franklin. *George Peabody: A Biography.* Nashville, 1971.

Pevsner, Nikolaus. *A History of Building Types.* Princeton, N.J., 1976.

Pierson, William H., Jr. *American Buildings and Their Architects: The Colonial and Neo-Classical Styles.* New York, 1970.

Ransom, David R. *George Keller, Architect.* Hartford, Conn., 1978.

Rhoads, William B. "The Colonial Revival and the Americanization of Immigrants." In *The Colonial Revival in America,* ed. Alan Axelrod. New York, 1985, 341–361.

Roth, Leland M. *McKim, Mead and White: Architects.* New York, 1983.

Roth, Rodris. "The New England, or 'Olde Tyme,' Kitchen Exhibit at Nineteenth-Century Fairs." In *The Colonial Revival in America,* ed. Alan Axelrod. New York, 1985, 159–183.

Rykwert, Joseph. "The Ecole des Beaux-Arts and the Classical Tradition." In *The Beaux-Arts and Nineteenth-Century French Architecture,* ed. Robin Middleton. Cambridge, Mass., 1982, 9–17.

Saddy, Pierre. *Henri Labrouste, architecte, 1801–1875.* Paris, 1977.

Said, Edward W. *Culture and Imperialism.* New York, 1993.

Saint, Andrew. *Richard Norman Shaw.* New Haven, 1976.

Sawyer, Mabel S. [Typescript description of the Braintree Public Library in the Braintree Historical Society]. Braintree, Mass., 1936.

Scheyer, Ernst. *The Circle of Henry Adams: Art and Artists.* Detroit, 1970.

Scully, Vincent J. *The Shingle Style and the Stick Style: Architectural Theory and Design from Downing to the Origins of Wright.* Rev. ed. New Haven, 1971.

Sekler, Edward. *Wren and His Place in European Architecture.* New York, 1956.

Shaffer, Robert B. "Ruskin, Norton, and Memorial Hall." *Harvard Library Bulletin* 3 (Spring 1949): 213–231.

Sharp, Katherine L. "Illinois Libraries." *University (of Illinois) Studies,* whole issue, 1906–1908.

Shelton, Brenda K. *Reformers in Search of Yesterday: Buffalo in the 1890s.* Albany, N.Y., 1976.

Shera, Jesse H. *Foundations of the Public Library.* Chicago, 1949.

Sherman, Paul. "The First Hundred Years: A History of the Cornell Public Library, Ithaca, New York and the Cornell Library Association 1864–1964." Typescript in the Tompkins County Public Library, Ithaca, N.Y., [1964?].

Shores, Louis. *Origins of the American College Library: 1638–1800.* Nashville, 1934.

Stannard, David E., ed. *Death in America.* Philadelphia, 1975.

Stein, Roger. *John Ruskin and Aesthetic Thought in America, 1840–1900.* Cambridge, Mass., 1967.

Stevenson, Gordon, and Judith Kramer-Greene, eds. *Melvil Dewey: The Man and the Classification.* Albany, N.Y., 1983.

Stone, Elizabeth. *American Library Development 1600–1899.* New York, 1977.

Story, Ronald. *The Forging of an Aristocracy: Harvard and the Boston Upper Class, 1800–1870.* Middletown, Conn., 1980.

Streeter, Burnett Hillman. *The Chained Library: A Survey of Four Centuries in the Evolution of the English Library.* London, 1931.

Stummvoll, Joseph, ed. *Geschichte der Österreichischen National-bibliothek,* vol. 1: *Die Hofbibliothek 1368–1922.* Vienna, 1968.

Summerson, John. *Architecture in Britain 1530 to 1830.* Harmondsworth, Eng., 1953; reprint, 1970.

Sutton, S. D. *Charles Sprague Sargent and the Arnold Arboretum.* Cambridge, Mass., 1970.

Tebbel, John William. *A History of Book Publishing in the United States.* 4 vols. New York, 1972–1981.

Thomas, Paul. *The Work of William Morris.* New York, 1967.

Tucci, Douglas Shand. *Built in Boston: City and Suburb 1800–1950.* Boston, 1978.

Turner, Paul Venable. *Campus: An American Planning Tradition.* Cambridge, Mass., 1984.

Van Slyck, Abigail A. "Free to All: Carnegie Libraries and the Transformation of American Culture, 1886–1917." Ph.D. diss., University of California at Berkeley, 1989.

Van Slyck, Abigail A. "'The Utmost Amount of Effectiv (*sic*) Accommodation': Andrew Carnegie and the Reform of the American Library." *JSAH* 50 (1991): 359–383.

Van Zanten, David T. "Architectural Composition at the Ecole des Beaux-Arts from Charles Percier to Charles Garnier." In *The Architecture of the Ecole des Beaux-Arts,* ed. Arthur Drexler. New York, 1977, 111–290.

Van Zanten, David T. "Architecture." In Philadelphia Museum of Art, *The Second Empire, 1852–1870: Art in France under Napoleon III.* Philadelphia, 1978, 35–73.

Van Zanten, David T. *Designing Paris: The Architecture of Duban, Labrouste, Duc and Vaudoyer.* Cambridge, Mass., 1987.

Van Zanten, David T. "Ornament." *VIA: The Journal of the Graduate School of Fine Arts of the University of Pennsylvania* 3 (1977): 49–54.

Van Zanten, David T. "Le Système des Beaux-Arts." In *A.D. Profiles 17: The Beaux-Arts.* London, n.d., 68–79.

Vidler, Anthony. "The Idea of Type: The Transformation of the Academic Ideal, 1750–1830." *Oppositions* 8 (1977): 95–115.

Vidler, Anthony. *The Writing of the Walls: Architectural Theory in the Late Enlightenment.* Princeton, 1987.

Viollet-le-Duc, Eugène-Emmanuel. *The Foundations of Architecture: Selections from the Dictionnaire raisonné.* Intro. Barry Bergdoll, trans. Kenneth D. Whitehead. New York, 1990.

Von Hoffman, Alexander. *Local Attachments: The Making of an American Urban Neighborhood, 1850 to 1920.* Baltimore, 1994.

Wadlin, Horace. *The Public Library of the City of Boston: A History.* Boston, 1911.

Wagner, Virginia L. "John Ruskin and Artistical Geology in America." *Winterthur Portfolio* 23 (1988): 151–167.

Wall, Joseph Frazier. *Andrew Carnegie.* New York, 1970.

Weingarten, Lauren S. "Naturalized Nationalism: A Ruskinian Discourse on the Search for an American Style of Architecture." *Winterthur Portfolio* 24 (1989): 43–68.

Wetherold, Houghton. "The Architectural History of the Newberry Library." *Newberry Library Bulletin* 6 (November 1962): 3–23.

Wheeler, Joseph L., and Alfred Morton Githens. *The American Public Library Building: Its Planning and Design with Special Reference to Its Administration and Service.* New York, 1941.

Whitehill, Walter Muir. *Boston Public Library: A Centennial History.* Cambridge, Mass., 1956.

Wiebe, Robert. *The Search for Order, 1877–1920.* New York, 1967.

Williamson, William Landram. *William Frederick Poole and the Modern Library Movement.* New York, 1963.

Wills, Garry. *Lincoln at Gettysburg: The Words That Remade America.* New York, 1992.

Wilson, Lynn Winfield. *History of Fairfield County, Connecticut: 1639–1928.* 3 vols. Chicago and Hartford, 1929.

Wilson, Richard Guy. "American Architecture and the Search for a National Style in the 1870s." *Nineteenth Century* 3 (Autumn 1977): 74–80.

Withey, Henry and Elsie R. *Biographical Dictionary of American Architects.* Los Angeles, 1956.

Wodehouse, Lawrence. "William Appleton Potter, Principal *Pasticheur* of Henry Hobson Richardson." *JSAH* 31 (1973): 175–192.

Woodford, Frank B. *Parnassus on Main Street: A History of the Detroit Public Library.* Detroit, 1965.

Woods, Mary N. "Henry Van Brunt: 'The Historic Styles, Modern Architecture.'" In *American Public Architecture: European Roots and Native Expressions,* ed. Craig Zabel and Susan Scott Munshower. Papers in Art History from Pennsylvania State University, vol. 5. University Park, Pa., 1989, 83–113.

Wright, Gwendolyn. *Moralism and the Model Home.* Chicago, 1980.

Wriston, Barbara. "The Architecture of Thomas Tefft." *Bulletin of the Museum of Art of the Rhode Island School of Design, Providence* 28 (November 1940): 37–45.

Yust, W. F. *A Bibliography of Justin Winsor.* Cambridge, Mass., 1902.

Zaitzevsky, Cynthia. *Frederick Law Olmsted and the Boston Park System.* Cambridge, Mass., 1982.

# Index

* *
*

Page numbers in italics refer to illustrations.

Abolitionism, 12, 38, 46
Adams, Ann Jensen, 188
Adams, Charles Francis, Jr., 27, 36, 43, 48, 65, 146, 276n18, 306n2
  on Crane Public Library, 21, 191, 266–268
  on history of Quincy, 20–21, 36, 251, 253
  on public education, 28, 177
  as Quincy Public Library trustee, 11, 21, 28–32, 34, 153, 155–156
Adams, Henry, 121, 137, 153, 276n20
Adams, John, 34
Adams, John Quincy, 34
Adams Academy (Quincy), 10, 34
Adams homesteads (Quincy), 176
Aesthetic movement, British, 131, 176, 216–217
Aiken, William Martin, 268
Albany (N.Y.)
  New York State Capitol, 4
Alberti, Leon Battista, 205
Alger, Horatio, stories, 35
Alger, Russell A., 252
Allen, Phineas, 92
*American Architect and Building News,* 14
  Crane Public Library (Quincy); *175*
  Dayton Public Library, 227
  on library design, 222, 257–260
  Nevins Memorial Library (Methuen), 227
  Woburn Public Library, 4, 114–120, 133, 152, 230; *112, 116–117, 119–120*
American Historical Association, 222
American Library Association (ALA)
  founding, 13
  on library design, 222–226, 256–261



**
*

Patton, Normand, at annual conference, 261
Poole, William, at annual conference, 222–224, 226–227
Van Brunt, Henry, at annual conference, 88, 250
Ames, Frederick Lothrop, 32, 36–37, 43, 65, 146, 153, 276n18, 282n91
Ames, Helen Angier, 153
Ames, Oakes Angier, 24, 37, 51, 153, 210
Ames, Oliver, Sr., 35
Ames, Oliver, II, 5, 24, 26, 28, 32, 36–37, 40, 51, 276n18
library bequest, 152–153
Saint-Gaudens relief of, 48, 166; 50
Ames, Oliver, III, 28
Ames, Sarah, 40, 153
Ames family, 32, 35, 38, 152, 306n2
connection with Union Pacific Railroad, 26–27, 37, 51, 276n18
Ames Free Library of Easton. *See* North Easton (Mass.): Ames Free Library of Easton
Ames Memorial Hall. *See* North Easton (Mass.): Oakes Ames Memorial Town Hall
Ames Monument (Sherman, Wyo.), 51–52, 188; 52
Amherst College Library (Amherst, Mass.), 111, 260
Andover (Mass.), 46
Memorial Hall, 43, 46, 106
André, Louis-Jules, 147, 182, 302n39
Ansonia (Conn.)
Memorial Library; *262*
Antin, Mary, 37
*Architectural Review,* 266
*Architectural Sketch Book*
MIT student designs for a memorial library, 93–100, 106, 114, 118, 121, 142, 177, 182–183, 265; *94–95, 100*
Turner Free Library (Randolph), 11, 89–92, 108, 121, 152–154; 89
*Architecture romane du Midi de la France* (Révoil), 141
Arles (France)
St.-Trophime, 304n16
Armories, National Guard, 27
Arnold, James, 136
Arnold, Matthew, 29–30, 217, 265
Arnold Arboretum (Boston), 136–137, 299n6
Art galleries. *See* Museums, in libraries
Arts and crafts movement, 131
Astor, John Jacob, 68, 70, 106, 221. *See also* New York: Astor Library
Athenaeums, 9. *See also* Boston: Boston Athenaeum; Pittsfield (Mass.): Berkshire Athenaeum; Portsmouth (N.H.): Athenaeum; Providence: Athenaeum
Atkinson, R. S.
design for a memorial library, 93–100, 106, 114, 121, 142, 177, 183, 265; 95
*Atlantic Monthly,* 148, 264
Auditoriums. *See* Lecture halls, in libraries
Austin, Henry, 63
Autun (France)
cathedral, 125; *127*

Bache, Alexander Dallas, tomb (Washington, D.C.), 209
Bacon, Francis H., 198
Ballard, Charles R., 26
Baltard, Victor, 145
Baltimore
Peabody Institute, 12, 77
Baltzell, E. Digby, 33
Bartol, George, 45

Bascom, John, 140
Bates, Joshua, 11–12, 71, 76
Bay City (Mich.), 220
Beaux-Arts style. *See* Ecole des Beaux-Arts
Bellemain, André, 99
Benjamin, Samuel G. W., 79, 191
Bentham, Jeremy, 68
Bernardston (Mass.)
  Cushman Library, 13, 237n32
Bertram, James, 35
*Bibliothéconomie* (Hesse), 63–65, 70–71, 79, 83, 121; *65*
Bibliothèque Nationale. *See* Paris: Bibliothèque Nationale
Bibliothèque Ste.-Geneviève. *See* Paris: Bibliothèque Ste.-Geneviève
Bicknell, Albion Harris, 30, 51, 115, 204–205, 212
Billings, Frederick, 240
Billings, Hammatt, 83; *85*
  Thayer Public Library (Braintree), 13, 83, 97, 152, 154, 282n96; *84*
Billings Memorial Library (University of Vermont), 180, 240, 243; *239–242*
Bissett, M., 99; *98*
Blodgett, Geoffrey, 30
Bond, Richard
  Gore Hall (Harvard University), 60–63, 71; *61–62*
Books
  lending of, 8, 12, 14, 16, 46, 70, 73–77, 127, 142, 221 (*see also* Library design: book delivery areas)
  public access to, 266
  segregation of public from, 68–71, 76, 79–81, 86, 92–93, 118, 127
  selection of, 29–31, 216
  size of early library collections, 9–10
Book storage
  alcove shelving, 57–69, 71, 76–77, 81–87, 89, 227, 284n11
    criticism of, 87, 224, 256, 258, 266, 289n52
    in Richardson's libraries, 121–127, 160, 173, 188, 198, 213, 240–243, 266
  compact storage, 86–88, 93, 118, 121, 177, 182, 230, 243
  early history, 56–58
  freestanding shelves, 89, 92, 118–121, 224, 226, 227–231, 237–243, 246, 264, 266
  galleries, 56, 60–68, 71, 76–77, 81–83, 121–127, 160, 173, 198, 227, 240–243, 290n64
    criticism of, 224, 256, 258, 260, 289n52
  hall libraries, 56, 57, 68–87
    criticism of, 86–87, 93, 222–225, 289n52
  panoptic shelving systems, 57, 68, 71, 79, 121, 125, 240; *68*
  segregation of public from, 68–71, 76, 79–81, 86, 92–93, 118, 127
  stack system, 67, 88–93, 121, 127, 177–178, 224, 246, 266, 268; *88*
Boston, 6–8, 82, 207
  Arnold Arboretum (Jamaica Plain), 136–137, 299n6
  Back Bay, 109
  Boston Athenaeum, 36, 60–67, 71, 77, 92, 112, 221; *64*
  Boston Public Library, 155, 221
    Bates Hall, 77, 86, 224; *74–75*
    Boston Public Library Act, 9
    Boylston Street building, 15, 73–79, 82–83, 86, 92; *72, 74–75*
    Copley Square building (McKim, Mead and White), 265; *265*
    founding, 6–9, 28, 37, 70–71



**
*

*Report of the Trustees* (1852), 6–8, 11–12, 73
Roxbury Branch, 86–88, 92, 96, 110–111, 121; *87*
Brattle Square Church, 109, 194, 205; *207*
Bunker Hill Monument, 292n72
as center of library movement, 14
Consumptives' Home (Roxbury), 38
Copley Square, 109
First Baptist Church, 41, 194 (*see also* Boston: Brattle Square Church)
Hayden Building, 4
Mercantile Library, 221
Mercantile Society, 70
New England Hospital for Women and Children (Roxbury), 38
New Old South Church, 109, 110, 115, 137
park system, 136
philanthropy in, 38
regional growth, 21
Temporary Home for the Destitute, 38
Trinity Church, 4, 40, 109–110, 114–115, 145, 185, 188, 205, 299n5; *5*
Boston and Albany Railroad, 26, 276n18
*Boston Evening Transcript,* 32
Botany. *See* Horticulture
Boullée, Etienne-Louis, 125, 305n25
Bradlee and Winslow
Roxbury Branch of the Boston Public Library, 86–88, 92, 96, 110–111, 121; *87*
Braintree (Mass.), 11, 33
Thayer Public Library, 13, 83, 97, 152, 154, 282n96; *84*
*Bread-Winner, The* (Hay), 27
Bridgewater (Mass.)
Public Library, 100; *103*
Brookline (Mass.)
Public Library, 13, 83, 97, 112, 293n16; *84–85*
Richardson home and studio, 109, 213; *214*
Brooks, Phillips, 40, 46, 48, 106, 191
Brown University Library (Providence, R.I.), 63, 65
Brunelleschi, Filippo, 125–127
Brush and Smith, 288n42
Buffalo (N.Y.)
Civil War Memorial project, 100; *101*
Young Men's Association Library, ix
*Building Superintendence* (Clark), 139
Bulfinch, Charles
Lancaster Meeting House, 45; *44*
Burgess, William, 131
Burgh, Thomas, 284n11
Byzantine style, 68, 145, 173, 190, 198–203, 205, 217

Cabot, Edward M., 65
Cabot and Dexter
Boston Athenaeum, 36, 60–67, 71, 77, 92, 112, 221; *64*
Calais (Me.)
Free Public Library; *263*
Cambridge (Mass.). *See also* Harvard University; Massachusetts Institute of Technology
Lawrence Institute, 12
Mount Auburn Cemetery, 41, 99, 292n72
Rindge Memorial Library, 266; *269*
Cambridge University
early alcove libraries, 57–58
Trinity College Library, 58–60
Capen, Edward, 110
Carnegie, Andrew, 14, 35–37, 51
Chaffin, William L., 39
Champney, Edwin, 275n8
Champney, Edwin G., 110

Champney, George M., 23, 30, 33, 48, 109–112, 114
Chandler, Francis W., 292n66
Chapin, Edwin Hubbell, 38, 40
Chicago, 245, 252–253, 266
Columbian Exposition, 265
Glessner House, 276n20, 301n28, 301n37, 305n23
Haymarket riot, 276n20
Public Library, 221, 231, 252, 308n21
Choate, Rufus, 36
Cincinnati
Public Library, 77, 93, 222, 224; *223*
Civil War, 12, 39, 41, 205, 207
memorials to, 43–48, 92–100, 106, 205, 210, 281n88; *42, 44, 47, 94, 95, 100–102, 210*
veterans, 27
Clark, Theodore Minot, 112, 139, 147
Classical principles of design, 93–99, 139, 145–148, 265–266
Cluny (France)
Romanesque townhouse, 133; *132*
Cogswell, Joseph Green, 68–69
Colonial revival, 33, 127–131, 160–166, 171–176, 198, 203, 213–216
churchyards, 208
kitchen at Woburn Public Library, 33–34
Concord (Mass.), 51, 82–83
Free Public Library, 13, 51, 79–83, 106, 108, 145, 293n16; *80–82*
Constantin, Leopold August. *See* Hesse, Leopold August Constantin
Converse, Elisha, 5, 23–24, 30–31, 33, 35–37, 51, 194, 203, 205, 217
Converse, Frank, 40, 194, 205
murder, 27, 217
portrait, 30, 48, 51, 204–205, 212–213
Converse, Harry S., 31
Converse, James W., 33, 194
Converse, Mary, 5, 23–24, 30, 36, 39–41, 51, 194, 203, 205
Converse, Parker, 107
Converse homestead (Woburn), 21–23, 33, 176, 203; *23*
Converse Memorial Building. *See* Malden (Mass.): Converse Memorial Building
Conway (Mass.)
Field Memorial Library, 266; *267*
Cook, Clarence, 160
Corey, Deloraine P., 29, 31
Cornell, Ezra, 307n5
Cornell University (Ithaca, N.Y.), 307n5
Couture, Thomas, 304n13
Crane, Albert, 21, 154, 156, 266–268
Crane, Benjamin F., 48
Crane, Clarissa L., 26, 38, 40, 48, 177
Crane, Thomas, 5, 20, 26, 32–34, 38, 48, 154. *See also* Quincy (Mass.): Thomas Crane Public Library
Crane family, 26, 32, 33, 154–156
*Crayon, The,* 148
Crédit Mobilier of America, 37
*Croquis d'architecture,* 96–99; 98
Cummings, Charles Amos, 109
Cummings, John, 24, 26, 32, 108–109
Cummings and Sears
in competition for Woburn Public Library, 4, 108–110, 114–121, 143, 177, 230; *116–117*
New Old South Church, 109, 110, 115, 137
Cutter, Charles Ammi, 96
Cutter, William R., 149

Dalzell, Robert, F., Jr., 38
Dana, John Cotton, 311n63

Danvers (Mass.)
Peabody Library, 12, 36
Davenport, A. H., 198
Davis, Alexander Jackson, 284n9
Dayton (Ohio)
Public Library, 227–230, 264; *228–229*
*Dayton Daily Democrat,* 227
Dean, William, 300n15
Deane and Woodward
Museum of Natural History (Oxford University), 137, 142, 145; *136–137*
Trinity College Library (Dublin), 60, 121, 284n11
Death, 27, 40–51, 203–217
*Decimal System for the Arrangement and Administration of Libraries* (Shurtleff), 73
Dedham (Mass.)
Public Library, 266; *268*
De Herrera, Juan, 56
Delessert, Benjamin, 65, 68, 71, 79, 121, 125, 240; *68*
Della Santa, Leopoldo, 65, 79
Determinist theory, French, 147–148
Detroit, 221
Public Library, 77, 307n5
Dewey, Melvil, 111
Dexter, George M., 65
*Dictionnaire raisonné de l'architecture française* (Viollet-le-Duc), 125, 133, 143, 159; *127, 132, 159*
Ditzion, Sidney, 6, 36
Douglas, Ann, 40, 217, 304n10
Downing, Andrew Jackson, 41, 134, 146
Dublin
Trinity College library, 60, 121, 284n11
Easthampton (Mass.)
Public Library, 309n38
Eastlake, Charles, 131, 134; *136–137*
Easton (Mass.). *See* North Easton (Mass.)
East Saginaw (Mich.), 221, 253
history, 220, 251–252
Hoyt Public Library
bequest for, 220–221
competition, 17, 227–246, 256
Jenney proposal for, 225
McKim, Mead and White proposal for, 230–237, 246, 256
Patton and Fisher proposal for, 233–237, 246, 251, 264; *234–235*
Peabody and Stearns proposal for, 230–233, 237, 245
Richardson proposal for, 17, 170–171, 182, 184, 237–245, 251, 256; *238, 244–245*
trustees, 220, 251–253, 256
Van Brunt and Howe building, 246–251, 253; *247–250*
Ecole des Beaux-Arts (Paris), 109, 153, 204–205, 265
curriculum at, 182–185
influence on MIT curriculum, 93–99
influence on Richardson, 16, 139, 146–148, 182–189
Edinburgh
University library, 284n11
Edwards, Edward, 77, 79
Egbert, Donald Drew, 301n37
Egyptian architecture, 189
Eidlitz, Leopold, 4
Emerson, George B., 137; *135*
Emerson, Ralph Waldo, 106, 289n49
*Encyclopédie d'architecture* (Planat), 97


**
*

*Entretiens sur l'architecture* (Viollet-le-Duc), 141, 188
Escorial, library, 56
Etlin, Richard A., 207
Everett, Edward, 6, 8, 28, 36, 65, 71, 155

Farnham, Captain Arthur, 27
Faxon, J. L., 231
Ferguson, John Day, 154
Field, Marshall, 266
Field Memorial Library (Conway), 266; 267
Fireproof construction in libraries, 69–70, 73, 88, 216, 224, 227–230, 250, 253
Fischer von Erlach, J. B., 127
Fletcher, William I., 260
Flint and Pere Marquette Railroad, 220
Flockton, Henry, 285n15
Florence (Italy)
Pitti Palace, 140
Santo Spirito, 127
Folsom, Charles, 65, 67
Ford, Edward R., 159
*Foundations of the Public Library* (Shera), 9
Foxboro (Mass.)
Public Library, 281n88
Framingham (Mass.)
Memorial Hall, 281n88
Franco-Prussian War, 99
Free Public Library Commission of Massachusetts, 51

Gambrill, Charles Dexter, 4, 108–109, 153
Gambrill and Richardson, 4, 108–109, 111–112, 114, 149, 230. *See also* Richardson, Henry Hobson
Garden of Academe, 134
Garnier, Charles, 204
Garrison, Dee, 14, 295n37, 307n8
Gärtner, Friedrich von
Munich Staatsbibliothek, 15, 65, 68, 71, 77, 287n29
Genealogy, 32–34, 216
Geology, 140–142, 146, 189–190
Georgetown (Mass.)
Peabody Institute, 12
Gettysburg (Pa.), 205
Gibbs, James, 57
Girouard, Mark, 216
Goodnow, John, 13
Goodwin, James B., House (Hartford), 295n38
"Gospel of Wealth" (Carnegie), 35
Gothic architecture, 139, 145, 190
*Gothic Forms Applied to Furniture, Metalwork and Decoration for Domestic Purposes* (Talbert), 131
Gothic revival, 60, 83, 92, 118, 145
*Grammar of Ornament* (Jones), 296n49
Grand Rapids (Mich.)
United States Court House and Post Office, 115
Gray, Asa, 134
Greek architecture, 189–190
at Paestum, 146–148
"Greek Lines" (Van Brunt), 148, 209
Greeley, Horace, 38
Green, Edward W., 27
Greenough, Henry, 109
Gregerson, James R., 109
Grenoble (France)
Musée-Bibliothèque, 97
Guadet, Julien, 145, 147, 184

Hale, Edward Everett, 67, 287n32
Hall, L. J., 231, 233, 237, 245
Hanaford, Phebe C., 281n81
*Handbuch der Bibliothekwissenschaft* (Schmidt), 63



**
*

*Harper's New Monthly Magazine,* 79, 83, 189, 191
*Harper's Weekly,* 5, 171, 256
Harris, Edward D., 45
Harris, Neil, 37, 208, 252–253
Hartford (Conn.)
Cheney Building, 4
Goodwin, James B., House, 295n38
Harvard University (Cambridge, Mass.), 15, 29, 33, 108–109, 134, 136, 153, 306n38
Arnold Arboretum, 136–137
Austin Hall, 109, 165; *169*
Botanic Garden, 136, 153
Boylston Hall, 145
early library rooms, 57
Gore Hall, 60–63, 71; *61–62*
stack addition to, 88, 93, 108, 121, 246; *88*
Houghton Library, Richardson drawings at, 48, 114, 156, 165, 177, 237, 243, 256; *49, 123, 126, 138, 162, 165, 169, 176, 178–181, 186–187, 196, 197, 201, 203, 238, 244–245*
Lawrence Scientific School, 109
Matthews Hall, 109
Memorial Hall, 43–45, 108, 137, 145, 205, 282n96; *42*
Sever Hall, 109
Thayer Commons, 45
Weld Hall, 108
Harvey, Laurence, 184
Hathorne, George
Springfield Public Library, 77, 266; *78*
Haverhill (Mass.)
Public Library, 110
Hay, John, 27, 276n20
Hayden, Edward D., 26–27, 32, 36, 43, 65, 108, 111–112, 121, 153
Hayden, Elizabeth, 294n23
Hayden, Ezekiel, 294n23
Hayden, John Cole, 294n23
Hayden, Julia, 294n23
Hesse, Leopold August Constantin
*Bibliothéconomie,* 63–65, 70–71, 79, 83, 121; *65*
Hill, L. Draper, 177
Hingham (Mass.)
Public Library, 11
*Hints on Household Taste* (Eastlake), 131, 134
Hitchcock, Henry-Russell, 145, 165, 176, 185, 198, 300n17
Hittorf, Jacques-Ignace, 182
Hoar, Ebenezer Rockwood, 82
Horticulture, 134–137, 153
Howard, Annie T., 311n1
Howard, Charles, 311n1
Howard, Frank T., 311n1
Howard Public Library. *See* New Orleans: Howard Public Library
Hoyt, Alfred M., 230
Hoyt, Jesse, 220–221, 230, 252
Hoyt Public Library. *See* East Saginaw (Mich.): Hoyt Public Library
Hubka, Thomas, 131
Hudson, Miss H. R., 83
Hunt, Richard Morris, 97, 108–109, 147–148
Huntington, David, 216
Hurd, D. Hamilton, 24

Immigration, 6, 15, 20–21, 34
Industrialization, 6, 13, 16, 20–26, 35–36, 40, 208, 213, 220, 251–252
*Inland Architect and Building News*
Scoville Institute (Oak Park); *232*
Iron, in library construction, 56, 63, 67, 68, 69, 76, 88, 121, 125, 160
Ithaca (N.Y.), 221
Cornell Library, 13, 237n32, 307n5

Cornell University, 307n5
Sage Women's College, 307n5

Jefferson, Thomas, 8, 57, 67
portrait, 30, 204
Jenney, William LeBaron, 225–226, 231, 233, 252–253
Jewett, Charles Coffin, 65, 67
John Evans and Co., 295n39, 300n21
Johnson, John, 48, 107
Jones, Horace, 131; *58*
Jones, Joseph C., 220

Kansas City (Mo.), 256
Katz, Michael, 6
Keller, George
Ansonia Memorial Library; *262*
Kirby, Charles Kirk, 73. *See also* Boston: Boston Public Library
Kirkland, Edward Chase, 32
Knights of Labor, 26
in Woburn, 275n15
Knights of St. Crispin, 26
Korb, Hermann, 57
Kusmer, Kenneth L., 37

Laborde, Léon de, 79
Labor unrest, 26–27, 36, 251–252
in Woburn, 275n15
Labrouste, Henri, 146–149. *See also* Paris: Bibliothèque Nationale; Paris: Bibliothèque Ste.-Geneviève
Labrouste, Théodore, 125, 127, 182
LaFarge, John, 48, 110
Lancaster (Mass.), 79
Common, 45; *44*
Meeting House, 45; *44*
Memorial Hall and Library, 43–45, 48, 79, 82, 93, 97; *44*
Larned, J. L., 310n50
Lasters' Protective Union, 26
Laurentium (Italy), 134
Lawrence, Amos, 67
Lears, T. J. Jackson, 39–40
Lecture halls, in libraries, 13, 159, 177–182, 226, 230, 237, 243
Leiden (Netherlands)
University library, 284n10
Letang, Eugène, 292n66
Levine, Lawrence W., 36–37
Levine, Neil, 146
Library design. *See also* Book storage
book delivery areas, 71–76, 81, 86–87, 92–96, 108, 110, 114–121, 127, 158, 171, 176–177, 186, 191, 194–198, 226, 230–231, 243, 256, 260 (*see also* Books: lending of)
fireproof construction in, 69–70, 73, 88, 216, 224, 227–230, 250, 253
hall libraries, 56, 57, 68–87
criticism of, 86–87, 93, 222–225, 289n52
iron, use of in, 56, 63, 67, 68, 69, 76, 88, 121, 125, 160
lighting, 14, 16, 76, 93, 127, 143, 149, 226–227, 243, 251, 257–260, 266–268
literature on, 13–14, 63–68, 70–79, 86–88, 97, 111, 222–227, 256–261, 266
reading rooms, disposition of, 56, 60–63, 67–86, 92–96, 106–107, 110, 114–118, 125–134, 142–143, 149, 152, 158, 166–168, 176–177, 182, 186, 191, 194, 226–231, 237–243, 246–250
*Library Journal,* 3–14, 111, 264
Poole, articles by, 222–230, 246; *225*
on Richardson's libraries, 149, 256, 258–260

Library legislation, 8–9, 31–32
Library philanthropy, 11–15, 20, 35–38, 51, 67–71, 82, 92
East Saginaw, 220–221
Malden, 26, 31, 38–40, 216–217
New Orleans, 256
North Easton, 26, 28, 32, 40, 152–153
Quincy, 10–11, 26, 38, 40, 154–156
Woburn, 26, 38, 106–107
Library profession. *See* American Library Association; Professionalization: of librarians
Lienau, Detlef, 147–149
Lincoln, Abraham, 205, 264
Lincoln (Mass.), 21, 32, 156
Lind, E. G., 288n42
Linderfelt, K. A., 313n17
Little, Arthur, 160
Little, Norman, 220
Littlfield, Josiah M., 293n16
Lloyd, Gordon, 310n48
Lockwood, J. L., 231
Logan, James, 56
London
British Museum Reading Room, 56, 71, 77, 79, 290n59
Guildhall Library, 60, 121, 131, 145; *58, 59*
New Zealand Chambers, 127
Long, John D., 27, 33, 38, 48, 205, 213
Lothrop, Harriet Mulford, 83
Loudon, John Claudius, 41
Louis XVI, 208
Lynn (Mass.), 26, 275n15

Malden (Mass.), 21, 24–26, 31, 36, 51, 194, 208–209, 212–213, 217
Boston Rubber Shoe Company, 24–26, 217
City Hospital, 38
Converse Memorial Building, 5, 14, 152, 182, 240–245; *39, 155, 196–197, 200–201*
art collection in, 30
book room, 198–201; *195, 199*
description, 194–203
entry porch, 201–203, 205–209; *202–203, 206*
expansion, 266
founding, 31, 194
memorial function of, 17, 27, 48–52, 203–209, 212–213, 217
Middlesex Society room, 198, 245
reading room hearth, 194–198, 213–216; *215*
First Baptist Church, 36, 39, 194; *39*
Home for the Aged, 38
Malden Bank, 27
murder of Frank Converse, 27
Public Library, 10, 29, 33–36, 194 (*see also* Malden (Mass.): Converse Memorial Building)
*Malden City Press,* 203–204, 208
*Malden Mirror,* 31
Manchester (Mass.)
Manchester Memorial Hall, 237, 264; *236–237*
Mann, Horace, 6, 70
*Manual of Public Libraries* (Rhees), 77
Marseilles
cathedral, 145
Marsh, George Perkins, 240
Marx, Karl, 37
Massachusetts, Free Public Library Commission, 51
Massachusetts Institute of Technology (Cambridge)
Department of Architecture, 93, 109
student designs for a memorial library, 93–100, 106, 114, 118, 121, 142, 177, 182–183, 265; *94–95, 100*

Massachusetts Railroad Commission, 276n18
Massachusetts Total Abstinence Society, 36
McKay, H. S., 39
McKim, Charles, 237
McKim, Mead and White
Boston Public Library, 264–265; *265*
Hoyt library competition (East Saginaw), 230–237, 246, 256
Hoyt summer house (Long Island), 230
Hoyt townhouse (New York), 230
Manchester Memorial Hall, 237, 264; *236–237*
McLaughlin, James H.
Cincinnati Public Library, 77, 93, 222, 224; *223*
Northampton Free Public Library, 13, 43, 46, 92–93, 96, 121; *47*
Melrose (Mass.), 24
*Mémoire sur la Bibliothèque Royale* (Delessert), 68
*Memoirs of Libraries* (Edwards), 77
Merrill, William F., 31
Methuen (Mass.)
Nevins Memorial Library, 51, 227
Middlesex Society (Malden), 198, 245
Milan
Ambrosian Library, 56
Milford (Conn.)
Taylor Memorial Library, *263*
Millet, Jean-François, 30
Milwaukee
Public Library, 313n17
Milwaukee and Northern Railroad, 306n2
Mitchell, John Ames
Turner Free Library (Randolph), 11, 89–92, 108, 121, 152–154; *89*
Moore, Charles, 217
Morienval (France)
church, 159; *159*
Morris, William, 131, 216
Mourning, 40–41, 46, 203–217
Munich (Germany)
Staatsbibliothek, 15, 65, 68, 71, 77, 287n29
Munroe, William, 51, 82, 106
Museums, in libraries, 13, 30, 63, 92, 107–110, 114, 118, 134, 137, 142–143, 149, 156, 159, 180, 198, 203–205, 237; *133*
*Museums, Libraries and Picture Galleries* (Papworth), 71
Muskegon (Mich.)
Hackley Public Library, 252, 261–264; *261*
Myers, Elijah E.
proposal for Hoyt Public Library (East Saginaw), 221, 230–233

*Nation, The,* 256
National Academy of Design (New York), 137
National Guard Association, 27. *See also* Armories, National Guard
Natural history collections. *See* Museums, in libraries
"Nature of Gothic" (Ruskin), 137
Neo-grec style, 97
Nesfield, Eden, 297n71
New Bedford (Mass.)
Public Library, 13
New Hampshire Public Library Act, 13
New London (Conn.)
Public Library, 266; *266*
New Orleans
Howard Public Library, 17, 256–258, 266; *257–259*
Newport (R.I.)
Redwood Library, 12, 56, 71
William Watts Sherman House, 4, 131, 171
New York, 34, 109, 154, 207, 220–221

Astor Library, 8, 15, 68–71, 76, 79, 221, 224; *69*
Central Park, 148
Hoyt townhouse, 230
Lenox Library, 97
National Academy of Design, 137
Society Library, 56
*New York Evening Post,* 68
Norcross, O. W., 159, 182
Norcross Brothers, 112, 139, 194, 300n21
Northampton (Mass.)
Free Public Library, 13, 43, 46, 92–93, 96, 121; *47*
*Northampton Courier,* 92
North Easton (Mass.), 11; *25*
Ames Free Library of Easton, 5, 11, 16, 24–26, 32, 168, 185–189, 243; *155, 157, 162–163, 211*
book room, 156, 160; *161*
book wing elevation, 159–160, 180, 201, 251; *161, 169*
description, 154–160
entryway, 100, 158–159, 205, 209; *158*
founding, 36–40, 152–153, 194
furnishings, 131, 160
geometric design, 185–189; *186–187*
memorial function, 48, 52, 100, 152, 166, 205, 209–210; *50*
reading room hearth, 48, 166; *50, 164–165*
Romanesque revival style, 190–191
Oakes Ames Memorial Town Hall, 24, 52, 153, 210, 227; *163, 211*
Old Colony Railroad Company, 152
Oliver Ames and Sons, 24–26, 275n12
Public School Committee, 28, 152
The Rockery, 100, 210; *102, 211*
Unitarian Society, 32, 38, 153, 282n98
Northrop, J. W.
Taylor Memorial Library (Milford); *263*
Norton, Charles Eliot, 29–30, 43, 140, 306n38
*Norton's Literary Gazette and Publishers' Circular,* 63, 67, 70–71, 81, 92, 121; *71*
Nourse, Henry Stedman, 51
Novak, Barbara, 141
Nuits (France), 99

Oak Park (Ill.)
Scoville Institute, 27, 231; *232*
Ochsner, Jeffrey Karl, 131, 276n18
O'Gorman, James F., 14, 17, 134, 145, 177, 182, 188, 209, 256, 302n49, 303n55
Old Colony Railroad, 152, 279n47
Olmsted, Frederick Law, 4, 17, 41–43, 134–137, 146, 148, 182, 296n49
work with Richardson at North Easton, 100, 153
work with Richardson at Malden, 194, 207–212; *102, 211*
Olmsted and Vaux, 148
*On Public Libraries and Public Education* (Adams), 28, 177
"On Romantic and Classic Architecture" (Lienau), 148
Orientalism, 217
Oswego (N.Y.)
City Library, 12–13
Oxford University
Bodleian Library, 57, 77
Corpus Christi College Library, 58
Magdalen College Library, 284n10
Merton College Library, 58, 309n37
Museum of Natural History, 137, 142, 145; *136–137*
Radcliffe Camera, 12, 57, 67, 79

Paestum (Italy)
Greek temples, 146–148
Palliser and Palliser, 231
Palmer, Thomas W., 252
Panofsky, Erwin, 207
Papworth, John and Wyatt, 71, 79
Paris (France). *See also* Ecole des Beaux-Arts
Bibliothèque Nationale, 16, 68, 121 (*see also* Paris: Bibliothèque Royale)
Salle des Imprimés (reading room), 125, 133–134, 208; *124*
stack system, 88, 127
Bibliothèque Royale, 65, 68, 71, 121, 125; *68* (*see also* Paris: Bibliothèque Nationale)
Bibliothèque Ste.-Geneviève, 15–16, 71, 77, 148, 184
book storage system, 88
facade elevation, 97, 125–127, 139, 142, 147; *99, 126, 129*
reading room, 121; *124*
vestibule, 133, 137, 143, 207–208
Chapelle Expiatoire, 208
Opéra, 204
St.-Augustin, 298n74
St.-Pierre de Montrouge, 297n71
tomb of Admiral Dumont d'Urville, 292n72
Parker, Francis W., 277n25
Parker, Theodore, 271n9
Patton, Normand S., 261, 264
Patton and Fisher
in competition for Hoyt Public Library (East Saginaw), 233–237, 246, 251, 264; *234–235*
Hackley Public Library (Muskegon), 252, 261–264; *261*
Scoville Institute (Oak Park), 27, 231; *232*
Peabody, George, 12–13, 36
Peabody, Robert Swain, 109, 131
Peabody (Mass.)
Peabody Institute, 12, 282n96
Peabody and Stearns, 108–109, 131
in competition for Hoyt Public Library (East Saginaw), 230–233, 237, 245
in competition for Turner Free Library (Randolph), 152–153
in competition for Woburn Public Library, 4, 114, 118–121, 177; *119–120*
Easthampton Public Library, 309n38
Matthews Hall (Harvard University), 109
Yarmouth Public Library, 108
Peter, James B., 220–221, 227, 230–237, 245–246
Peters and Burns
Dayton Public Library, 227–230, 264; *228–229*
Philadelphia
Centennial Exposition, 13, 33, 131, 160
Library Company, 56
Loganian Library, 56
Ridgeway Branch Library, 106
Society Library, 71
Pisa
Campo Santo, 208
Pittsburgh
Allegheny County Court House, 185
Pittsfield (Mass.)
Berkshire Athenaeum, 13, 92, 96, 115, 141, 145; *90–91*
Plato, 208
Pliny the Younger, 134
Poole, William Frederick, 92–93, 252–253, 290n64
as consultant to Hoyt Public Library (East Saginaw), 17, 221–224, 230–237, 245–246, 250, 256, 264, 266

on design of small library buildings, 225–231, 243; *225*
*Poole's Guide to Periodical Literature,* 222
Portsmouth (N.H.)
Athenaeum, 57
Post Mills (Vt.)
Peabody Library, 12
Potter, Henry, Sr., 220
Potter, Henry C., Jr., 220
Potter, William A.
Berkshire Athenaeum (Pittsfield), 92, 96, 115, 141, 145; *90–91*
United States Court House and Post Office (Grand Rapids), 115
Poussin, Nicolas, 207
Pratt and Koppe, 307n5
Professionalization
of architects, 17, 37, 253
of librarians, 13–14, 17, 79, 253 (*see also* American Library Association)
of middle class, 252–253
Protestantism, 38–40, 46–48, 194
Providence
Athenaeum, 56
Public education, 6–8, 15, 28–29, 152, 177
*Public Libraries in the United States of America* (U.S. Department of Interior), 13, 88, 111
*Public Library and the Common Schools, The* (Adams), 28
Public library movement, 6–14, 70
Public parks, 41–43, 136
Public schools. *See* Public education

Quatremère de Quincy, Antoine Chrysostome, 208
Queen Anne style, 127–131, 160, 176, 198
Questal, C. A., 97
Quincy, Josiah, 60
Quincy (Mass.), 26, 28, 31–33
Adams Academy, 10, 34
Adams homesteads, 176
Crane family and, 154, 217, 253, 268
Historical Society, 34
history, 20–21, 24, 36
Public Library, 10–11, 26, 28–29, 31–32, 34 (*see also* Quincy (Mass.): Thomas Crane Public Library)
Thomas Crane Public Library, 16, 251, 264; *7, 155, 167–168*
and Adams, Charles Francis, Jr., 21, 152–156, 177, 191, 266–268
book room, 171–173, 198, 313n17; *172–174*
book wing elevation, 166–168; *169*
early designs for, 177–182, 184, 201, 240, 243; *176, 178–179, 181*
entry arch, 100, 158–159, 170, 205, 209; *170*
founding, 10–11, 26, 153–156, 221
furnishings in, 176–177
landscaping of grounds around, 209–210, 237
and library typology, 182–185, 189–191, 243, 264–265
memorial function of, 34, 48, 52, 100, 154, 209
reaction to, in popular press, 5–6, 14, 152, 171, 191
reading room hearth, 48, 176; *175*
*Quincy Patriot Ledger,* 154, 156, 177, 191

Railroads, 24–27, 37, 51, 152, 220, 253, 276n18, 276n19, 279n47, 306n2
Randolph (Mass.)
Turner Free Library, 11, 89–92, 108, 121, 152–154; *89*
*Readers Guide to Periodical Literature,* 222

Renaissance basilicas, 127
*Report on the Trees and Shrubs . . . of Massachusetts* (Emerson), 137; *135*
Republican Party, 30–31
Révoil, Henry Antoine, 141
*Revue générale de l'architecture,* 97–99, 207; *126, 129*
Rhees, William, 77
Richardson, A. E., 182
Richardson, Henry Hobson, 4–6, 9, 16–17, 26, 28–29, 31–32, 38–43, 46, 60, 83, 109, 250; *3. See also* Malden (Mass.): Converse Memorial Building; North Easton (Mass.): Ames Free Library of Easton; Quincy (Mass.): Thomas Crane Public Library; Woburn (Mass.): Woburn Public Library
  and aesthetic movement, 216–217
  Agwam Bank (Springfield), 299n5
  Allegheny County Court House (Pittsburgh), 185
  Ames Monument (Sherman, Wyo.), 51–52, 188; *52*
  Austin Hall (Harvard University), 109, 165; *169*
  Bache, Alexander Dallas, tomb (Washington, D.C.), 209
  Billings Memorial Library (University of Vermont), 180, 240, 243; *239–242*
  Brattle Square Church (Boston), 109, 194, 205; *207*
  Browne, Reverend Percy, house (Marion), 185
  Byzantine ornament, 173, 190, 198–203, 205, 217
  Cheney Building (Hartford), 4
  Civil War Memorial project (Buffalo), 100; *101*
  Civil War Memorial project (Worcester), 100
  colonial revival, interpretation of, 127–131, 160–166, 171–176, 198, 203, 213–216
  criticism of his library designs, 191, 256–260, 266–269
  and development of library typology, 182–185, 189–191, 243, 264–265
  drawings, in Houghton Library (Harvard University), 48, 114, 156, 165, 177, 237, 243, 256; *49, 123, 126, 138, 162, 165, 169, 176, 178–181, 186–187, 196–197, 201, 203, 238, 244–245*
  Ecole des Beaux-Arts, influence of, 139, 182–189
  in Europe, 121–125, 137, 147, 182
  First Baptist Church (Malden), design for, 39, 194; *39*
  and French romanticism, 146–149
  Glessner House (Chicago), 276n20, 301n28, 301n37, 305n23
  Goodwin, James B., House (Hartford), 295n38
  Hayden Building (Boston), 4
  Hay House (Washington, D.C.), 276n20
  home and studio (Brookline), 83, 213; *214*
  Howard Public Library (New Orleans), 17, 256–258, 266; *257–259*
  Hoyt Public Library (East Saginaw)
    invitation to participate in competiton for, 230–233
    proposal for, 17, 170–171, 182, 184, 237–245, 251, 256; *238, 244–245*
  naturalistic ornament, 133–139, 212
  New York State Capitol (Albany), 4
  Oakes Ames Memorial Town Hall (North Easton), 24, 52, 153, 210, 227; *163, 211*
  and Olmsted, 17, 134–137, 146, 148, 153, 194, 207–212
  Romanesque style, interpretation of, 4, 114–115, 145–149, 171, 189–191
  and Sargent, 135–137, 153
  Sever Hall (Harvard University), 109

Trinity Church (Boston), 4, 40, 109–110, 114–115, 145, 185, 188, 205, 299n5; *5*
Unity Church (Springfield), 299n5
Watts Sherman House, William (Newport), 4, 131, 171
Western Railroad Offices (Springfield), 299n5
Young Men's Association Library (Buffalo), design for, ix
Richardson, W. C.
design for a memorial library, 97–100, 106, 142, 265; *100*
Richardsonian Romanesque, 115–118, 237, 264, 266; *261–263, 266, 268–269*. *See also* Romanesque revival
Richmond (Ind.)
Morrisson Library, 13
Rimini (Italy)
Tempio Malatestiano, 205
Robinson, George D., 213
Roche, Robert, 303n3
Rogers, Isaiah, 284n12
Romanesque architecture, 125, 131–133, 143, 147, 189
Romanesque revival architecture, 4, 68, 115–118, 145. *See also* Richardsonian Romanesque
Richardson's interpretation of, 4, 114–115, 145–149, 171, 189–191
Rome
Arch of Titus, 189
Pantheon, 57
Root, John Welborn, 253
Rotch, Arthur, 100
Rotch and Tilden
Bridgewater Public Library, 100; *103*
Rowley, Reverend Francis H., 41
Rumrill, Charles Augustus, 276n18
*Rundbogenstil,* 68, 145. *See also* Romanesque revival architecture
Rural cemeteries, 41–43, 99, 208, 292n72
Rush, James, 106
Ruskin, John, 16, 29, 70, 92, 216
"Lamp of Power," 140, 189–191
"Lamp of Truth," 131
on masonry, 140–141, 146
and nature, 148, 271
on ornament, 134, 137–139, 173, 210
Ryder and Harris
Lancaster Memorial Hall and Library, 43–45, 48, 79, 82, 93, 97; *44*

*Saalbibliotheken,* 79, 127. *See also* Library design: hall libraries
Saeltzer, Alexander
Astor Library (New York), 8, 15, 68–71, 76, 79, 221, 224; *69*
Sage, Henry, 221
Saginaw (Mich.). *See* East Saginaw (Mich.)
Said, Edward, 51
Saint-Gaudens, Augustus, 48, 165; *50*
Sargent, Charles Sprague, 134, 136–137, 153, 276n18
Schmidt, J. A. F., 63, 65
Schrettinger, Martin, 65
Schulze, Paul, 145
Schuyler, Montgomery, 68, 152, 158, 165
Scoville, James, 27
Sears, Willard T., 109
*Seven Lamps of Architecture* (Ruskin), 173, 190
Shaw, Richard Norman, 127, 131
Shepley, George, 245
Shepley, Rutan and Coolidge
Field Memorial Library (Conway), 266; *267*
Howard Public Library (New Orleans), 17, 256–258, 266; *257–259*
New London Public Library, 266; *266*
Springfield Public Library, 266

Shera, Jesse, 6, 8
Shipley Hall (England), 297n71
Shurtleff, Nathaniel B., 73, 77, 114, 293n16
Siege of Paris, 99
Sleeper, Jonathan, 212, 217
"Small Library Buildings" (Poole), 226
Smith, Gerritt, 12
Snell, George, 109
Snell and Gregerson
  in competition for Woburn Public Library, 4, 108–109, 114
  Free Public Library of Concord, 13, 51, 79–83, 106, 108, 142, 145, 293n16; *80–82*
Sorosis Club, 40
South Danvers (Mass.). *See* Peabody (Mass.)
Springfield (Mass.)
  Agwam Bank, 299n5
  Public Library, 77, 266; *78*
  Unity Church, 299n5
  Western Railroad Offices, 299n5
Springfield (Ohio)
  Public Library, 266
Stamford (Conn.)
  Crane home, 154
  Public Library, 154, 300n12
Stearns, John Goddard, 109
Stickney, F. W.
  design for a memorial library, 93–97, 106, 114, 121, 142, 177, 183, 265; *94*
Stockbridge (Mass.)
  Public Library, 13
*Stones of Venice* (Ruskin), 141, 173
Storey, Joseph, 41
Storey, Ronald, 26
Strickland, William, 56
Stuart, Gilbert, 30, 204
Sudbury (Mass.)
  Goodnow Memorial Library, 13
Taine, Hippolyte, 147
Talbert, Bruce, 131
Tarascon (France)
  Ste.-Marthe, 296n43
Tarsney, Timothy E., 220, 252
Tefft, Thomas A.
  American Antiquarian Society (Worcester), 67–68, 287n32
  Lawrence Hall (Williams College), 67–68, 71, 88, 92, 121; *66*
Temperance movement, 36
Thayer, Christopher, 45
Thayer, Nathaniel, 43, 65, 79, 97
Thayer, Samuel F. J., 153
  Nevins Memorial Library (Methuen), 51, 227
  proposal for Turner Free Library (Randolph), 152–153
Thiele, Joel, 303n5
Thomas, Albert, 33
Thornton, William, 56
*Three Episodes of Massachusetts History* (Adams), 20
Ticknor, George, 6–8, 28, 36–37, 65, 69, 71, 77, 156
Tilden, George, 100
Tilton, Edward L., 310n50
Topeka (Kan.)
  Public Library, 290n61, 312n14
Transcendentalism, 17, 43, 82–83, 134, 148, 207, 217
Tufts College (Medford), 38
Turner, Colonel Royal, 92

Union Pacific Railroad, 26–27, 37, 51, 276n19
Universalism, 38
University of Michigan (Ann Arbor), 253
  library, 246
University of North Carolina library (Salem), 284n9

University of South Carolina library (Columbia), 63
University of Vermont (Burlington)
Billings Memorial Library, 180, 240; *239–242*
University of Virginia library (Charlottesville), 57, 67

Van Brunt, Henry, 108, 209, 261, 264. *See also* Van Brunt and Howe; Ware and Van Brunt
on Bibliothèque Ste.-Geneviève (Paris), 97, 142, 148
on tomb of Admiral Dumont d'Urville, 292n72
Van Brunt and Howe, 264. *See also* East Saginaw (Mich.): Hoyt Public Library
Public Library (Dedham), 266; *268*
Rindge Memorial Library (Cambridge), 266; *269*
Van Rensselaer, Mariana Griswold
on collaboration of Richardson and Olmsted, 209–210
on Converse Memorial Building (Malden), 194, 209–210
on Crane Public Library (Quincy), 177
on Richardson's masonry style, 139–140
on Richardson's mastery of the *esquisse,* 183–185
on Richardson's ornament, 190
on Richardson's use of the Romanesque style, 114, 146
on Woburn Public Library, 143, 158–159
Van Zanten, David, 16, 134, 142, 146
Vaudoyer, Léon, 145
Vaudremer, J.-A., 145
Vinal, A. H.
Free Public Library (Calais); *263*
Viollet-le-Duc, Eugène-Emmanuel, 125, 133, 141, 143, 147, 159, 188–189; *127, 132, 158*
Walterboro (S.C.)
Society Library, 56
Ware, William Robert, 93, 108–109
Ware and Van Brunt, 108–109
Adams Academy (Quincy), 10, 34
in competition for Woburn Public Library, 4, 114, 121
Gore Hall (Harvard University), stack addition, 88, 93, 108, 121, 246; *88*
Memorial Hall (Harvard University), 43–45, 108, 137, 145, 205; *42*
Topeka Public Library, 290n61, 312n14
University of Michigan Library (Ann Arbor), 246
Weld Hall (Harvard University), 108
Washington (D.C.)
Hay House, 276n20
Wayland (Mass.)
Public Library, 9
Webber, William L., 220–221, 252
Weissbein, Louis
Brookline Public Library, 13, 83, 97, 112, 293n16; *84–85*
Wellesley College (Wellesley, Mass.), 38
Wellman, Arthur H., 35
West Bay City (Mich.), 220–221
Sage Public Library, 221
White, Stanford, 131; *165*
Whitehead, Walter Muir, 12
Whitney, James L., 310n50
Wiebe, Robert, 252–253
Wight, Peter Bonnett, 137, 253
Williams College (Williamstown, Mass.)
Lawrence Hall, 67–68, 71, 88, 92, 121; *66*
Wills, Garry, 264
Windsor style of furniture, 176, 198, 213
Winn, Charles Bowers, 4, 11, 24–28, 32, 100
bequest, 38, 48, 106–107, 143

painting collection, 30
Winn, Jonathan Bowers, 10, 35, 48, 100, 106–107
Winn, Timothy, 10
Winn family, 21, 26, 111
Winsor, Justin
and design of Roxbury Branch of Boston Public Library, 86–88, 92, 96, 110–111, 121; *87*
and design of stack addition to Gore Hall, 88, 93, 108, 121, 246; *88*
on library design, 86–87, 114, 118, 177, 222–224, 289n52
Winthrop, John, 33
Woburn (Mass.), 194; *22*
Converse homestead, 21–23, 33, 176, 203; *23*
growth, 21–26
labor unrest in, 275n15
Woburn Public Library, 4, 13, 15–16, 26, 112–145, 149, 152, 303n3, 313n17; *112, 113, 115, 133, 138, 155*
book room, 121–127, 134, 227, 243; *122–123, 126, 128*
book wing, 133, 139–142; *169*
colonial kitchen in, 33–34
competition for, 4, 16, 92, 107–121, 149, 153, 230 (*see also* Cummings and Sears; Peabody and Stearns; Snell and Gregerson; Ware and Van Brunt)
cost, 112
criticism of, 258
early history, 10–11, 28–29, 33, 106
entry porch, 100, 143; *49, 144*
furnishings in, 127–131
makeup of board, 32
masonry work at, 139–142
memorial function of, 48–52, 100, 143; *49*
naturalistic ornamentation, 133–139, 212
and other Richardson libraries, 152–165, 173–183, 185, 188–190, 198, 203
picturesque massing, 142–145
reading room hearth, 131–133; *130*
Winn bequest for, 4, 26, 106–107
Winn painting collection in, 30
*Woburn Advertiser,* 30
Wolfenbüttel (Germany)
Ducal Library, 57, 79
*Woman Churning Butter* (Millet), 30
Women's Christian Temperance Union, 36
Women's National Relief Association, 38
*Wooden and Brick Buildings with Details* (Bicknell), 115
Worcester (Mass.)
American Antiquarian Society, 67–68, 287n32
Civil War Memorial project, 100
Wren, Sir Christopher
Trinity College Library (Cambridge University), 58–60
Wren, Thomas Ward, 11
Wright, Gwendolyn, 213

Yale University (New Haven)
libraries, 57, 60–63, 71
Yarmouth (Mass.)
Public Library, 108

Zoller, Edmund von, 79



**
*